Shugo Chara!

6

PEACH-PIT

Translated by
Satsuki Yamashita

Adapted by
Nunzio DeFilippis and Christina Weir

Lettered by
North Market Street Graphics

BALLANTINE BOOKS · NEW YORK

Shugo Chara! volume 6 is a work of fiction. Names, characters, places, and incidents are the products of the author's imagination or are used fictitiously. Any resemblance to actual events, locales, or persons, living or dead, is entirely coincidental.

A Del Rey Manga/Kodansha Trade Paperback Original

Published in the United States by Del Rey, an imprint of The Random House Publishing Group, a division of Random House, Inc., New York.

Publication rights arranged through Kodansha Ltd.

First published in Japan in 2008 by Kodansha Ltd., Tokyo

ISBN 978-0-345-51032-7

Original cover design by Akiko Omo

Printed in the United States of America

www.delreymanga.com

9 8 7 6 5 4 3 2 1

Translator: Satsuki Yamashita
Adapters: Nunzio DeFilippis and Christina Weir
Lettering: North Market Street Graphics

Contents

Honorifics Explained

Throughout the Del Rey Manga books, you will find Japanese honorifics left intact in the translations. For those not familiar with how the Japanese use honorifics and, more important, how they differ from American honorifics, we present this brief overview.

Politeness has always been a critical facet of Japanese culture. Ever since the feudal era, when Japan was a highly stratified society, use of honorifics—which can be defined as polite speech that indicates relationship or status—has played an essential role in the Japanese language. When addressing someone in Japanese, an honorific usually takes the form of a suffix attached to one's name (example: "Asuna-san"), is used as a title at the end of one's name, or appears in place of the name itself (example: "Negi-sensei," or simply "Sensei").

Honorifics can be expressions of respect or endearment. In the context of manga and anime, honorifics give insight into the nature of the relationship between characters. Many English translations leave out these important honorifics and therefore distort the feel of the original Japanese. Because Japanese honorifics contain nuances that English honorifics lack, it is our policy at Del Rey not to translate them. Here, instead, is a guide to some of the honorifics you may encounter in Del Rey Manga.

-san: This is the most common honorific and is equivalent to Mr., Miss, Ms., or Mrs. It is the all-purpose honorific and can be used in any situation where politeness is required.

-sama: This is one level higher than "-san" and is used to confer great respect.

-dono: This comes from the word "tono," which means "lord." It is an even higher level than "-sama" and confers utmost respect.

-kun: This suffix is used at the end of boys' names to express familiarity or endearment. It is also sometimes used by men among friends, or when addressing someone younger or of a lower station.

-chan:	This is used to express endearment, mostly toward girls. It is also used for little boys, pets, and even among lovers. It gives a sense of childish cuteness.
Bozu:	This is an informal way to refer to a boy, similar to the English terms "kid" and "squirt."
Sempai/ Senpai:	This title suggests that the addressee is one's senior in a group or organization. It is most often used in a school setting, where underclassmen refer to their upperclassmen as "sempai." It can also be used in the workplace, such as when a newer employee addresses an employee who has seniority in the company.
Kohai:	This is the opposite of "sempai" and is used toward underclassmen in school or newcomers in the workplace. It connotes that the addressee is of a lower station.
Sensei:	Literally meaning "one who has come before," this title is used for teachers, doctors, or masters of any profession or art.
-[blank]:	This is usually forgotten in these lists, but it is perhaps the most significant difference between Japanese and English. The lack of honorific means that the speaker has permission to address the person in a very intimate way. Usually, only family, spouses, or very close friends have this kind of permission. Known as *yobisute*, it can be gratifying when someone who has earned the intimacy starts to call one by one's name without an honorific. But when that intimacy hasn't been earned, it can be very insulting.

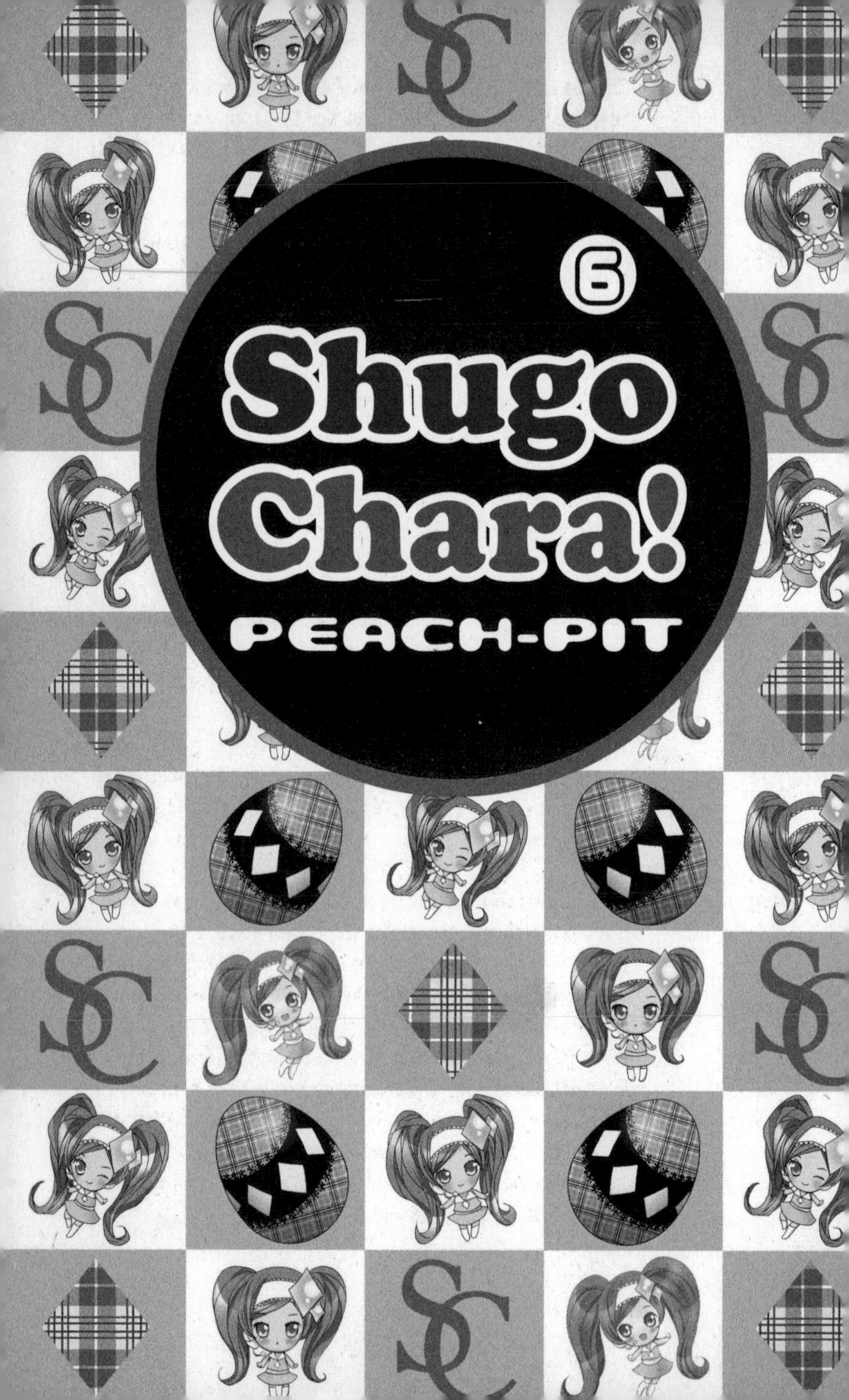
6
Shugo Chara!
PEACH-PIT

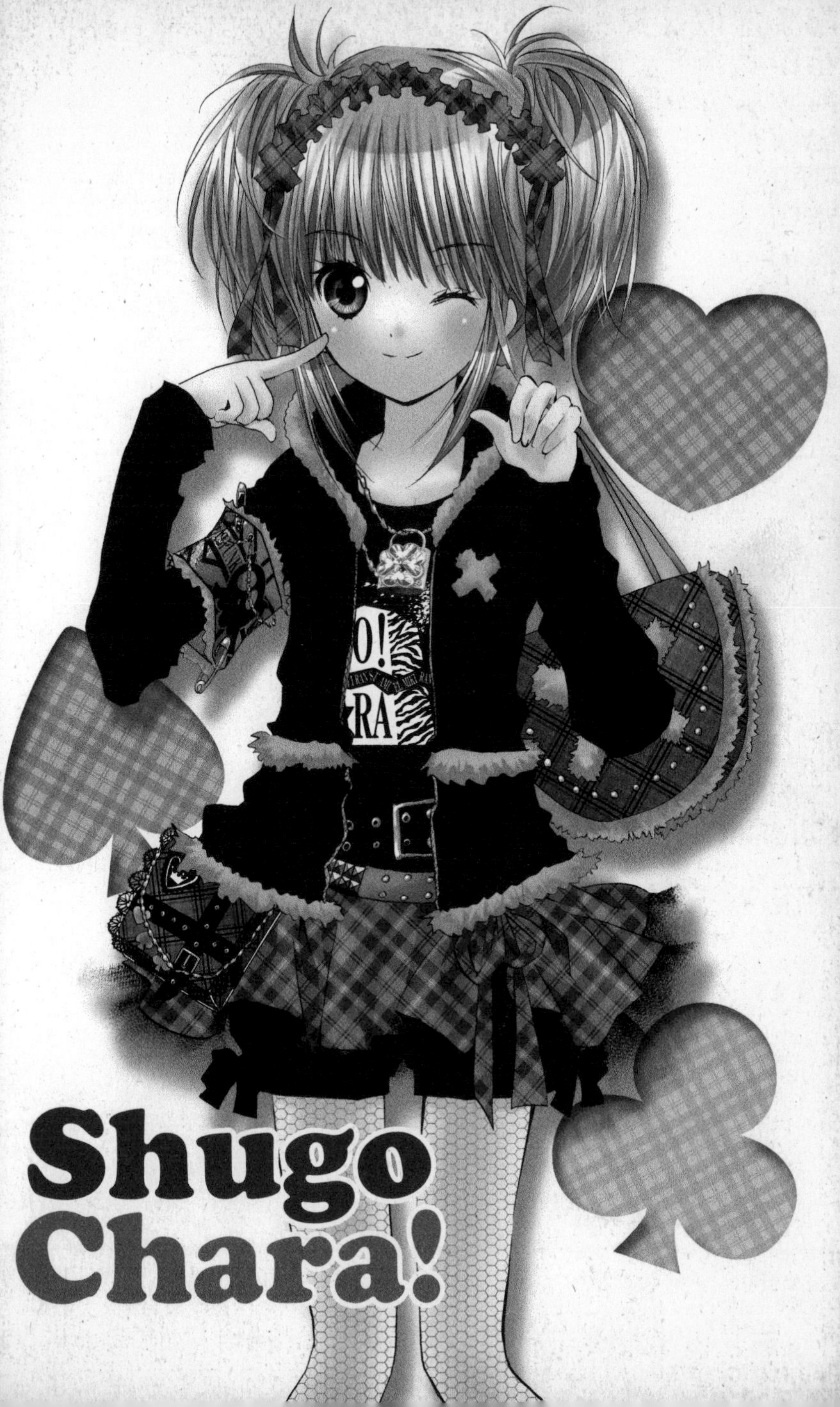
Shugo
Chara!

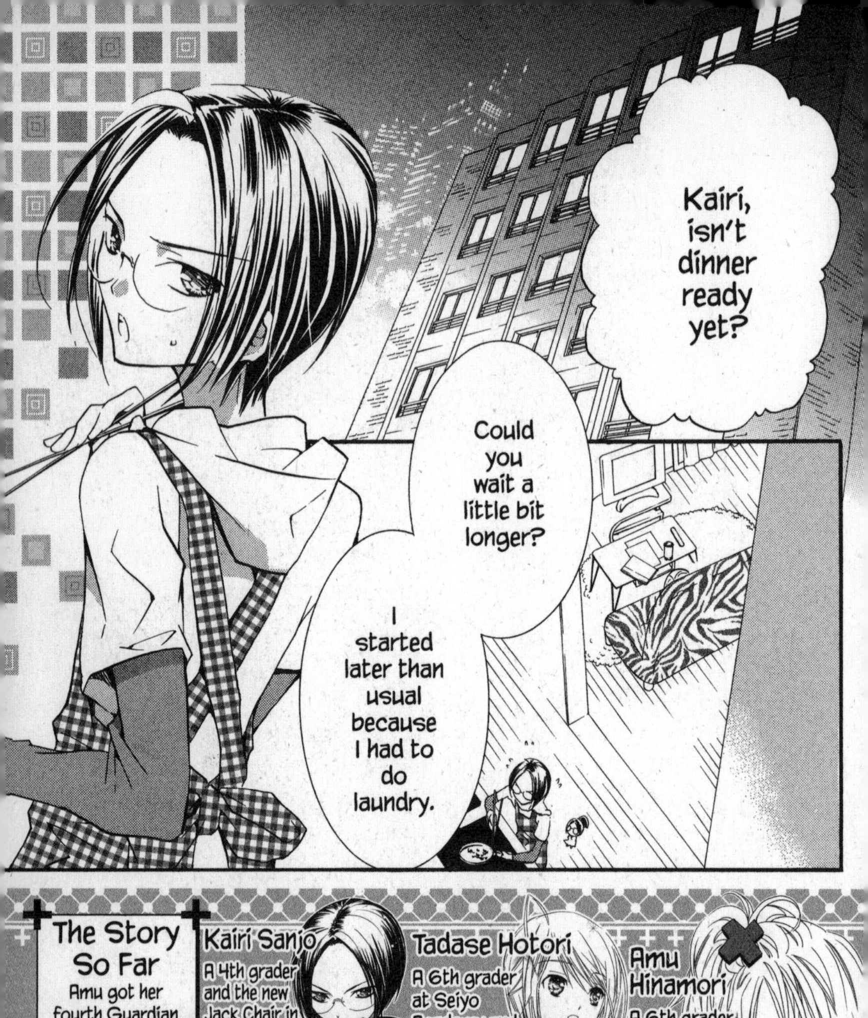
Kairi, isn't dinner ready yet?
Could you wait a little bit longer?
I started later than usual because I had to do laundry.

The Story So Far

Amu got her fourth Guardian Egg, but since she was feeling blue, the Egg turned into an X Egg and ran away! She's getting to know the new Queen Chair, Rima, and the new Jack Chair, Kairi. But what is the relationship between Kairi and Sanjo-san from the Easter Corporation!?

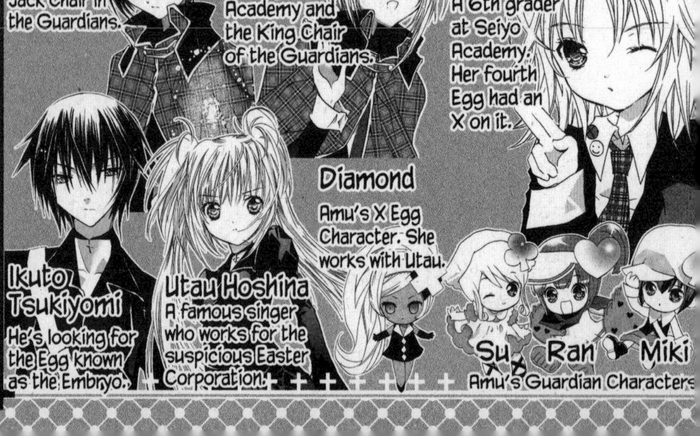
Amu Hinamori
A 6th grader at Seiyo Academy. Her fourth Egg had an X on it.
Tadase Hotori
A 6th grader at Seiyo Academy and the King Chair of the Guardians.
Kairi Sanjo
A 4th grader and the new Jack Chair in the Guardians.
Diamond
Amu's X Egg Character. She works with Utau.
Utau Hoshina
A famous singer who works for the suspicious Easter Corporation.
Ikuto Tsukiyomi
He's looking for the Egg known as the Embryo.
Su
Ran
Miki
Amu's Guardian Characters

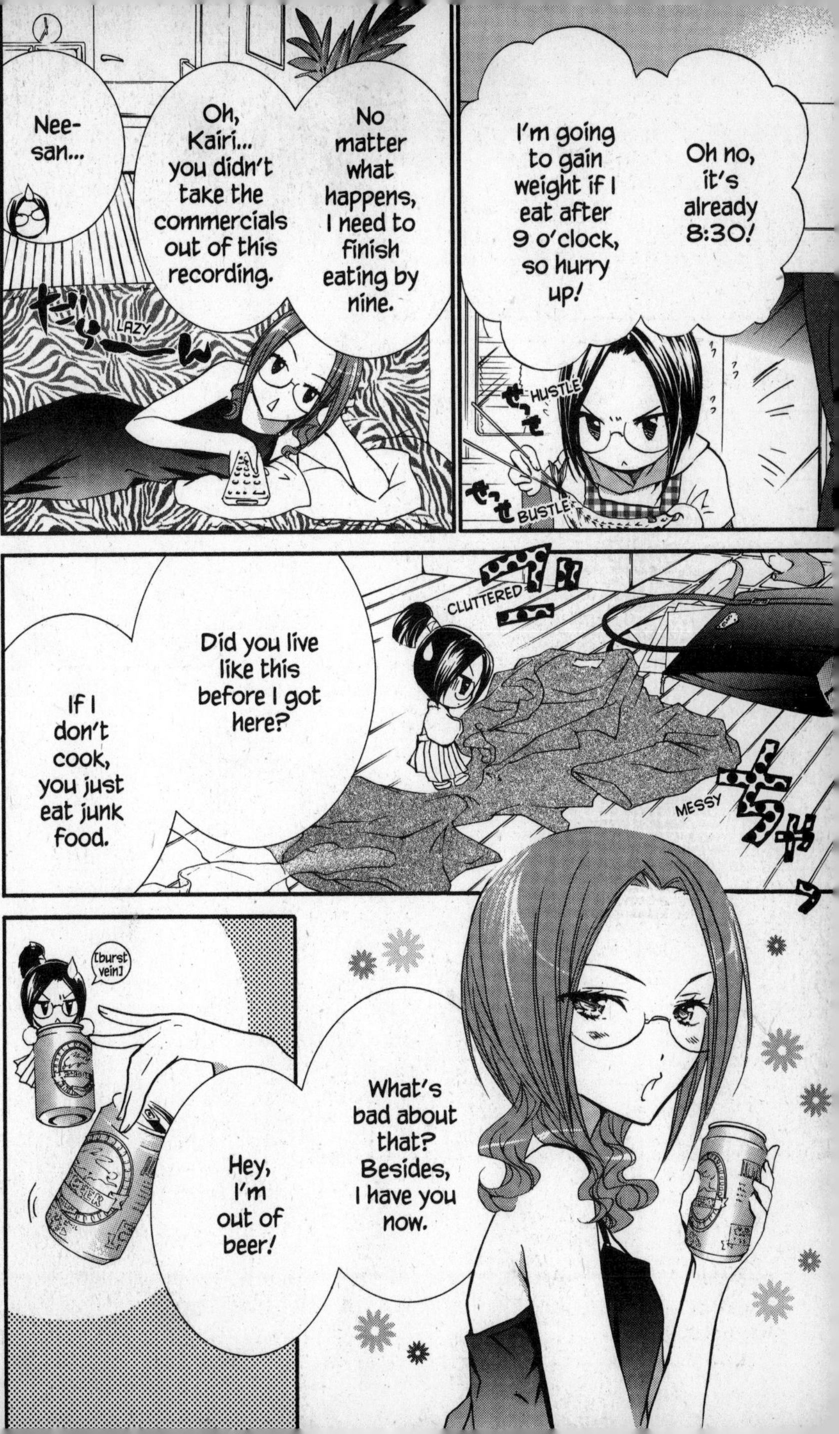
Oh no, it's already 8:30!
I'm going to gain weight if I eat after 9 o'clock, so hurry up!
HUSTLE
BUSTLE
No matter what happens, I need to finish eating by nine.
Oh, Kairi... you didn't take the commercials out of this recording.
Nee-san...
LAZY
CLUTTERED
MESSY
Did you live like this before I got here?
If I don't cook, you just eat junk food.
What's bad about that? Besides, I have you now.
Hey, I'm out of beer!
[burst vein]

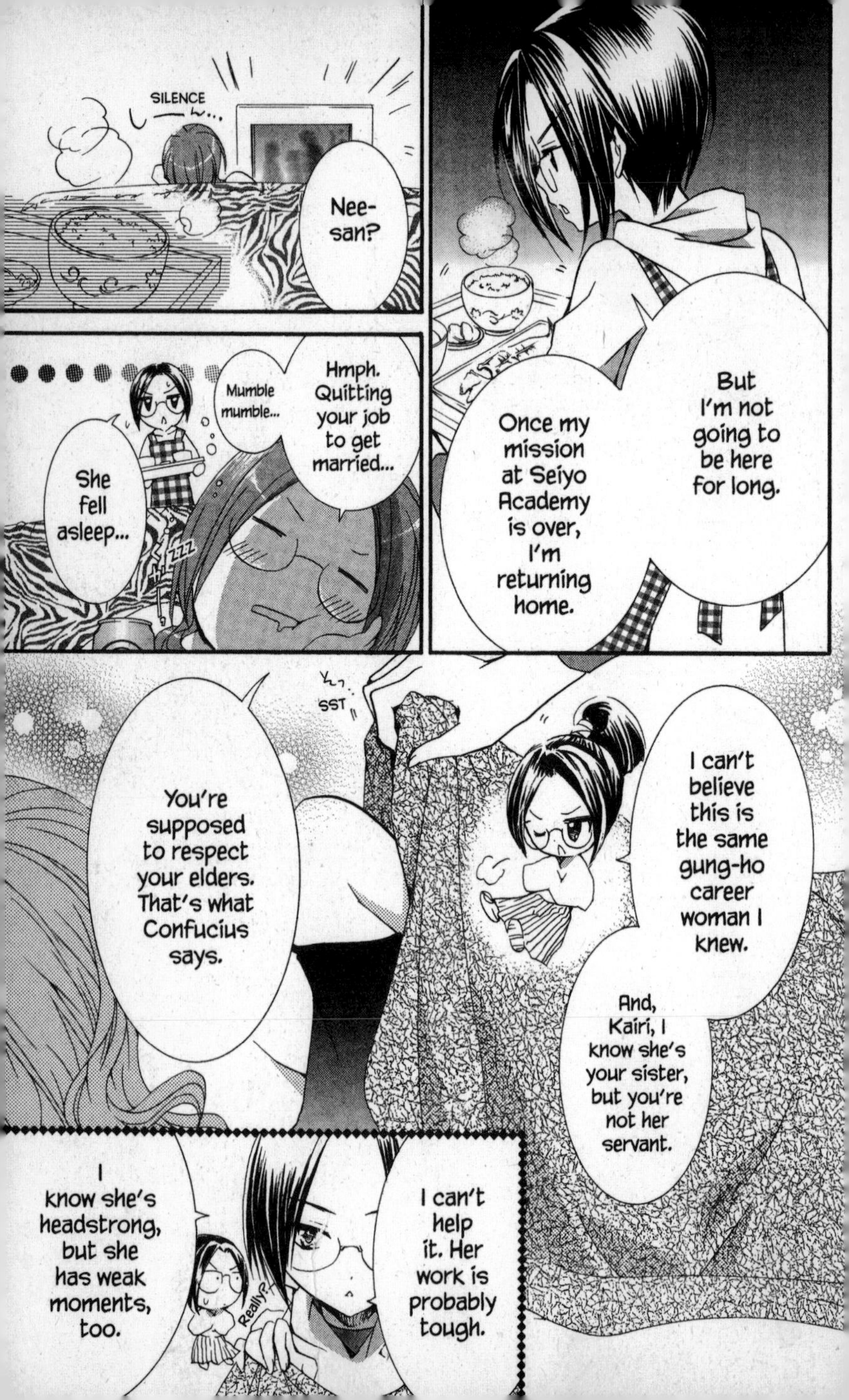
But I'm not going to be here for long.
Once my mission at Seiyo Academy is over, I'm returning home.
SILENCE
Nee-san?
Hmph. Quitting your job to get married...
Mumble mumble...
She fell asleep...
SST
I can't believe this is the same gung-ho career woman I knew.
You're supposed to respect your elders. That's what Confucius says.
And, Kairi, I know she's your sister, but you're not her servant.
I can't help it. Her work is probably tough.
I know she's headstrong, but she has weak moments, too.
Really?

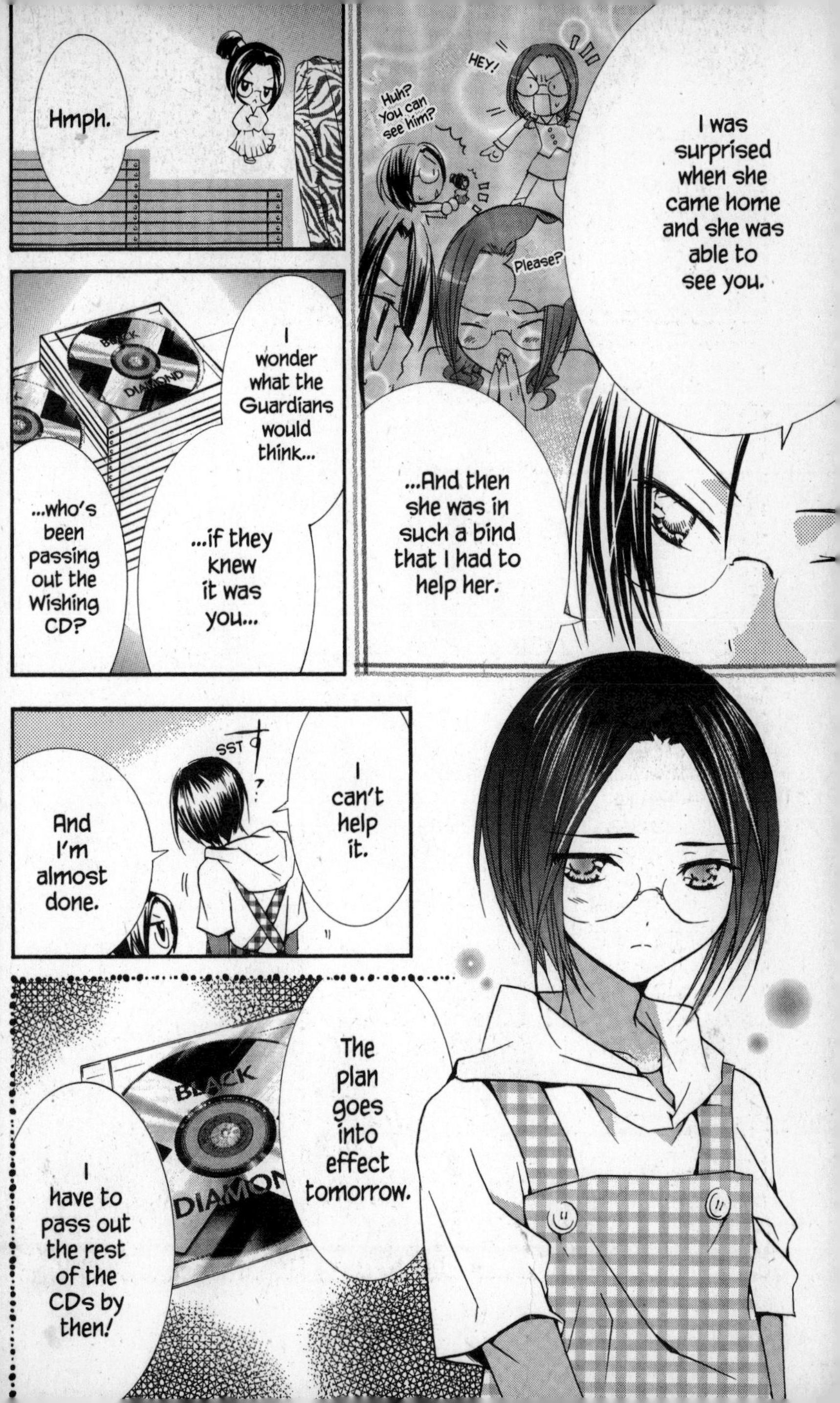
I was surprised when she came home and she was able to see you.
HEY!
Huh? You can see him?
Please?
...And then she was in such a bind that I had to help her.
Hmph.
I wonder what the Guardians would think...
...if they knew it was you...
...who's been passing out the Wishing CD?
BLACK DIAMOND
I can't help it.
SST
And I'm almost done.
The plan goes into effect tomorrow.
I have to pass out the rest of the CDs by then!
BLACK DIAMON

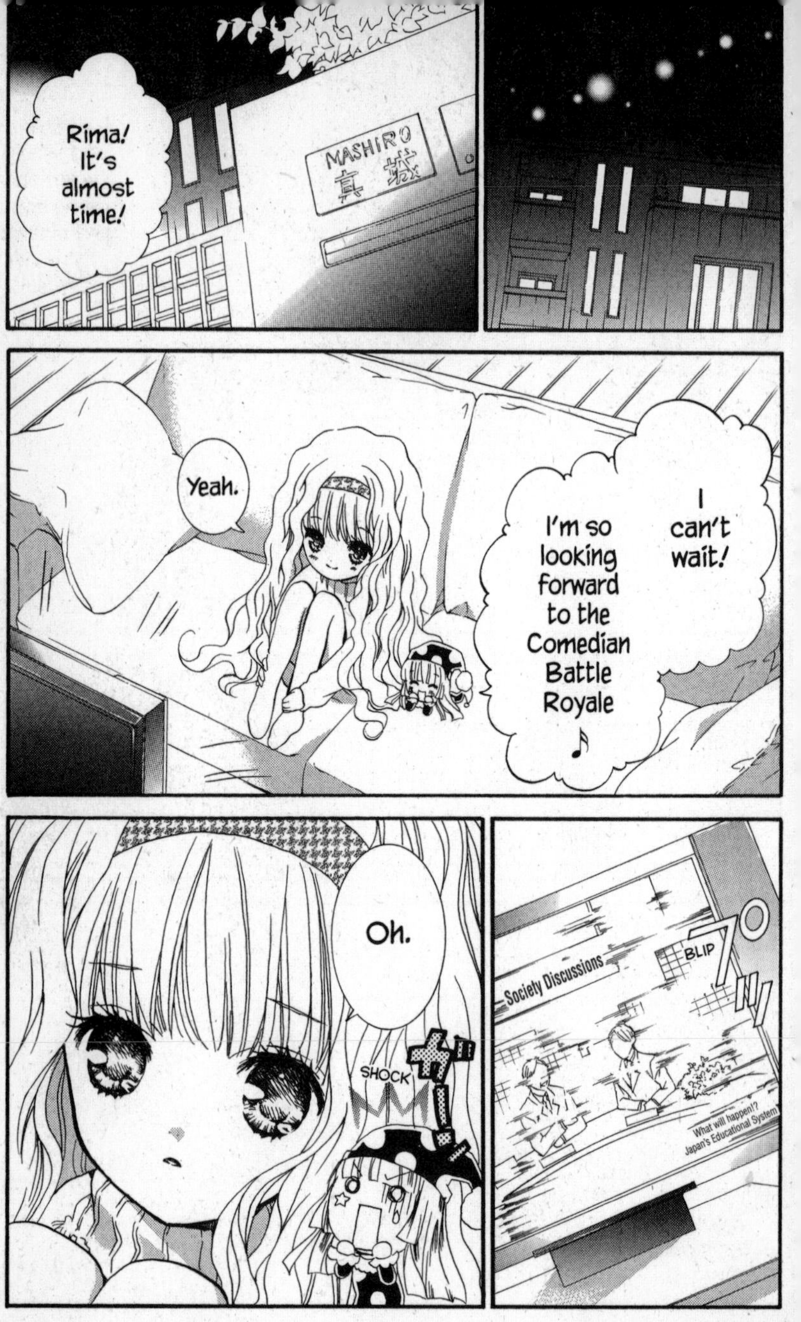
Rima! It's almost time!
MASHIRO 真城
I can't wait!
I'm so looking forward to the Comedian Battle Royale ♪
Yeah.
BLIP
Society Discussions
What will happen!? Japan's Educational System
Oh.
SHOCK

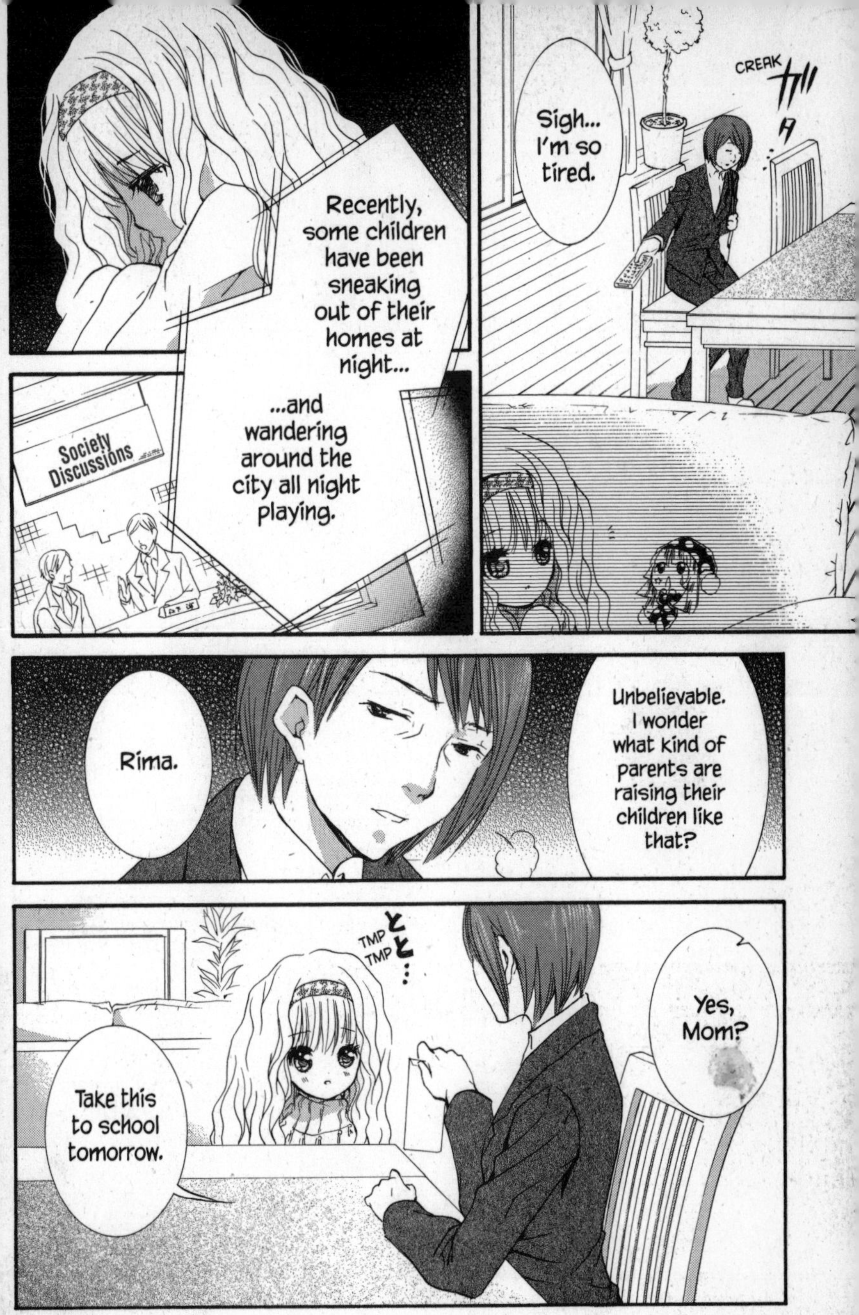

Sigh... I'm so tired.
CREAK
Recently, some children have been sneaking out of their homes at night...
Society Discussions
...and wandering around the city all night playing.
Unbelievable. I wonder what kind of parents are raising their children like that?
Rima.
Yes, Mom?
TMP とと TMP
Take this to school tomorrow.

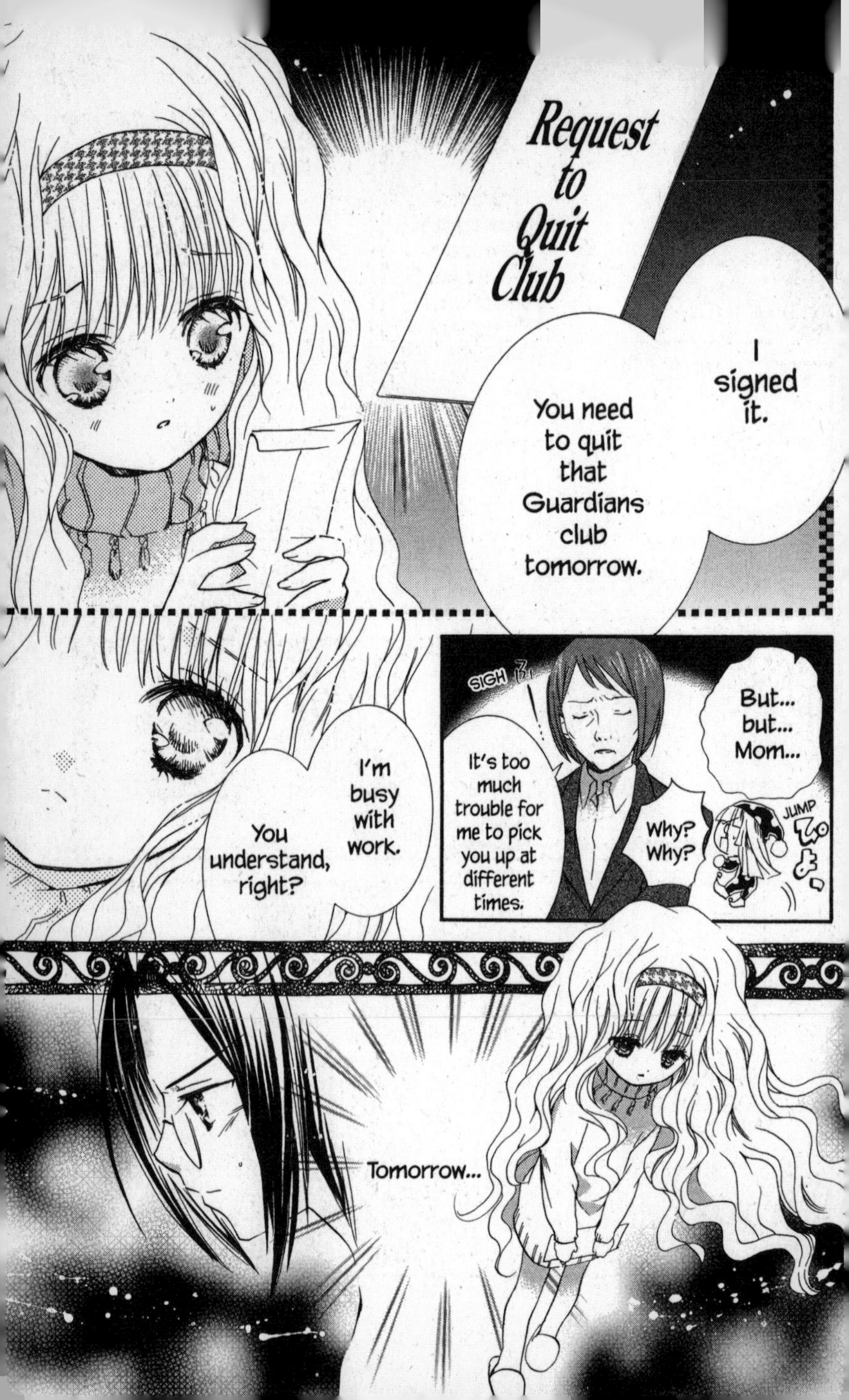
Request to Quit Club
I signed it.
You need to quit that Guardians club tomorrow.
But... but... Mom...
JUMP
Why? Why?
SIGH
It's too much trouble for me to pick you up at different times.
I'm busy with work.
You understand, right?
Tomorrow...

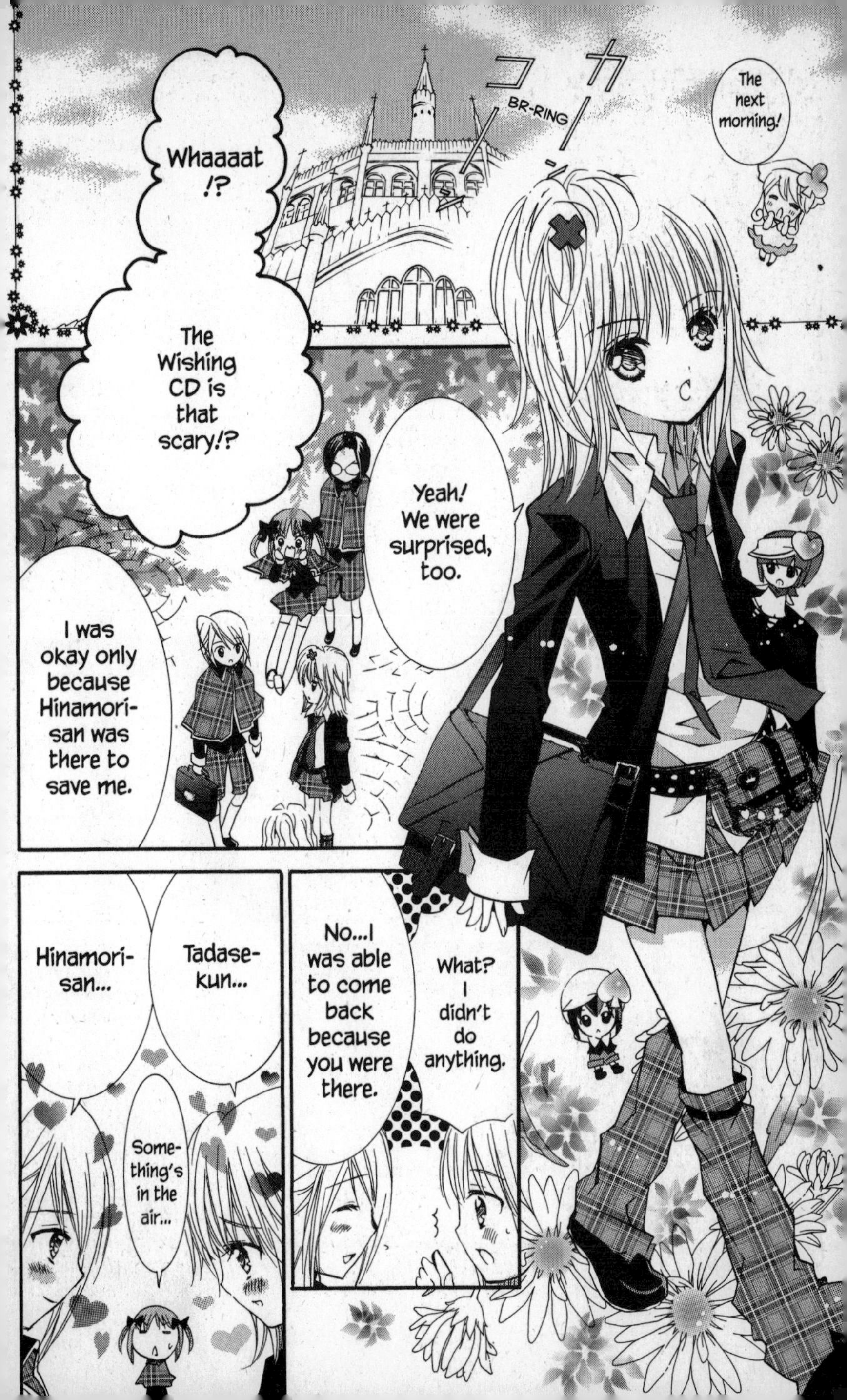
The next morning!
BR-RING
Whaaaat!?
The Wishing CD is that scary!?
Yeah! We were surprised, too.
I was okay only because Hinamori-san was there to save me.
What? I didn't do anything.
No...I was able to come back because you were there.
Tadase-kun...
Hinamori-san...
Something's in the air...

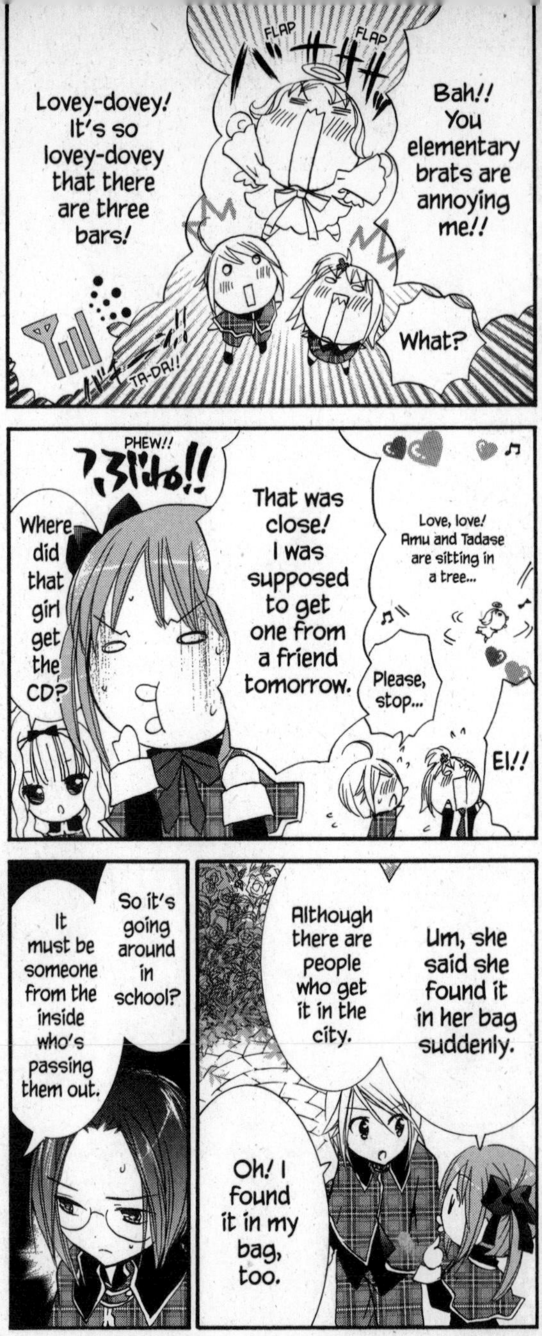
FLAP
FLAP
Bah!! You elementary brats are annoying me!!
Lovey-dovey! It's so lovey-dovey that there are three bars!
What?
TA-DA!!
Love, love! Amu and Tadase are sitting in a tree...
Please, stop...
Ei!!
That was close! I was supposed to get one from a friend tomorrow.
PHEW!!
Where did that girl get the CD?
Um, she said she found it in her bag suddenly.
Although there are people who get it in the city.
Oh! I found it in my bag, too.
So it's going around in school?
It must be someone from the inside who's passing them out.

character profile

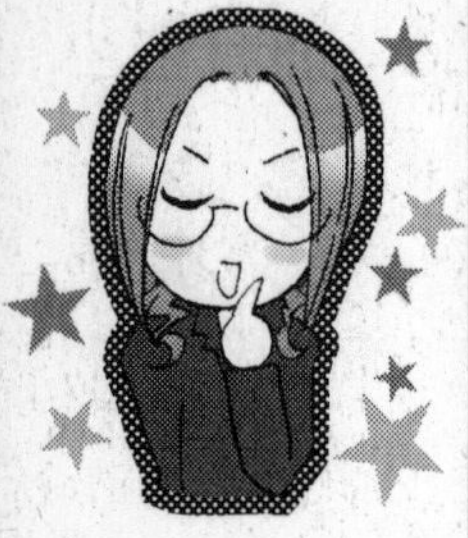

Yukari Sanjo

Birthday: 8/7
Blood Type: B
Sign: Leo

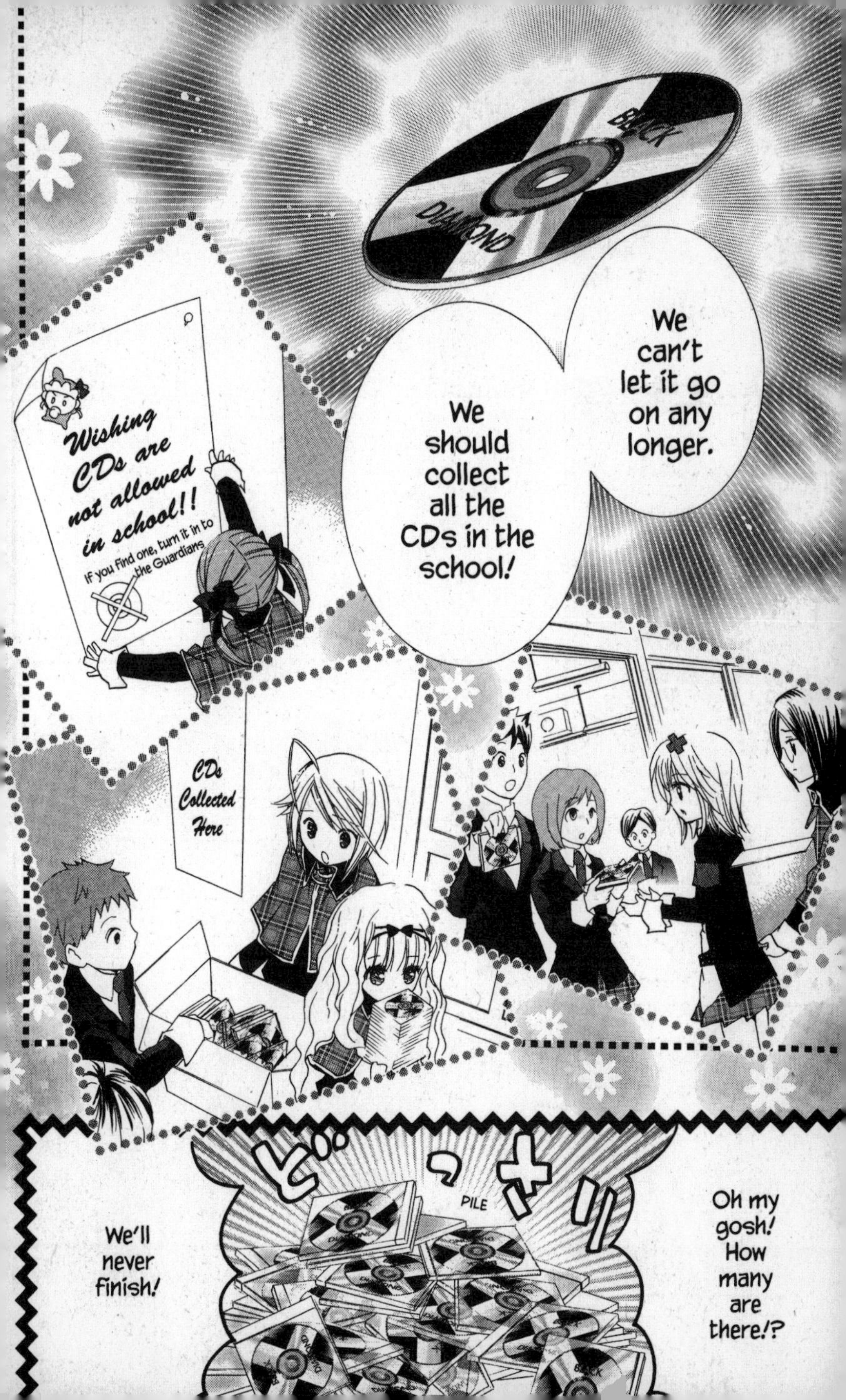
BLACK
DIAMOND
We can't let it go on any longer.
We should collect all the CDs in the school!
Wishing CDs are not allowed in school!!
If you find one, turn it in to the Guardians
CDs Collected Here
PILE
Oh my gosh! How many are there!?
We'll never finish!

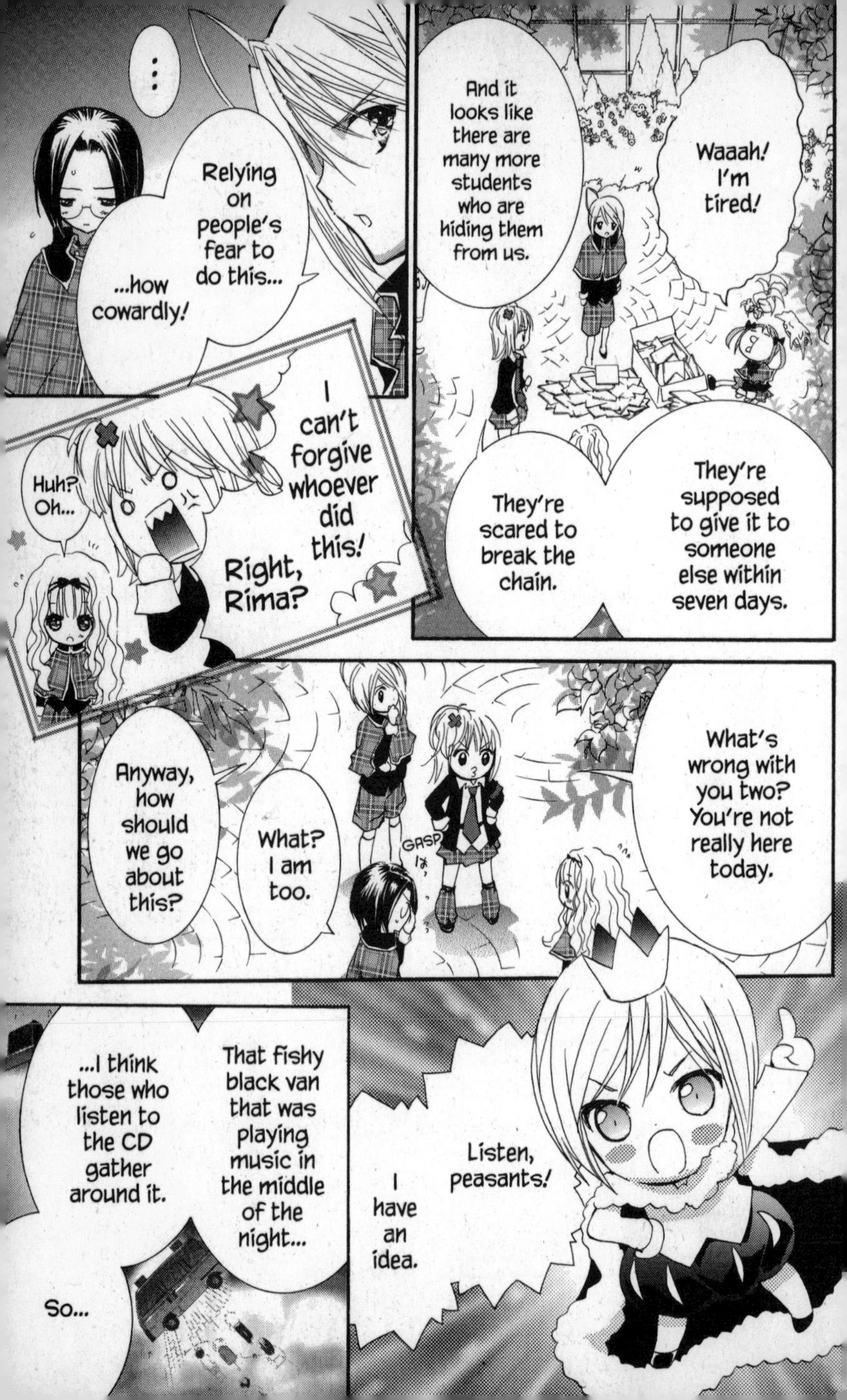
Waaah! I'm tired!
And it looks like there are many more students who are hiding them from us.
They're supposed to give it to someone else within seven days.
They're scared to break the chain.
...
Relying on people's fear to do this...
...how cowardly!
I can't forgive whoever did this!
Right, Rima?
Huh? Oh...
What's wrong with you two? You're not really here today.
GASP
What? I am too.
Anyway, how should we go about this?
Listen, peasants!
I have an idea.
That fishy black van that was playing music in the middle of the night...
...I think those who listen to the CD gather around it.
So...

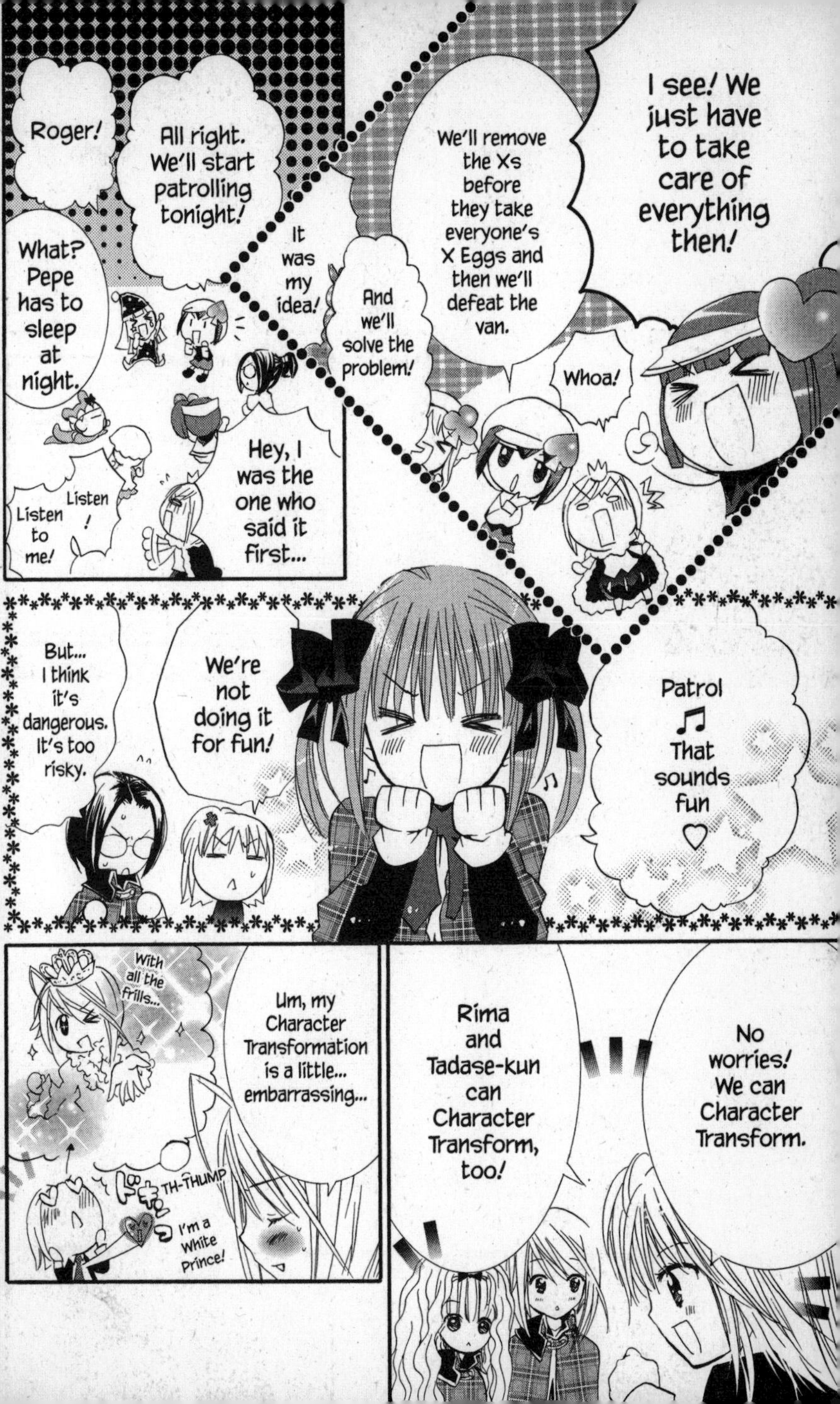
I see! We just have to take care of everything then!
We'll remove the Xs before they take everyone's X Eggs and then we'll defeat the van.
Whoa!
And we'll solve the problem!
It was my idea!
All right. We'll start patrolling tonight!
Roger!
What? Pepe has to sleep at night.
Hey, I was the one who said it first...
Listen!
Listen to me!
Patrol ♫ That sounds fun ♡
We're not doing it for fun!
But... I think it's dangerous. It's too risky.
No worries! We can Character Transform.
Rima and Tadase-kun can Character Transform, too!
Um, my Character Transformation is a little... embarrassing...
With all the frills...
TH-THUMP
I'm a White Prince!

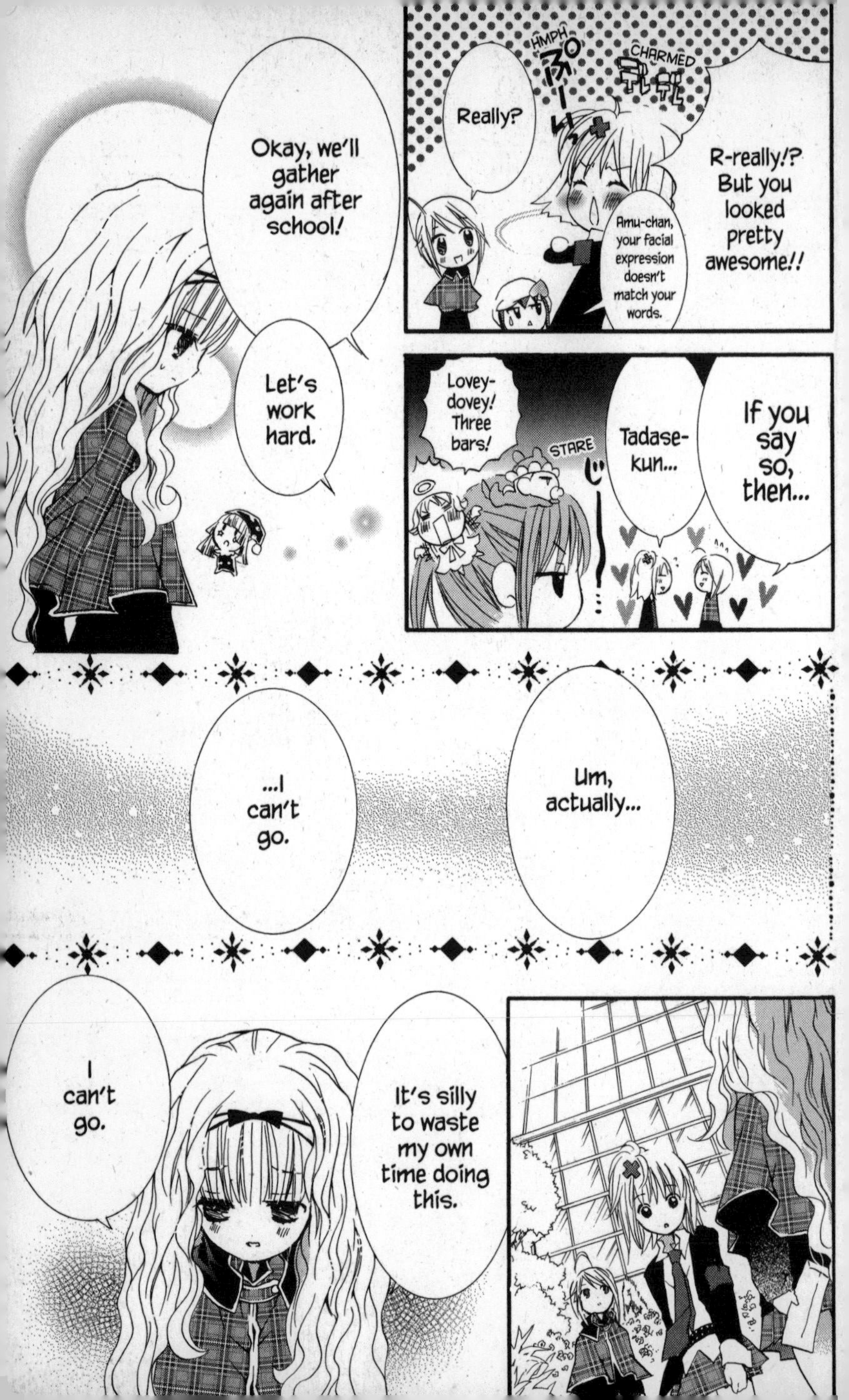
CHARMED
HMPH
R-really!? But you looked pretty awesome!!
Amu-chan, your facial expression doesn't match your words.
Really?
If you say so, then...
Tadase-kun...
STARE
Lovey-dovey! Three bars!
Okay, we'll gather again after school!
Let's work hard.
Um, actually...
...I can't go.
It's silly to waste my own time doing this.
I can't go.

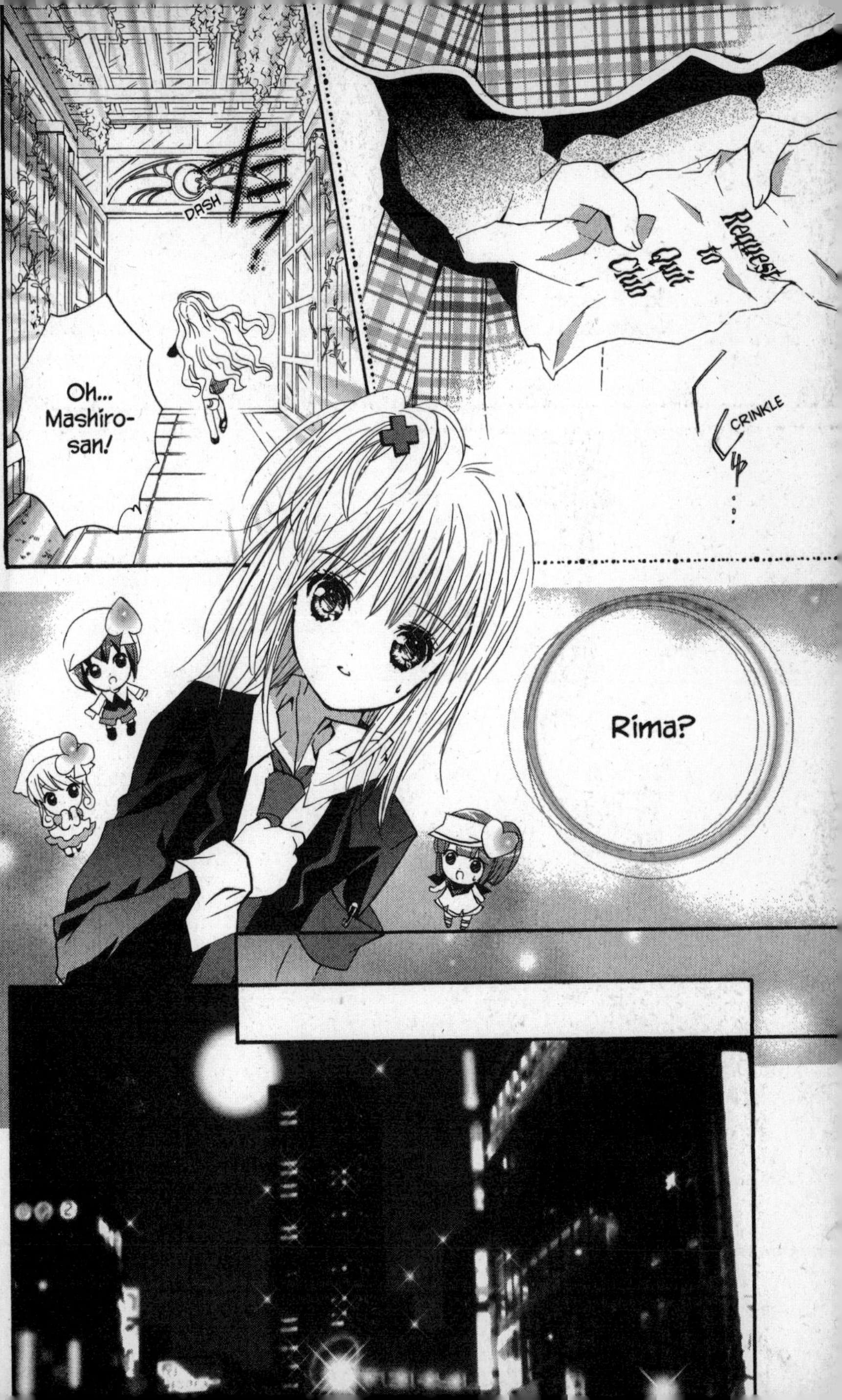
Request to Quit Club
CRINKLE
DASH
Oh... Mashiro-san!
Rima?

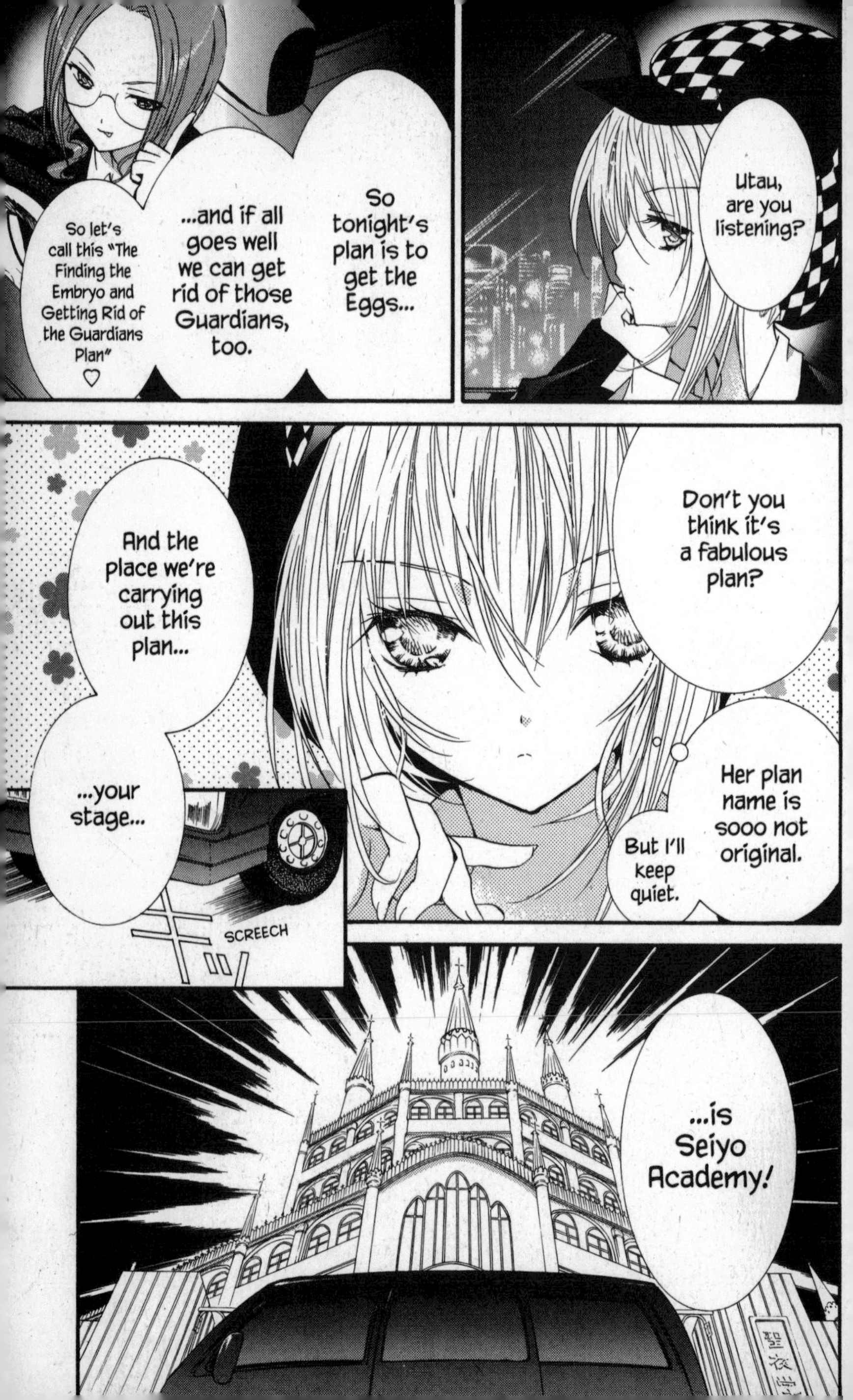
Utau, are you listening?
So tonight's plan is to get the Eggs...
...and if all goes well we can get rid of those Guardians, too.
So let's call this "The Finding the Embryo and Getting Rid of the Guardians Plan" ♡
Don't you think it's a fabulous plan?
Her plan name is sooo not original.
But I'll keep quiet.
And the place we're carrying out this plan...
...your stage...
SCREECH
...is Seiyo Academy!

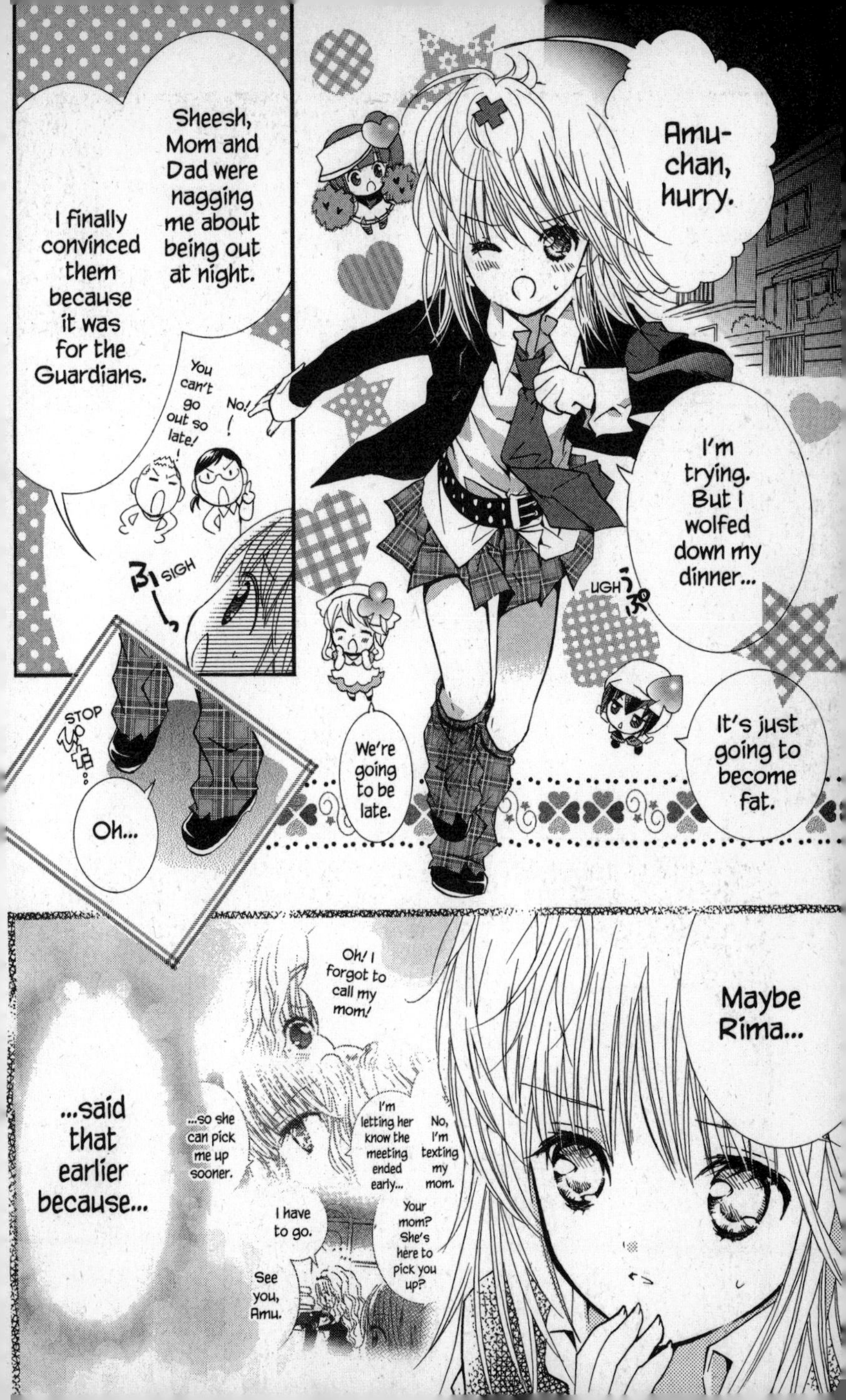
Amu-chan, hurry.
I'm trying. But I wolfed down my dinner...
UGH
It's just going to become fat.
We're going to be late.
Sheesh, Mom and Dad were nagging me about being out at night.
I finally convinced them because it was for the Guardians.
No!
You can't go out so late!
SIGH
STOP
Oh...
Maybe Rima...
Oh! I forgot to call my mom!
No, I'm texting my mom.
Your mom? She's here to pick you up?
I'm letting her know the meeting ended early...
...so she can pick me up sooner.
I have to go.
See you, Amu.
...said that earlier because...

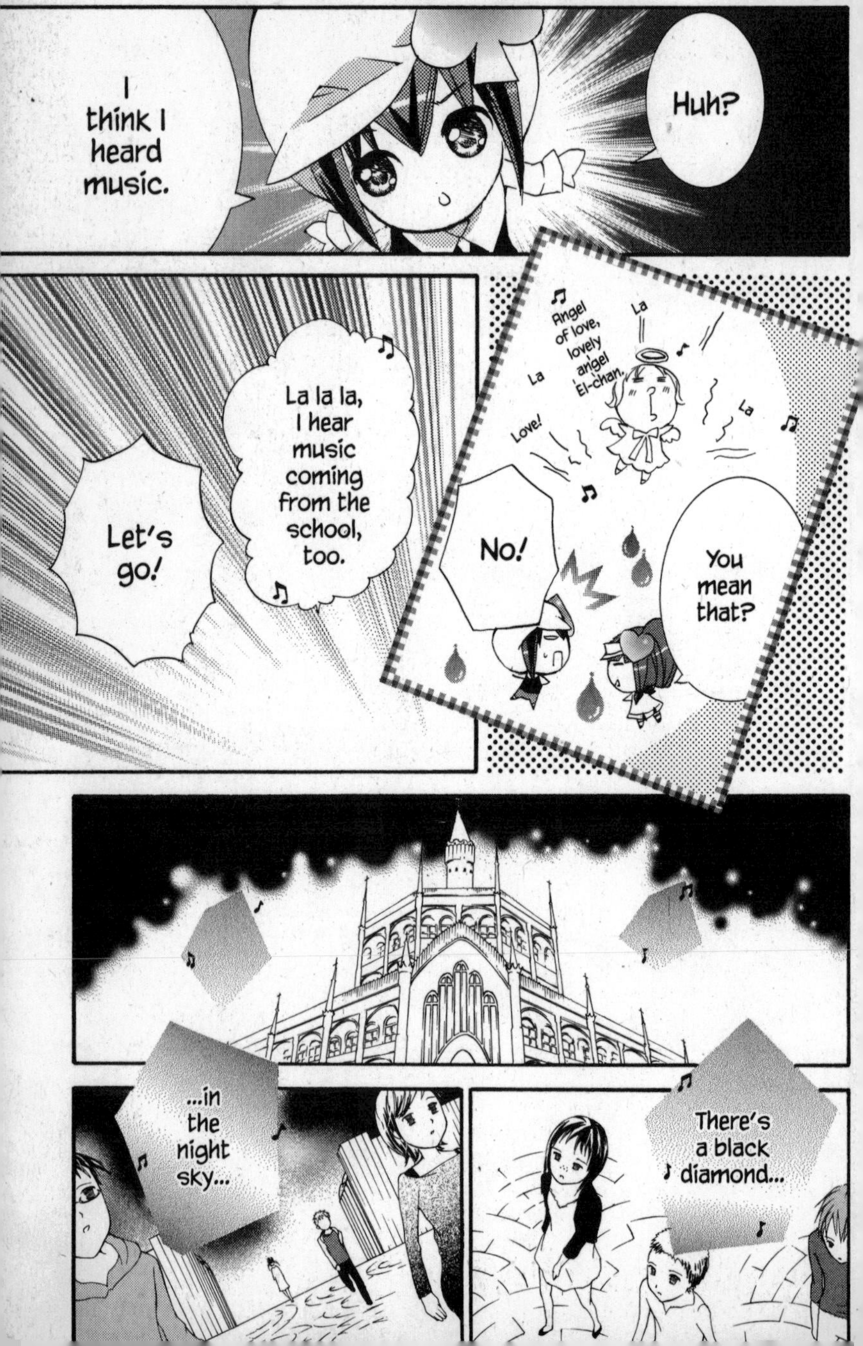
Huh?
I think I heard music.
La
Angel of love, lovely angel El-chan.
La
La
Love!
You mean that?
No!
La la la, I hear music coming from the school, too.
Let's go!
There's a black diamond...
...in the night sky...

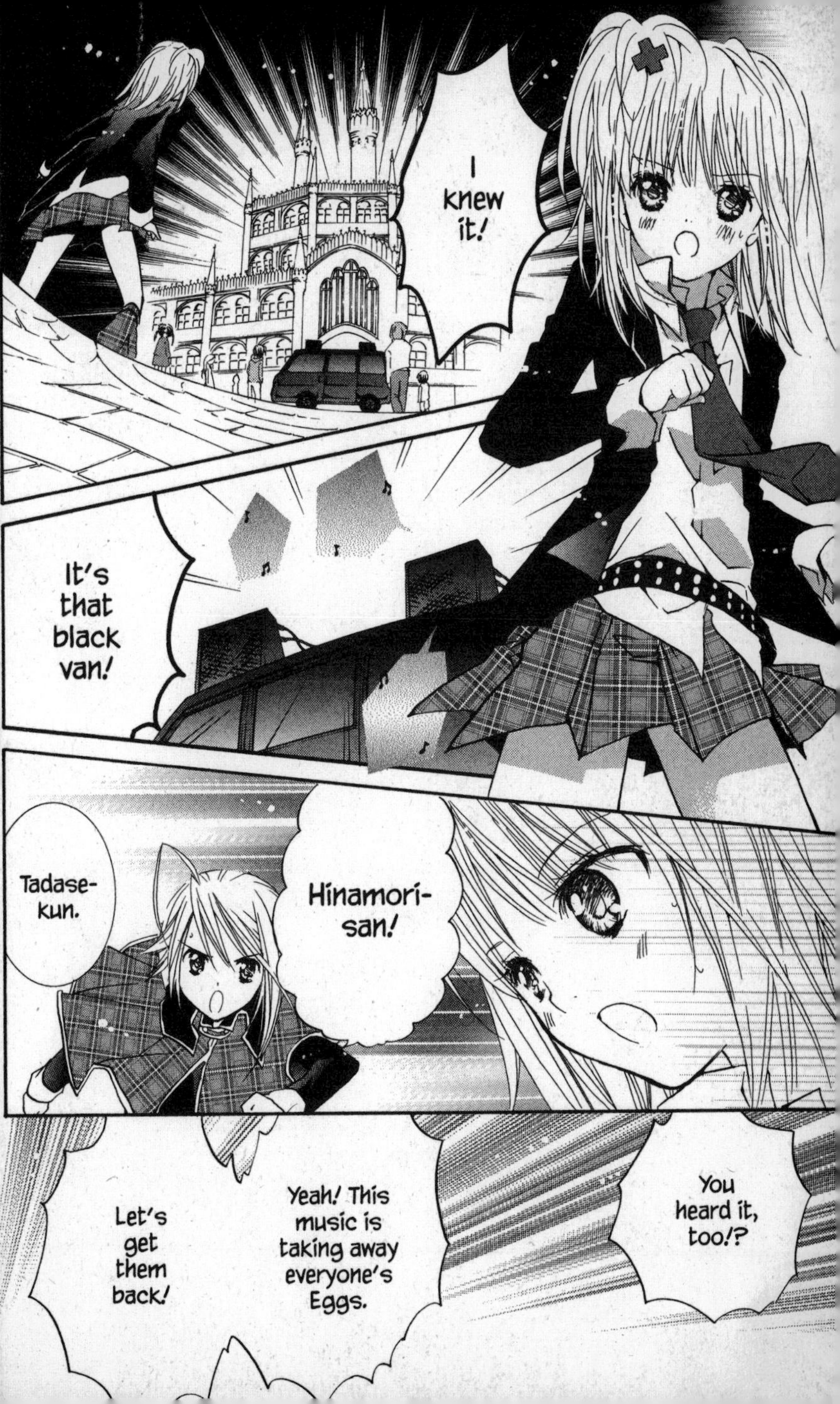
I knew it!
It's that black van!
Hinamori-san!
Tadase-kun.
You heard it, too!?
Yeah! This music is taking away everyone's Eggs.
Let's get them back!

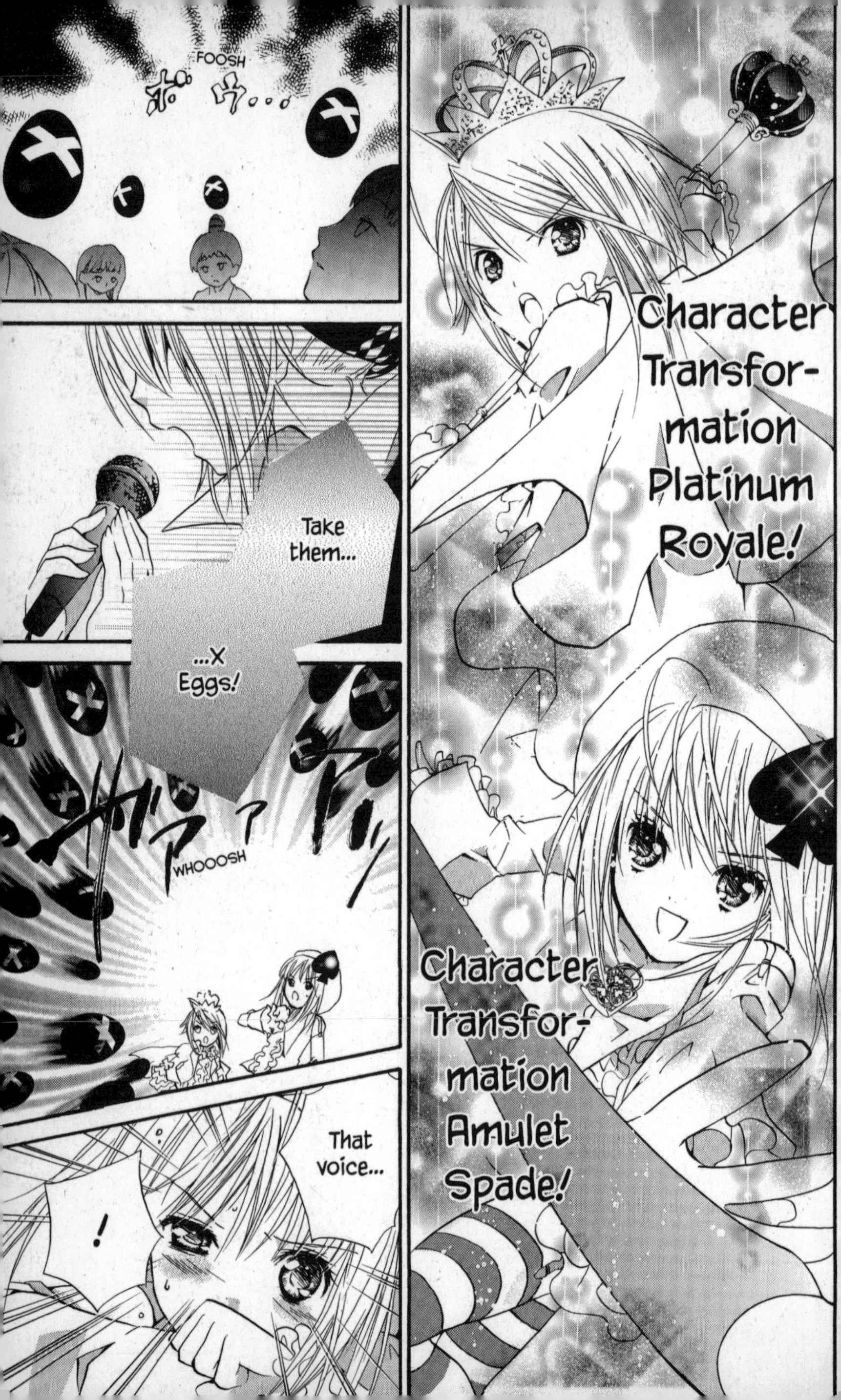
Character Transfor-mation Platinum Royale!
Character Transfor-mation Amulet Spade!
FOOSH
Take them...
...X Eggs!
WHOOOSH
That voice...
!

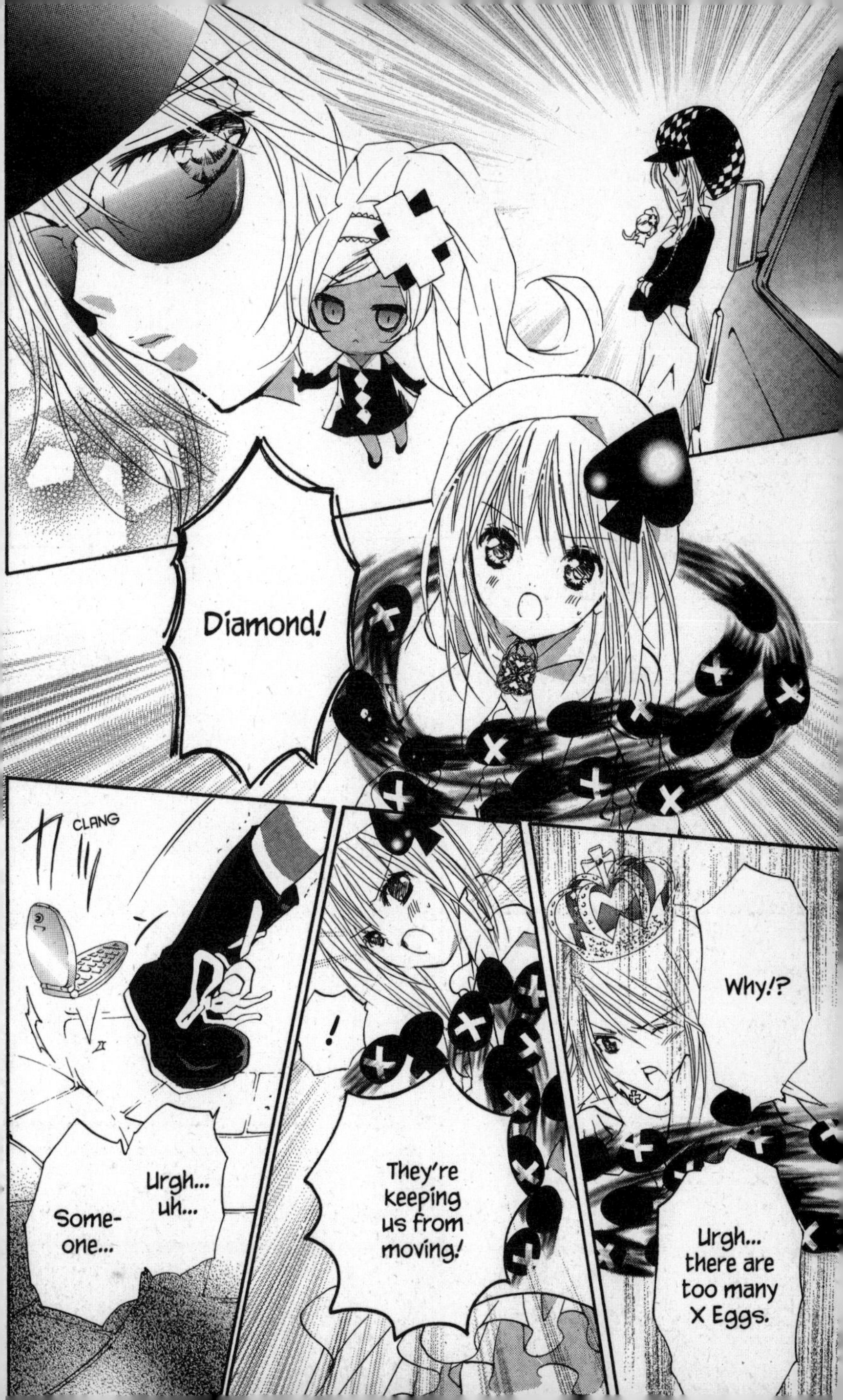
Diamond!
Why!?
Urgh... there are too many X Eggs.
!
They're keeping us from moving!
CLANG
Urgh... uh...
Some-one...

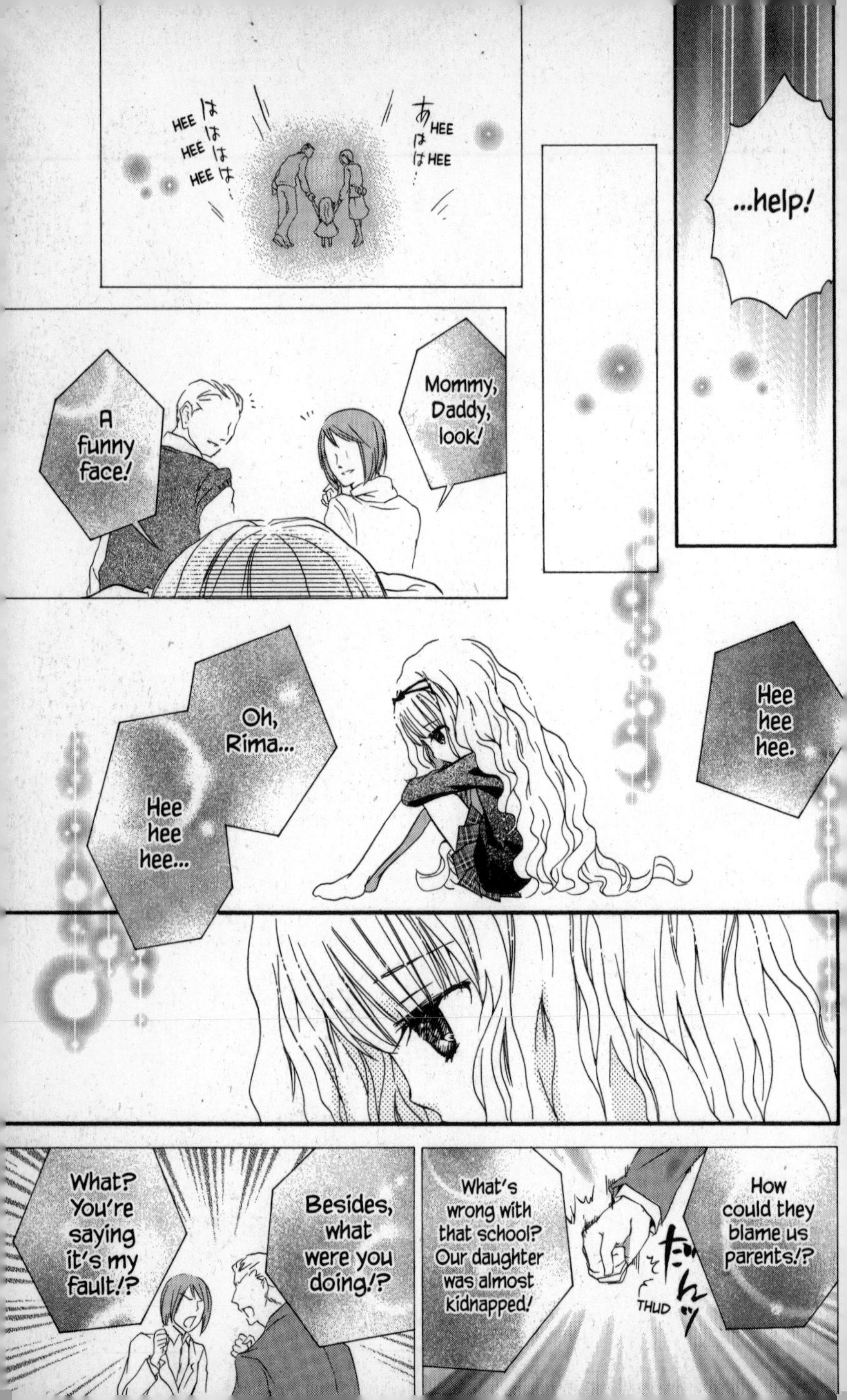
...help!
あはは…
HEE
HEE
ははは…
HEE
HEE
HEE
Mommy, Daddy, look!
A funny face!
Hee hee hee.
Oh, Rima...
Hee hee hee...
How could they blame us parents!?
だんッ
THUD
What's wrong with that school? Our daughter was almost kidnapped!
Besides, what were you doing!?
What? You're saying it's my fault!?

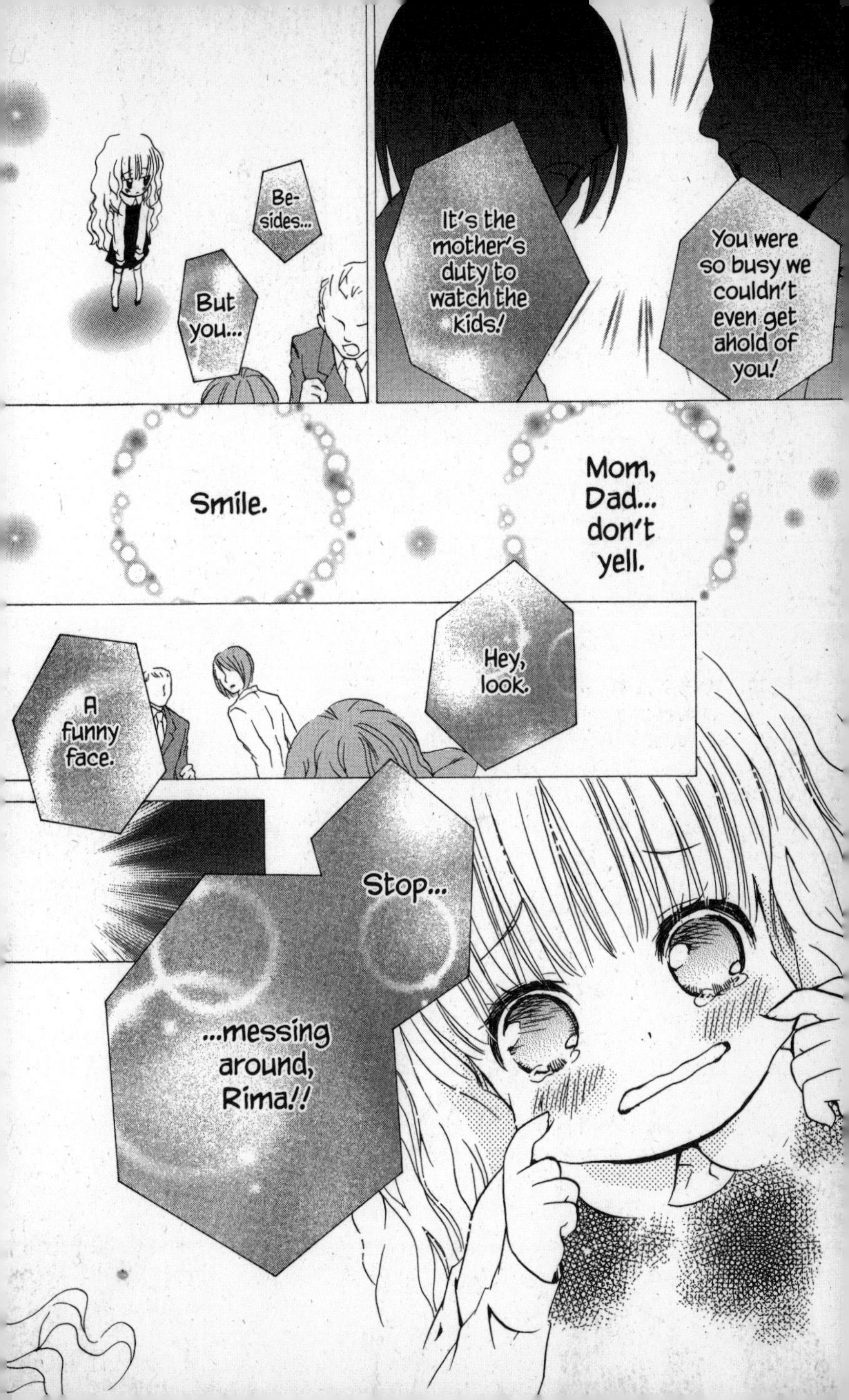
You were so busy we couldn't even get ahold of you!
It's the mother's duty to watch the kids!
Be-sides...
But you...
Mom, Dad... don't yell.
Smile.
Hey, look.
A funny face.
Stop...
...messing around, Rima!!

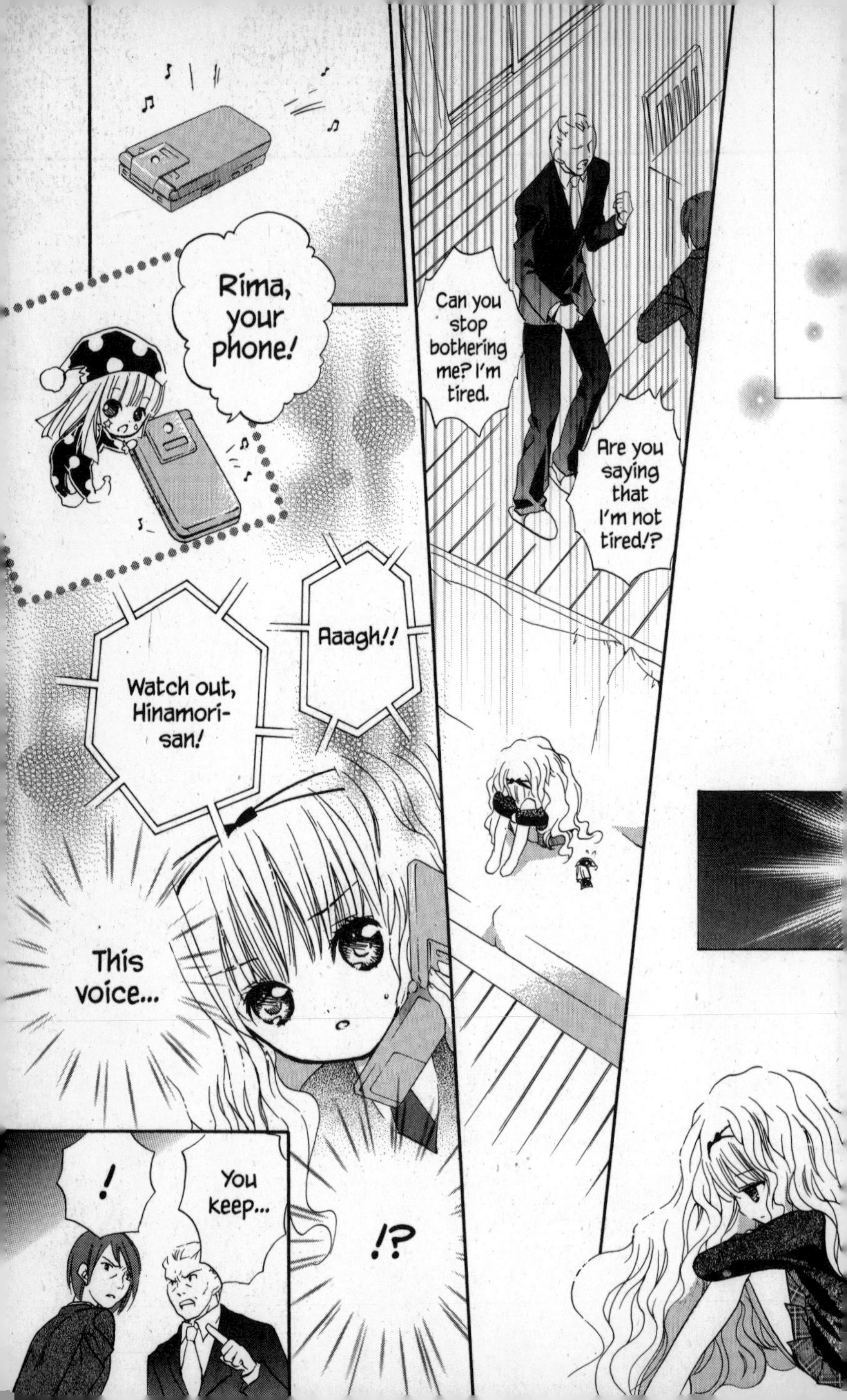
Can you stop bothering me? I'm tired.
Are you saying that I'm not tired!?
Rima, your phone!
Aaagh!!
Watch out, Hinamori-san!
This voice...
!?
You keep...
!

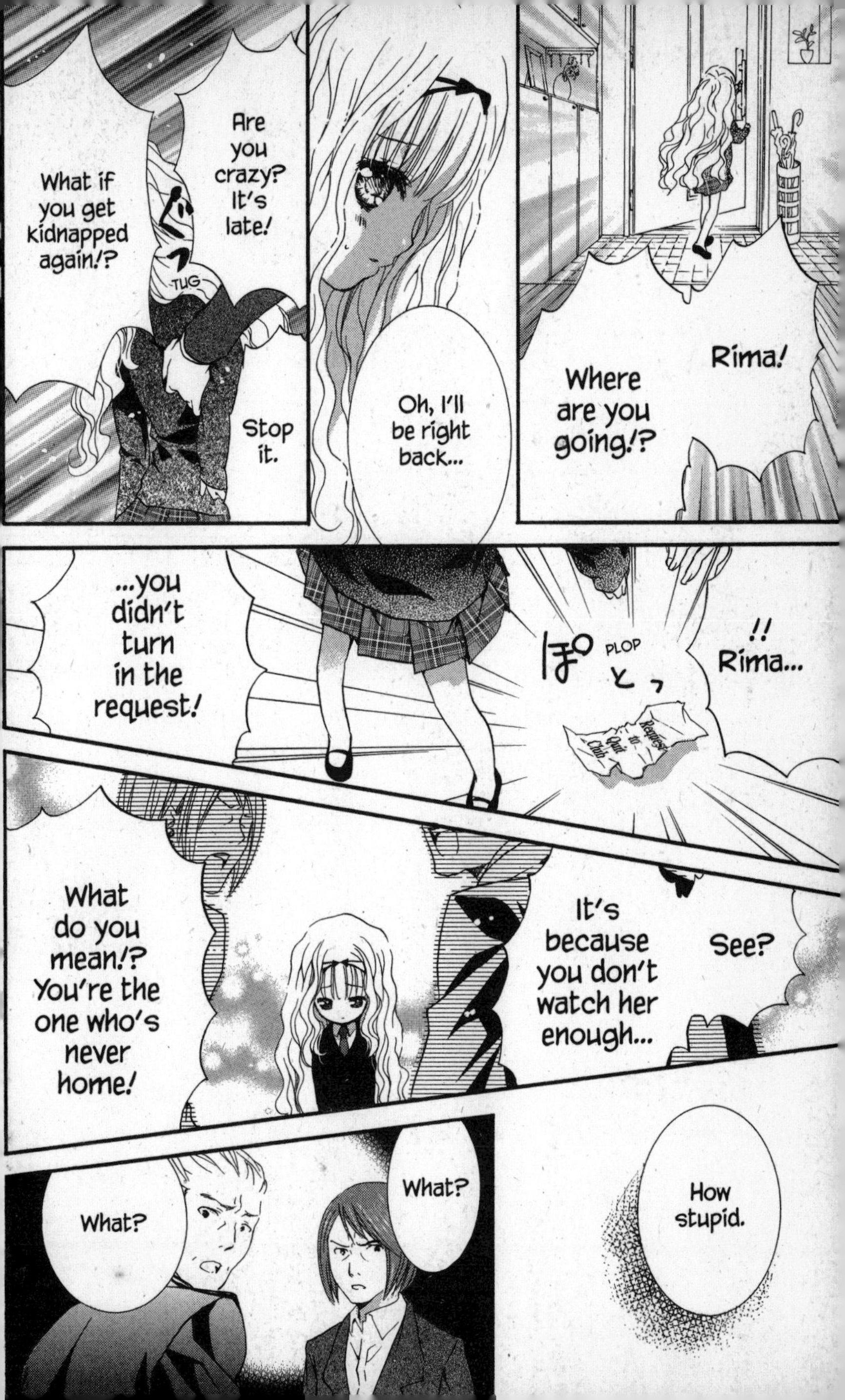
Rima!
Where are you going!?
Oh, I'll be right back...
Are you crazy? It's late!
What if you get kidnapped again!?
TUG
Stop it.
!! Rima...
ぽとっ
PLOP
Request to Quit Club
...you didn't turn in the request!
See?
It's because you don't watch her enough...
What do you mean!? You're the one who's never home!
How stupid.
What?
What?

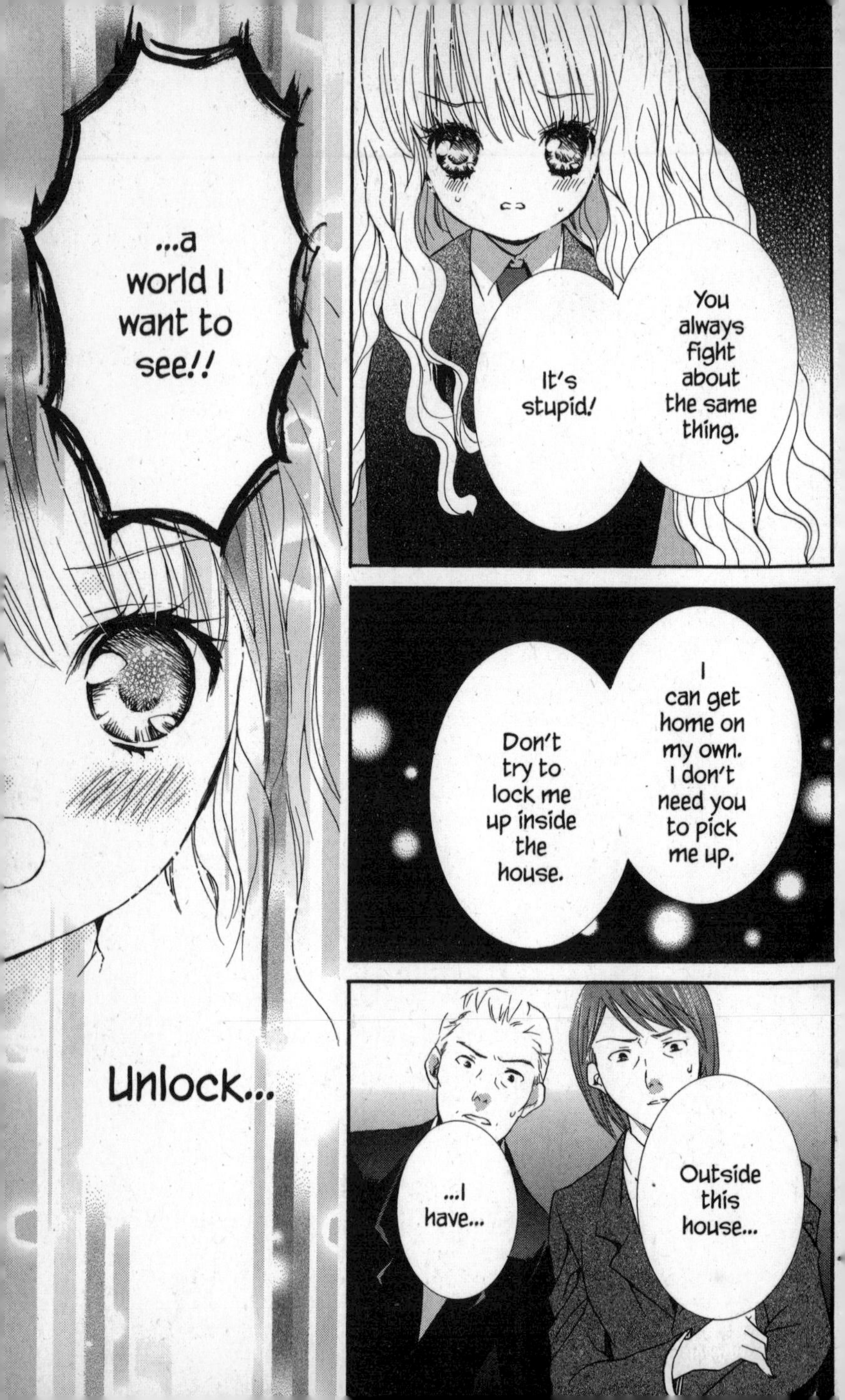
You always fight about the same thing.
It's stupid!
I can get home on my own. I don't need you to pick me up.
Don't try to lock me up inside the house.
Outside this house...
...I have...
...a world I want to see!!
Unlock...

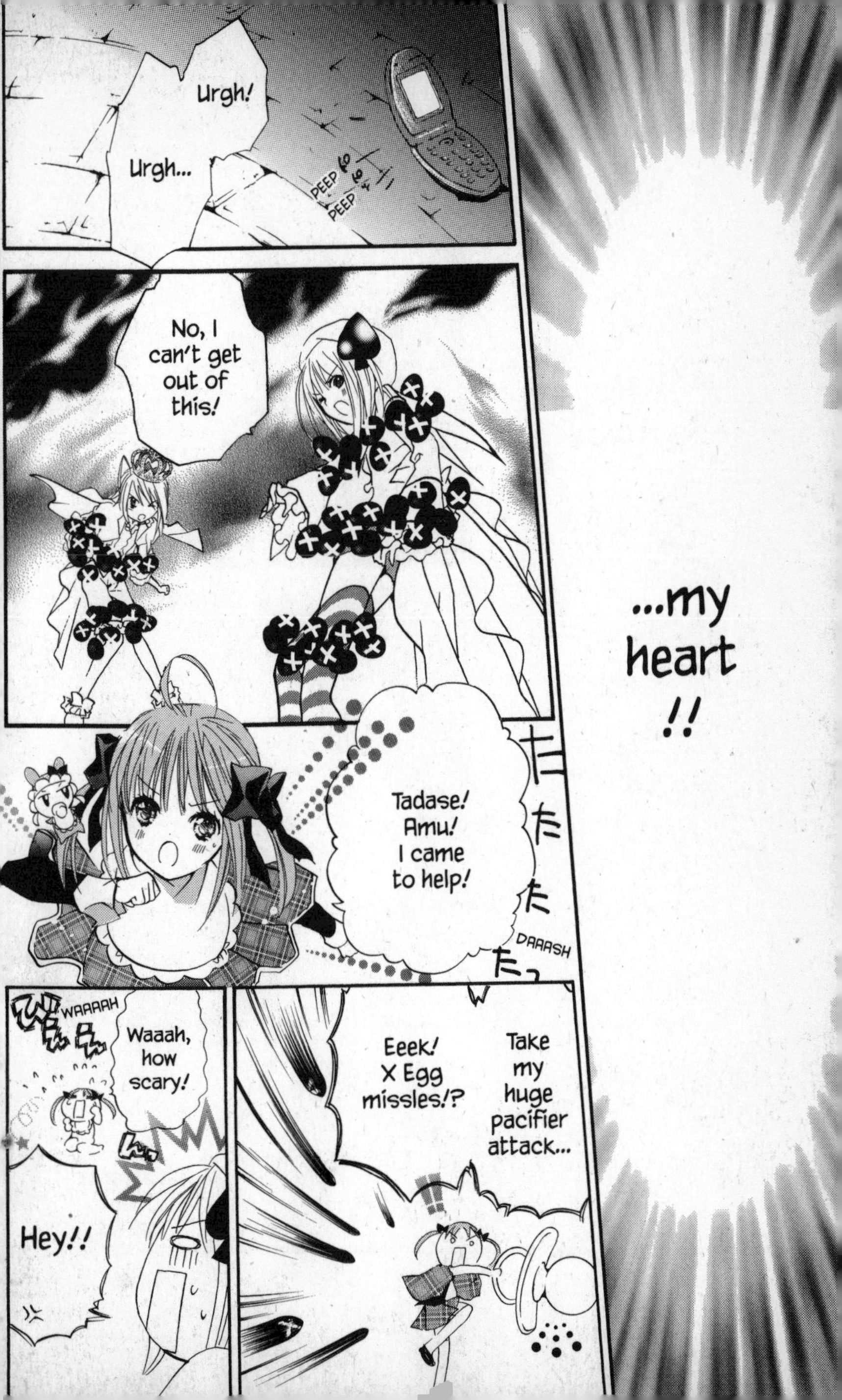
...my heart!!
Urgh!
Urgh...
PEEP PEEP
No, I can't get out of this!
Tadase! Amu! I came to help!
DAAASH
Take my huge pacifier attack...
Eeek! X Egg missles!?
WAAAAH
Waaah, how scary!
Hey!!

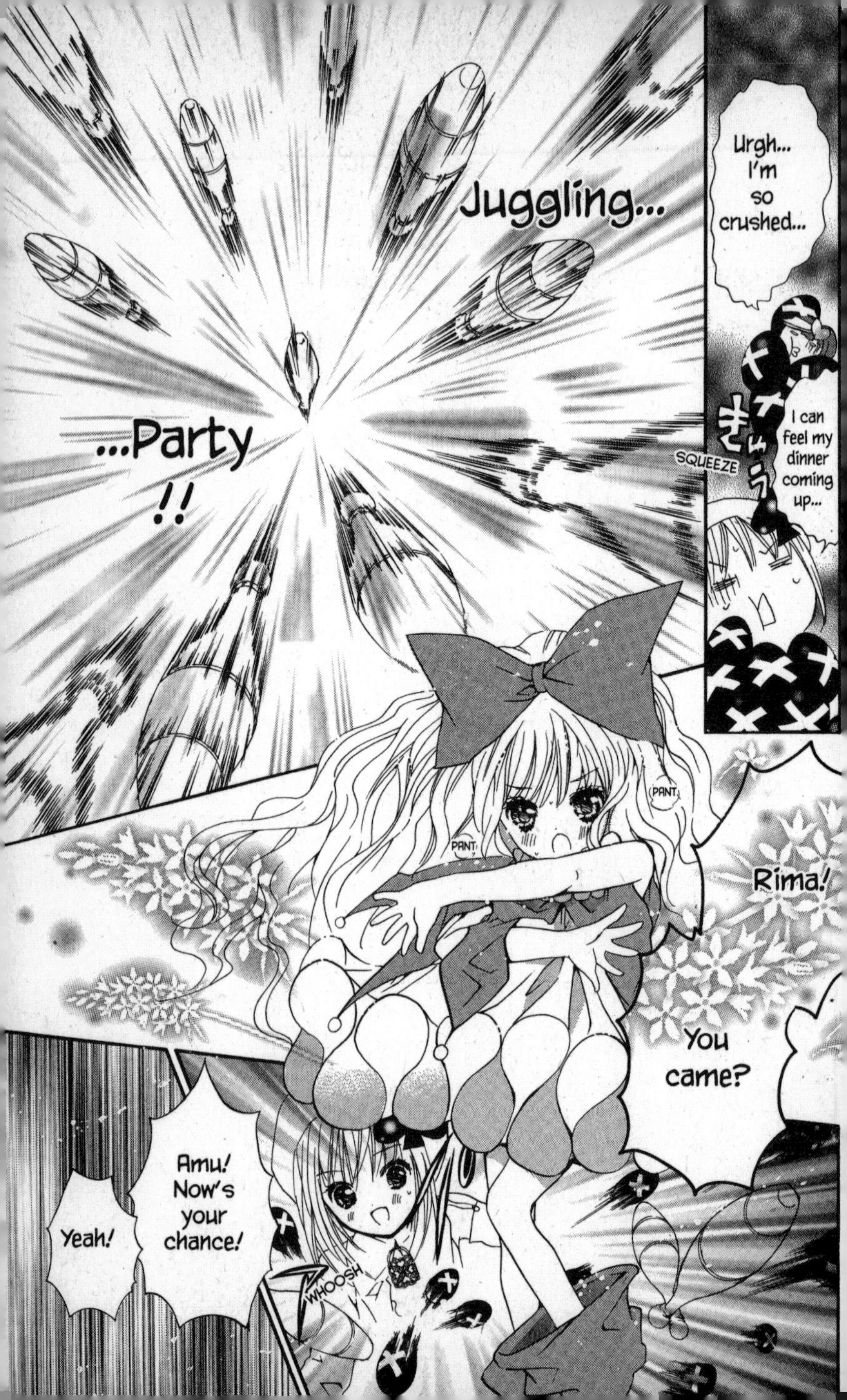
Urgh... I'm so crushed...
I can feel my dinner coming up...
SQUEEZE
Juggling...
...Party !!
PANT
PANT
Rima!
You came?
Amu! Now's your chance!
Yeah!
WHOOSH

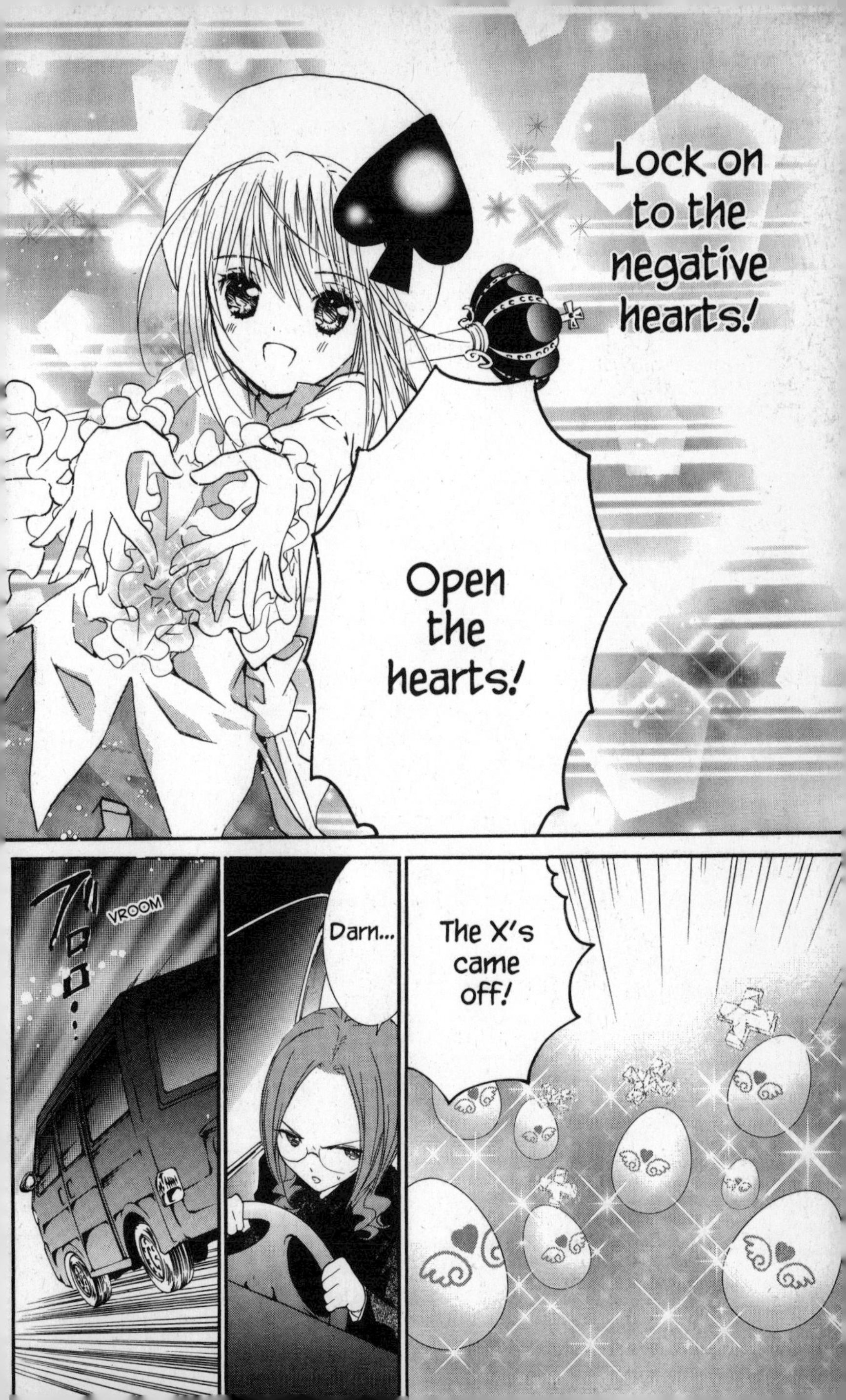
Lock on to the negative hearts!
Open the hearts!
The X's came off!
Darn...
VROOM

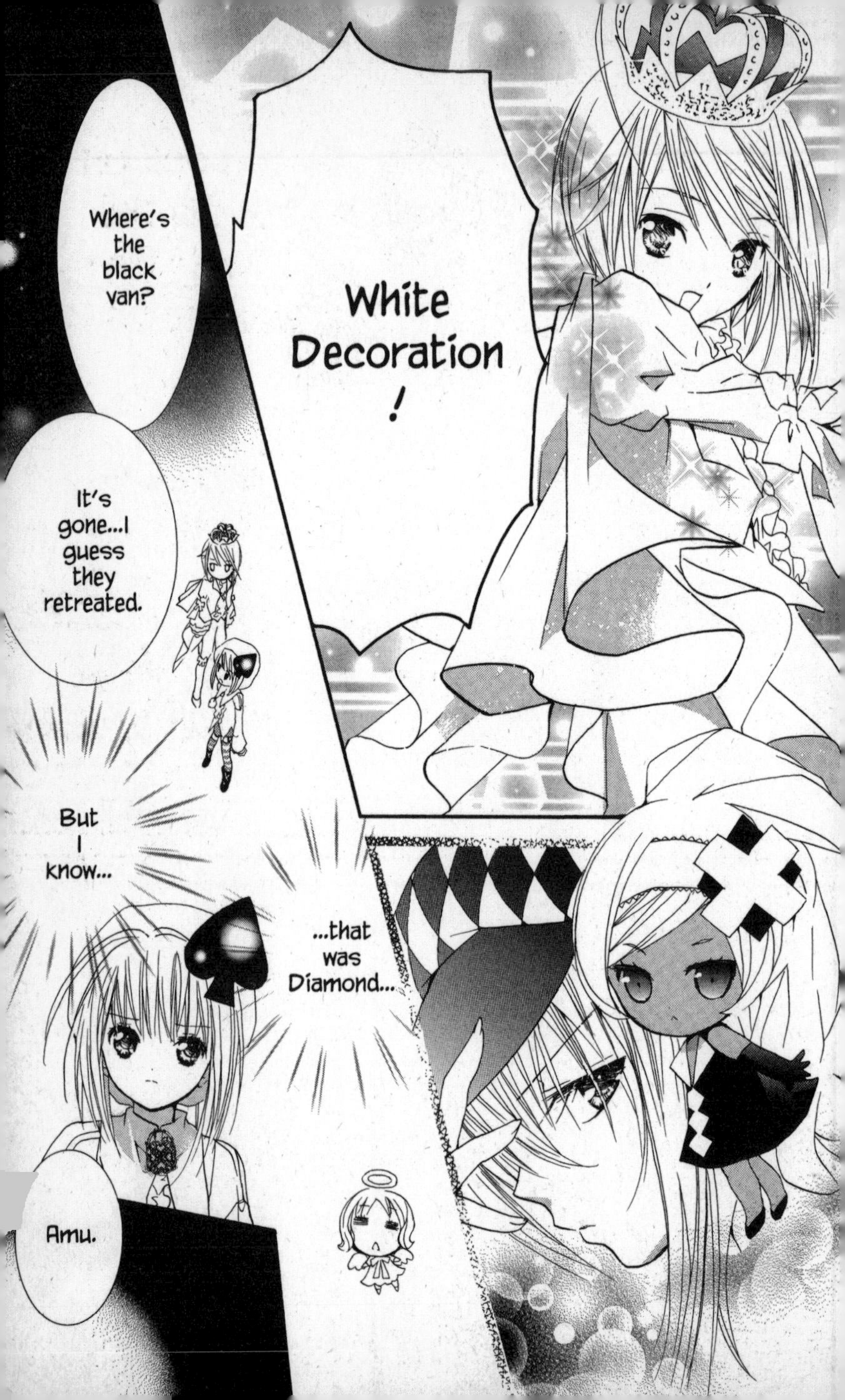
White Decoration!
Where's the black van?
It's gone...I guess they retreated.
But I know...
...that was Diamond...
Amu.

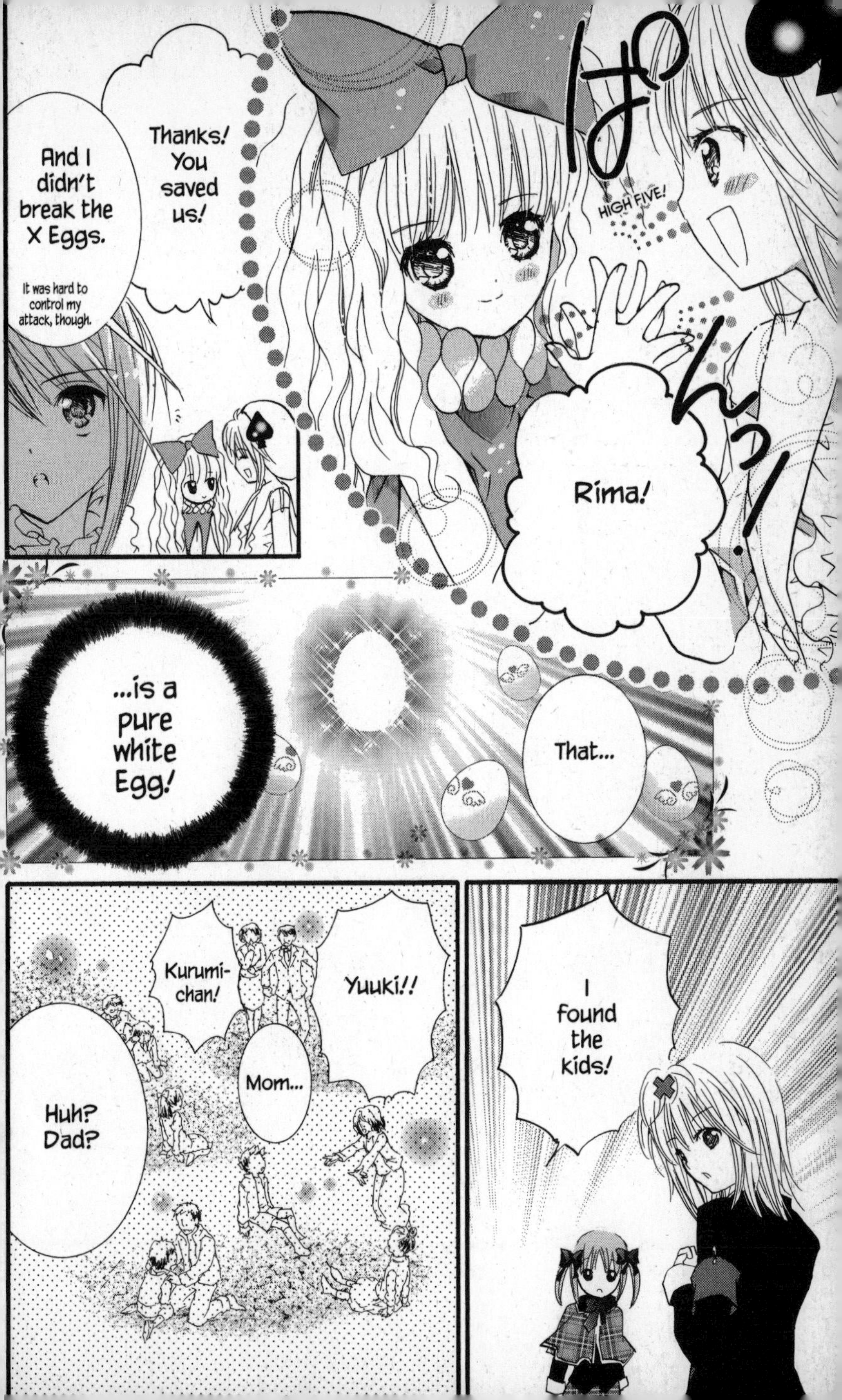
ぱんっ!
HIGH FIVE!
Rima!
Thanks! You saved us!
And I didn't break the X Eggs.
It was hard to control my attack, though.
That...
...is a pure white Egg!
I found the kids!
Yuuki!!
Kurumi-chan!
Mom...
Huh? Dad?

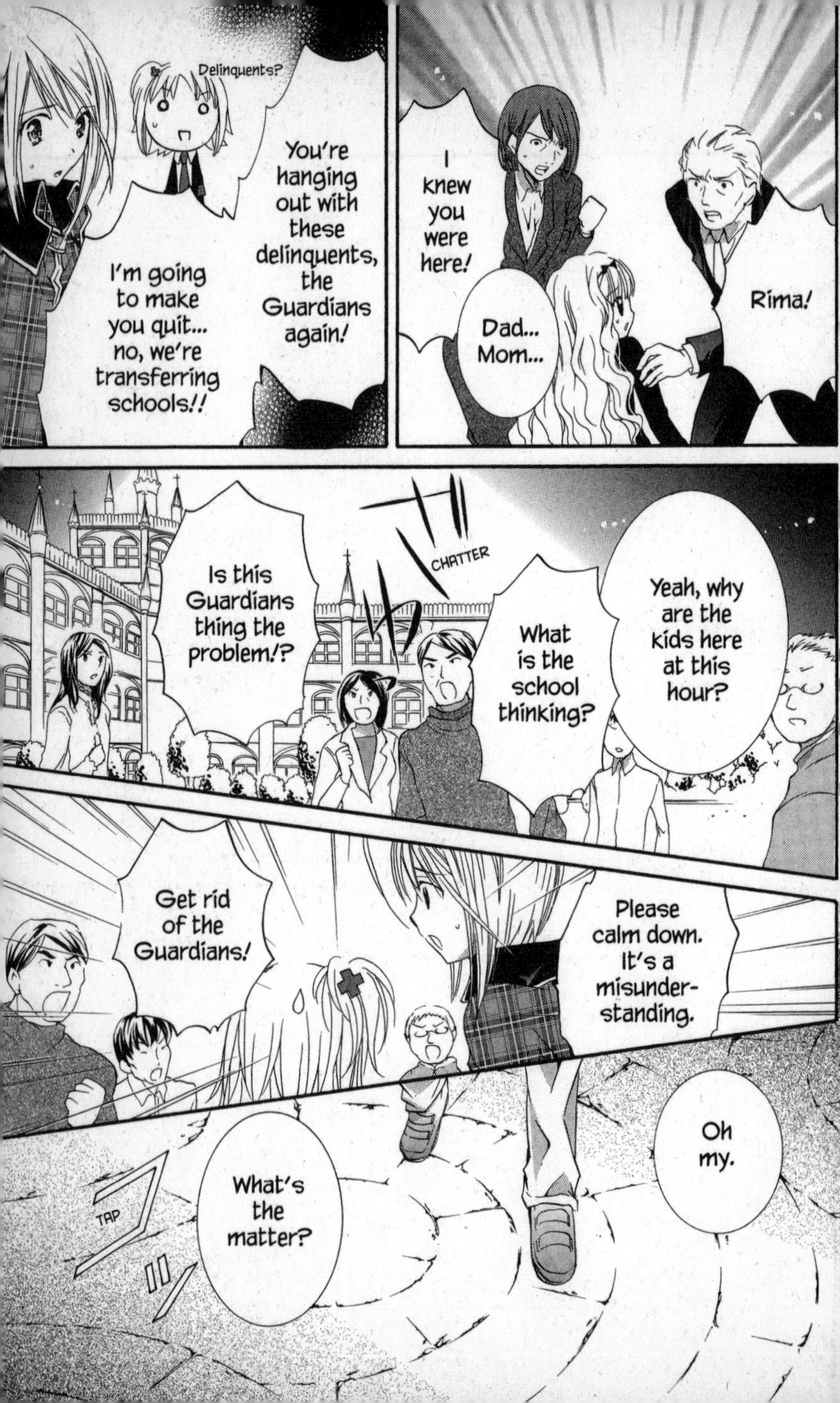

Rima!
I knew you were here!
Dad... Mom...
You're hanging out with these delinquents, the Guardians again!
I'm going to make you quit... no, we're transferring schools!!
Delinquents?
CHATTER
Yeah, why are the kids here at this hour?
What is the school thinking?
Is this Guardians thing the problem!?
Please calm down. It's a misunderstanding.
Get rid of the Guardians!
Oh my.
What's the matter?
TAP

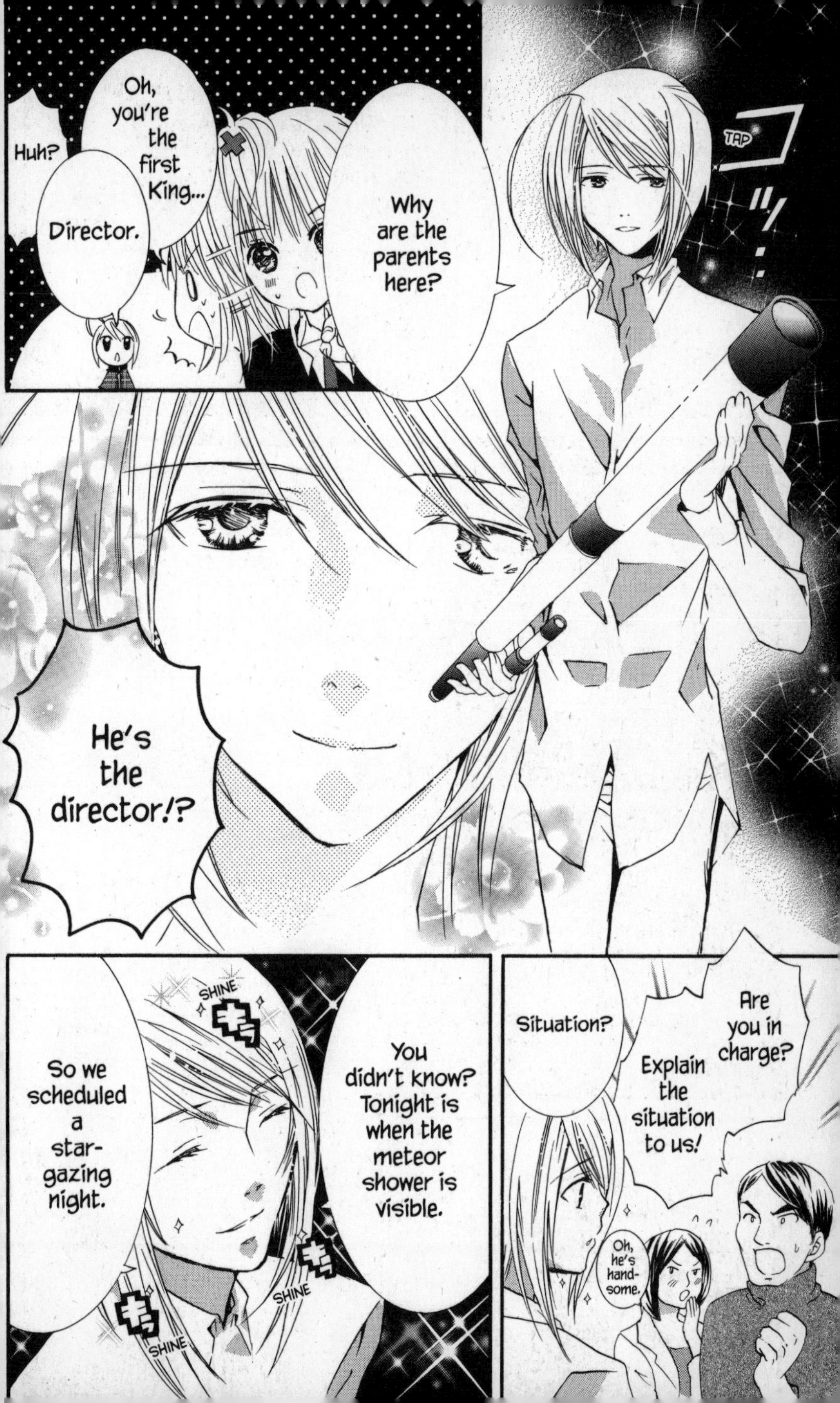
TAP
Why are the parents here?
Oh, you're the first King...
Huh?
Director.
He's the director!?
Are you in charge?
Explain the situation to us!
Situation?
Oh, he's hand-some.
SHINE
You didn't know? Tonight is when the meteor shower is visible.
So we scheduled a star-gazing night.
SHINE
SHINE

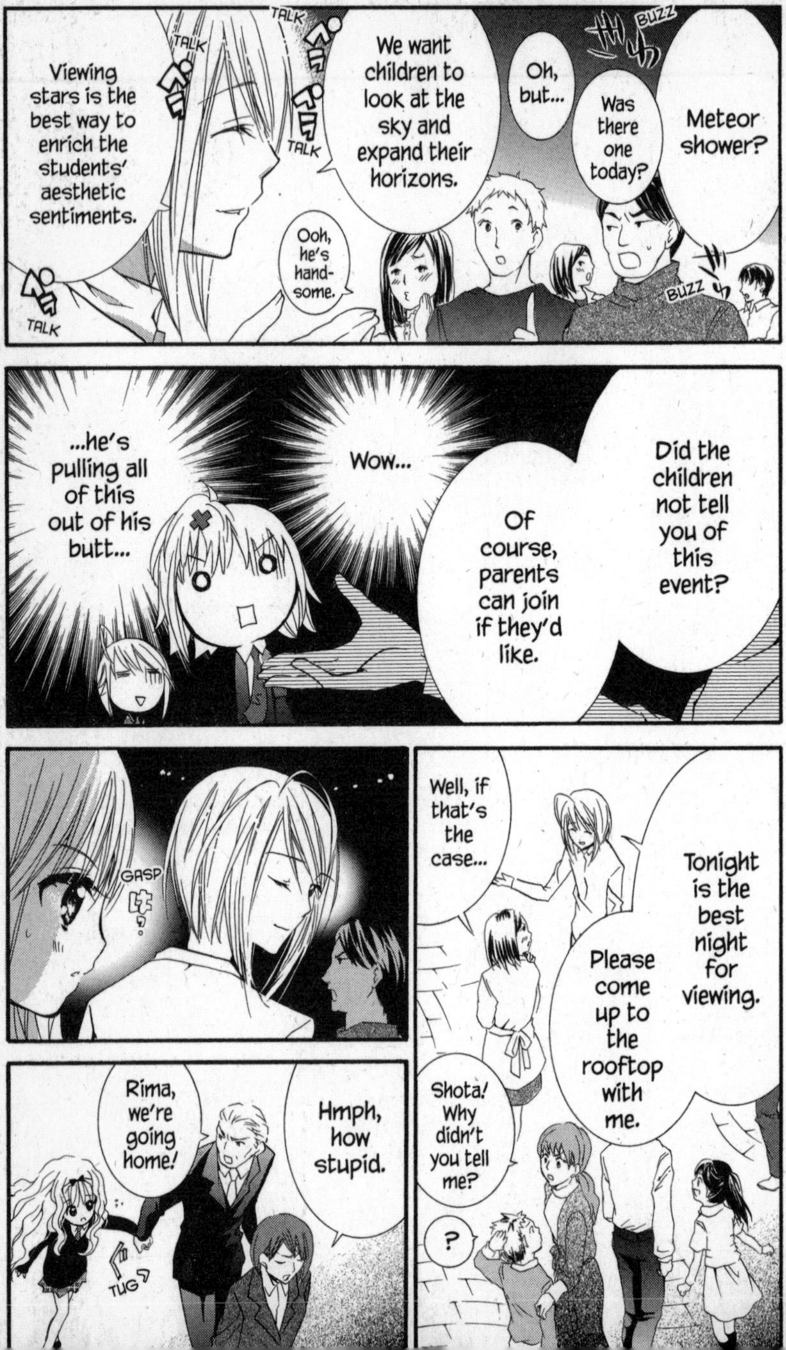
BUZZ
Meteor shower?
Was there one today?
Oh, but...
BUZZ
TALK
TALK
We want children to look at the sky and expand their horizons.
TALK
Ooh, he's handsome.
Viewing stars is the best way to enrich the students' aesthetic sentiments.
TALK
Did the children not tell you of this event?
Of course, parents can join if they'd like.
Wow...
...he's pulling all of this out of his butt...
Tonight is the best night for viewing.
Please come up to the rooftop with me.
Well, if that's the case...
Shota! Why didn't you tell me?
?
GASP
Hmph, how stupid.
Rima, we're going home!
TUG

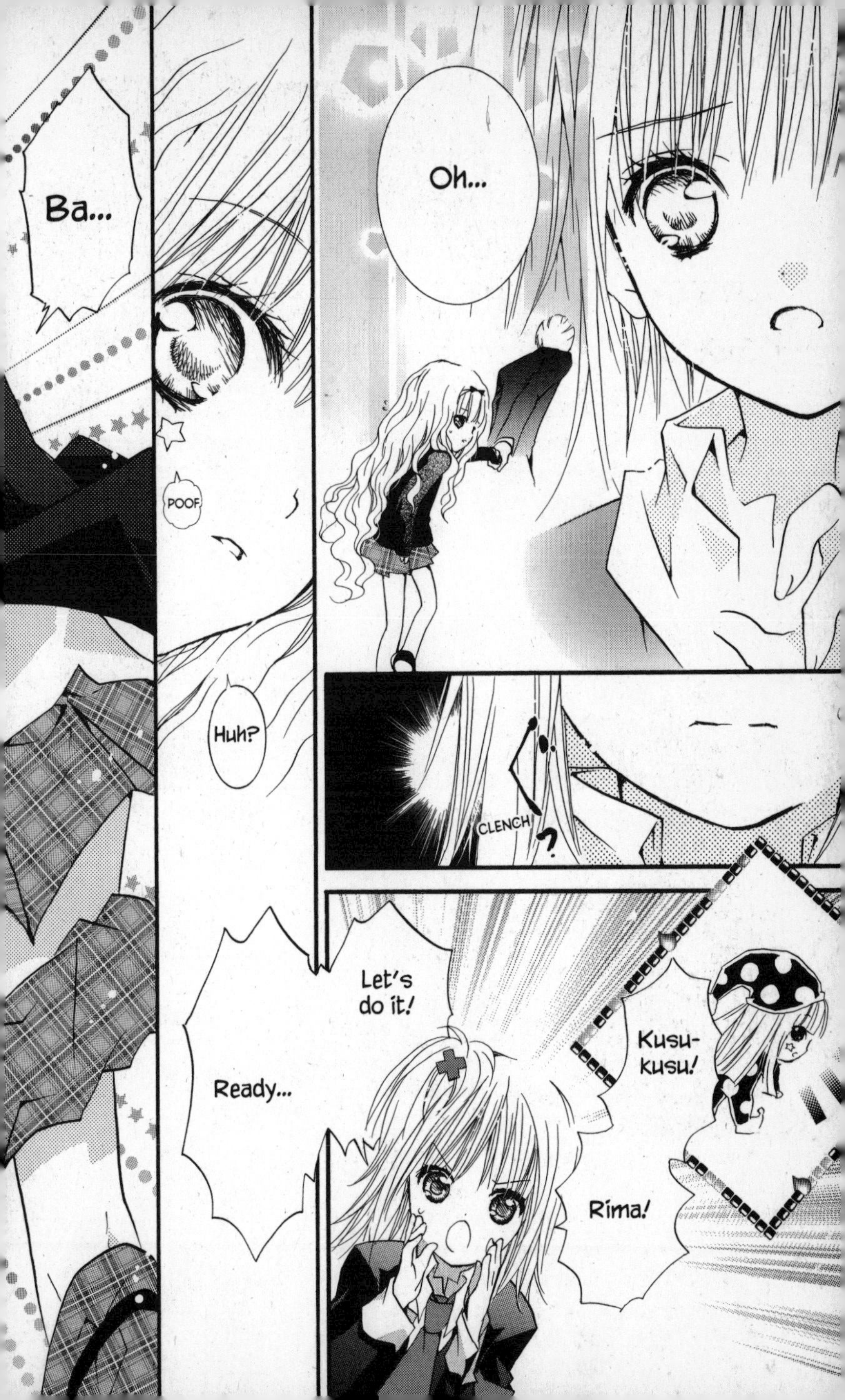
Oh...
CLENCH
?
Kusu-kusu!
Rima!
Let's do it!
Ready...
POOF
Huh?
Ba...

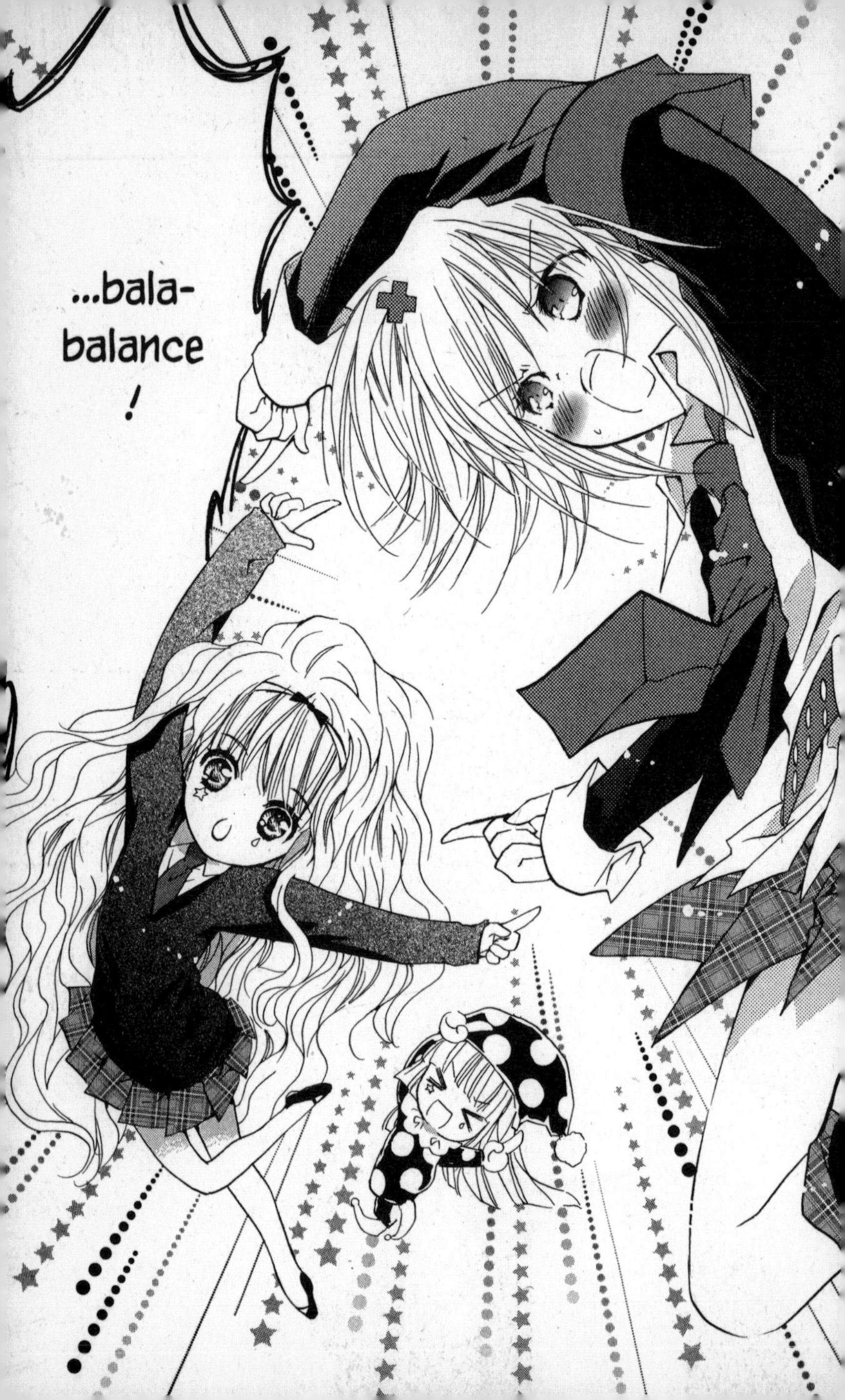
...bala-
balance
!

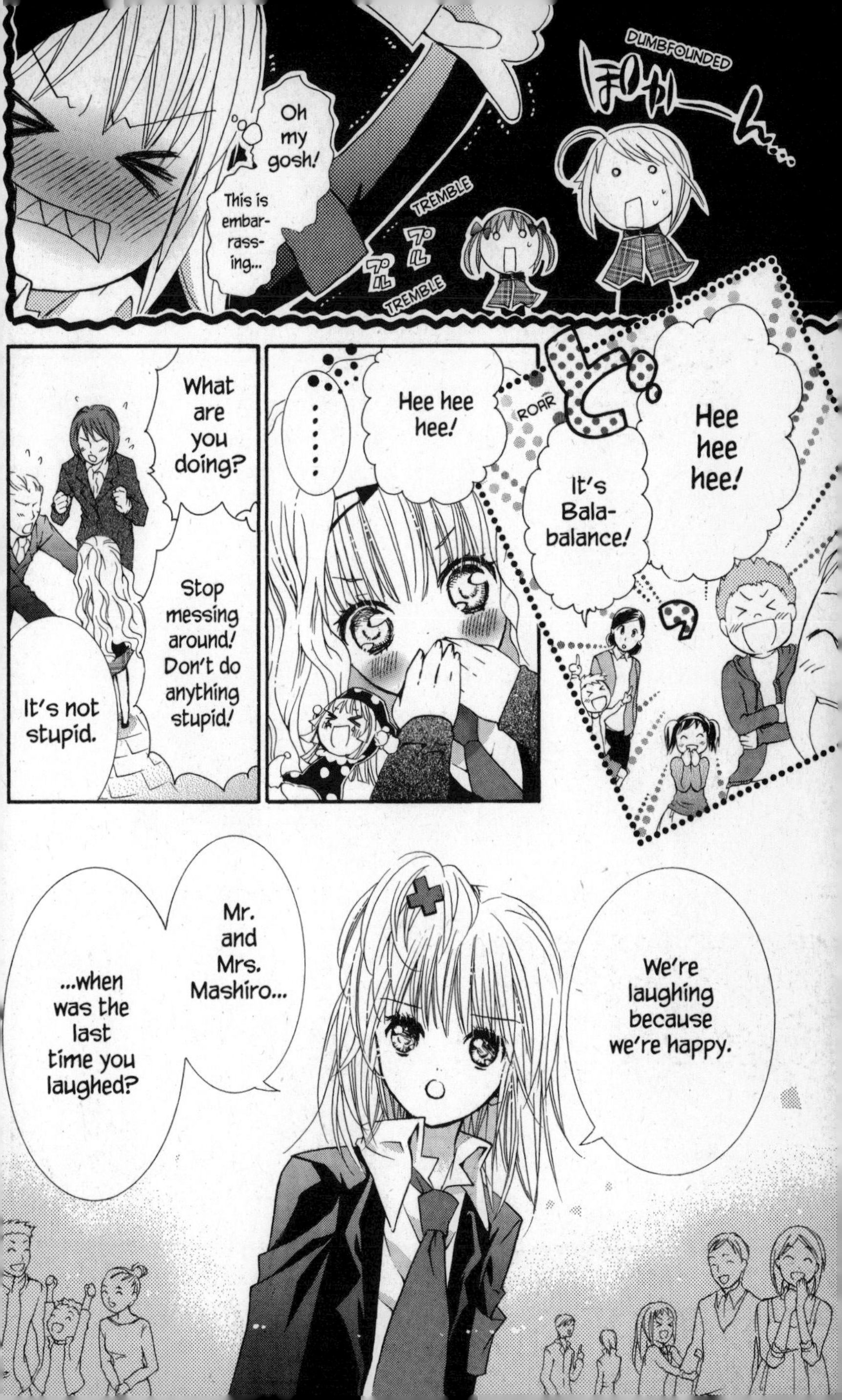

DUMBFOUNDED
TREMBLE
TREMBLE
Oh my gosh!
This is embar-rass-ing...
ROAR
Hee hee hee!
It's Bala-balance!
Hee hee hee!
......
What are you doing?
Stop messing around! Don't do anything stupid!
It's not stupid.
We're laughing because we're happy.
Mr. and Mrs. Mashiro...
...when was the last time you laughed?

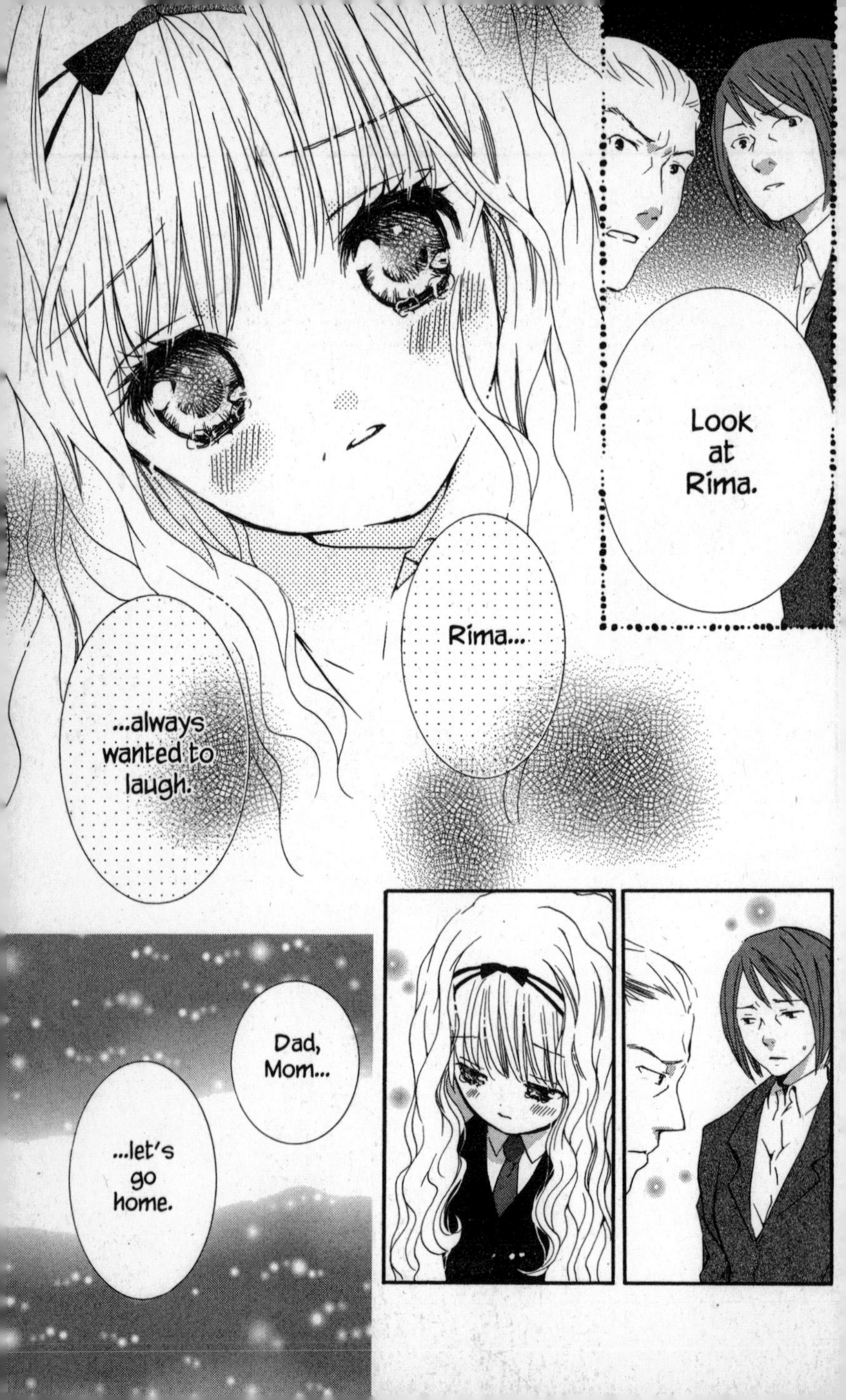
Look at Rima.
Rima...
...always wanted to laugh.
Dad, Mom...
...let's go home.

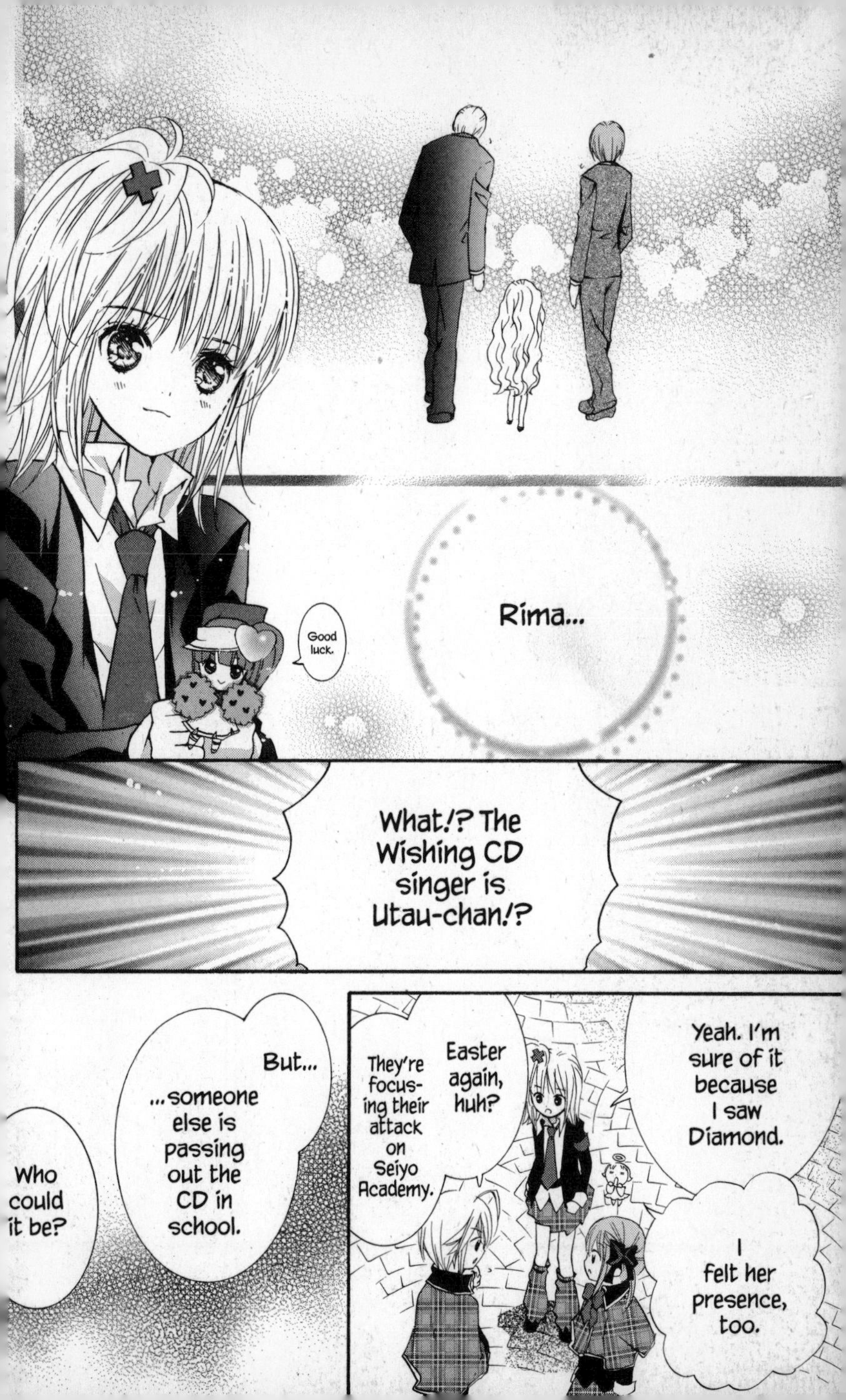

Rima...
Good luck.
What!? The Wishing CD singer is Utau-chan!?
Yeah. I'm sure of it because I saw Diamond.
I felt her presence, too.
Easter again, huh?
They're focusing their attack on Seiyo Academy.
But...
...someone else is passing out the CD in school.
Who could it be?

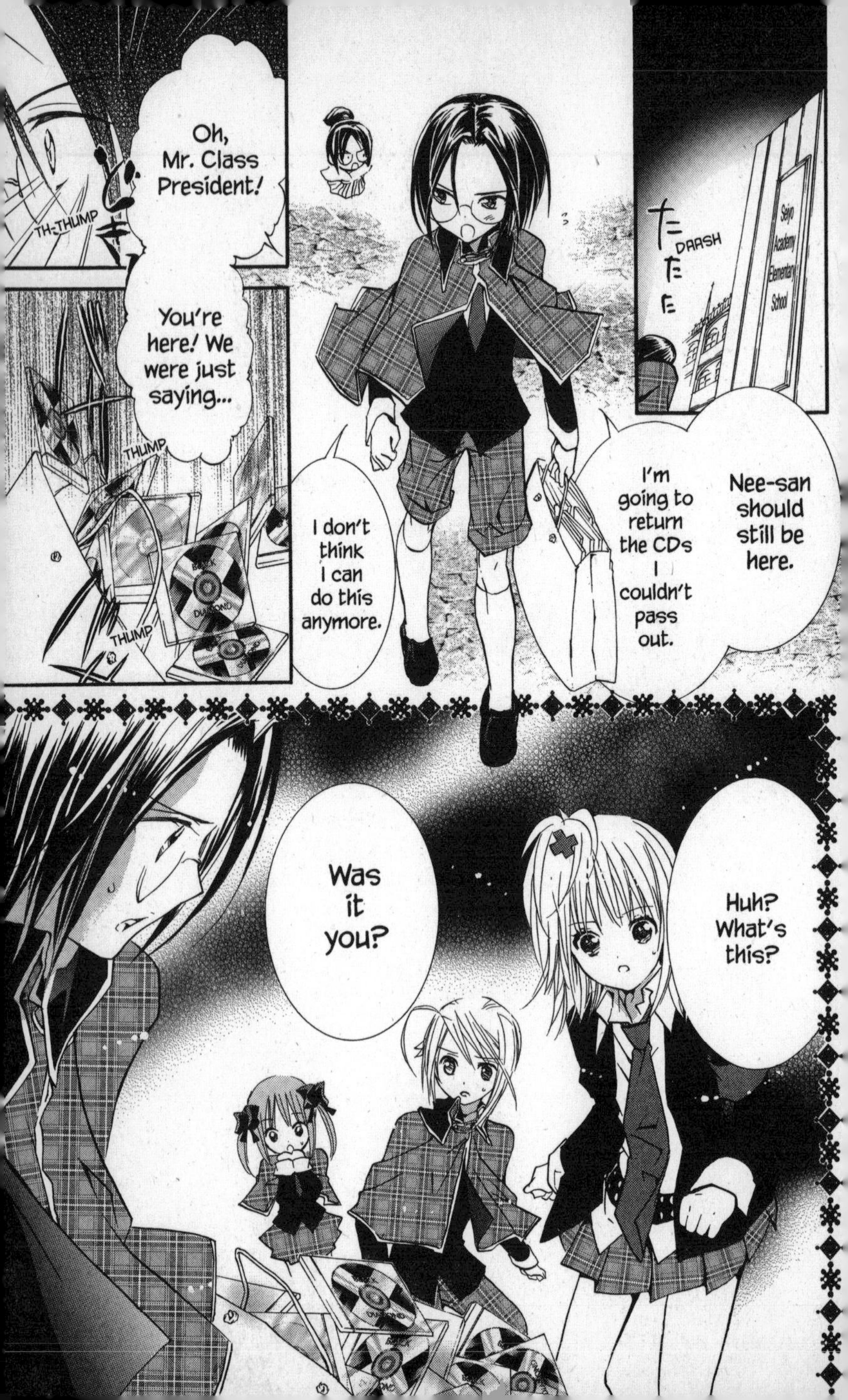

たたた
DAASH
Seiyo Academy Elementary School
Nee-san should still be here.
I'm going to return the CDs I couldn't pass out.
I don't think I can do this anymore.
Oh, Mr. Class President!
TH-THUMP
You're here! We were just saying...
THUMP
THUMP
Huh? What's this?
Was it you?

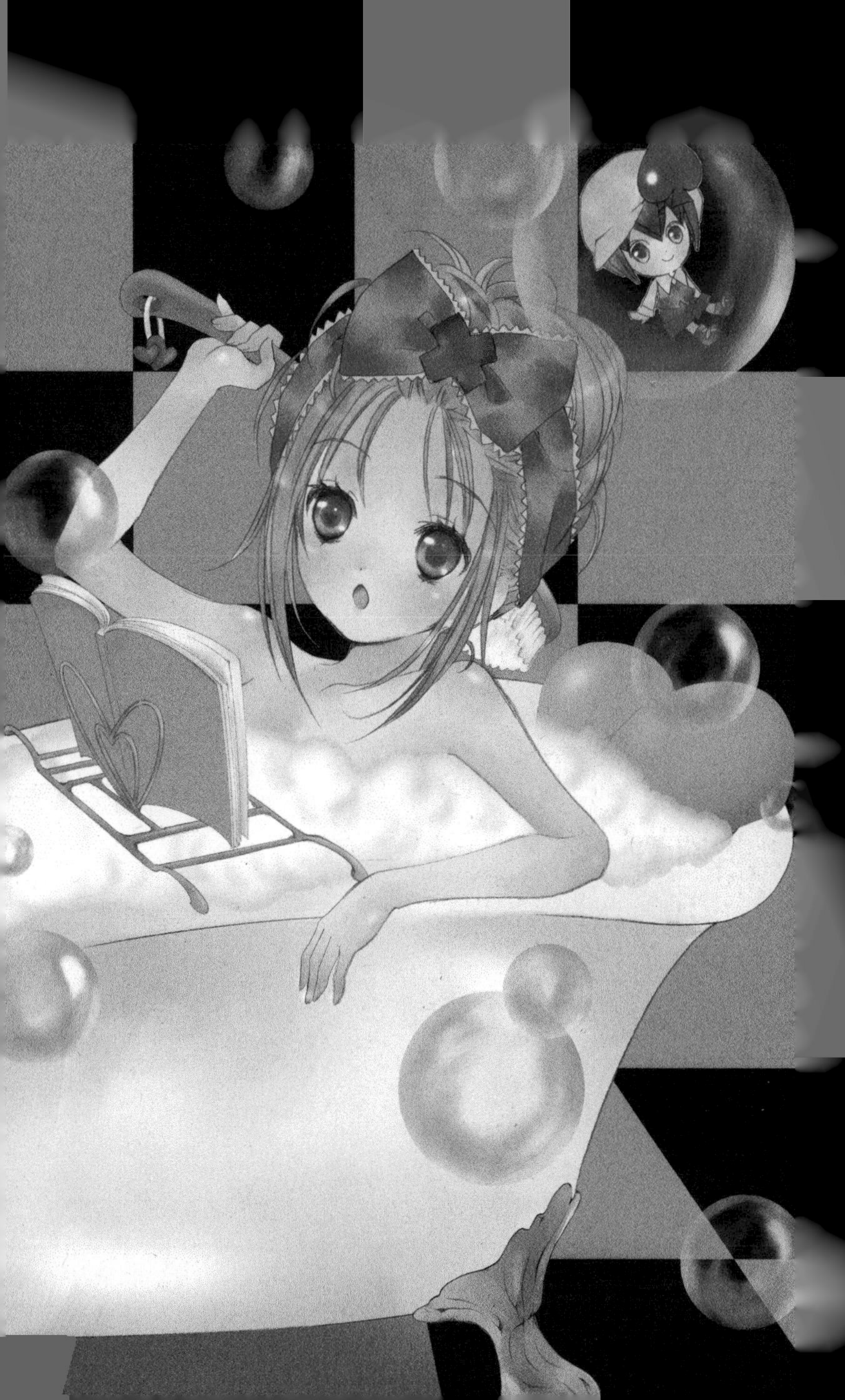

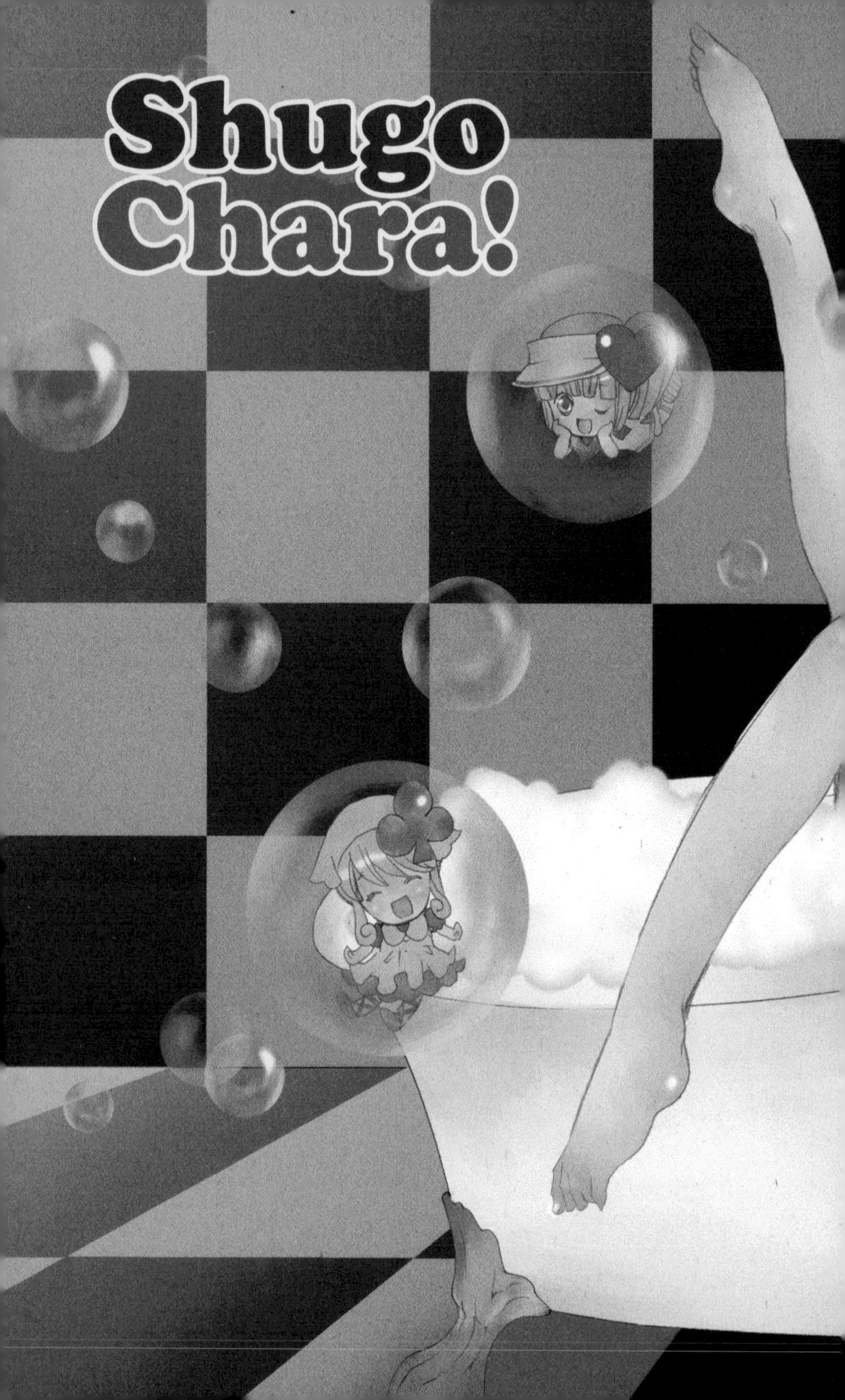
Shugo Chara!

Shugo Chara!

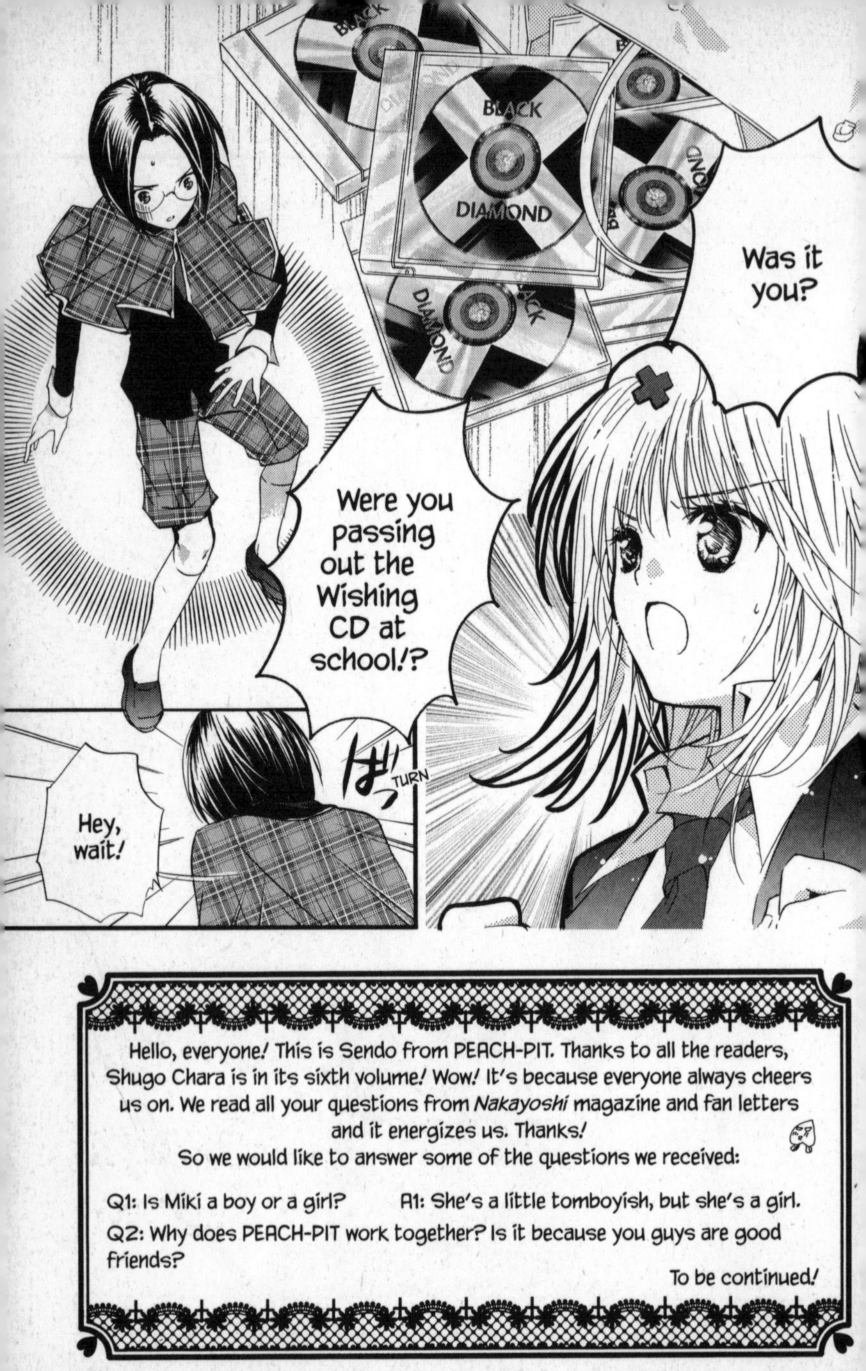
BLACK DIAMOND
Was it you?
Were you passing out the Wishing CD at school!?
ぱっ TURN
Hey, wait!

Hello, everyone! This is Sendo from PEACH-PIT. Thanks to all the readers, Shugo Chara is in its sixth volume! Wow! It's because everyone always cheers us on. We read all your questions from *Nakayoshi* magazine and fan letters and it energizes us. Thanks!

So we would like to answer some of the questions we received:

Q1: Is Miki a boy or a girl? A1: She's a little tomboyish, but she's a girl.

Q2: Why does PEACH-PIT work together? Is it because you guys are good friends?

To be continued!

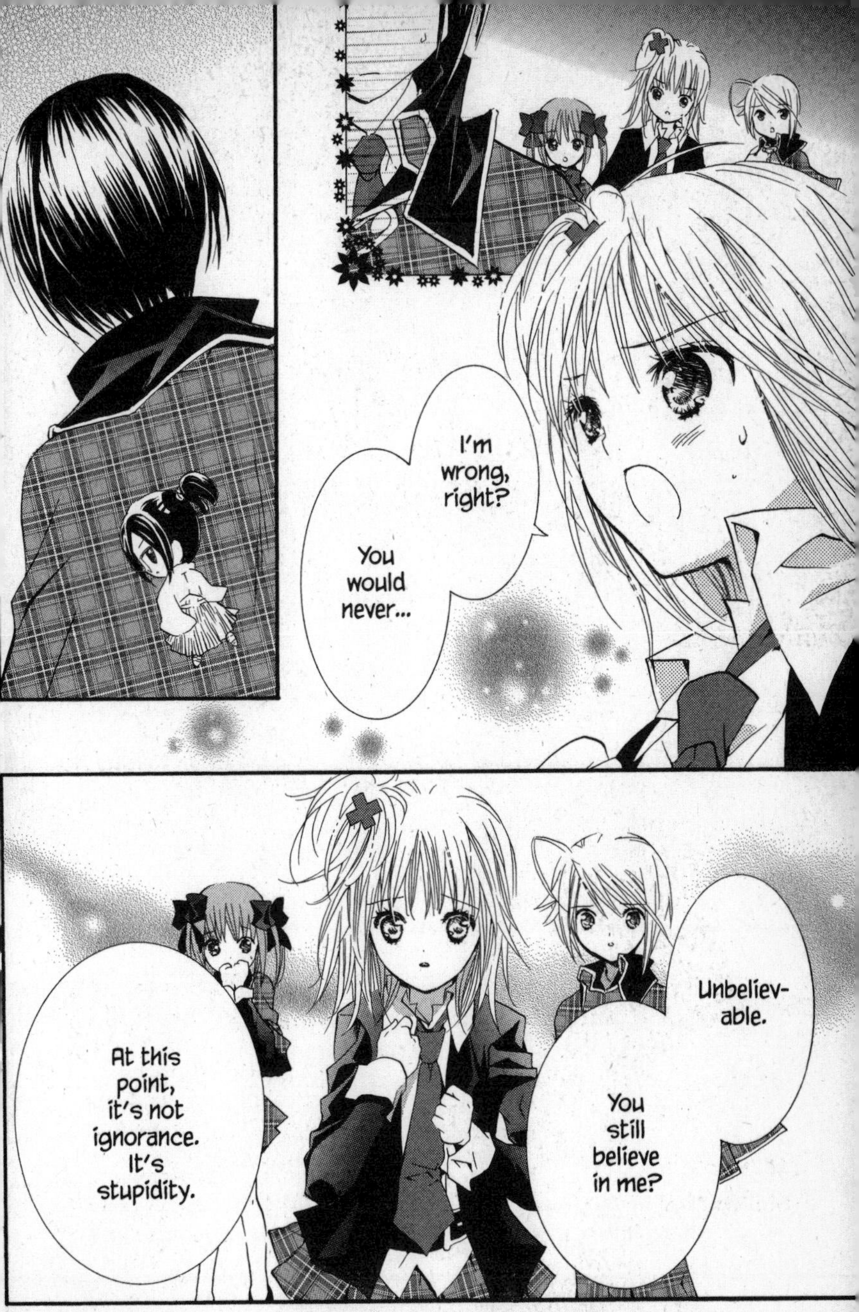
I'm wrong, right?
You would never...
Unbelievable.
You still believe in me?
At this point, it's not ignorance. It's stupidity.

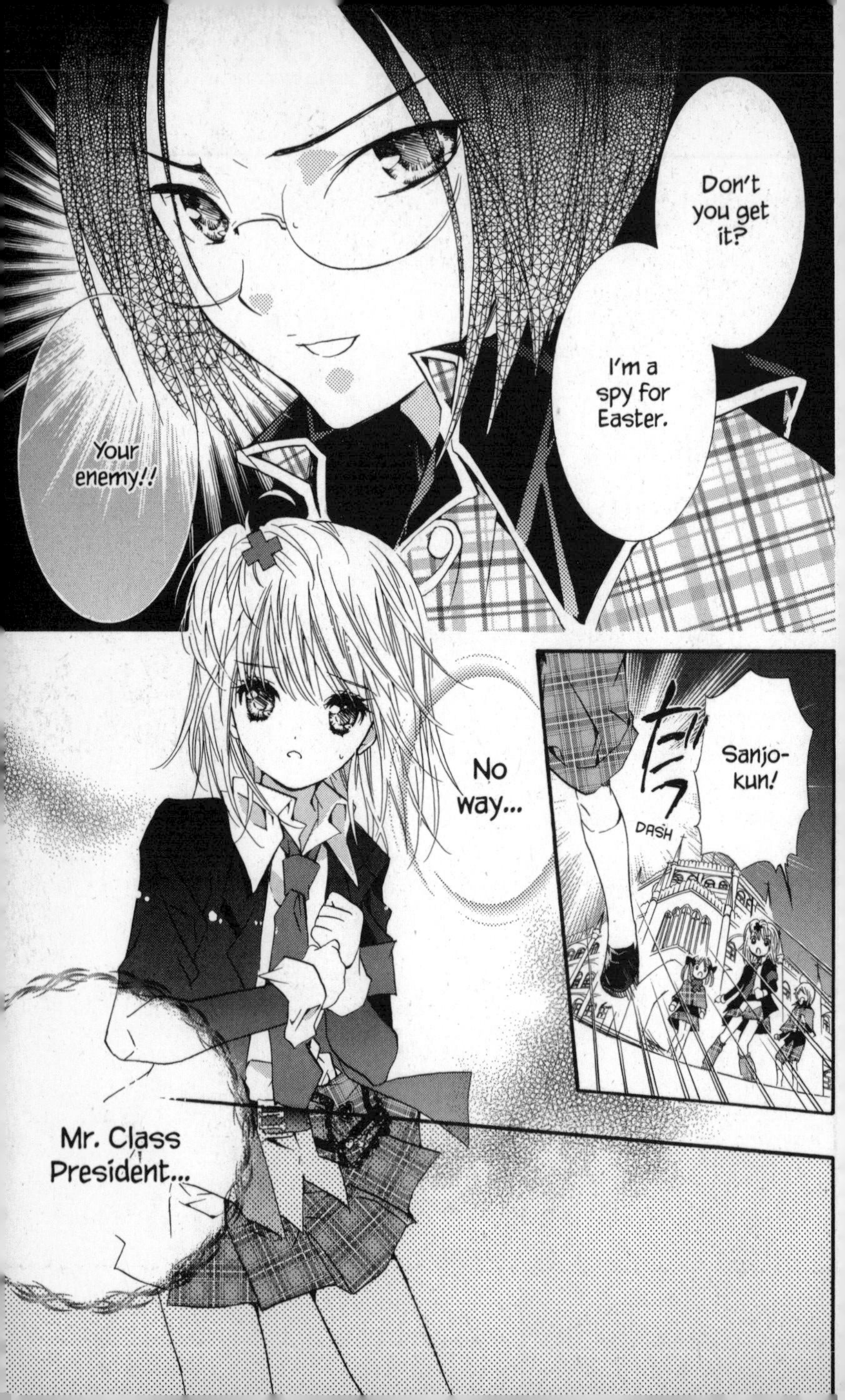
Don't you get it?
I'm a spy for Easter.
Your enemy!!
Sanjo-kun!
DASH
No way...
Mr. Class President...

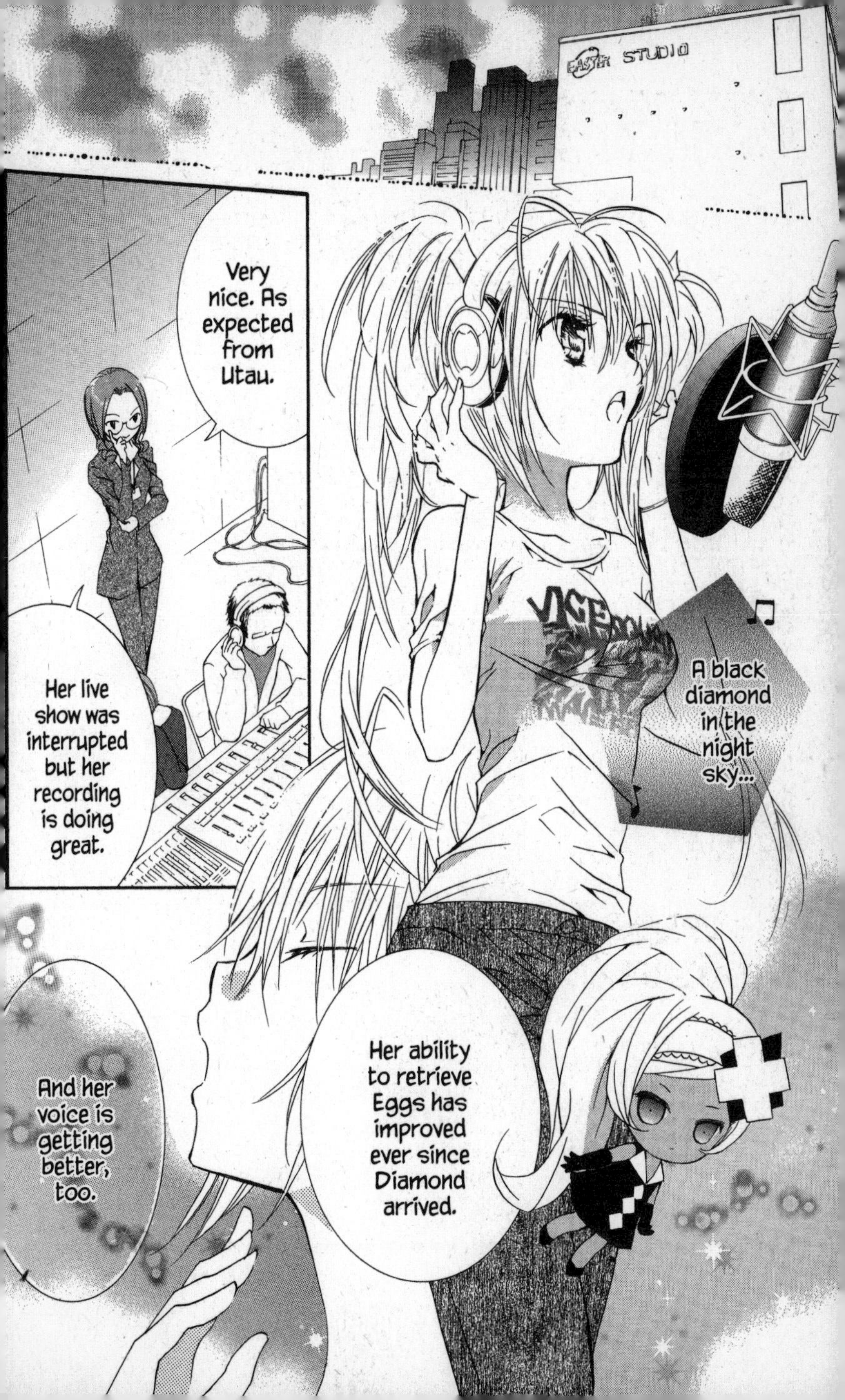
EASTER STUDIO
A black diamond in the night sky...
Very nice. As expected from Utau.
Her live show was interrupted but her recording is doing great.
Her ability to retrieve Eggs has improved ever since Diamond arrived.
And her voice is getting better, too.

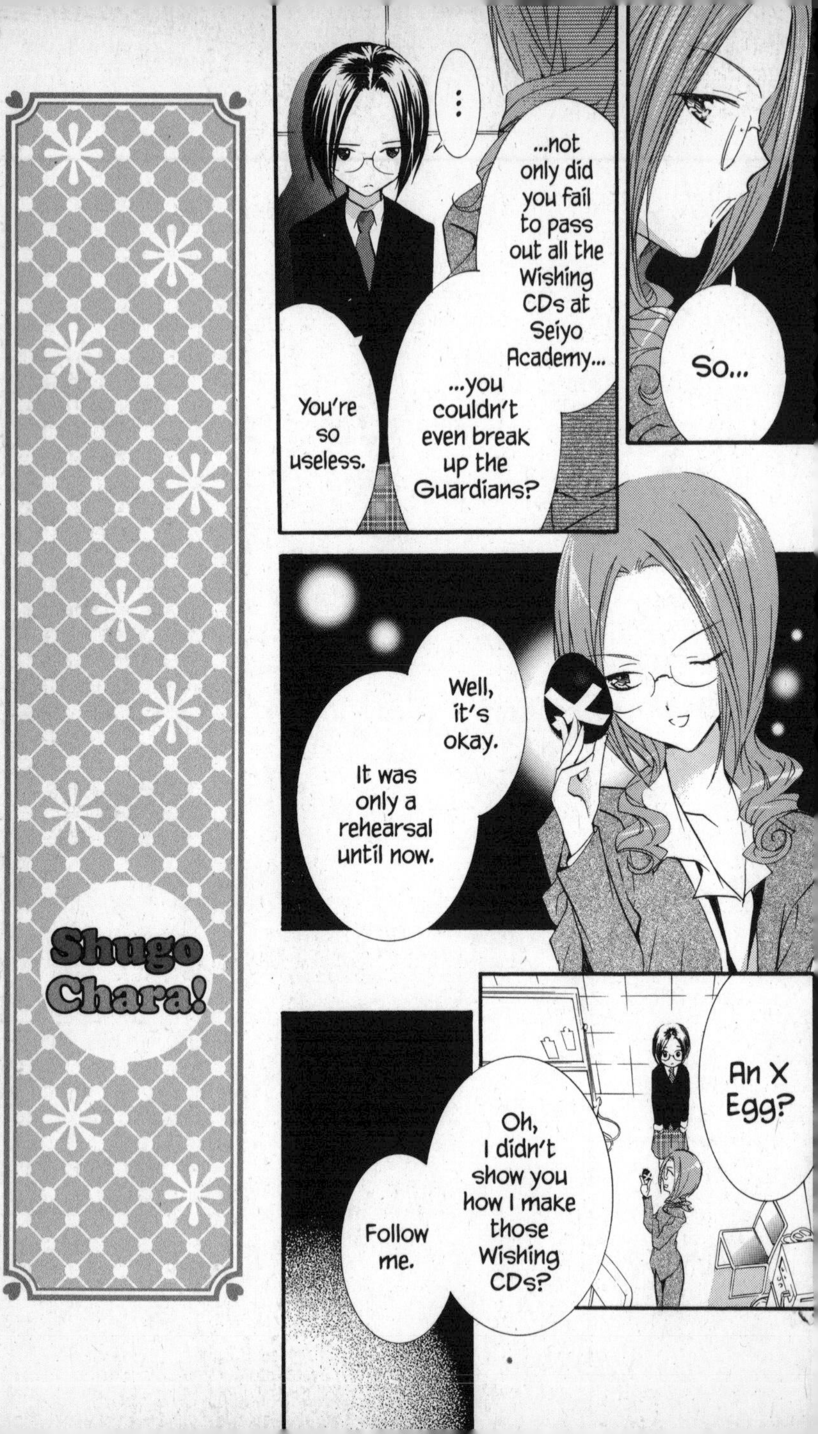
So...
...
...not only did you fail to pass out all the Wishing CDs at Seiyo Academy...
...you couldn't even break up the Guardians?
You're so useless.
Well, it's okay.
It was only a rehearsal until now.
An X Egg?
Oh, I didn't show you how I make those Wishing CDs?
Follow me.

Shugo Chara!

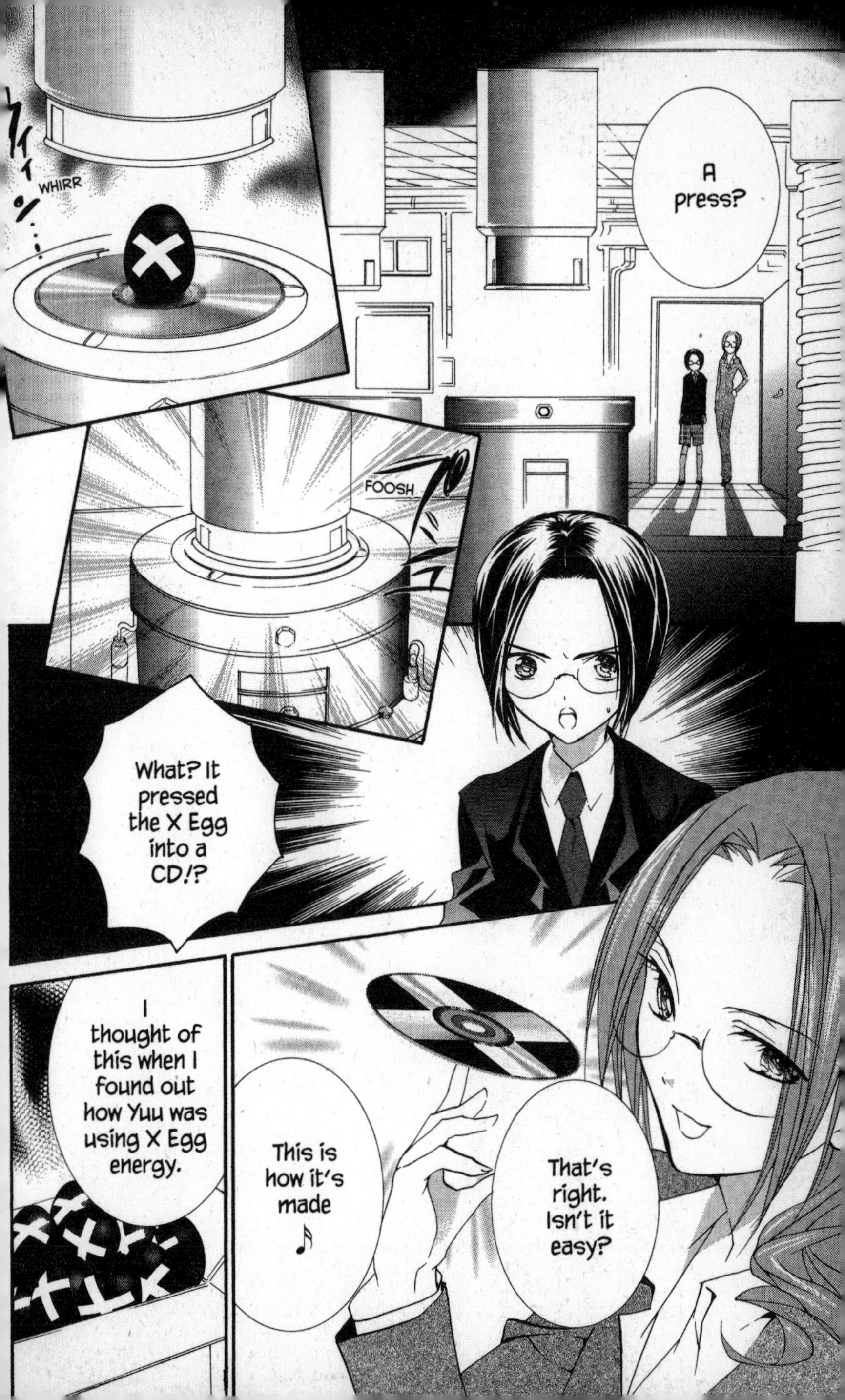
A press?
What? It pressed the X Egg into a CD!?
WHIRR
FOOSH
That's right. Isn't it easy?
This is how it's made ♪
I thought of this when I found out how Yuu was using X Egg energy.

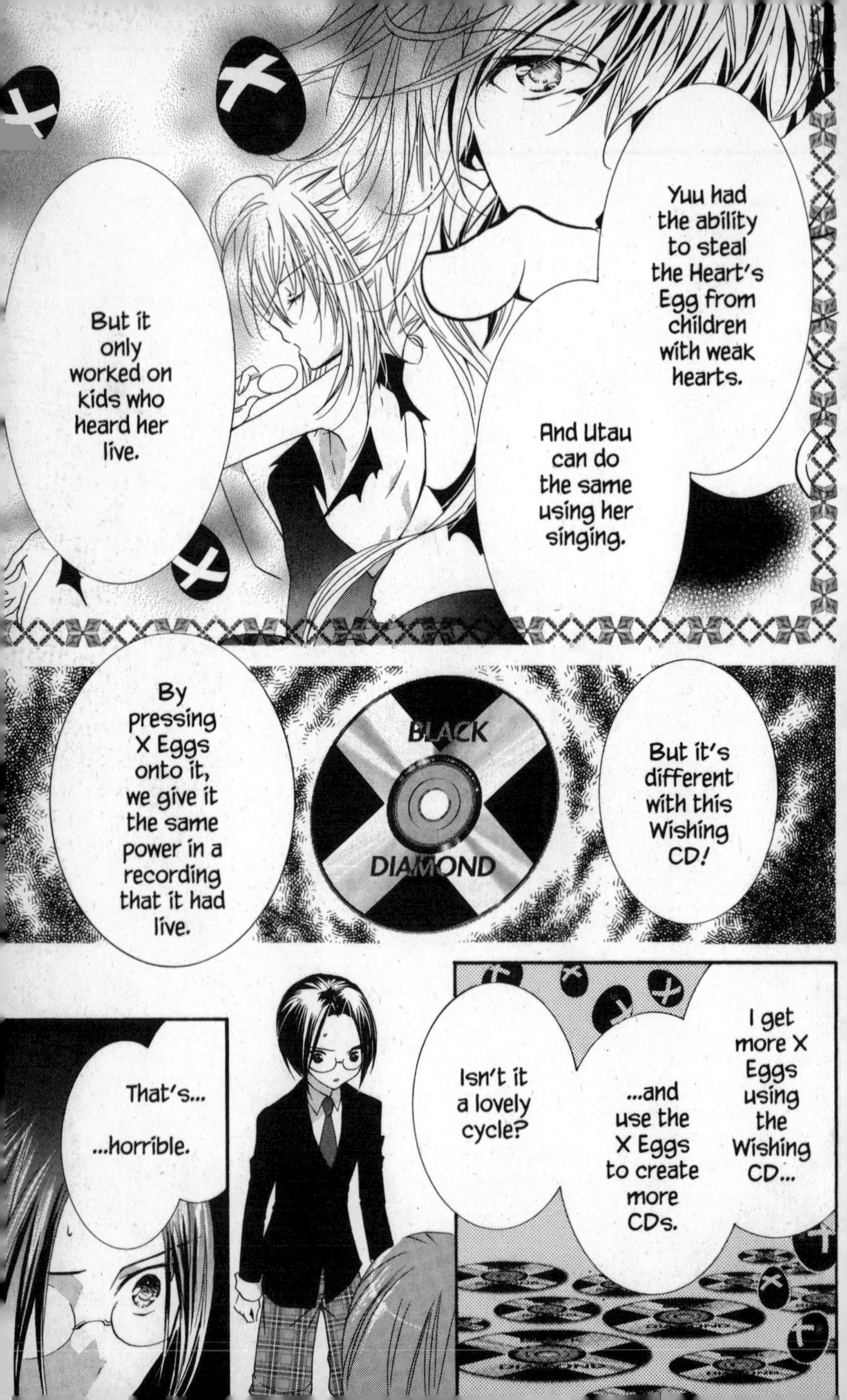
Yuu had the ability to steal the Heart's Egg from children with weak hearts.
And Utau can do the same using her singing.
But it only worked on kids who heard her live.
But it's different with this Wishing CD!
BLACK DIAMOND
By pressing X Eggs onto it, we give it the same power in a recording that it had live.
I get more X Eggs using the Wishing CD...
...and use the X Eggs to create more CDs.
Isn't it a lovely cycle?
That's...
...horrible.

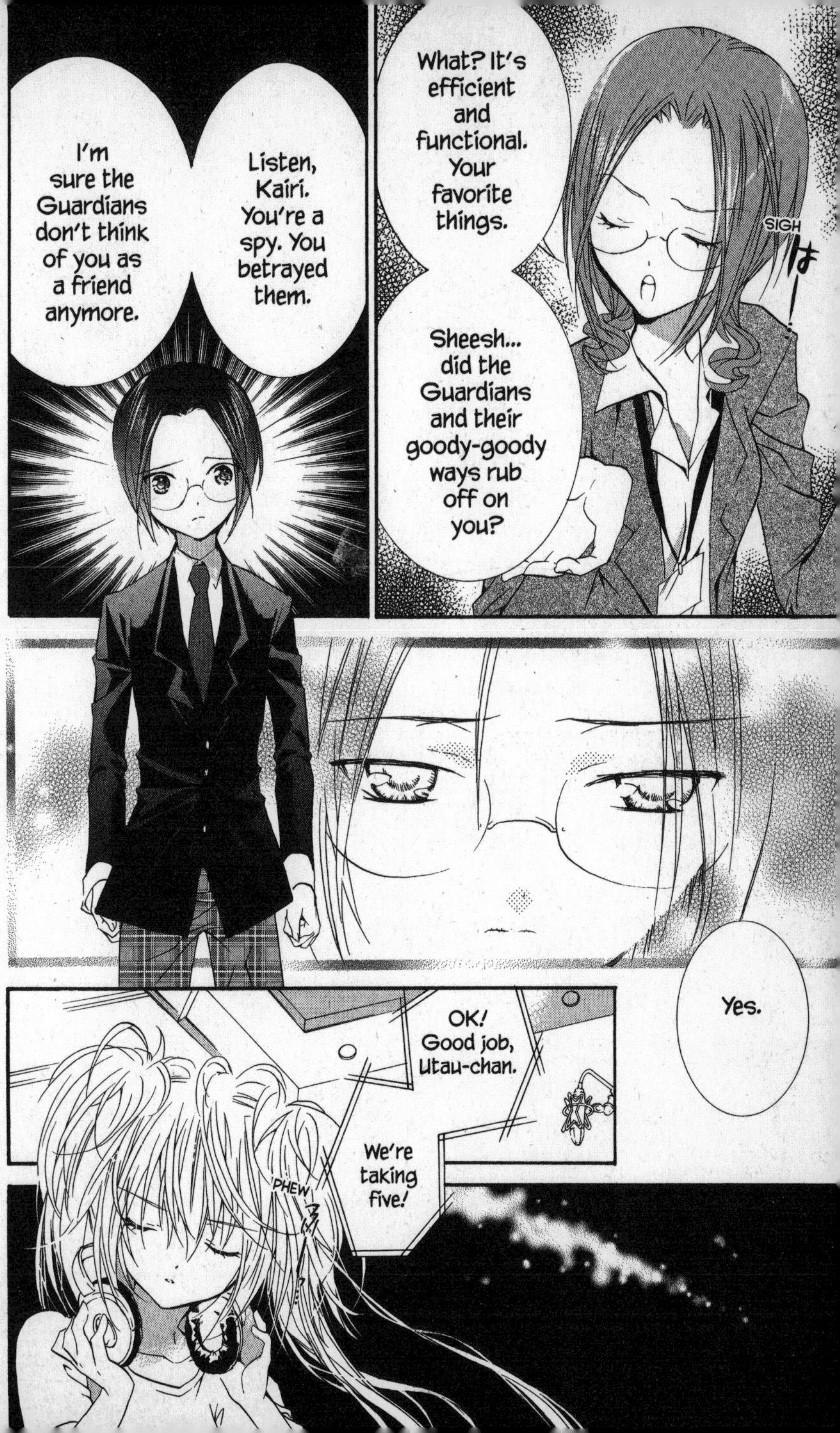
What? It's efficient and functional. Your favorite things.
SIGH
Sheesh... did the Guardians and their goody-goody ways rub off on you?
Listen, Kairi. You're a spy. You betrayed them.
I'm sure the Guardians don't think of you as a friend anymore.
Yes.
OK! Good job, Utau-chan.
We're taking five!
PHEW

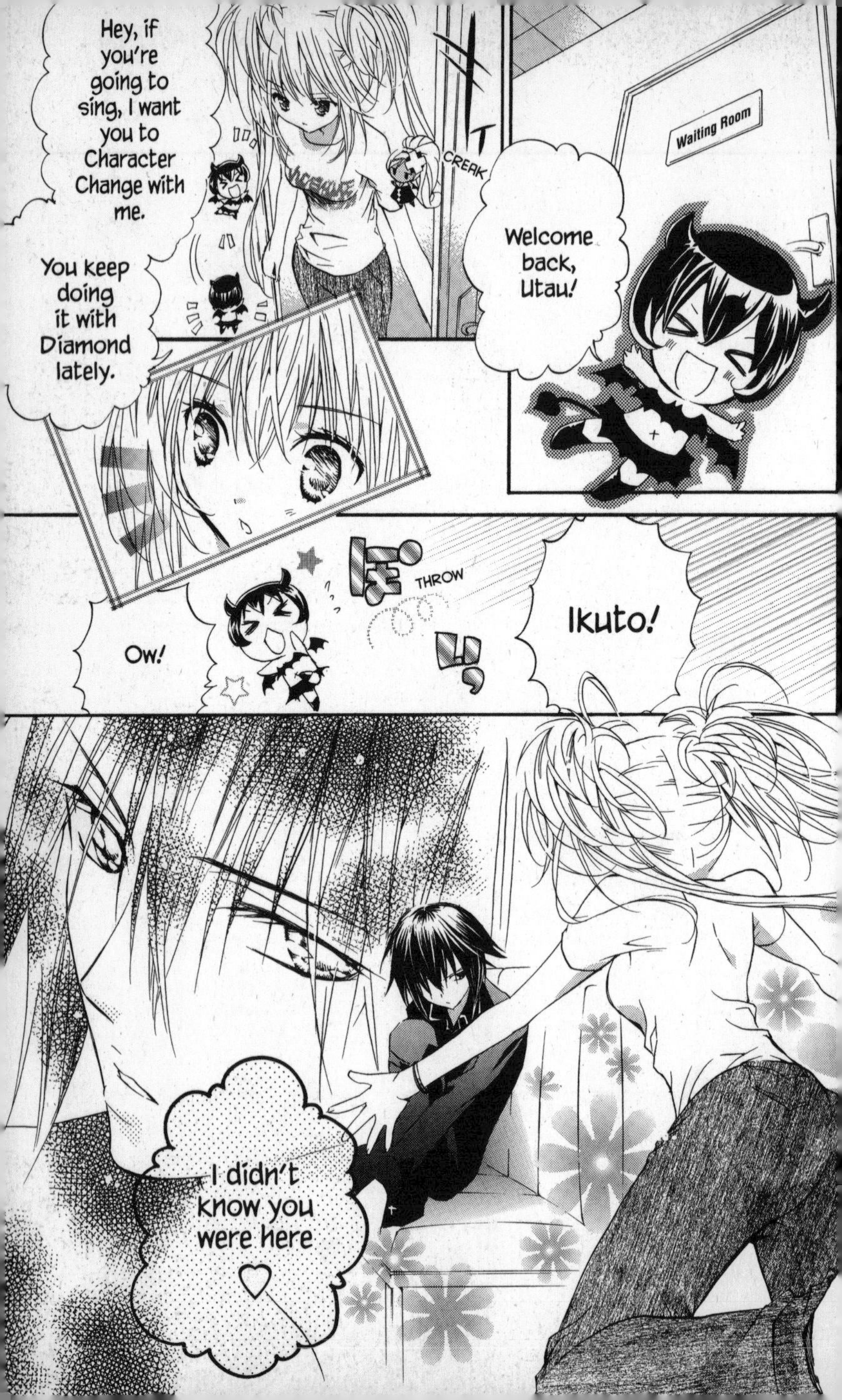
Waiting Room
Welcome back, Utau!
CREAK
Hey, if you're going to sing, I want you to Character Change with me.
You keep doing it with Diamond lately.
Ikuto!
THROW
Ow!
I didn't know you were here ♡

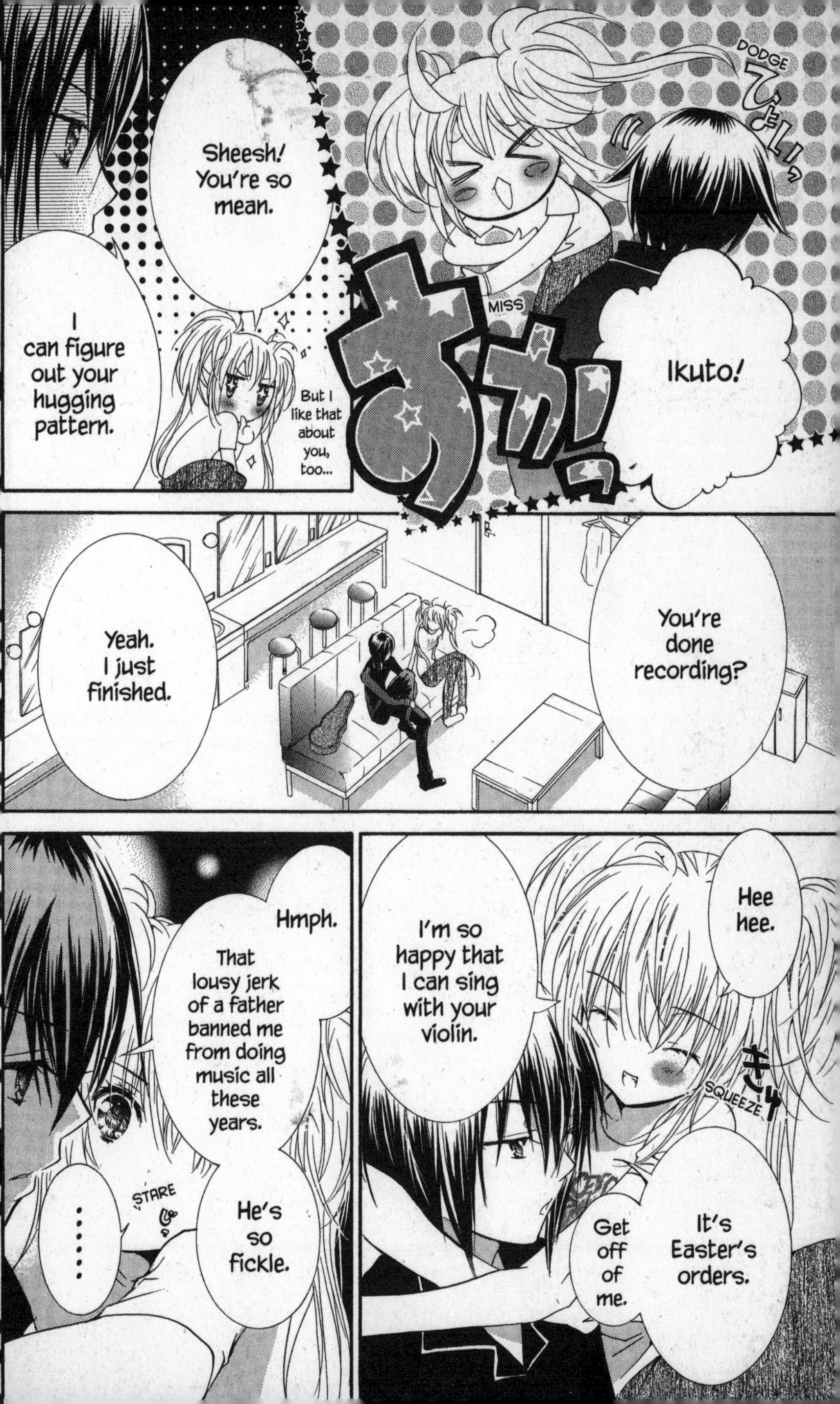

DODGE
Ikuto!
MISS
Sheesh! You're so mean.
I can figure out your hugging pattern.
But I like that about you, too...
You're done recording?
Yeah. I just finished.
Hee hee.
SQUEEZE
I'm so happy that I can sing with your violin.
It's Easter's orders.
Get off of me.
Hmph.
That lousy jerk of a father banned me from doing music all these years.
He's so fickle.
STARE
......

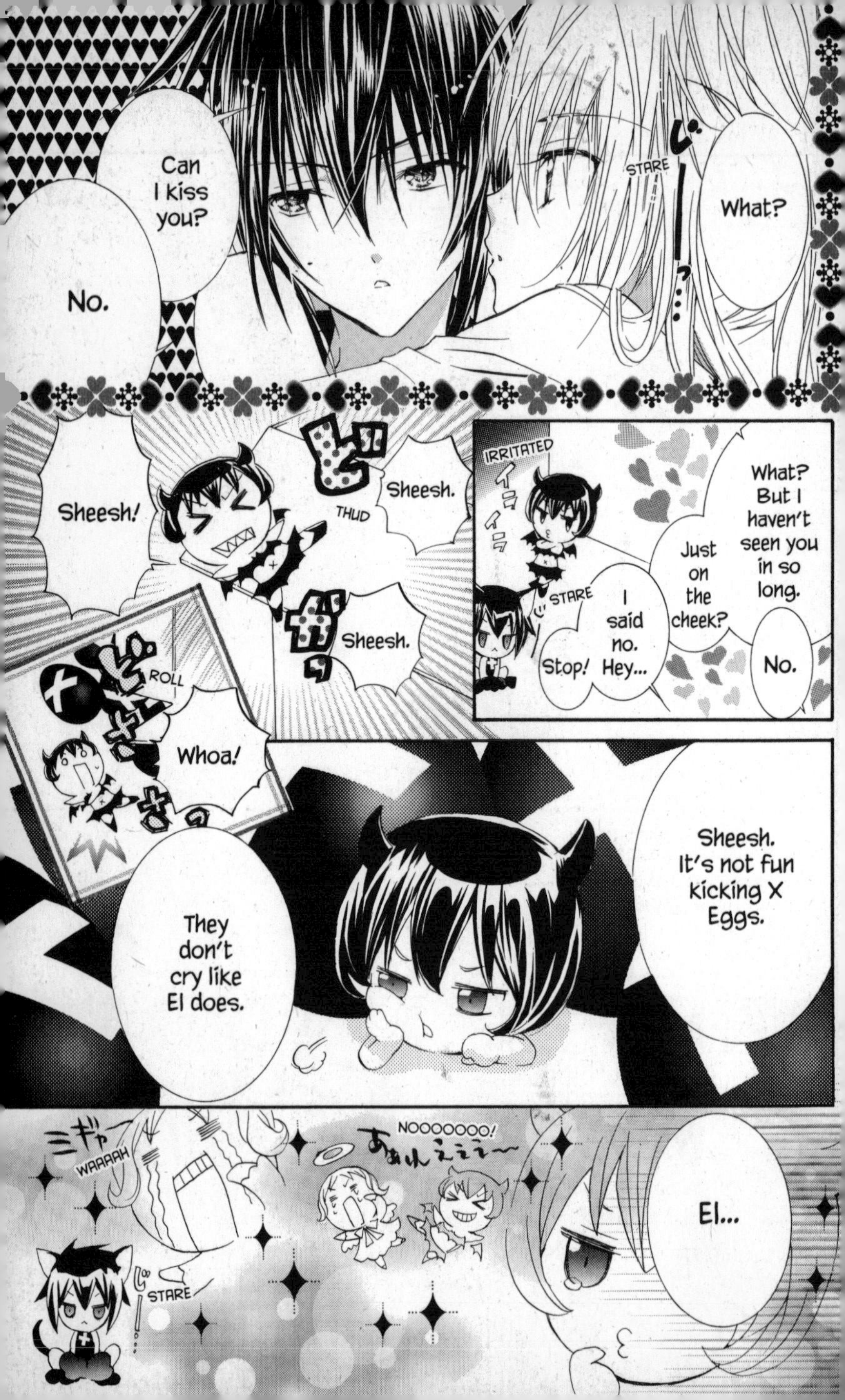
STARE
What?
Can I kiss you?
No.
IRRITATED
What? But I haven't seen you in so long.
Just on the cheek?
No.
I said no. Hey...
STARE
Stop!
Sheesh.
THUD
Sheesh!
Sheesh.
ROLL
Whoa!
Sheesh. It's not fun kicking X Eggs.
They don't cry like El does.
El...
NOOOOOOO!
WAAAAH
STARE

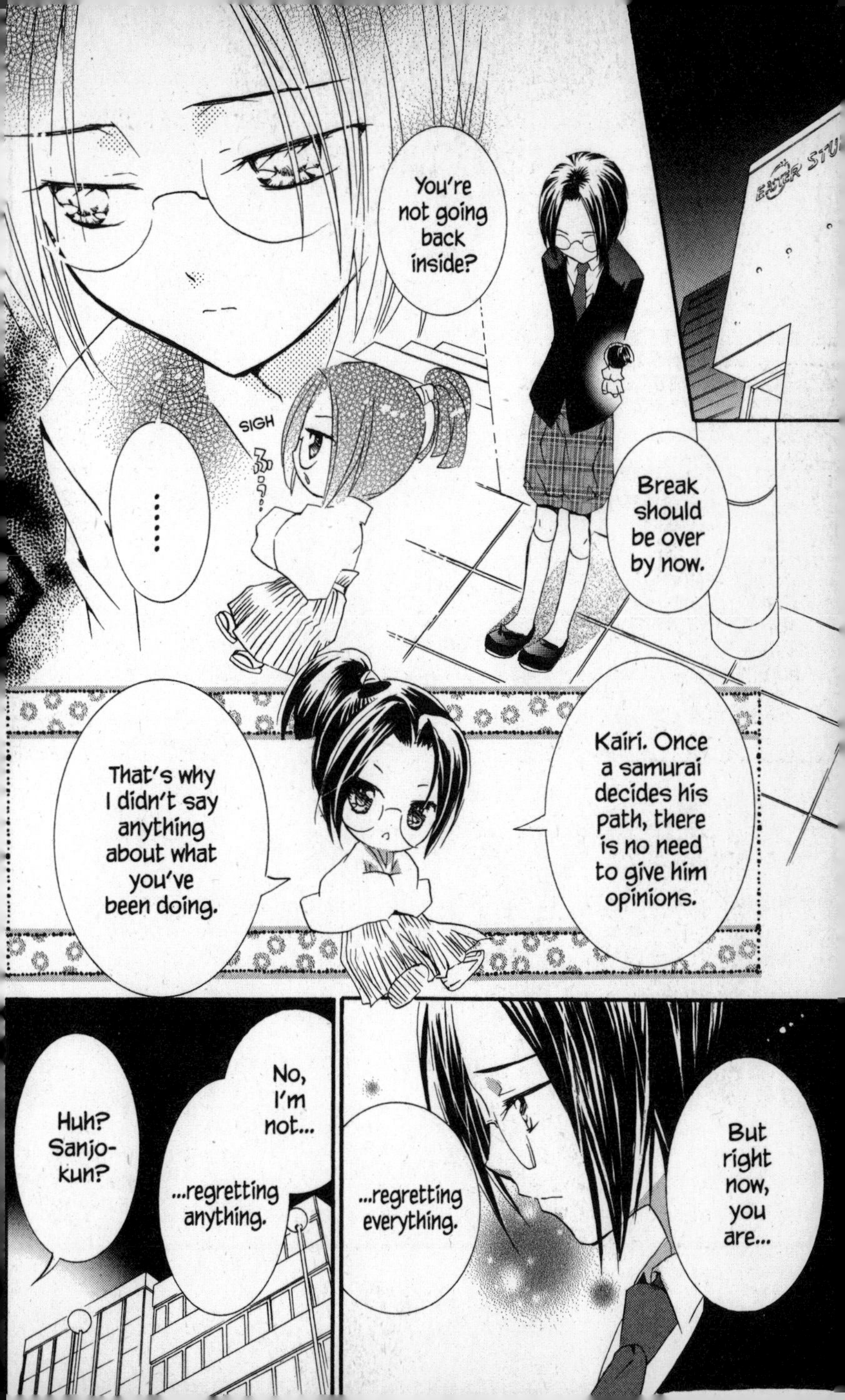

You're not going back inside?
Break should be over by now.
SIGH
......
Kairi. Once a samurai decides his path, there is no need to give him opinions.
That's why I didn't say anything about what you've been doing.
But right now, you are...
...regretting everything.
No, I'm not...
...regretting anything.
Huh? Sanjo-kun?

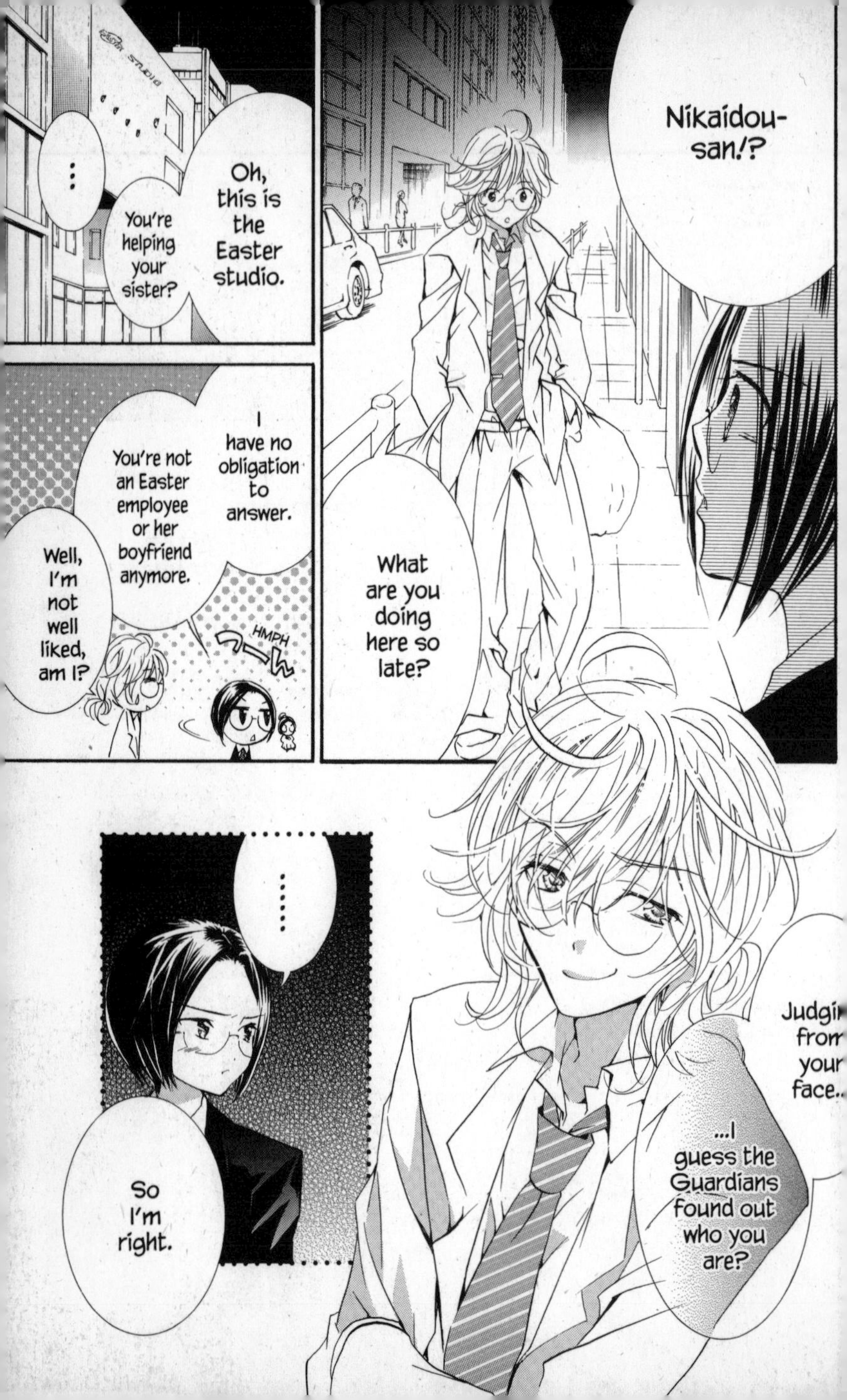
Nikaidou-san!?
What are you doing here so late?
Oh, this is the Easter studio.
You're helping your sister?
…
I have no obligation to answer.
You're not an Easter employee or her boyfriend anymore.
HMPH
Well, I'm not well liked, am I?
Judgi from your face..
...I guess the Guardians found out who you are?
......
So I'm right.

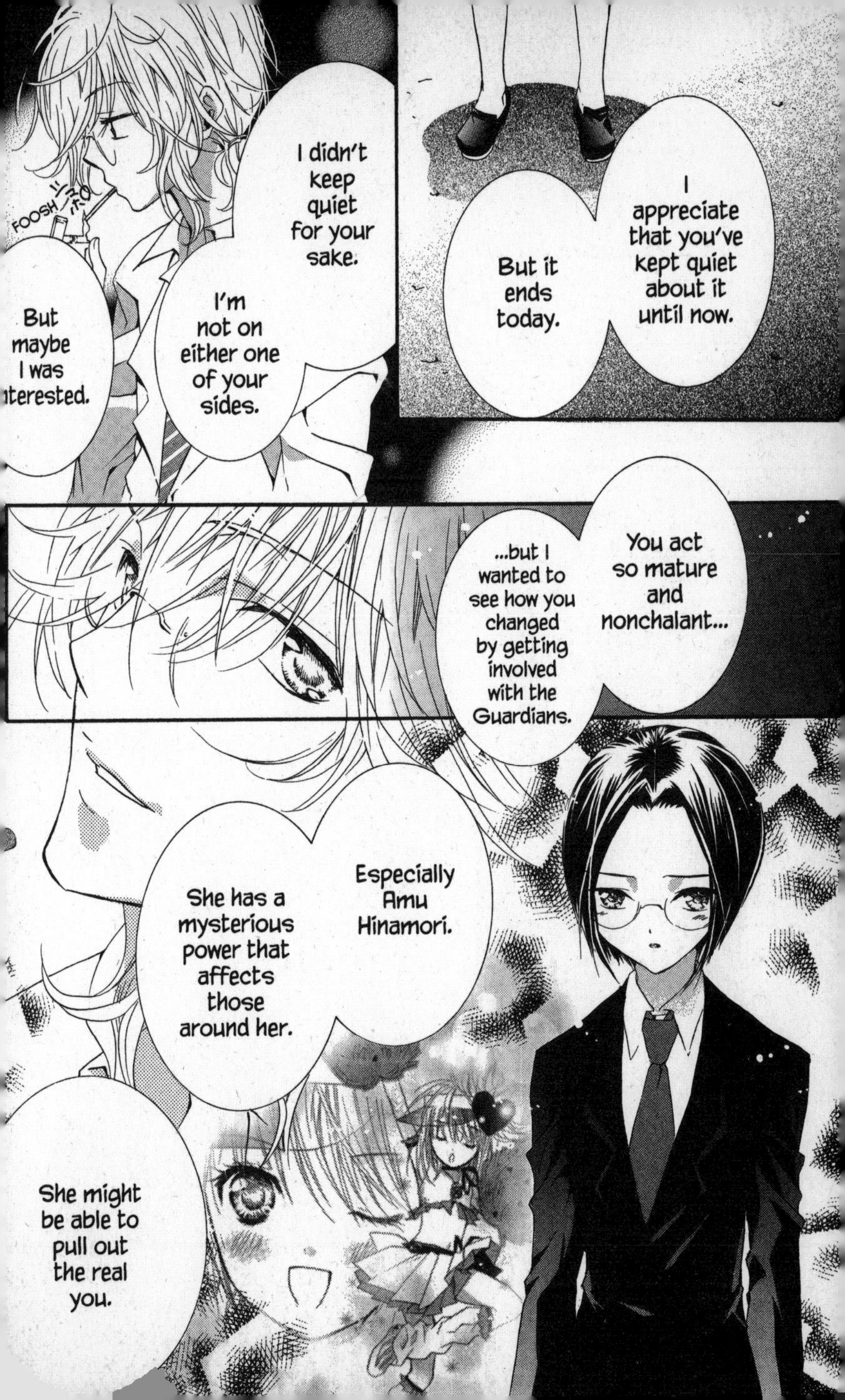
I appreciate that you've kept quiet about it until now.
But it ends today.
I didn't keep quiet for your sake.
I'm not on either one of your sides.
FOOSH
But maybe I was terested.
You act so mature and nonchalant...
...but I wanted to see how you changed by getting involved with the Guardians.
Especially Amu Hinamori.
She has a mysterious power that affects those around her.
She might be able to pull out the real you.

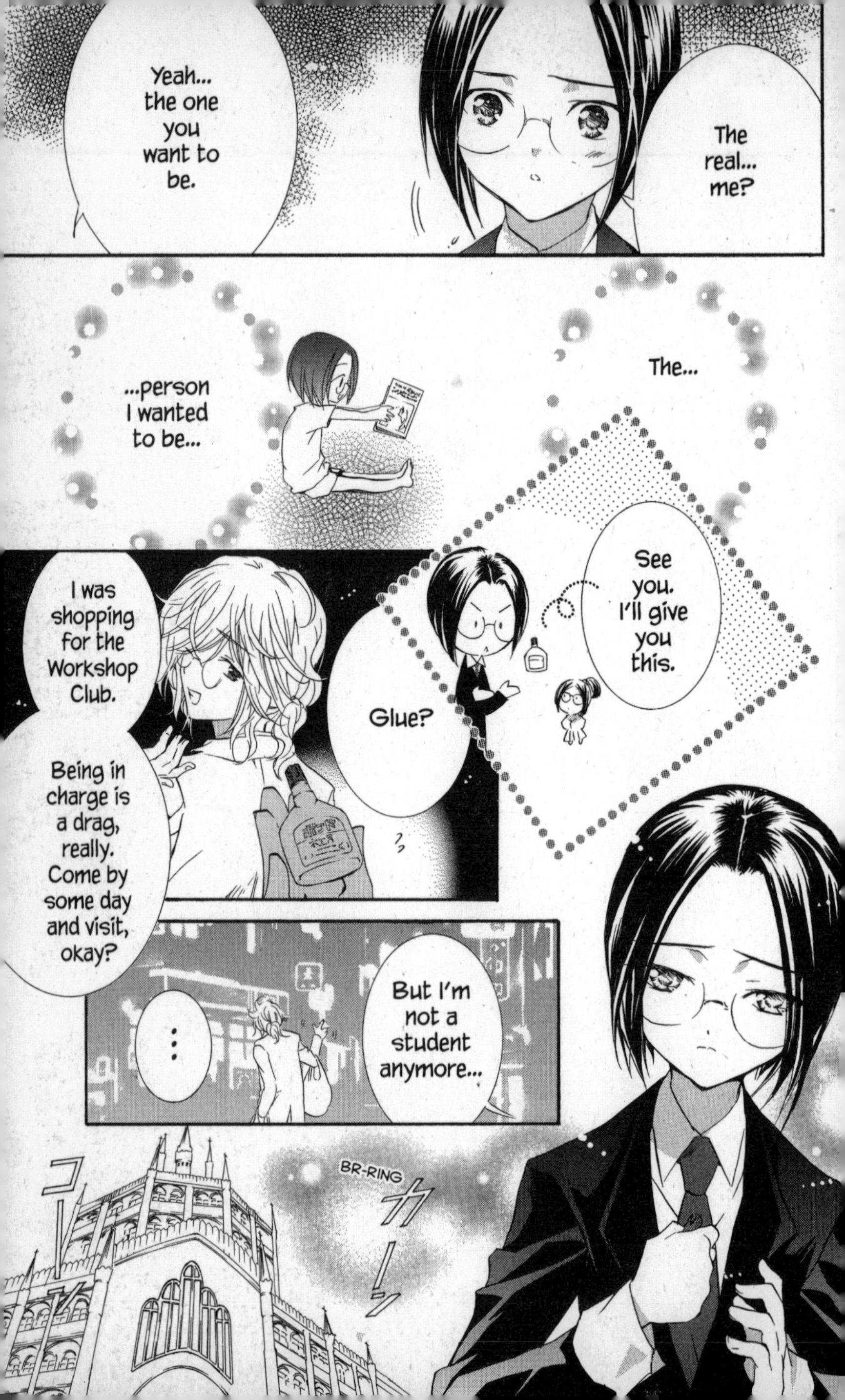
The real... me?
Yeah... the one you want to be.
The...
...person I wanted to be...
See you. I'll give you this.
Glue?
I was shopping for the Workshop Club.
Being in charge is a drag, really. Come by some day and visit, okay?
But I'm not a student anymore...
...
BR-RING

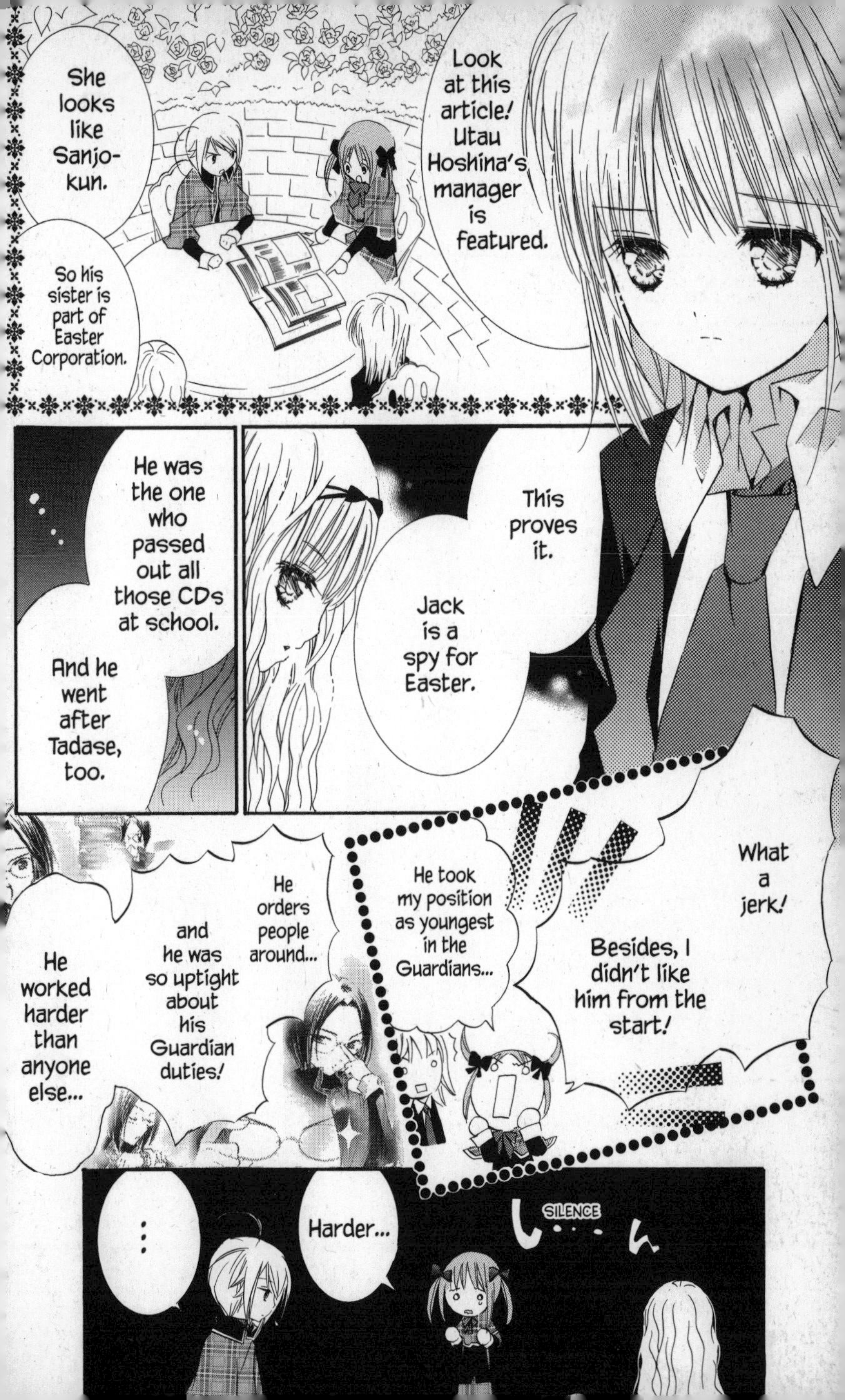

Look at this article! Utau Hoshina's manager is featured.
She looks like Sanjo-kun.
So his sister is part of Easter Corporation.
This proves it.
Jack is a spy for Easter.
He was the one who passed out all those CDs at school.
And he went after Tadase, too.
What a jerk!
Besides, I didn't like him from the start!
He took my position as youngest in the Guardians...
He orders people around...
and he was so uptight about his Guardian duties!
He worked harder than anyone else...
SILENCE
Harder...
...

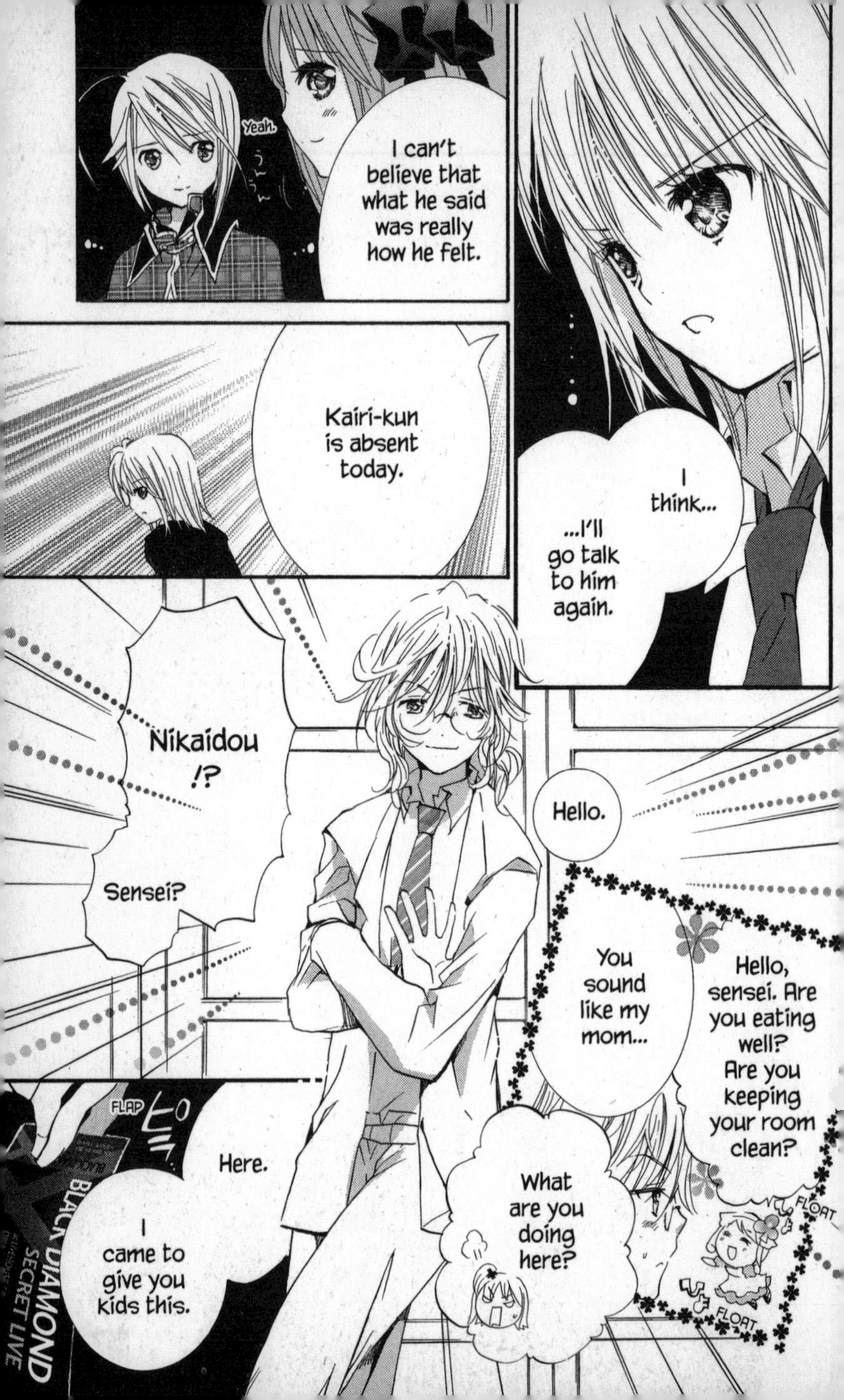
I think...
...I'll go talk to him again.
Yeah.
うんうん
I can't believe that what he said was really how he felt.
Kairi-kun is absent today.
Hello.
Nikaidou !?
Sensei?
Hello, sensei. Are you eating well? Are you keeping your room clean?
You sound like my mom...
FLOAT
FLOAT
What are you doing here?
FLAP
Here.
I came to give you kids this.
BLACK DIAMOND SECRET LIVE

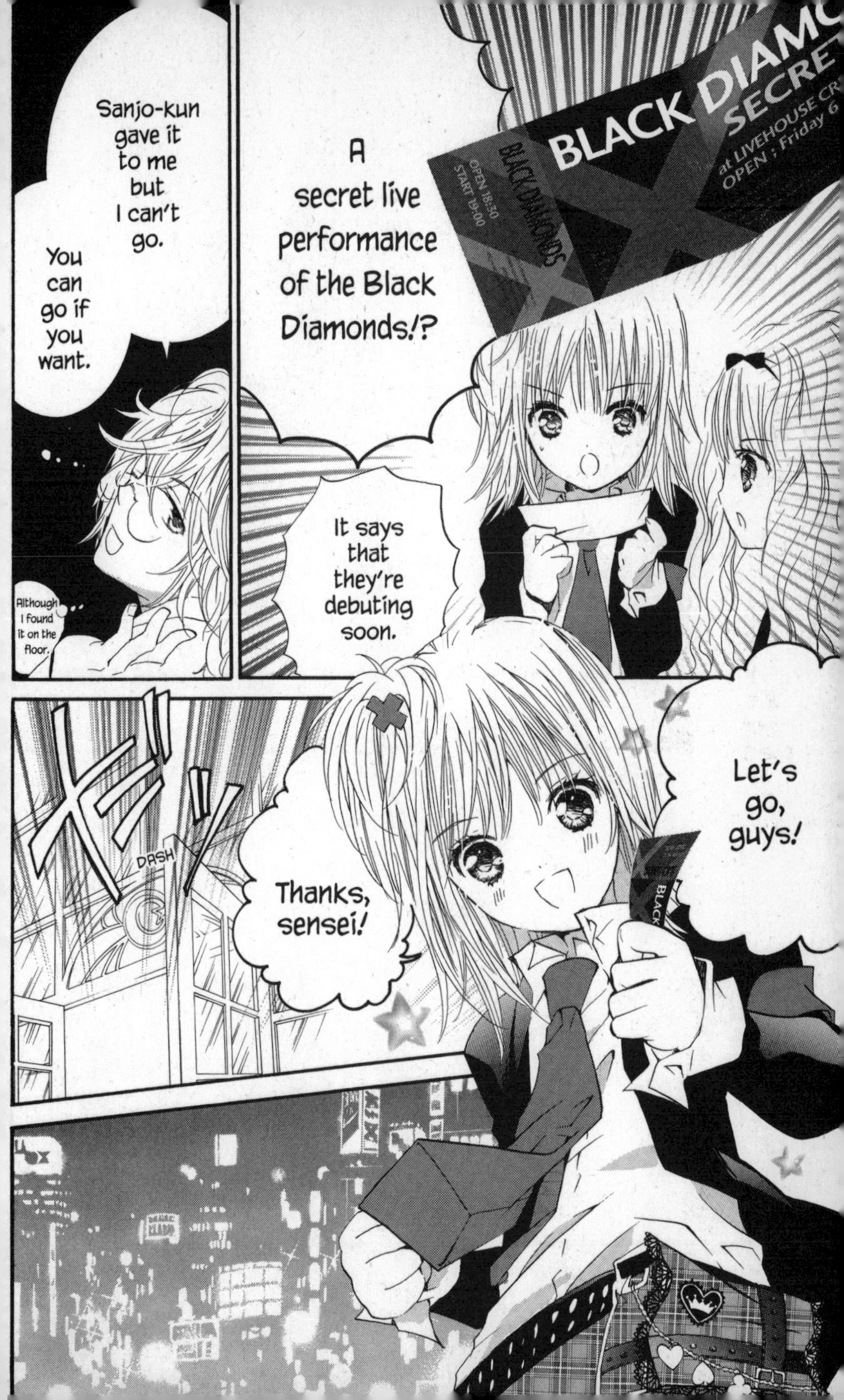
BLACK DIAMONDS
OPEN 18:30
START 19:00
A secret live performance of the Black Diamonds!?
It says that they're debuting soon.
Sanjo-kun gave it to me but I can't go.
You can go if you want.
Although I found it on the floor.
Let's go, guys!
Thanks, sensei!
DASH

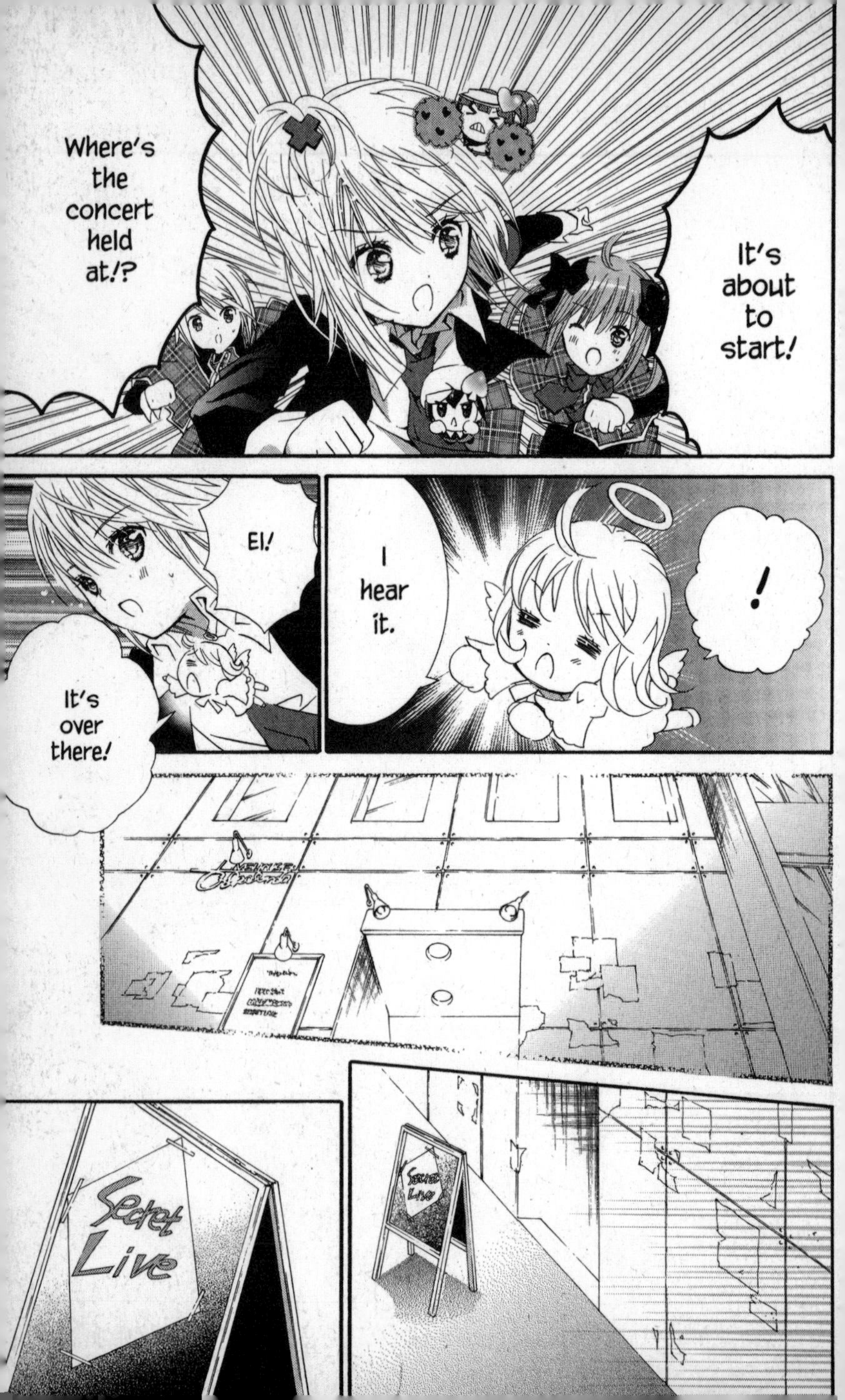

It's about to start!
Where's the concert held at!?
!
I hear it.
Ei!
It's over there!
Secret Live
Secret Live

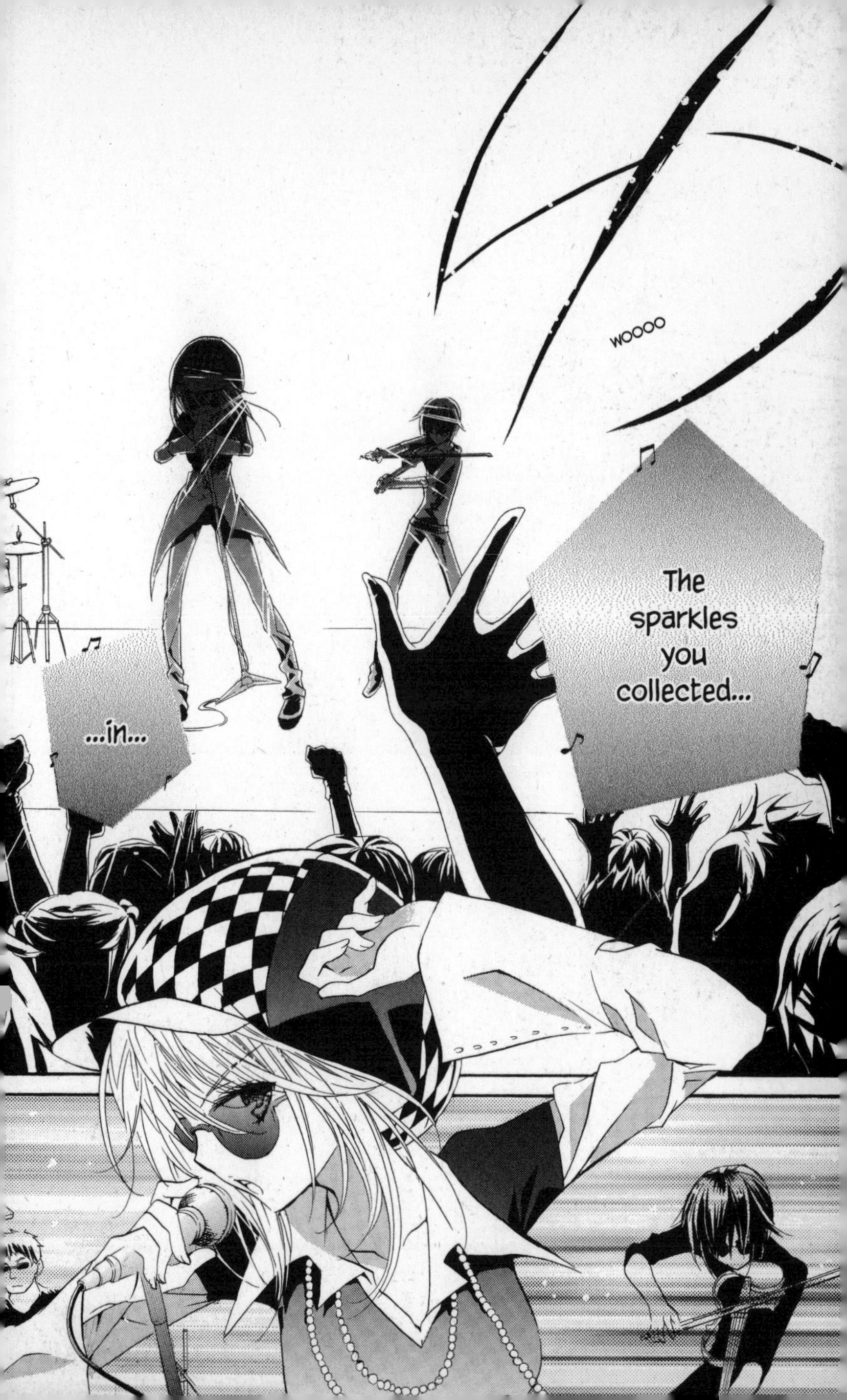
WOOOO
The sparkles you collected...
...in...

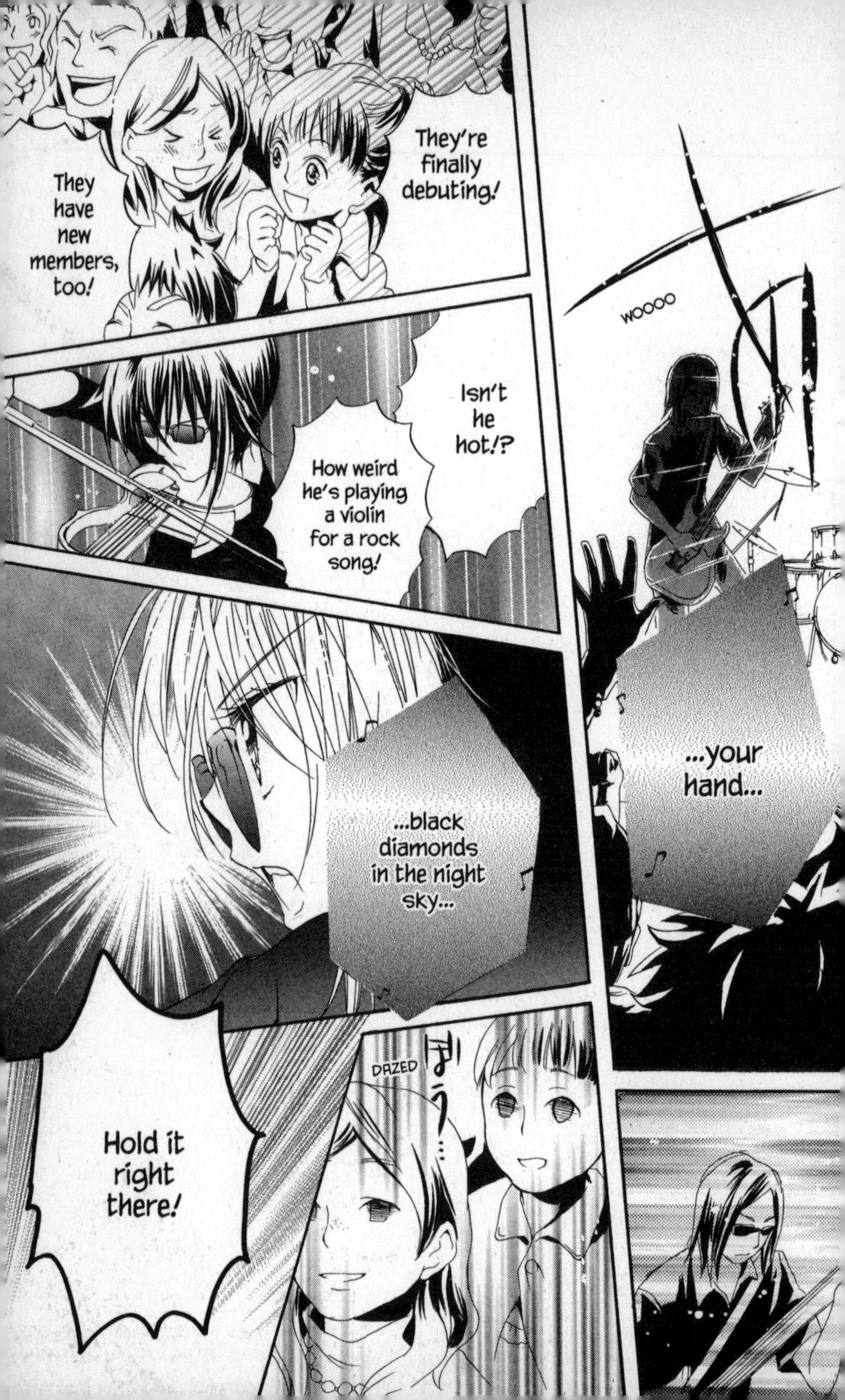
WOOOO
...your hand...
They're finally debuting!
They have new members, too!
Isn't he hot!?
How weird he's playing a violin for a rock song!
...black diamonds in the night sky...
DAZED
ぼう…
Hold it right there!

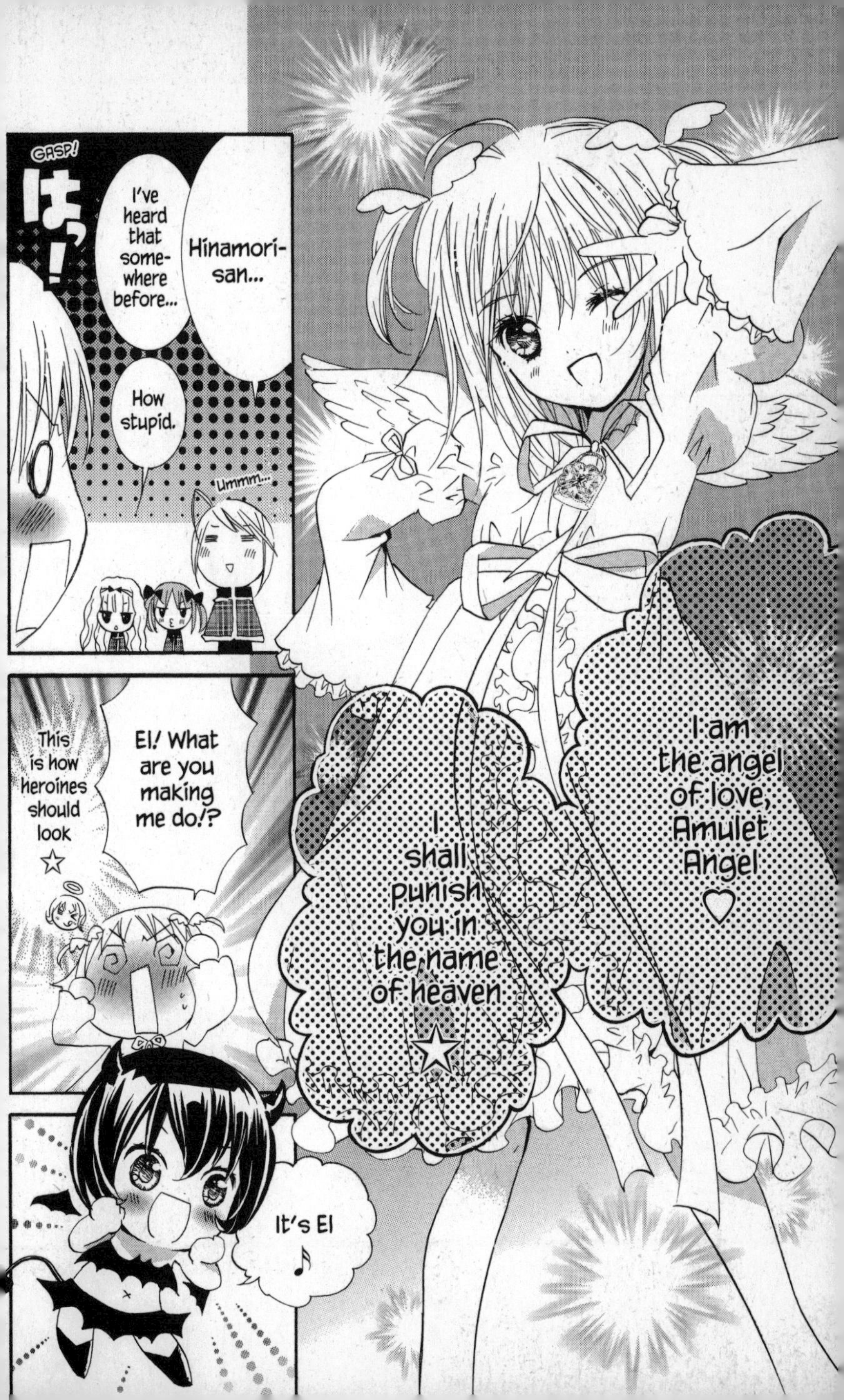
I am the angel of love, Amulet Angel ♡
I shall punish you in the name of heaven ☆
Hinamori-san...
I've heard that somewhere before...
GASP!
はっ!
How stupid.
Ummm...
El! What are you making me do!?
This is how heroines should look ☆
It's El ♪

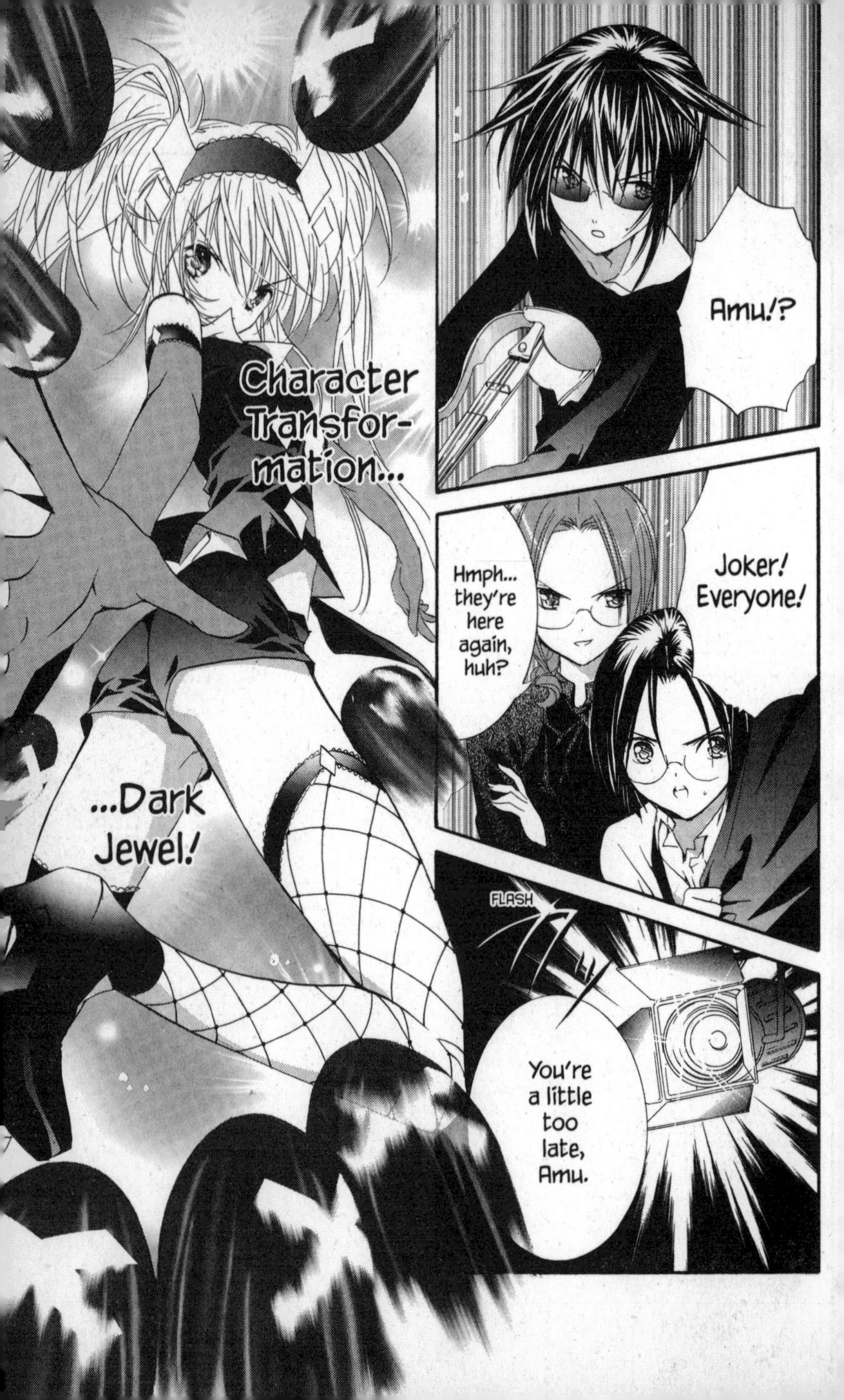
Amu!?
Joker! Everyone!
Hmph... they're here again, huh?
FLASH
You're a little too late, Amu.
Character Transformation...
...Dark Jewel!

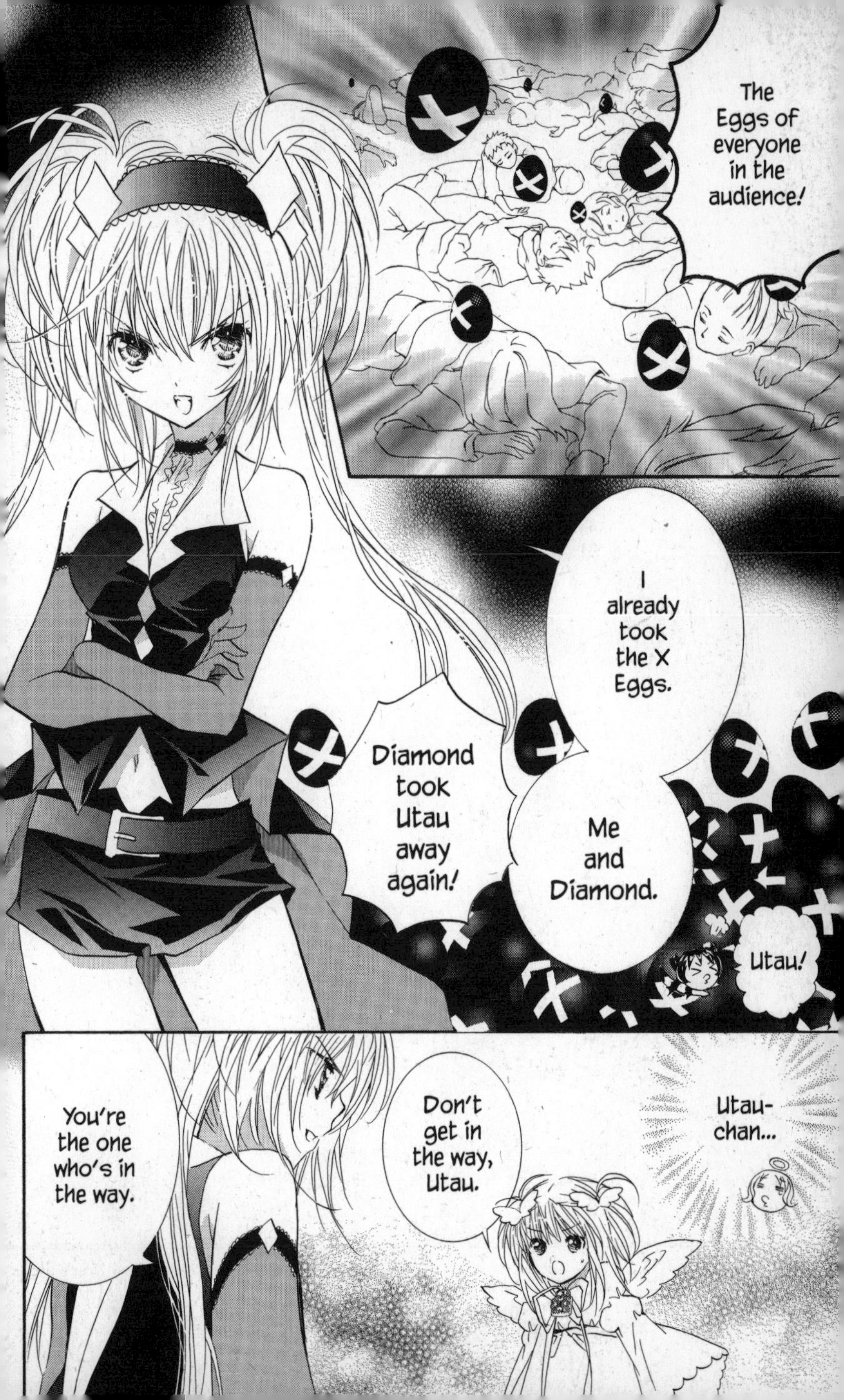
The Eggs of everyone in the audience!
I already took the X Eggs.
Me and Diamond.
Utau!
Diamond took Utau away again!
Utau-chan...
Don't get in the way, Utau.
You're the one who's in the way.

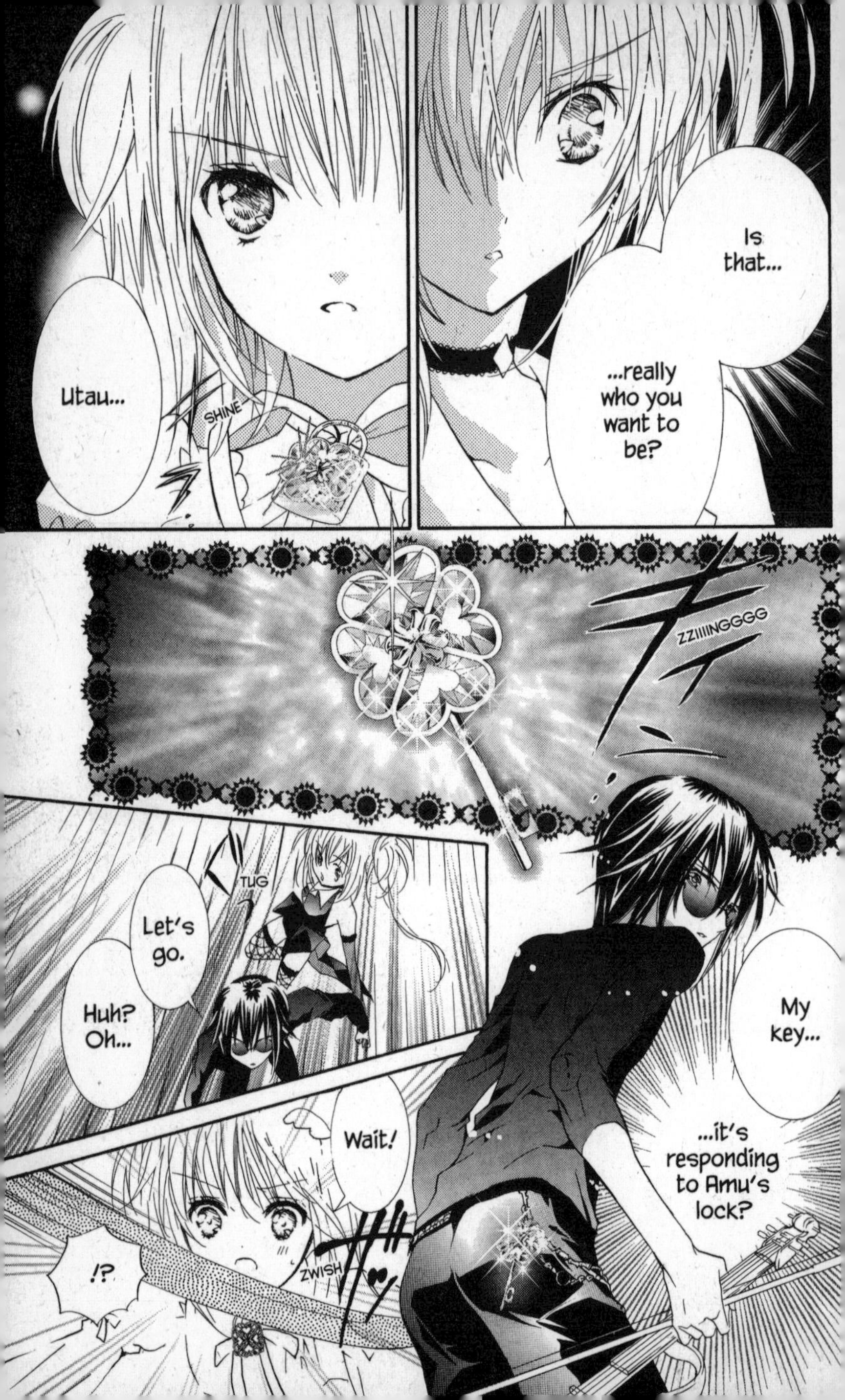

Is that...
...really who you want to be?
Utau...
SHINE
ZZIIIINGGGG
My key...
...it's responding to Amu's lock?
TUG
Let's go.
Huh? Oh...
Wait!
ZWISH
!?

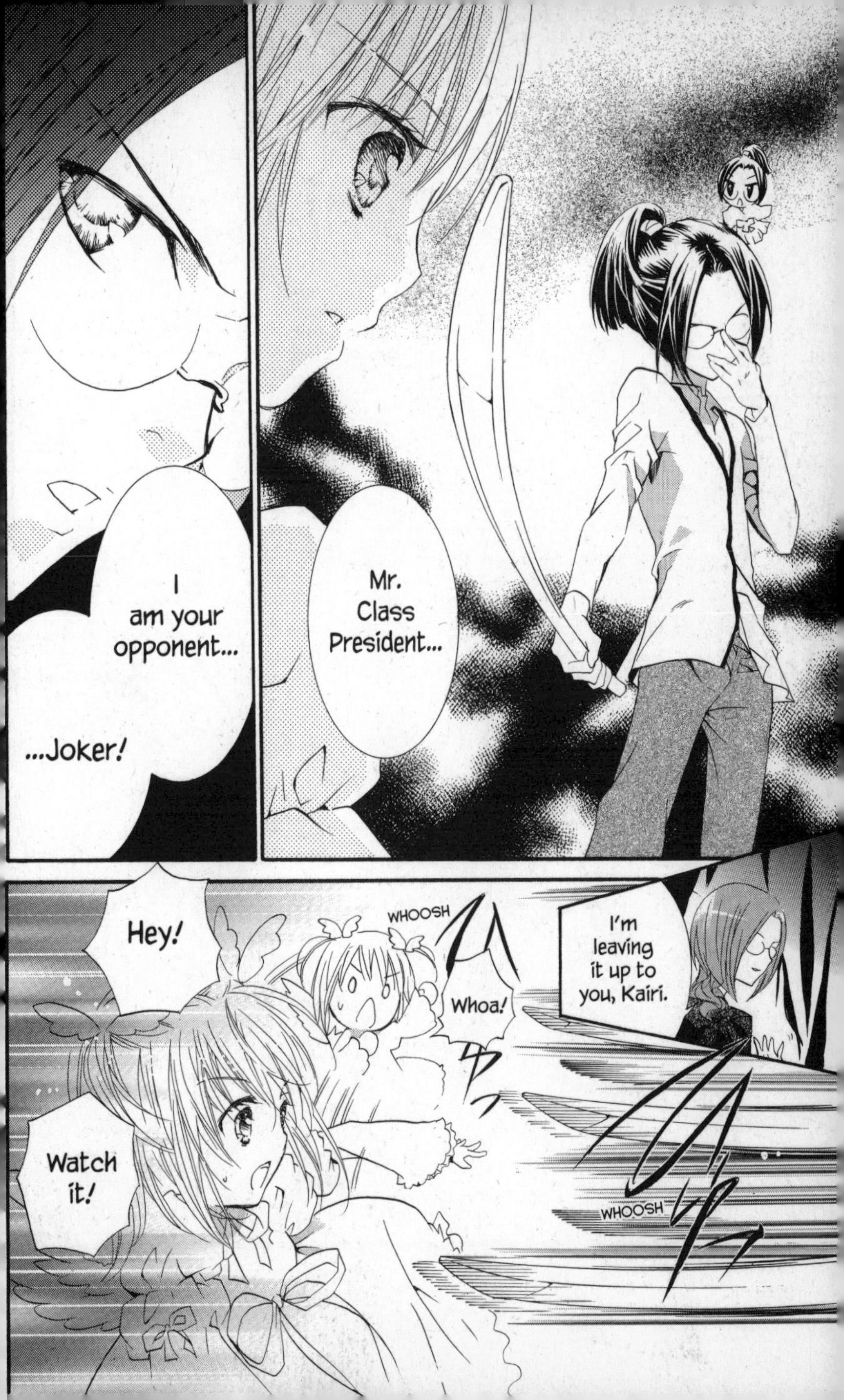
Mr. Class President...
I am your opponent...
...Joker!
I'm leaving it up to you, Kairi.
WHOOSH
Whoa!
Hey!
WHOOSH
Watch it!

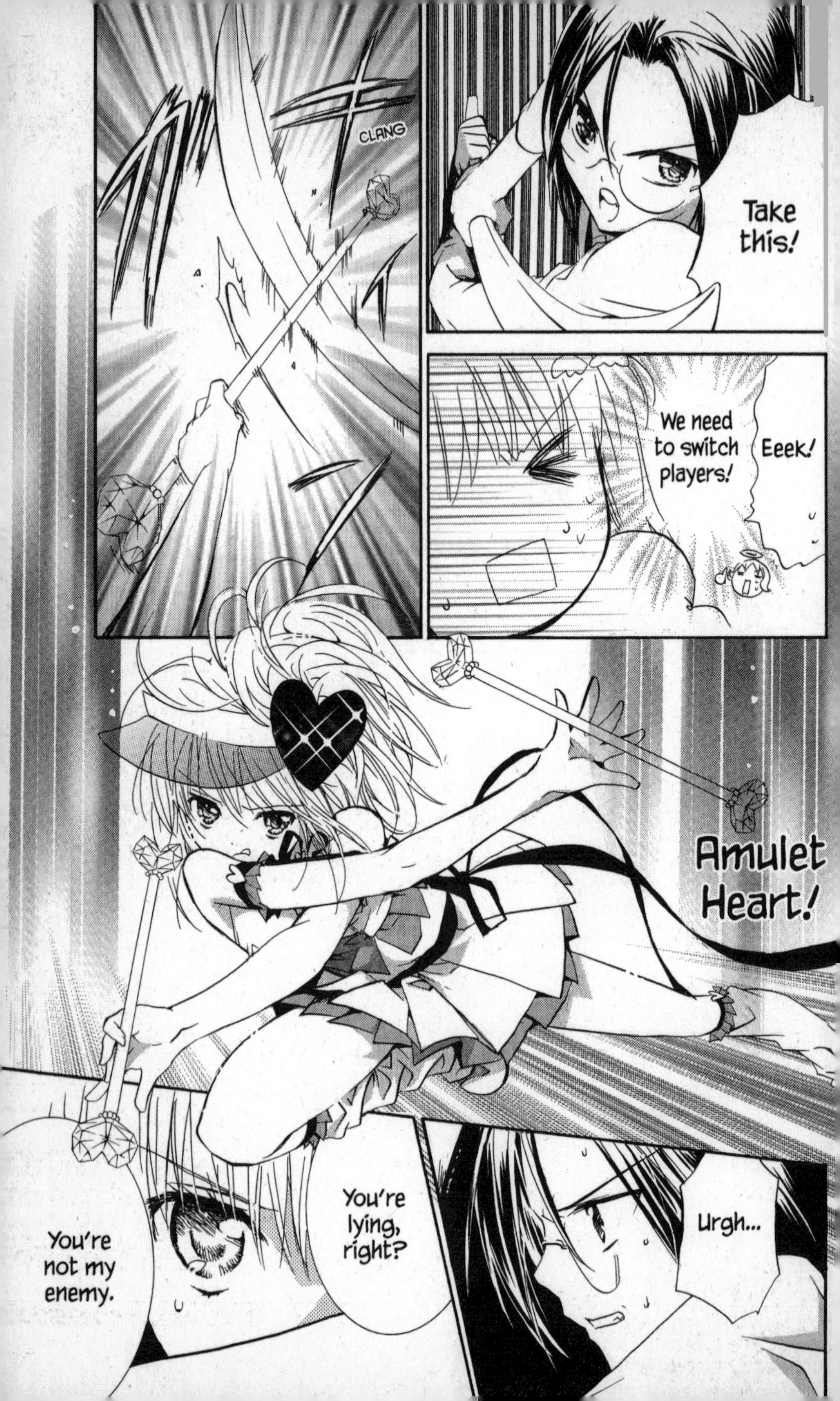
Take this!
Eeek!
We need to switch players!
CLANG
Amulet Heart!
Urgh...
You're lying, right?
You're not my enemy.

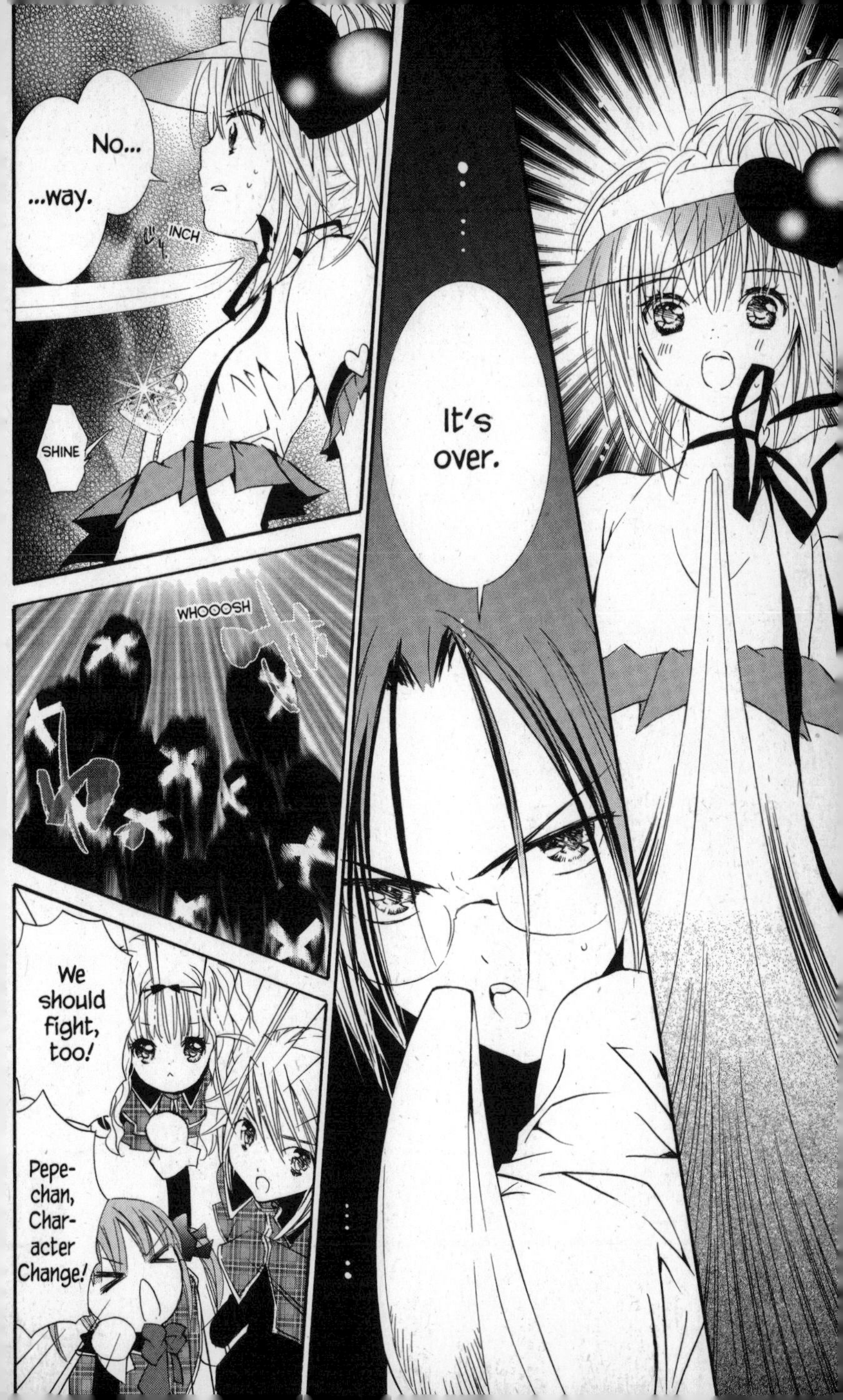

It's over.
No...
...way.
INCH
SHINE
WHOOOSH
We should fight, too!
Pepe-chan, Character Change!

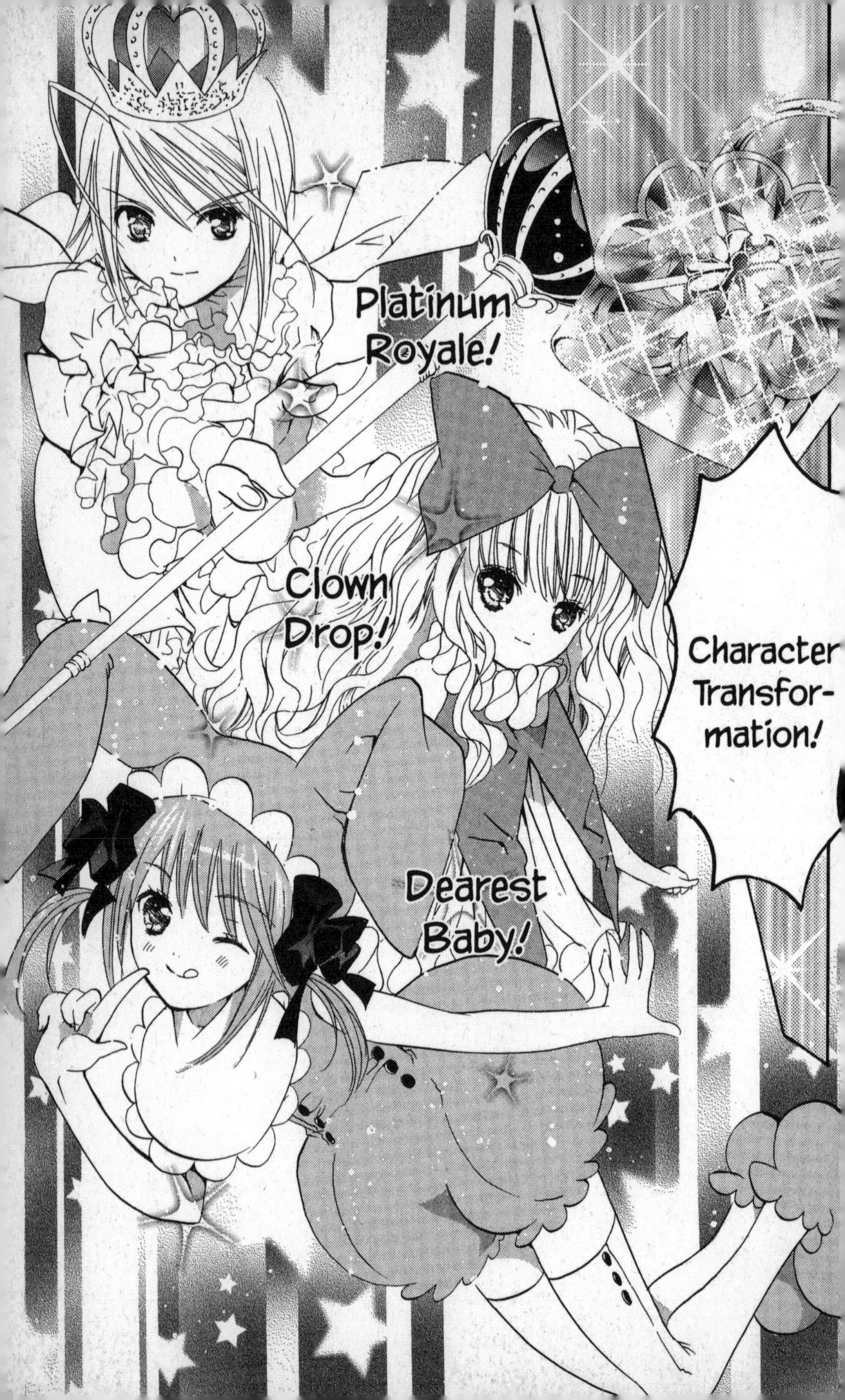
Character Transformation!
Platinum Royale!
Clown Drop!
Dearest Baby!

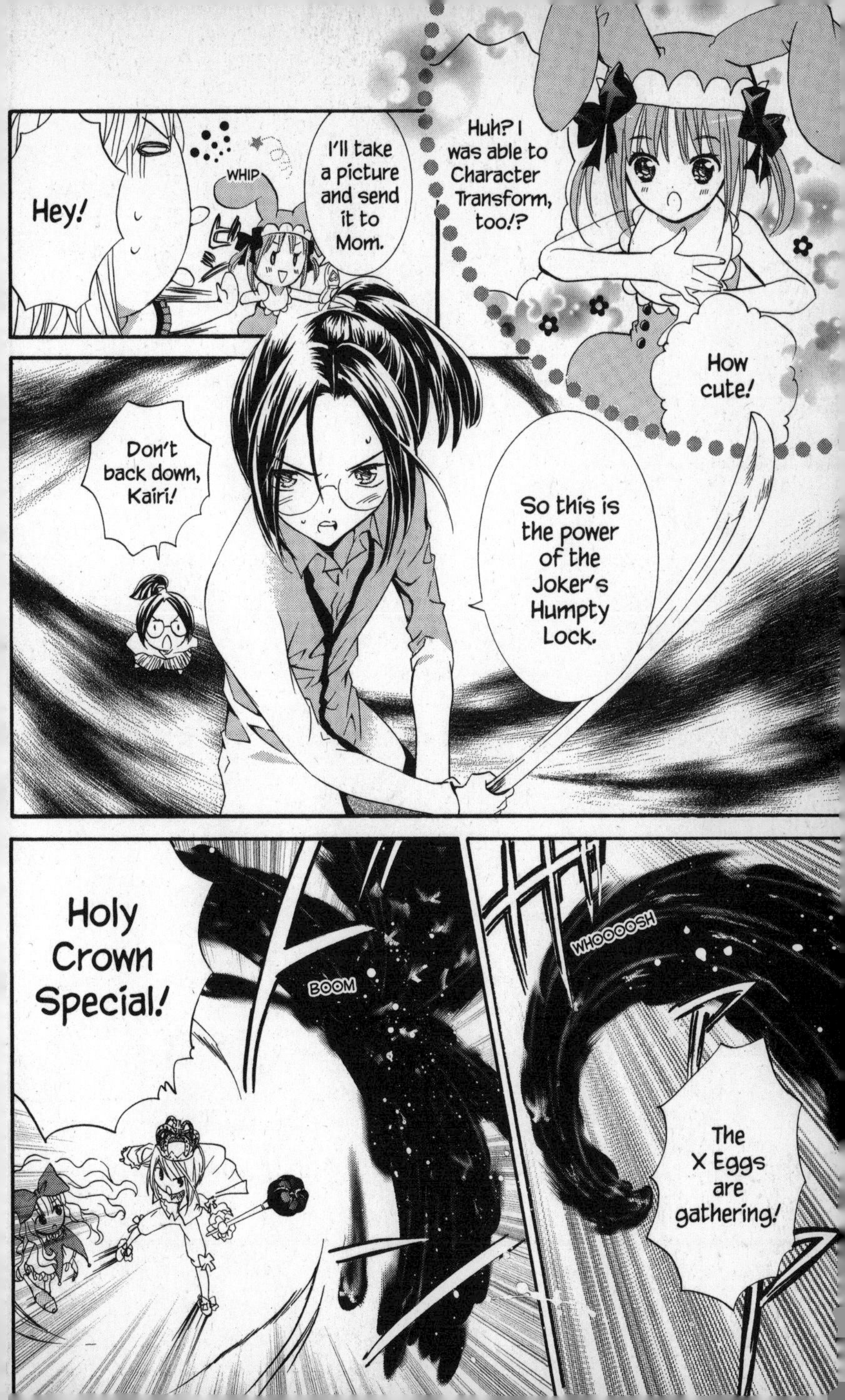
Huh? I was able to Character Transform, too!?
How cute!
I'll take a picture and send it to Mom.
WHIP
Hey!
So this is the power of the Joker's Humpty Lock.
Don't back down, Kairi!
WHOOOOSH
The X Eggs are gathering!
Holy Crown Special!
BOOM

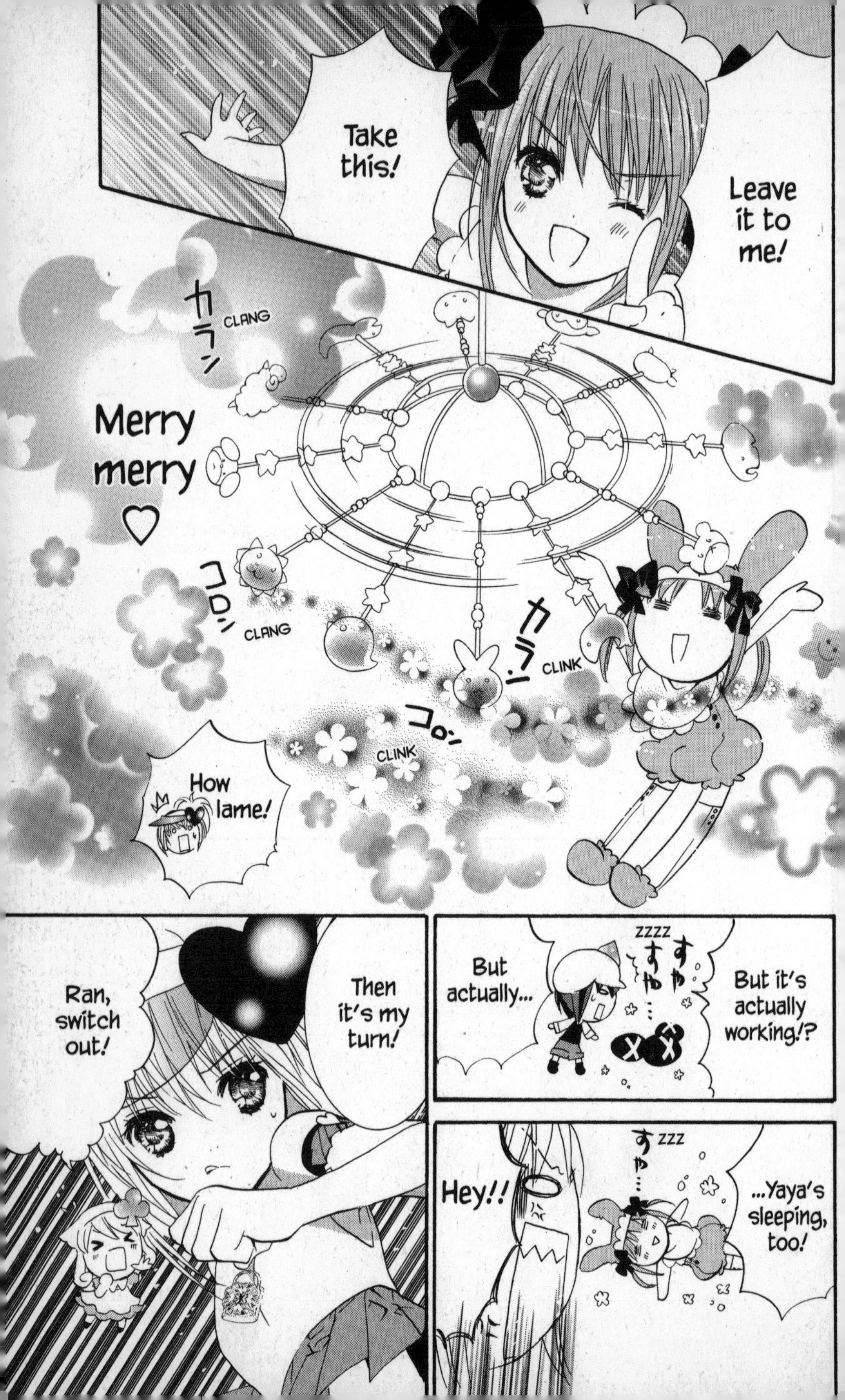
Leave it to me!
Take this!
カラン
CLANG
Merry merry ♡
コロン
CLANG
カラン
CLINK
コロン
CLINK
How lame!
But it's actually working!?
すやすや…
ZZZZ
But actually...
...Yaya's sleeping, too!
すや…
ZZZ
Hey!!
Then it's my turn!
Ran, switch out!

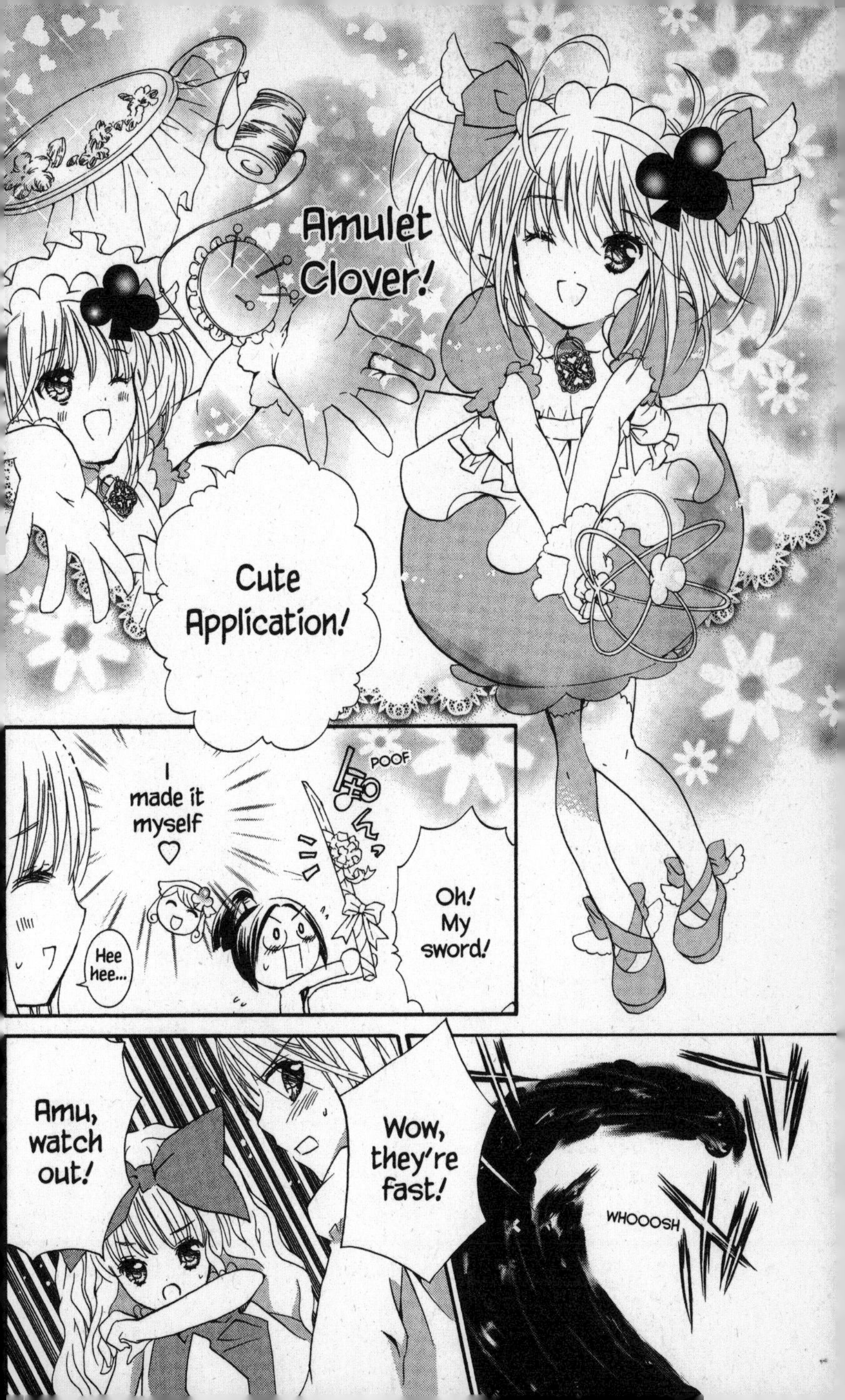
Amulet Clover!
Cute Application!
POOF
Oh! My sword!
I made it myself ♡
Hee hee...
WHOOOSH
Wow, they're fast!
Amu, watch out!

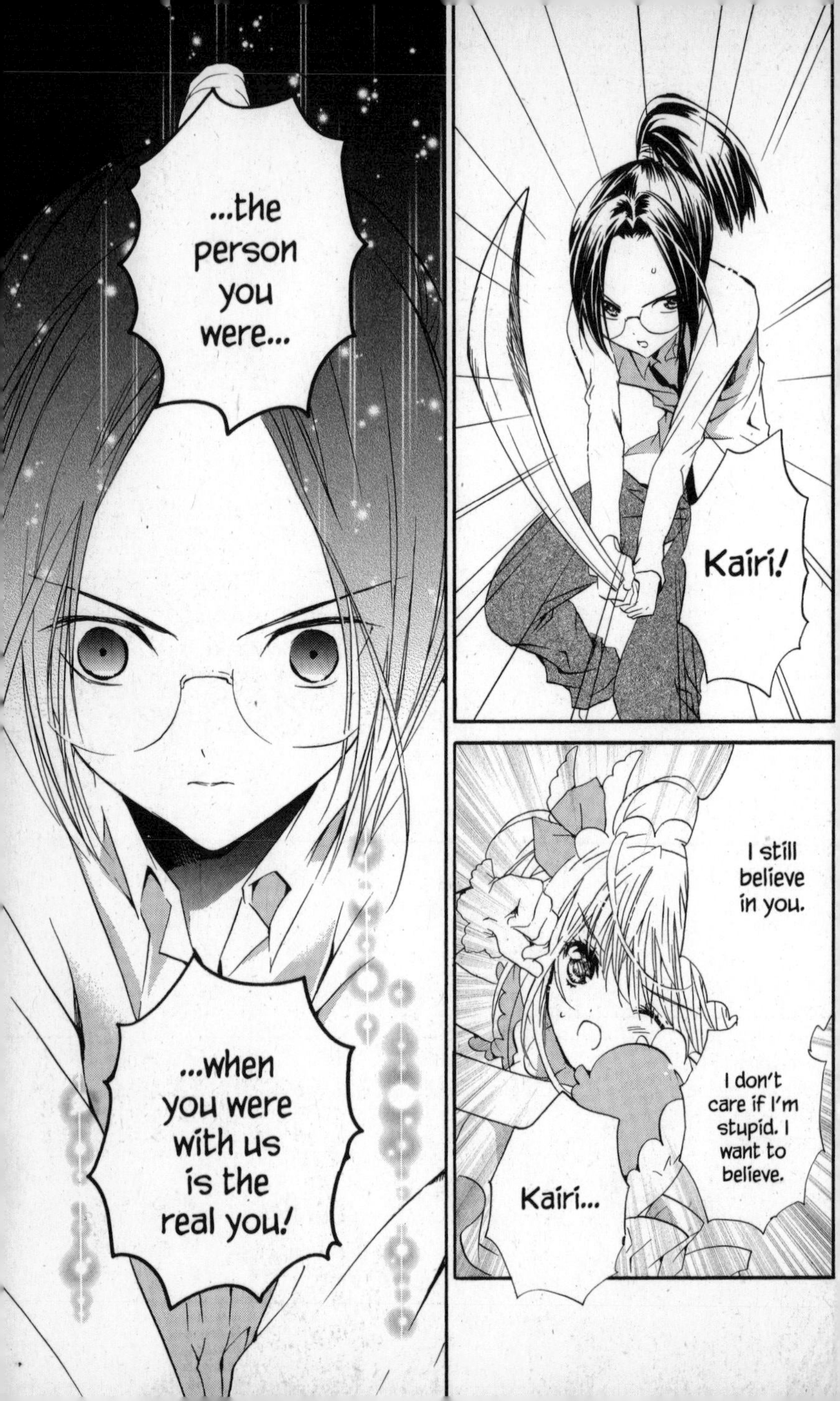
Kairi!
I still believe in you.
I don't care if I'm stupid. I want to believe.
Kairi...
...the person you were...
...when you were with us is the real you!

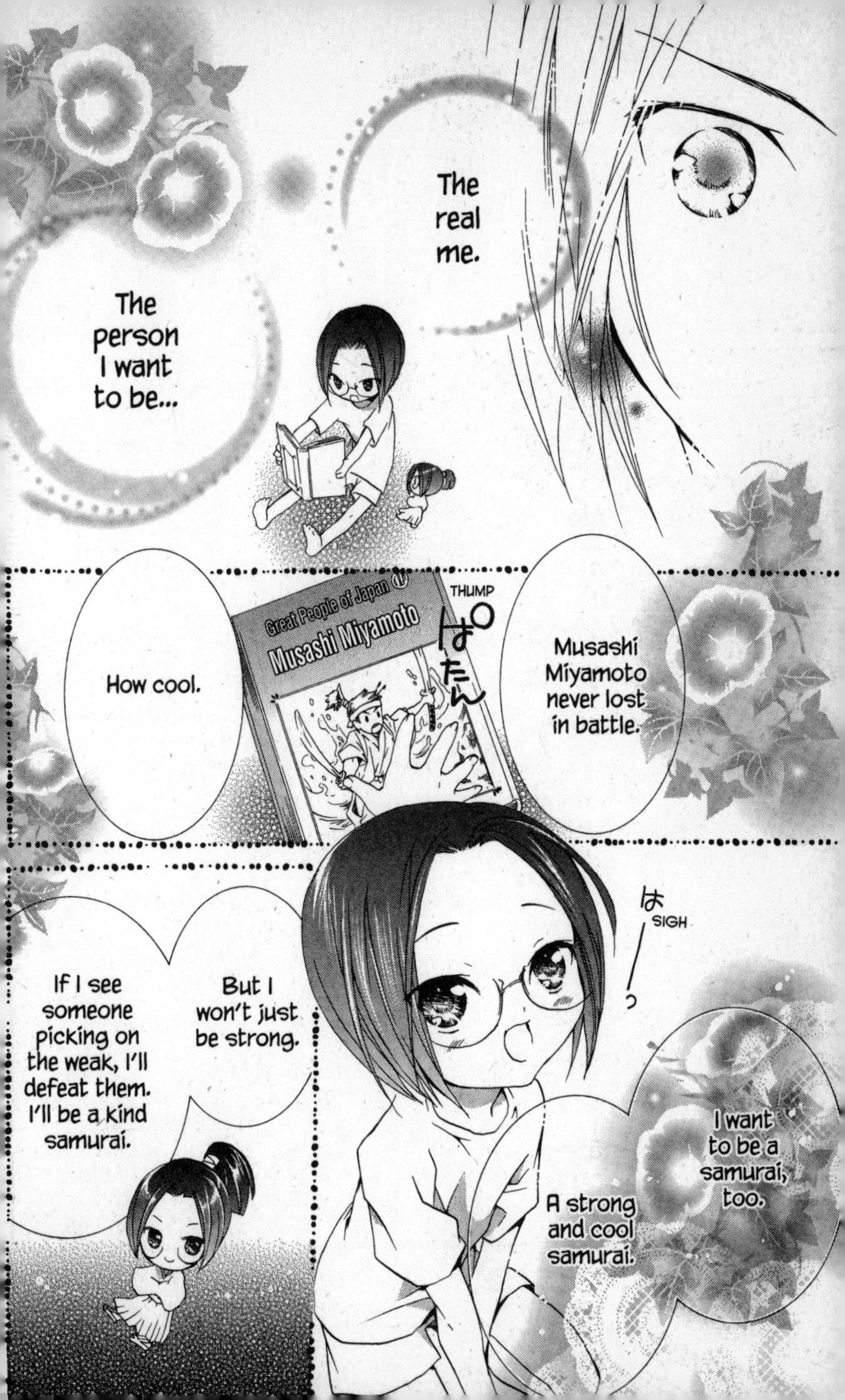
The real me.
The person I want to be...
Musashi Miyamoto never lost in battle.
ぱたん
THUMP
Great People of Japan (1)
Musashi Miyamoto
How cool.
は
SIGH
I want to be a samurai, too.
A strong and cool samurai.
But I won't just be strong.
If I see someone picking on the weak, I'll defeat them. I'll be a kind samurai.

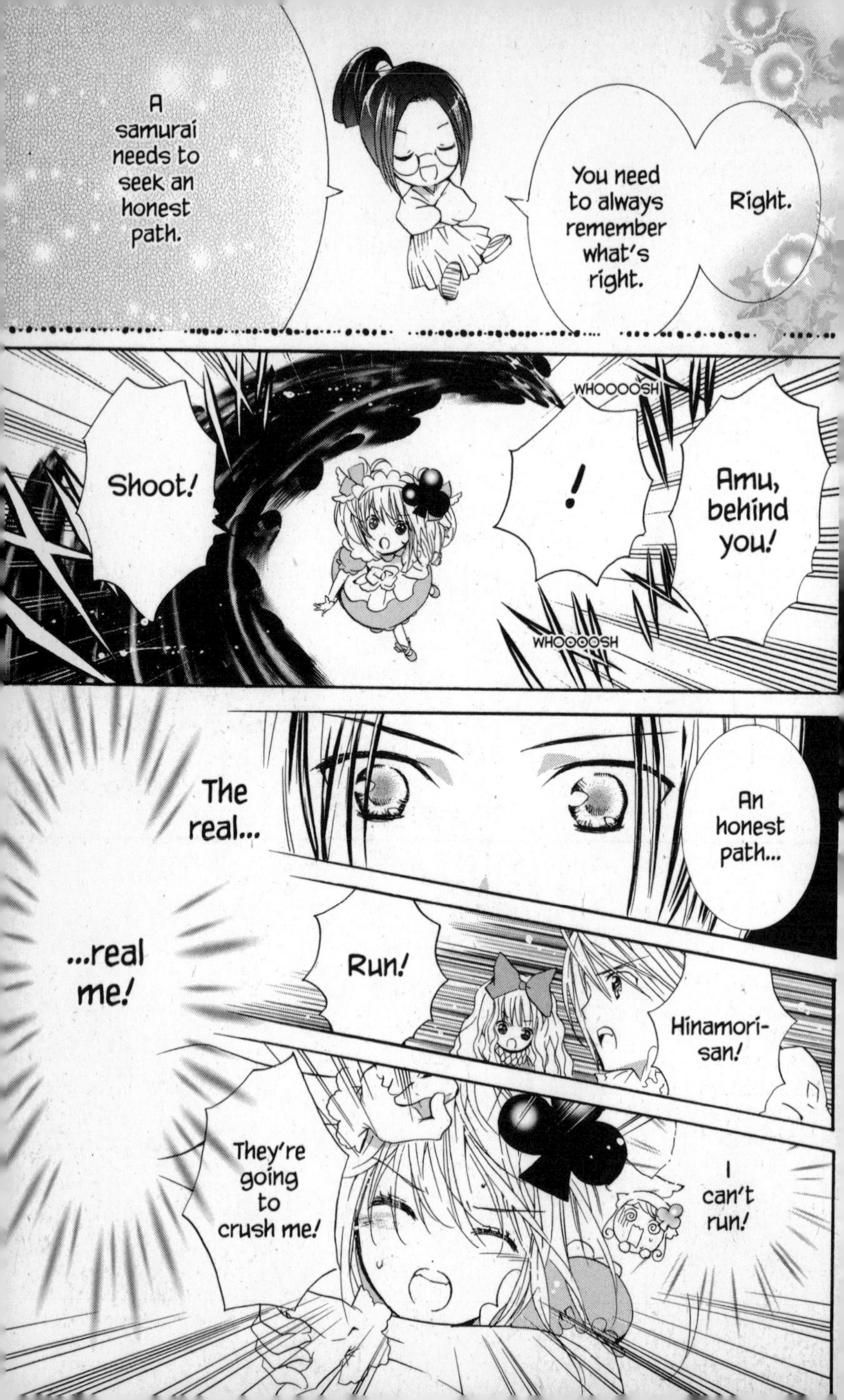
Right.
You need to always remember what's right.
A samurai needs to seek an honest path.
WHOOOOSH
Amu, behind you!
!
WHOOOOSH
Shoot!
An honest path...
Hinamori-san!
Run!
I can't run!
They're going to crush me!
The real...
...real me!

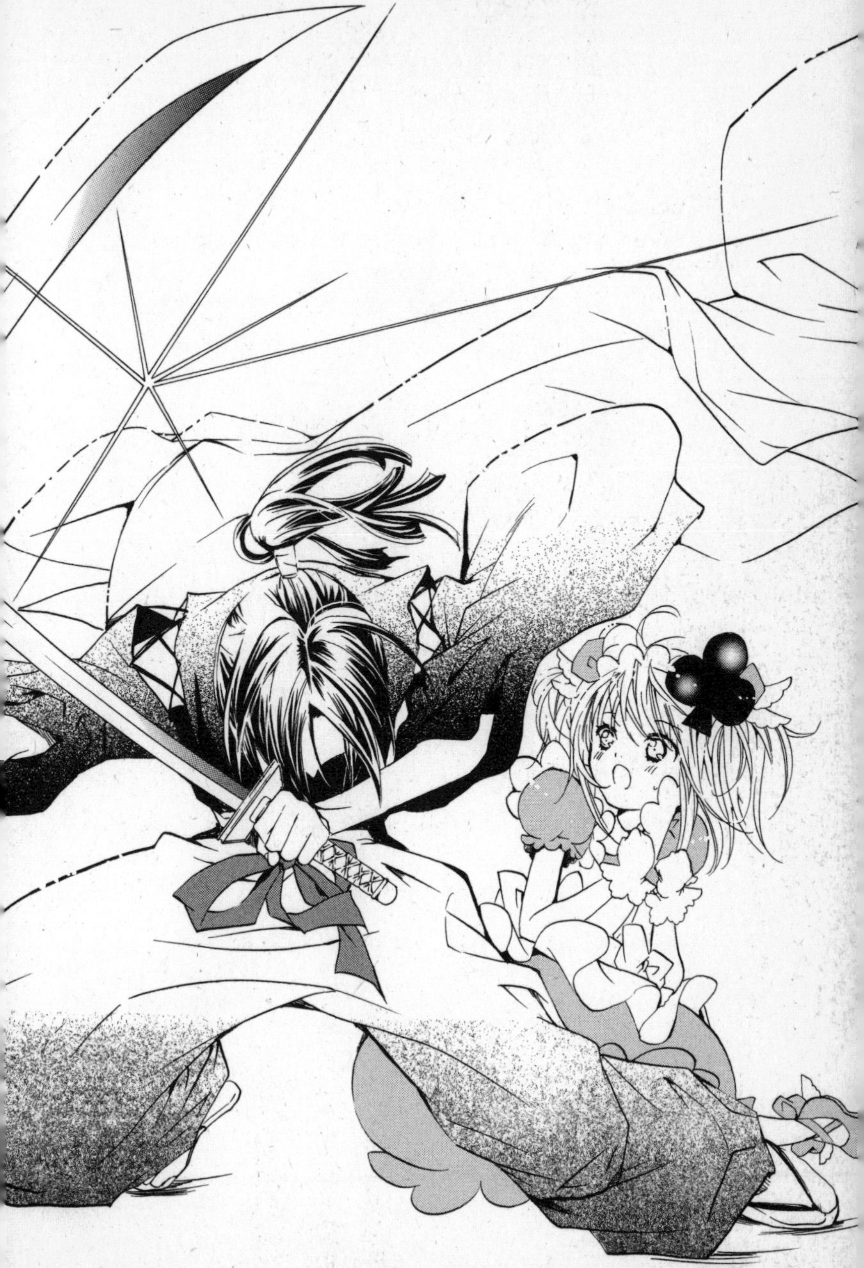

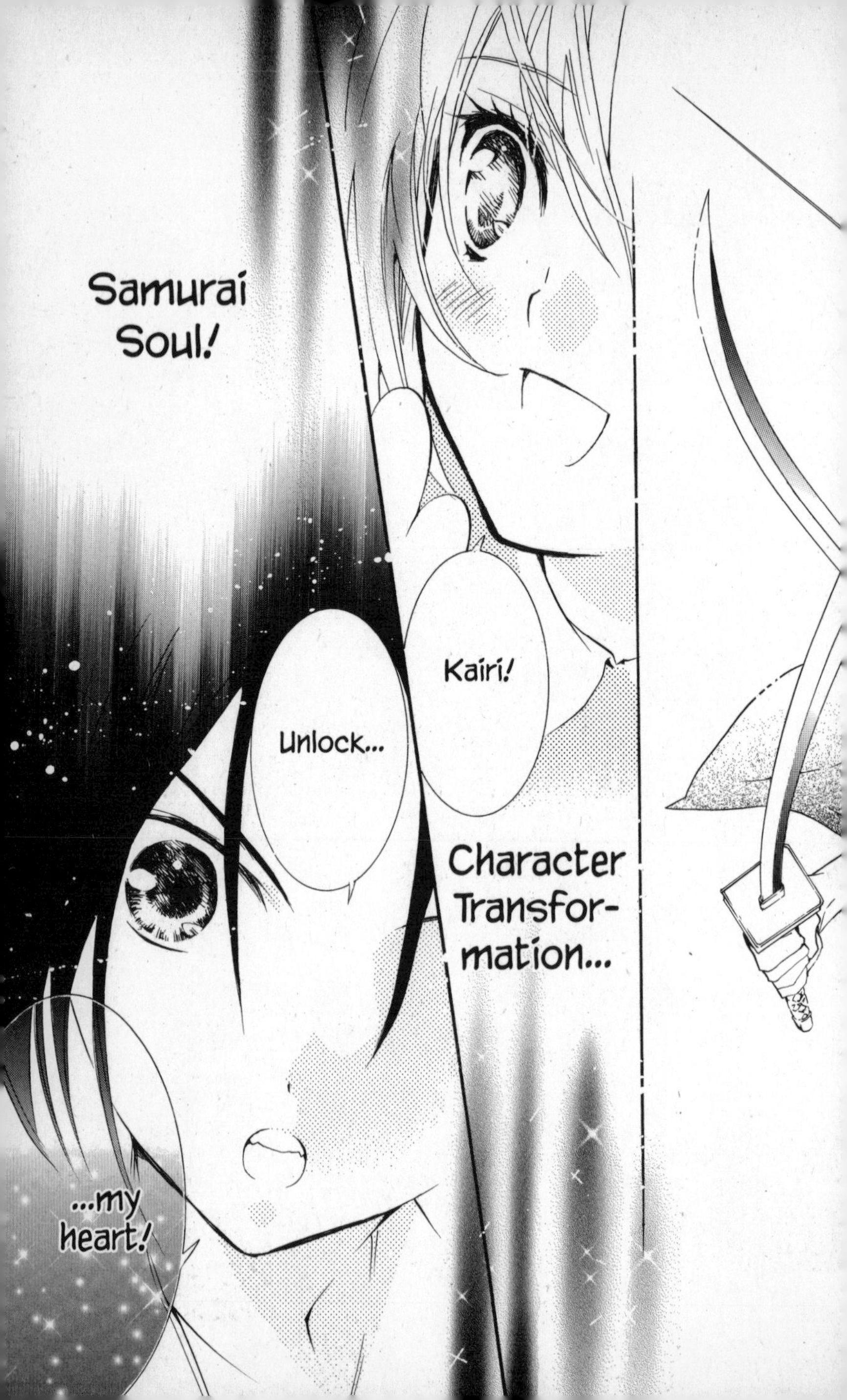
Kairi!
Unlock...
...my heart!
Character Transformation...
Samurai Soul!

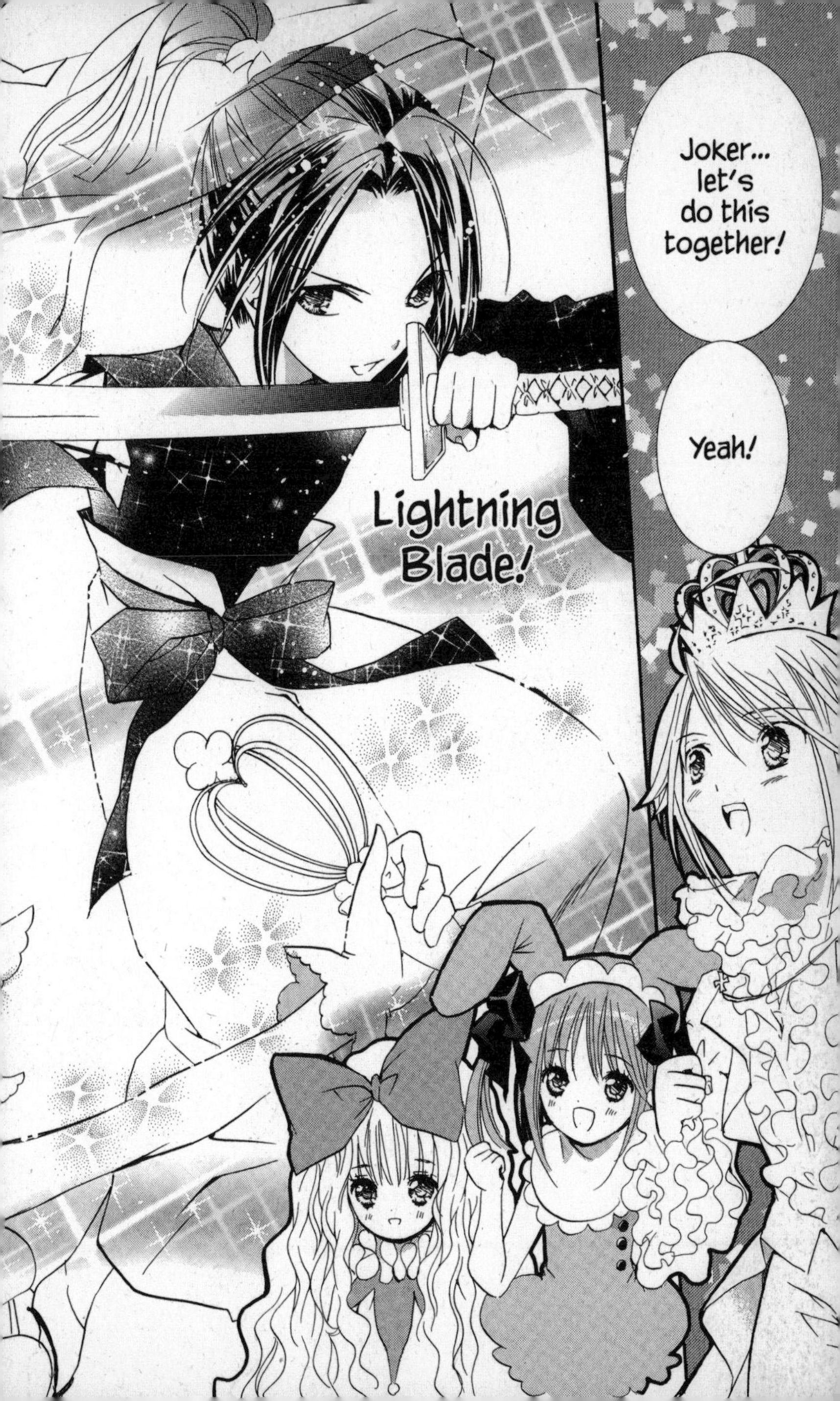
Joker... let's do this together!
Yeah!
Lightning Blade!

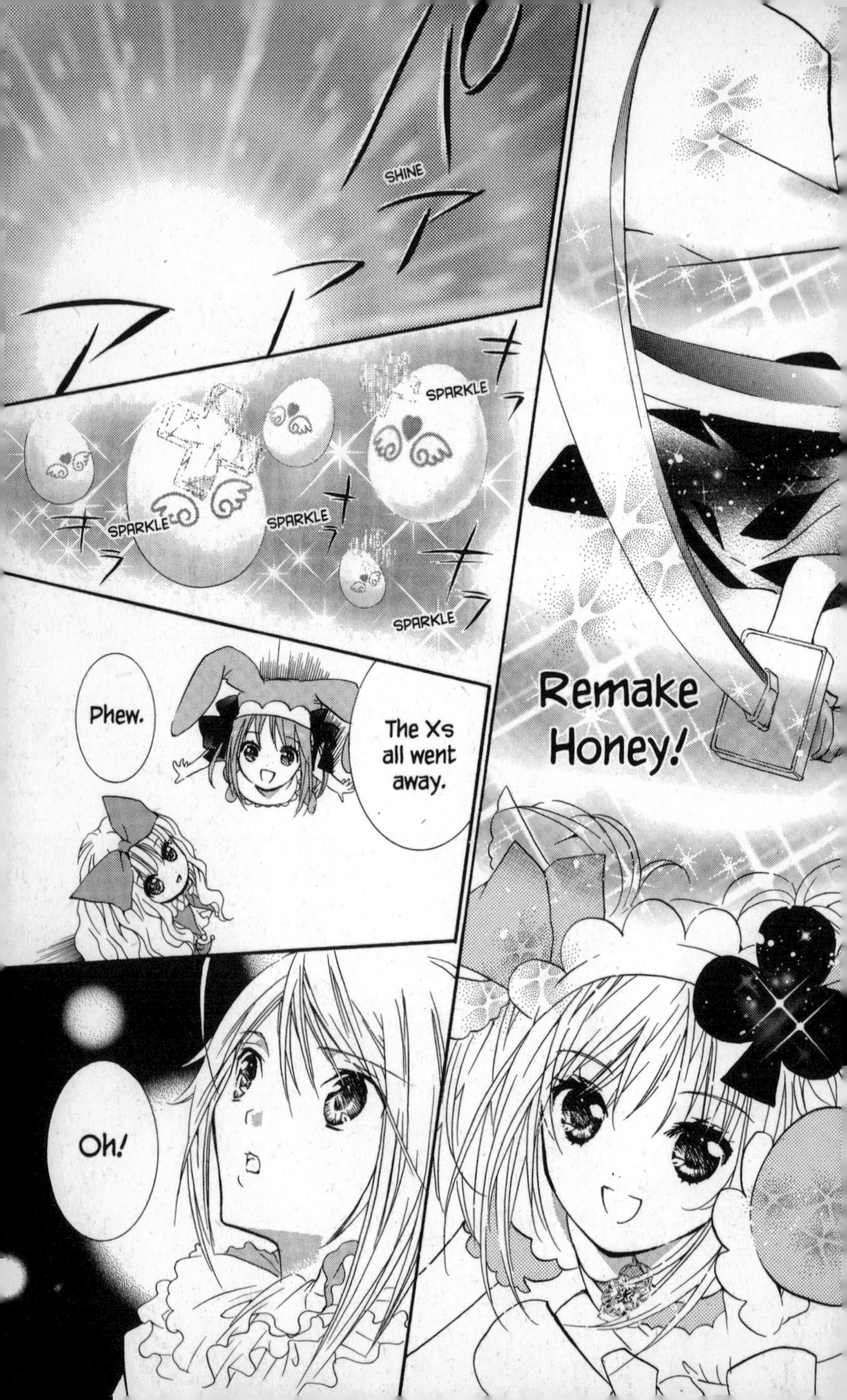

Remake Honey!
SHINE
SPARKLE
SPARKLE
SPARKLE
SPARKLE
The Xs all went away.
Phew.
Oh!

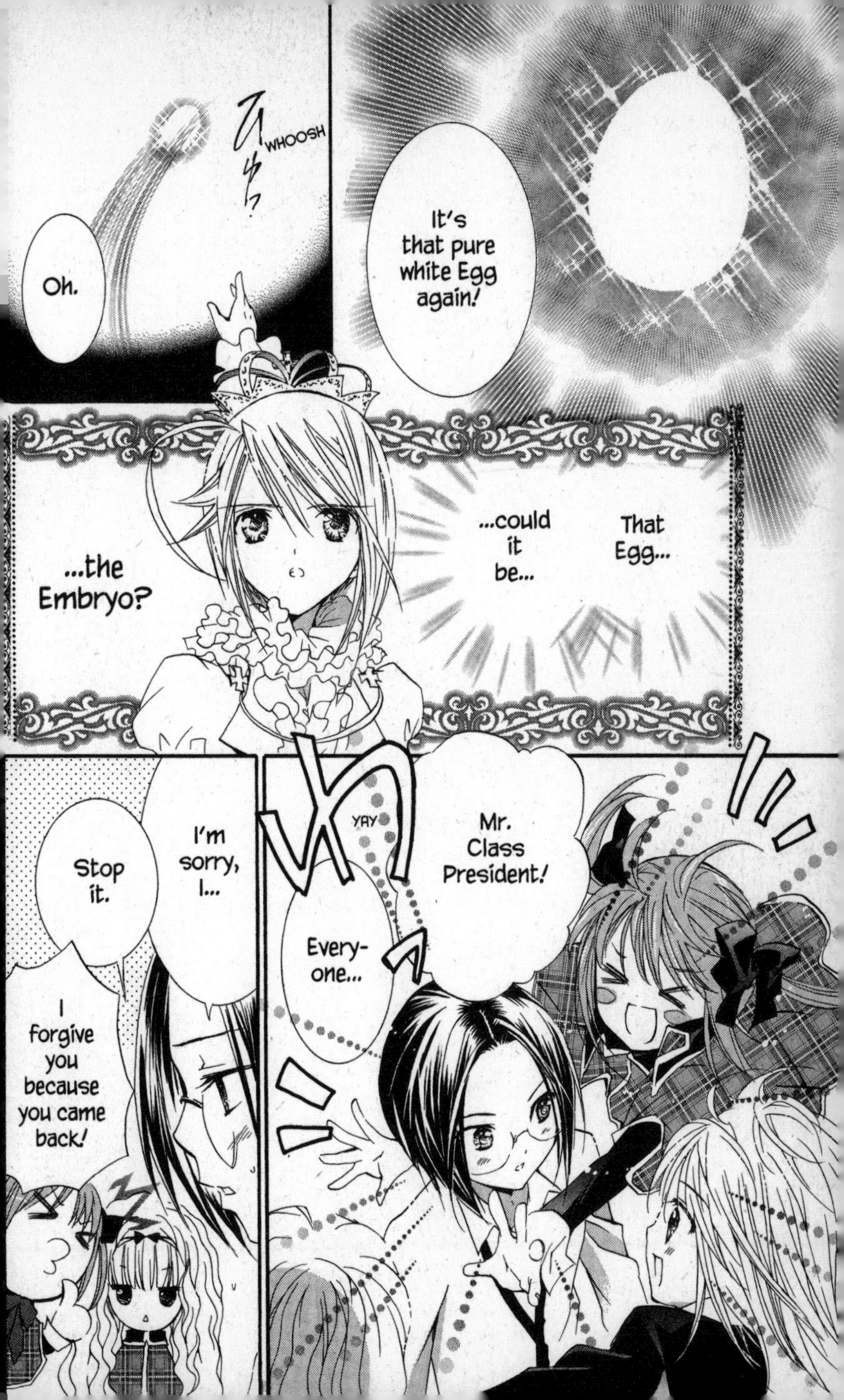
It's that pure white Egg again!
WHOOSH
Oh.
That Egg...
...could it be...
...the Embryo?
Mr. Class President!
YAY
Every-one...
I'm sorry, I...
Stop it.
I forgive you because you came back!

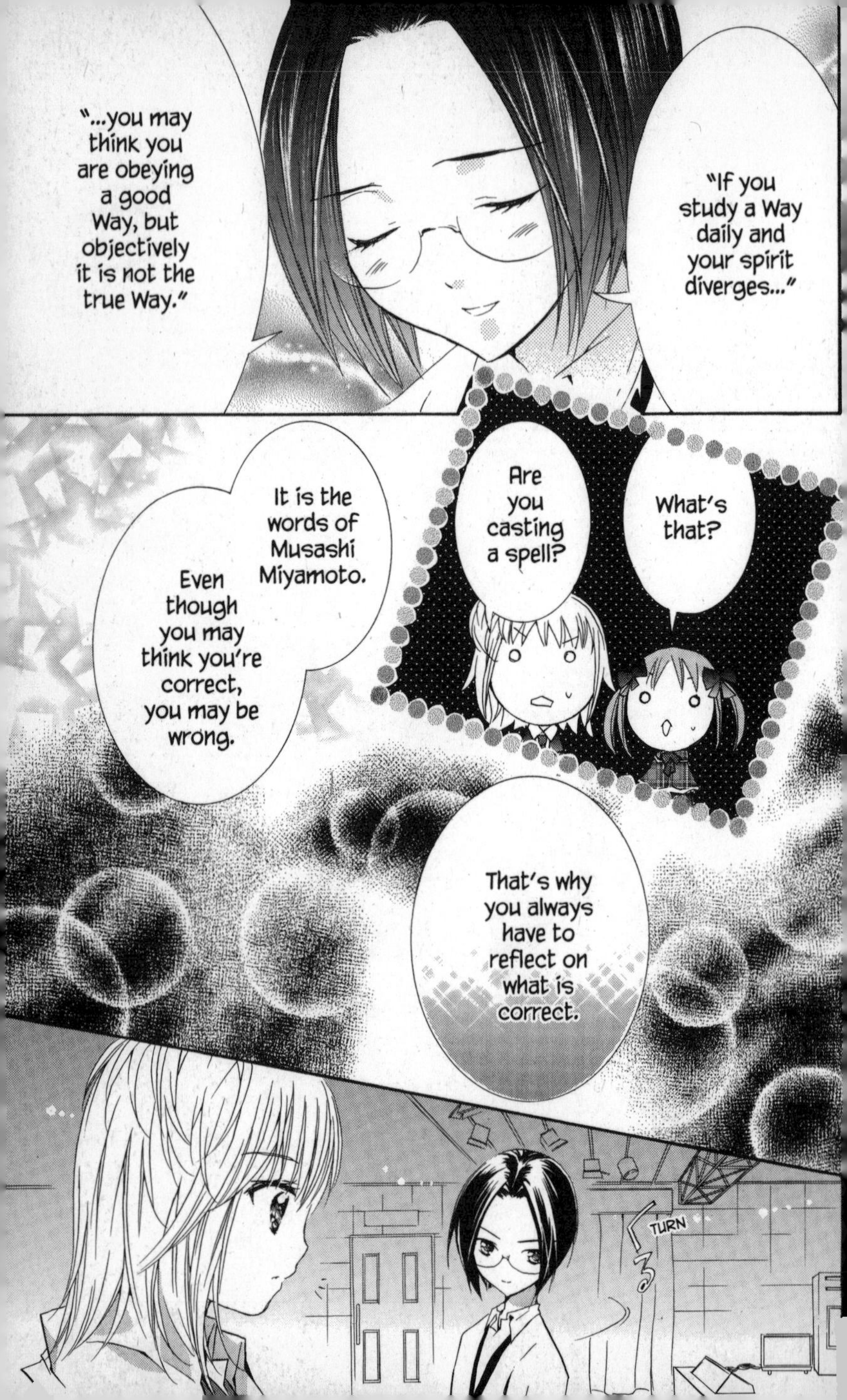
"If you study a Way daily and your spirit diverges..."
"...you may think you are obeying a good Way, but objectively it is not the true Way."
What's that?
Are you casting a spell?
It is the words of Musashi Miyamoto.
Even though you may think you're correct, you may be wrong.
That's why you always have to reflect on what is correct.
TURN

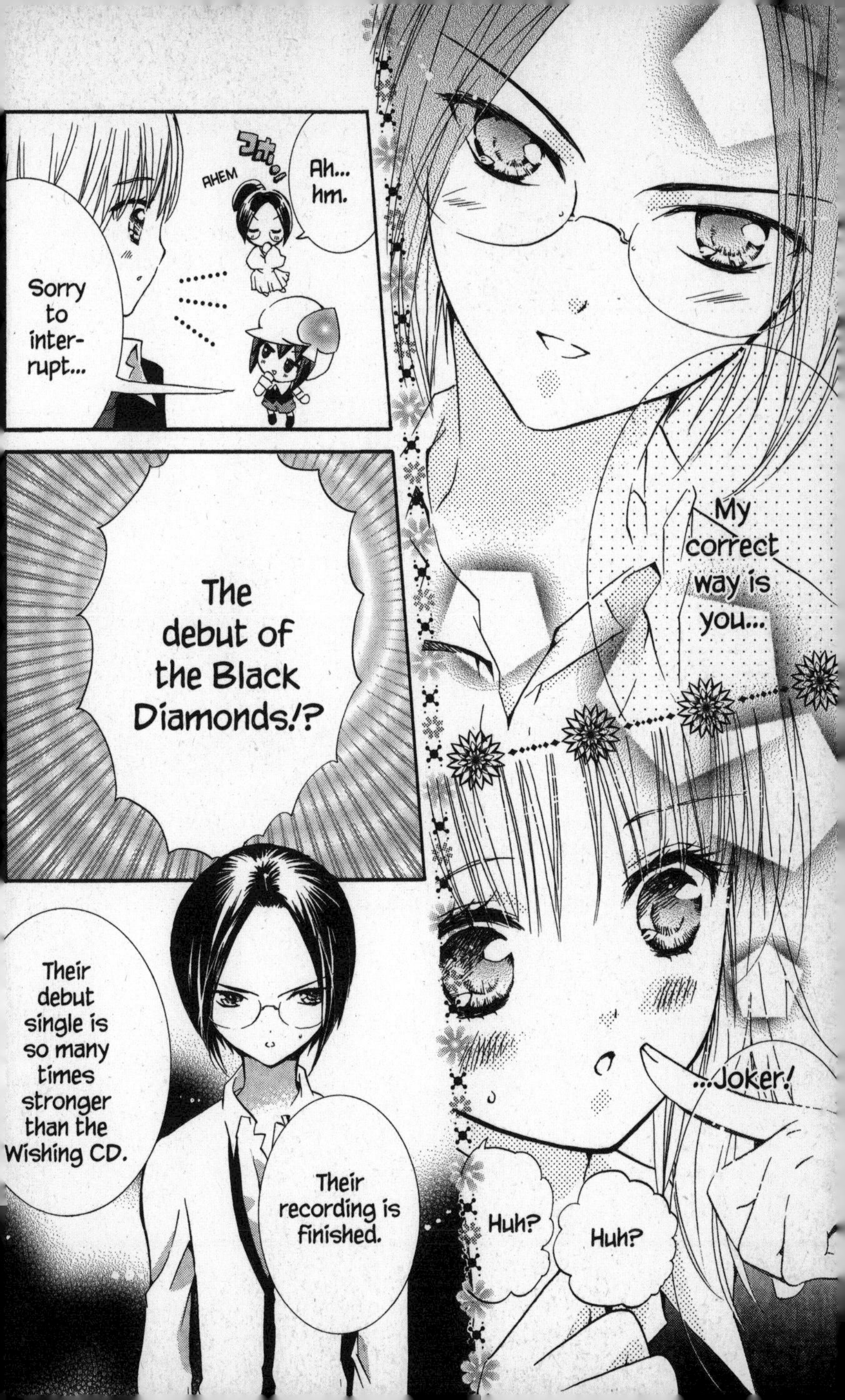
My correct way is you...
...Joker!
Huh?
Huh?
Ah... hm.
AHEM
Sorry to interrupt...
The debut of the Black Diamonds!?
Their recording is finished.
Their debut single is so many times stronger than the Wishing CD.

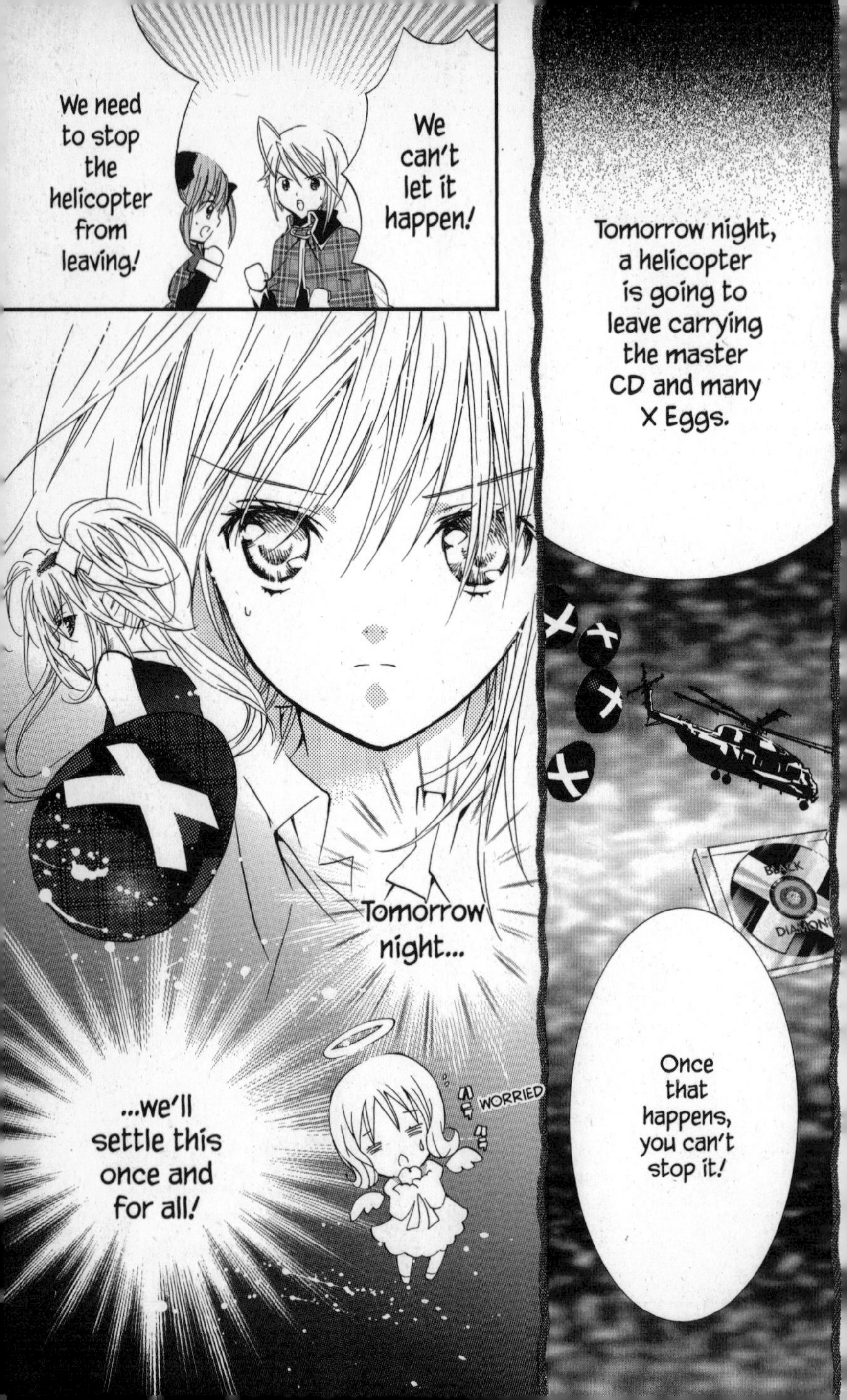
Tomorrow night, a helicopter is going to leave carrying the master CD and many X Eggs.
Once that happens, you can't stop it!
We can't let it happen!
We need to stop the helicopter from leaving!
Tomorrow night...
WORRIED
...we'll settle this once and for all!

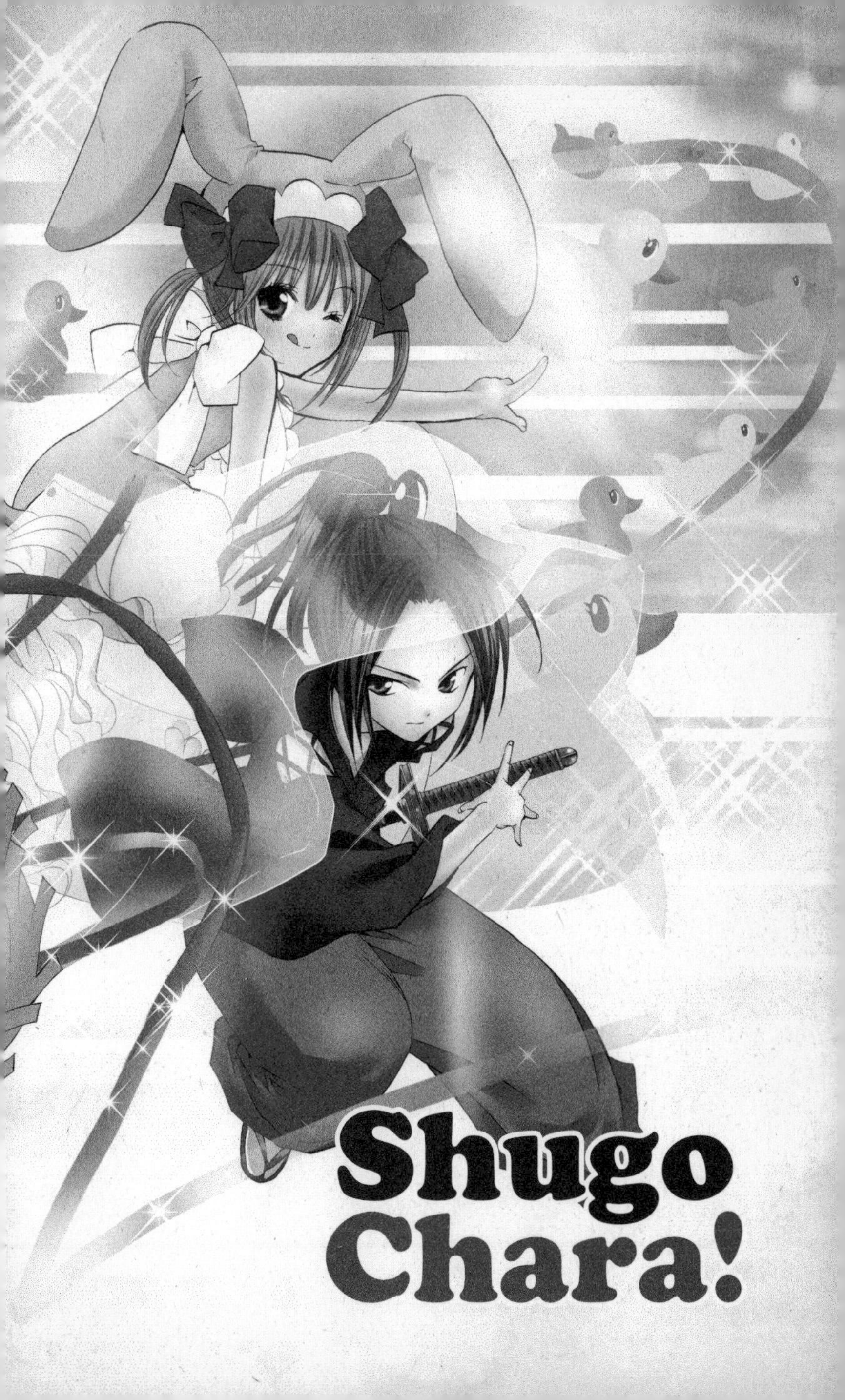
Shugo
Chara!

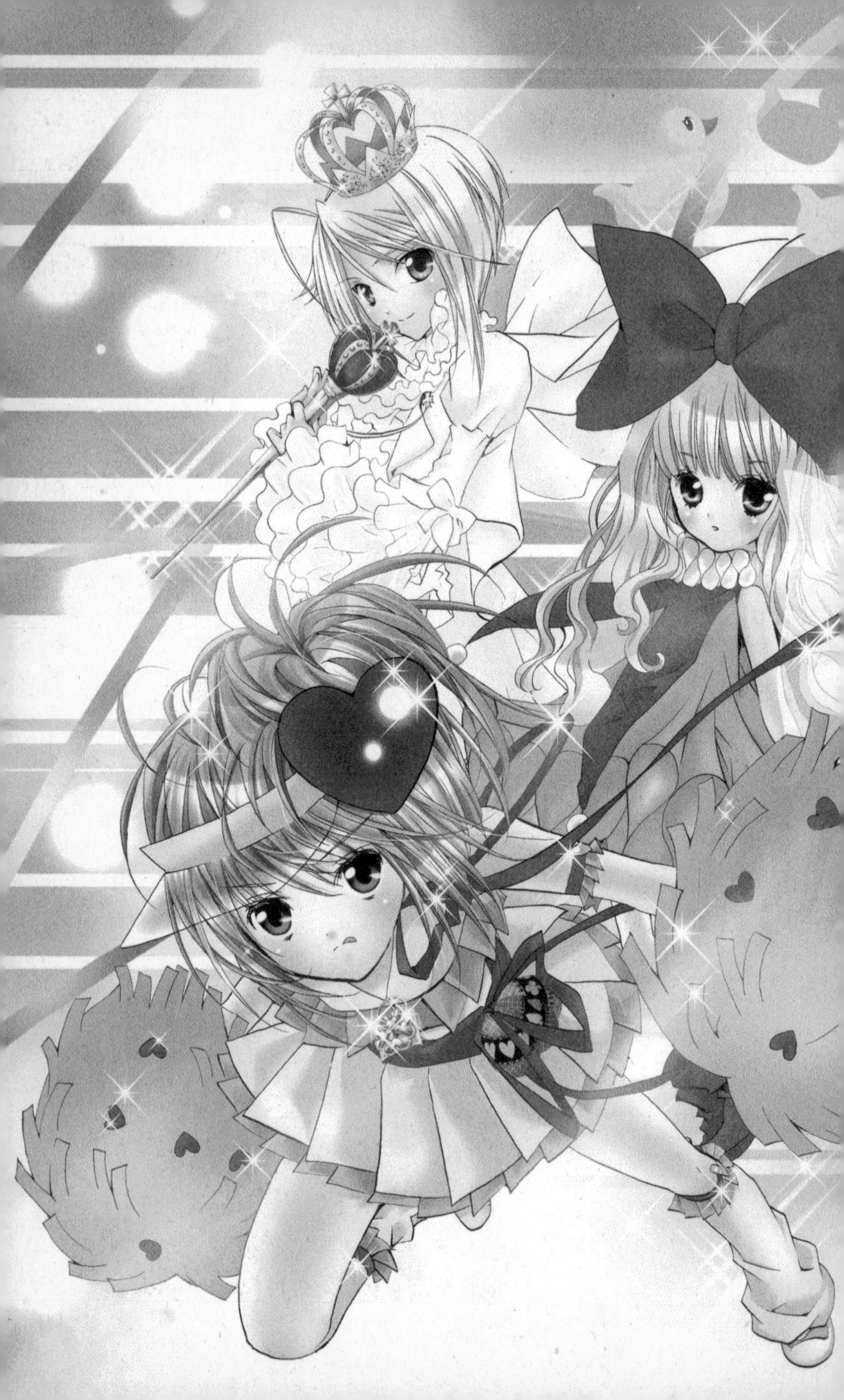

Shugo Chara!

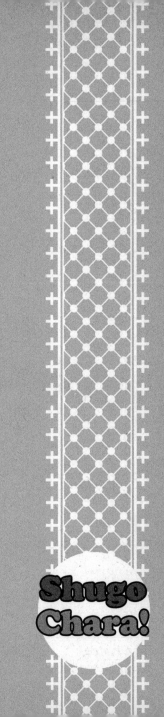

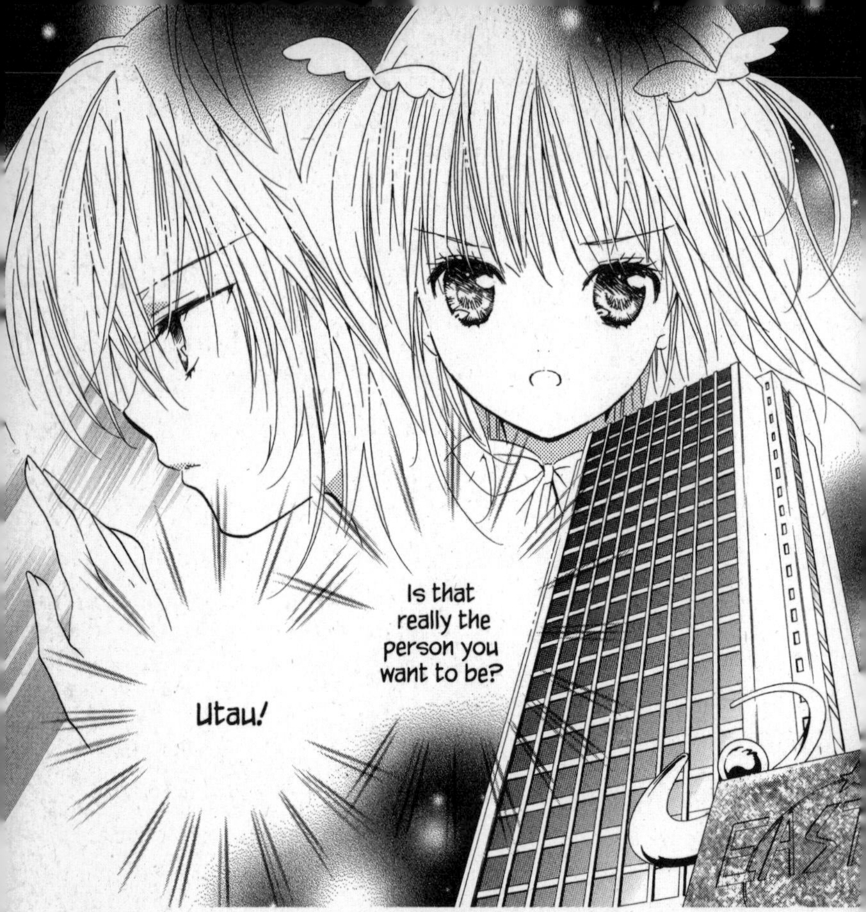
Is that really the person you want to be?
Utau!

continued

A2: It's because we're really good friends! We've been friends since elementary school, so we're really like sisters!

Q3: Do you have any tips for drawing better?
A3: Hmm, that's a hard question! Maybe put your feelings in it? Like "look cute!" or "look awesome!" But...drawing is hard, isn't it? We always struggle, too. I think it's important to keep trying to improve your drawing...

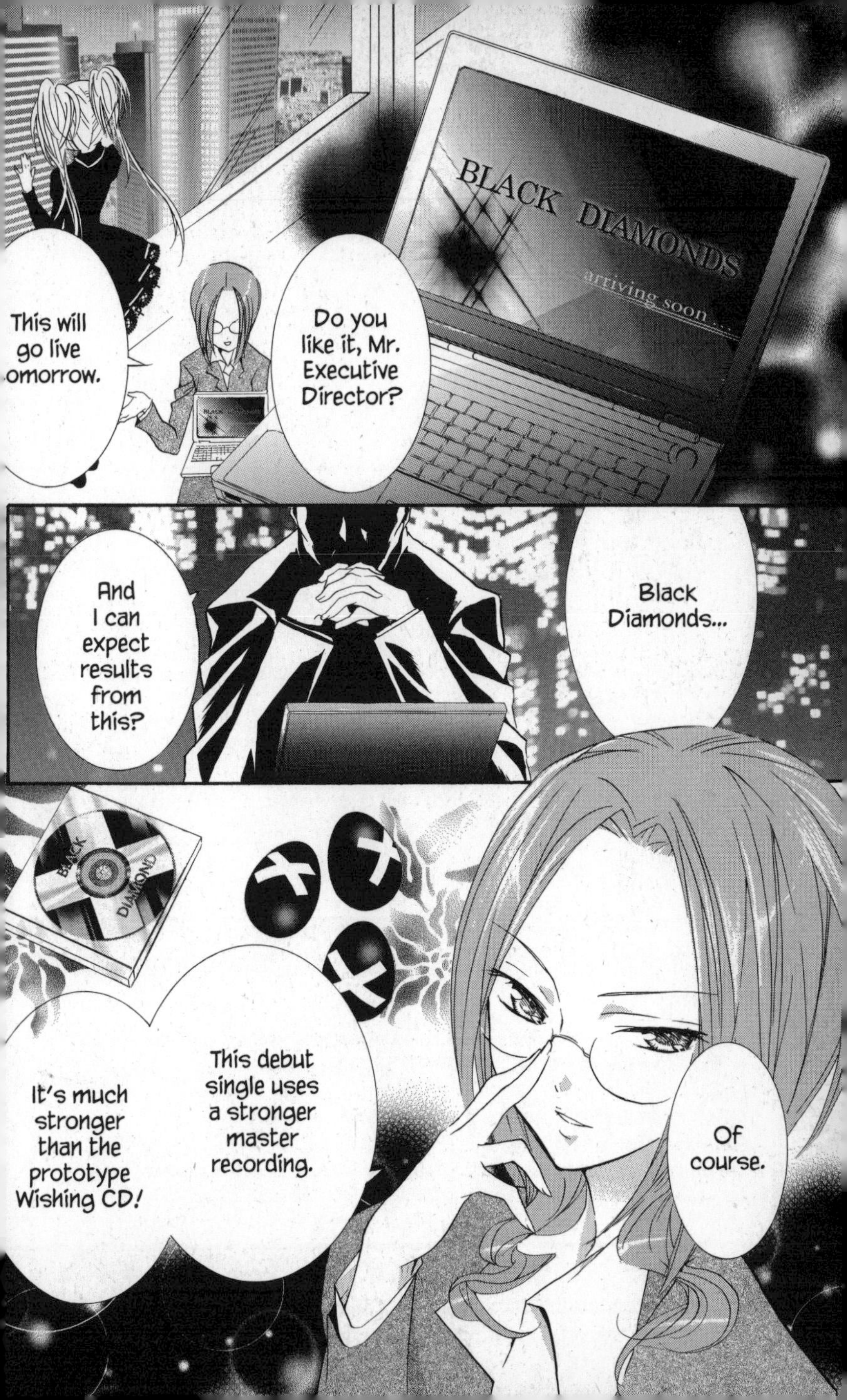

BLACK DIAMONDS
arriving soon...
Do you like it, Mr. Executive Director?
This will go live omorrow.
Black Diamonds...
And I can expect results from this?
BLACK DIAMOND
Of course.
This debut single uses a stronger master recording.
It's much stronger than the prototype Wishing CD!

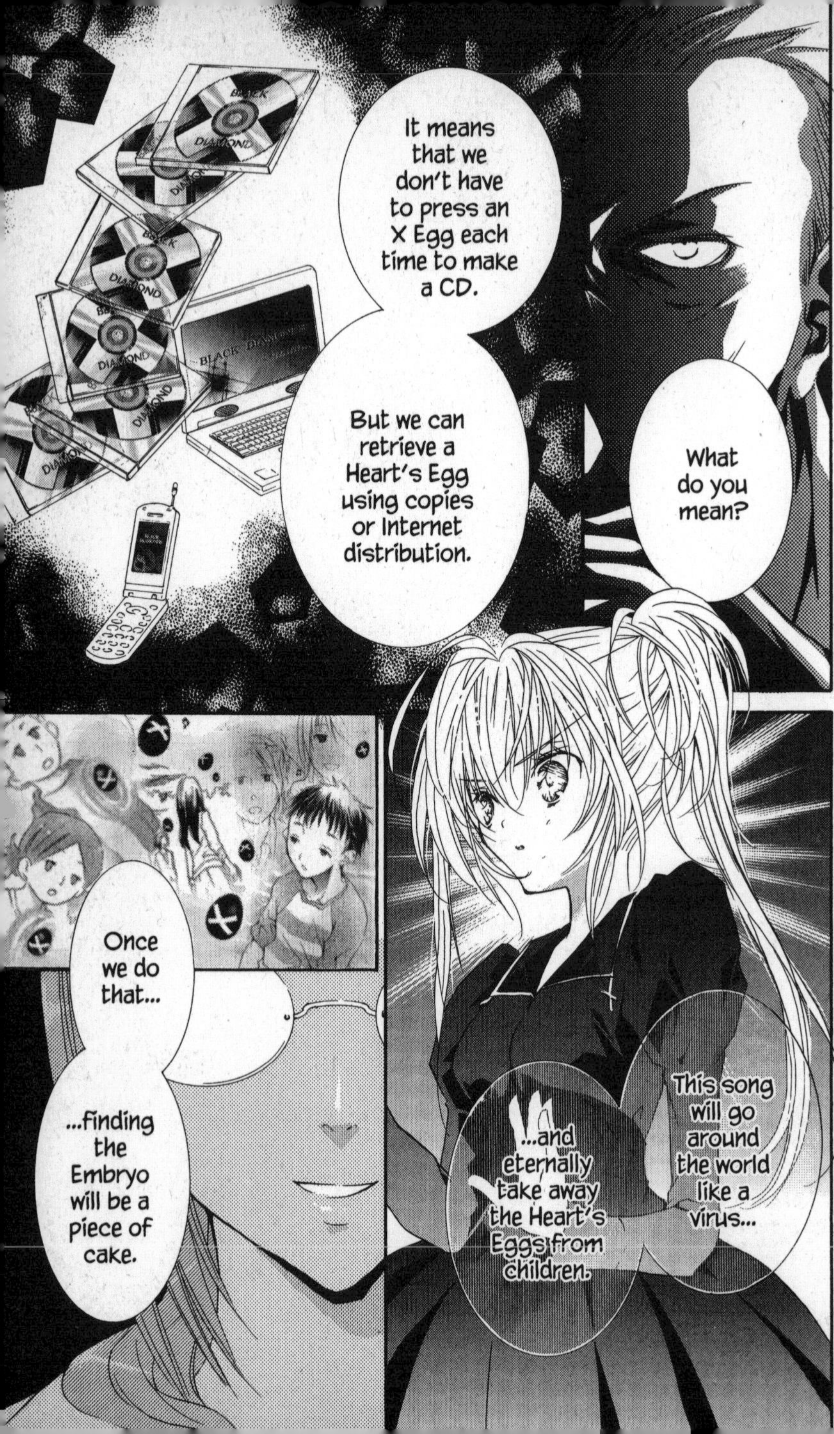
What do you mean?
It means that we don't have to press an X Egg each time to make a CD.
But we can retrieve a Heart's Egg using copies or Internet distribution.
This song will go around the world like a virus...
...and eternally take away the Heart's Eggs from children.
Once we do that...
...finding the Embryo will be a piece of cake.

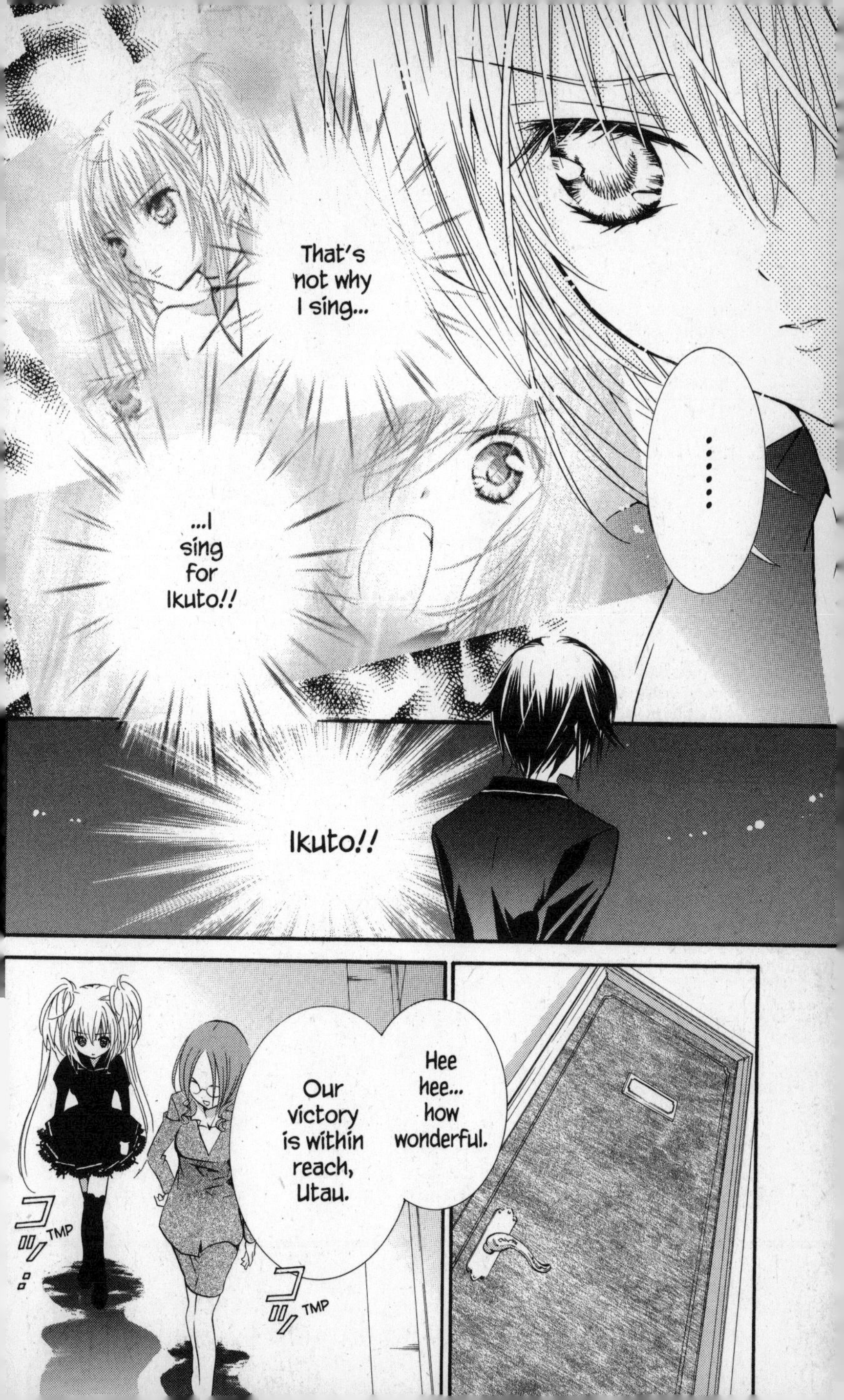
......
That's not why I sing...
...I sing for Ikuto!!
Ikuto!!
Hee hee... how wonderful.
Our victory is within reach, Utau.
TMP
TMP

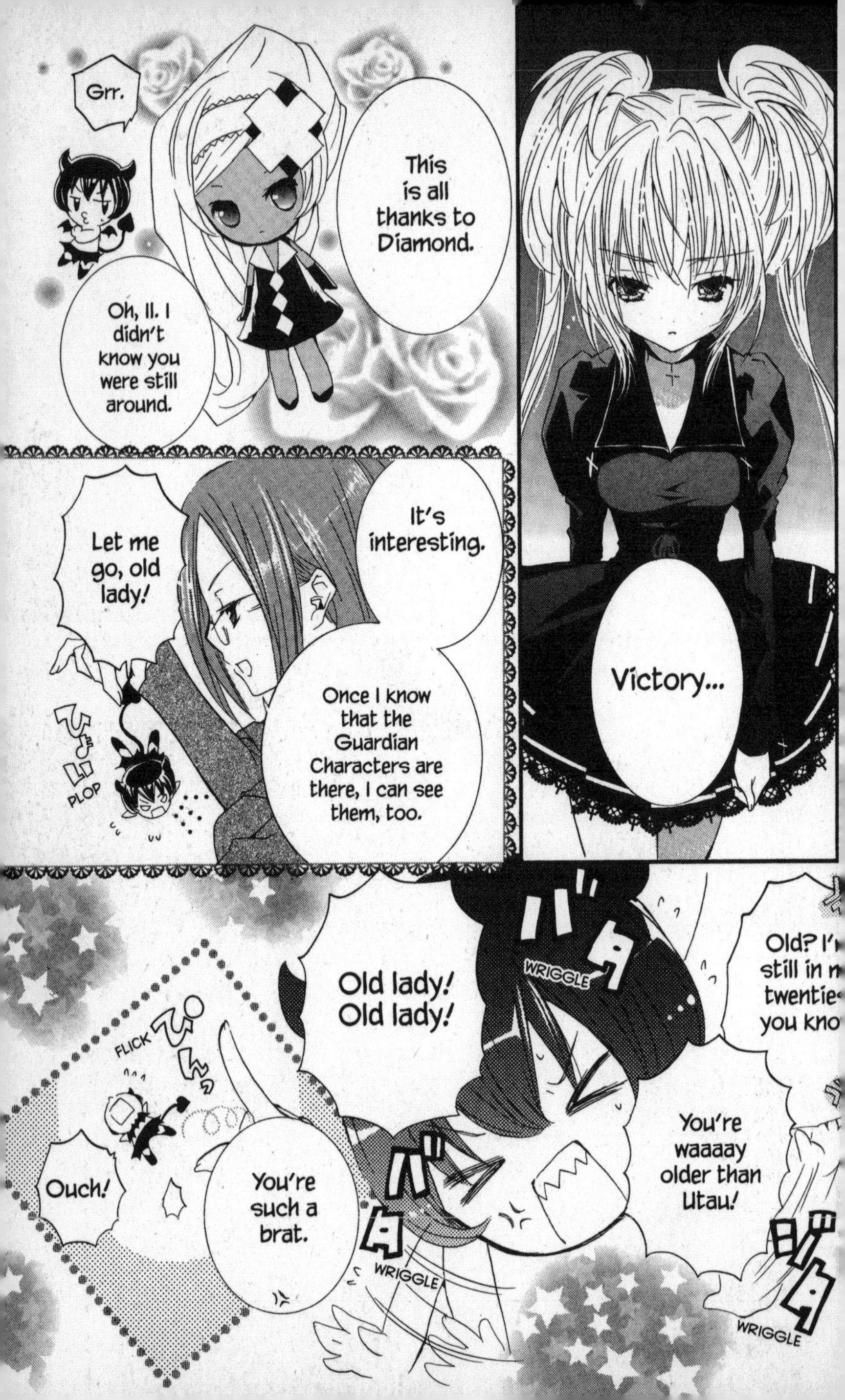
Victory...
This is all thanks to Diamond.
Grr.
Oh, Il. I didn't know you were still around.
It's interesting.
Once I know that the Guardian Characters are there, I can see them, too.
Let me go, old lady!
PLOP
Old? I' still in m twentie you kno
WRIGGLE
Old lady! Old lady!
You're waaaay older than Utau!
WRIGGLE
FLICK
You're such a brat.
Ouch!
WRIGGLE

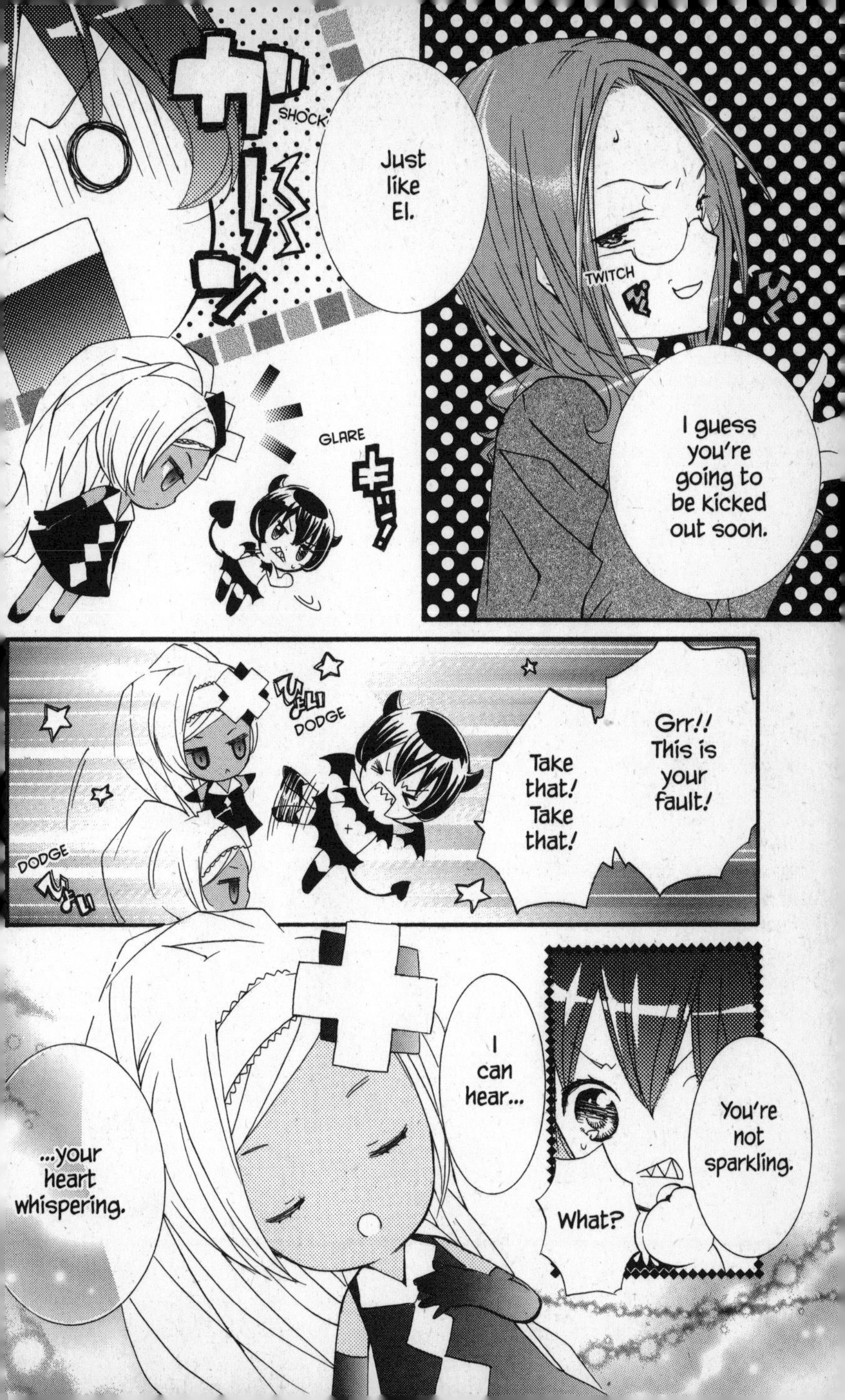
TWITCH
I guess you're going to be kicked out soon.
Just like El.
SHOCK
GLARE
Grr!! This is your fault!
Take that! Take that!
DODGE
DODGE
You're not sparkling.
What?
I can hear...
...your heart whispering.

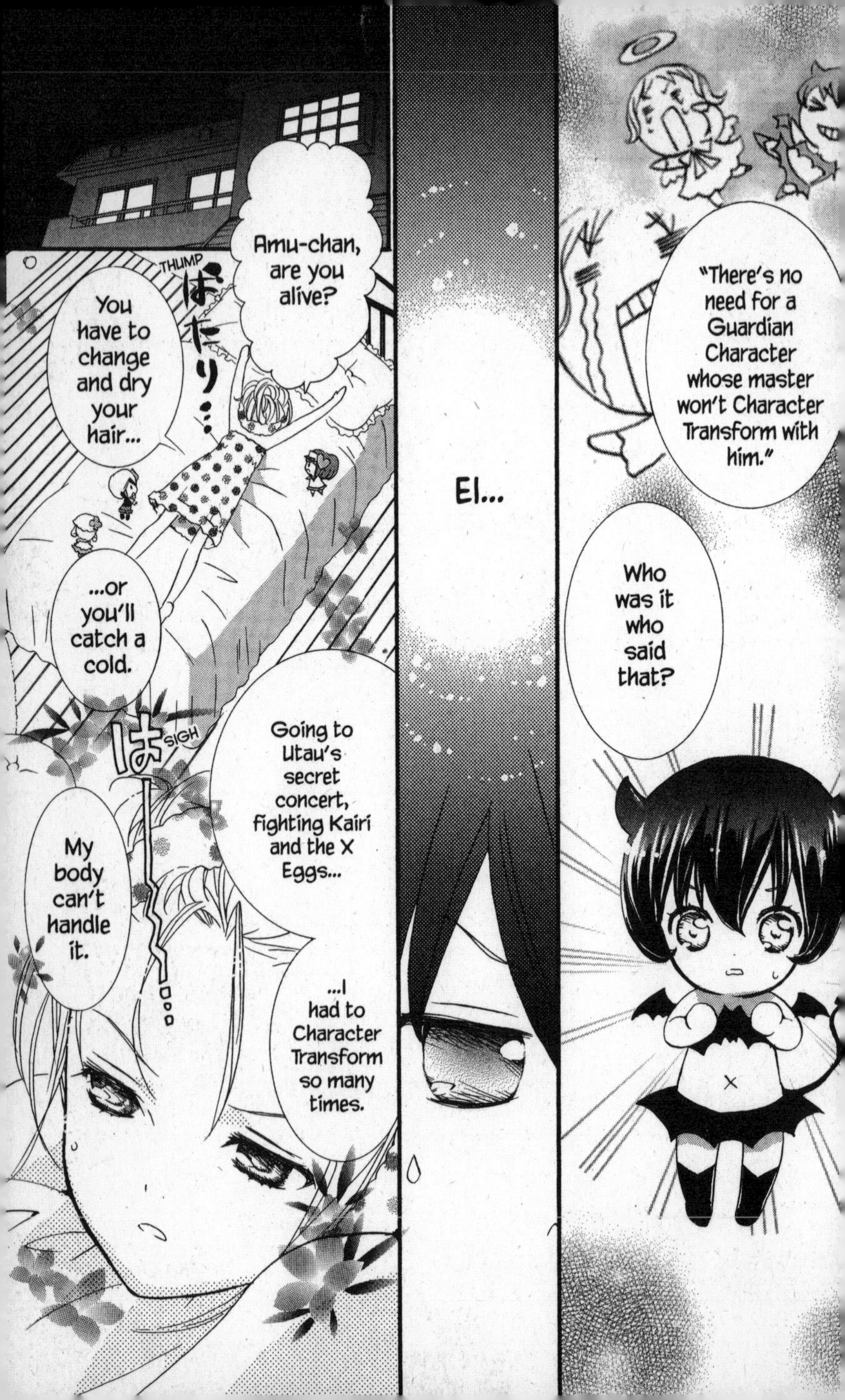
"There's no need for a Guardian Character whose master won't Character Transform with him."
Who was it who said that?
El...
Amu-chan, are you alive?
THUMP
ぱたり
You have to change and dry your hair...
...or you'll catch a cold.
Going to Utau's secret concert, fighting Kairi and the X Eggs...
SIGH
はーー
...I had to Character Transform so many times.
My body can't handle it.

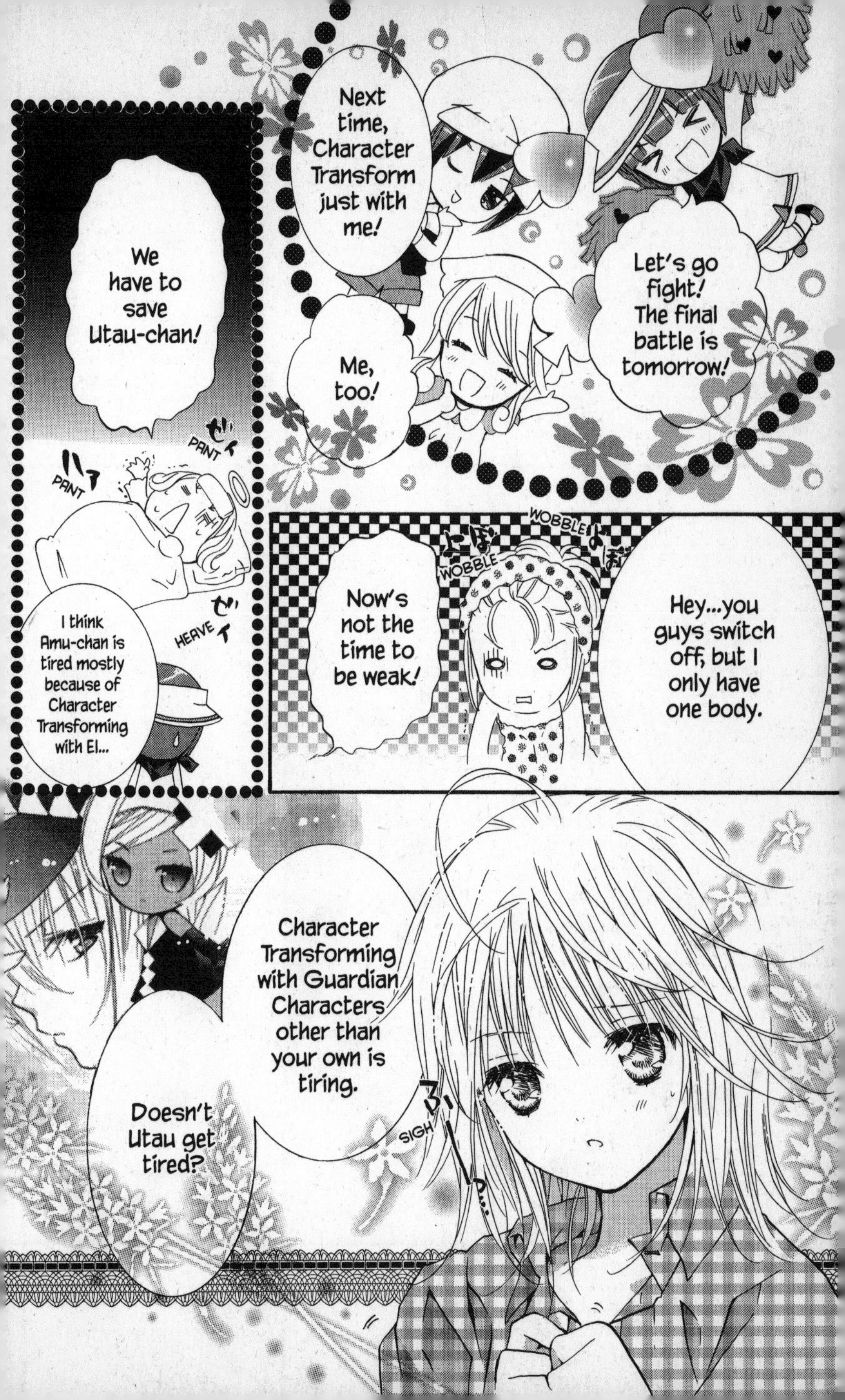
Let's go fight! The final battle is tomorrow!
Next time, Character Transform just with me!
Me, too!
WOBBLE
WOBBLE
Hey...you guys switch off, but I only have one body.
Now's not the time to be weak!
We have to save Utau-chan!
PANT
PANT
HEAVE
I think Amu-chan is tired mostly because of Character Transforming with El...
Character Transforming with Guardian Characters other than your own is tiring.
SIGH
Doesn't Utau get tired?

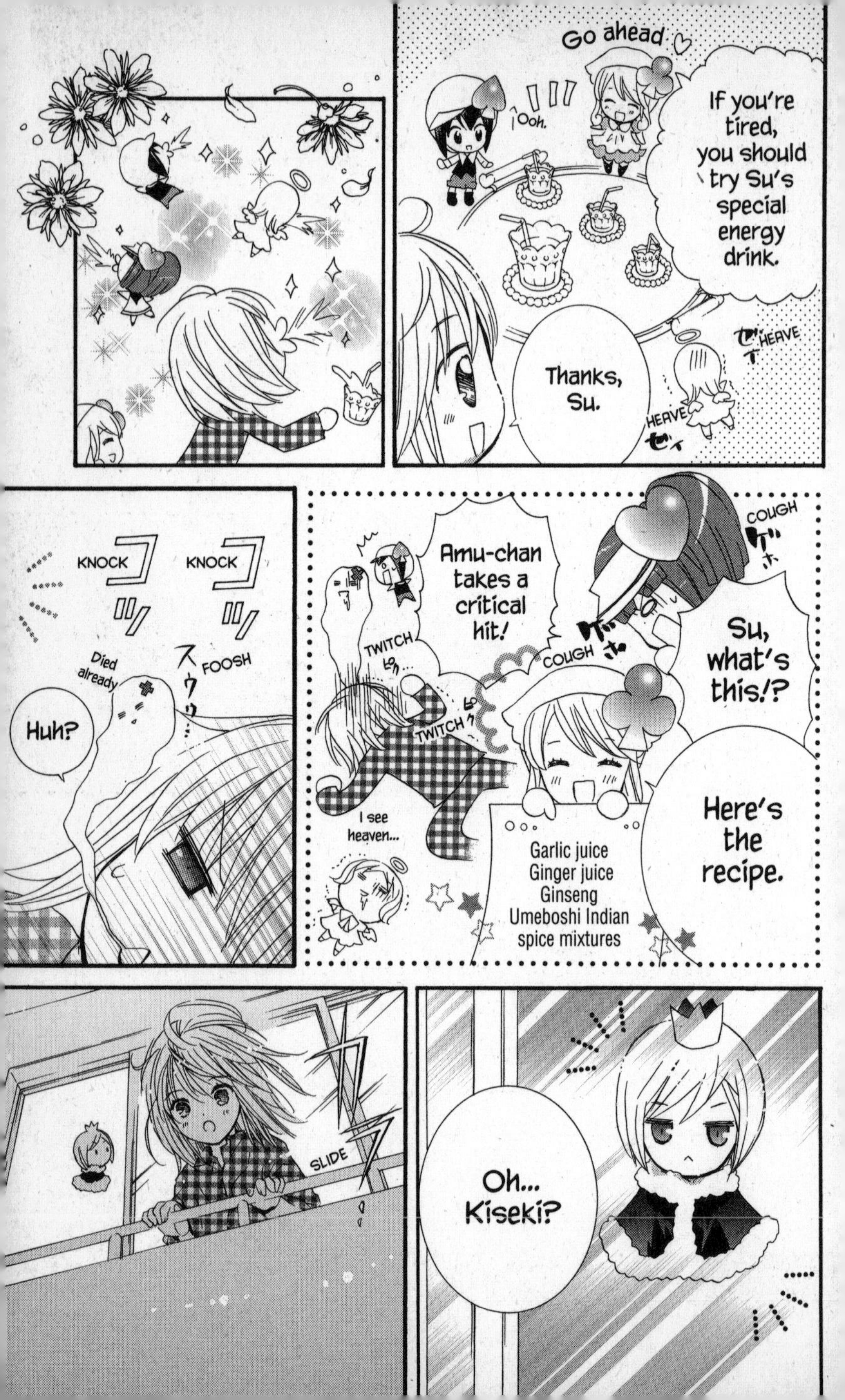

Go ahead ♡
If you're tired, you should try Su's special energy drink.
!!!
Ooh.
Thanks, Su.
HEAVE
HEAVE
COUGH
Su, what's this!?
Amu-chan takes a critical hit!
COUGH
TWITCH
TWITCH
Here's the recipe.
Garlic juice
Ginger juice
Ginseng
Umeboshi Indian spice mixtures
I see heaven...
KNOCK
KNOCK
FOOSH
Died already
Huh?
Oh... Kiseki?
SLIDE

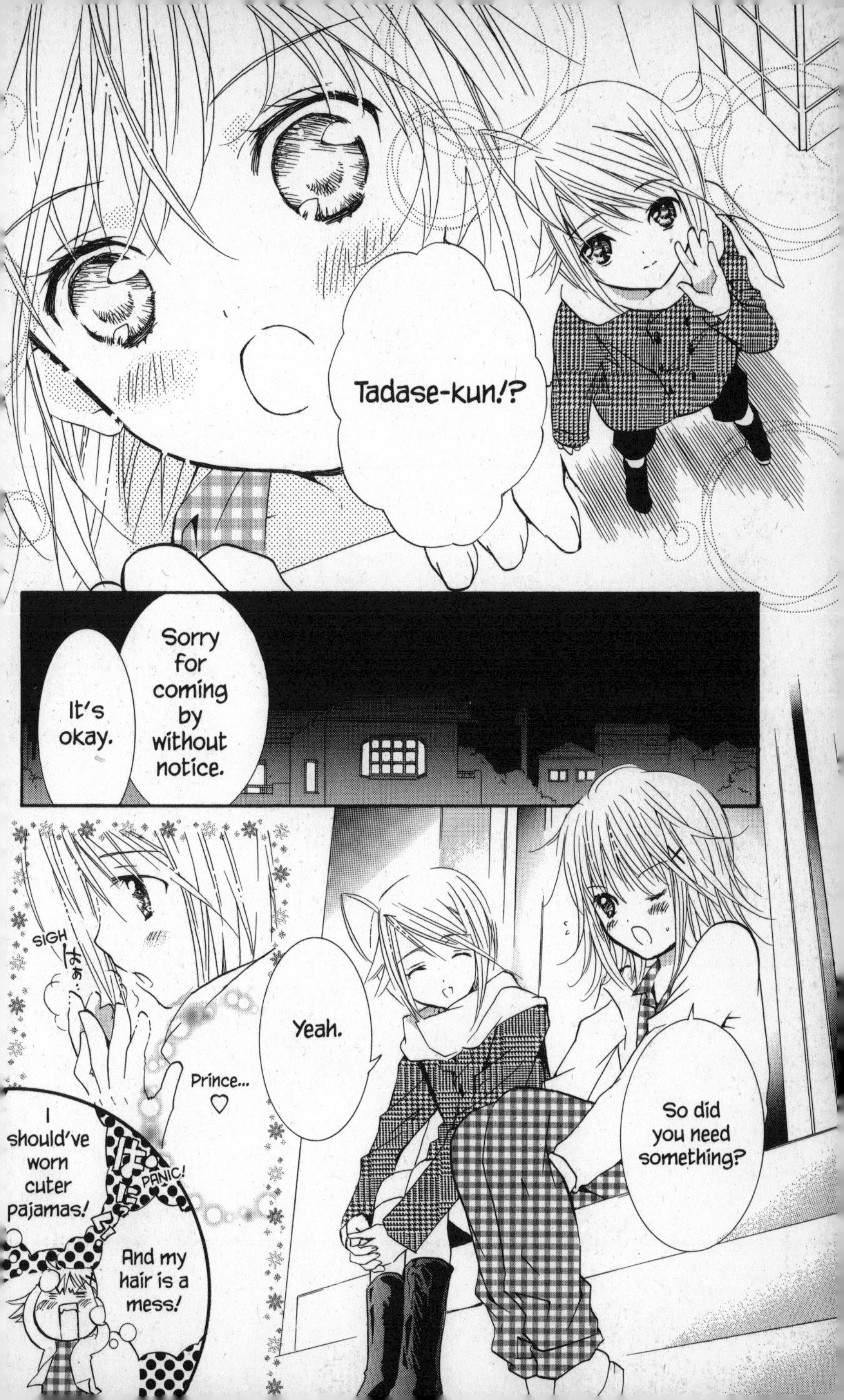
Tadase-kun!?
Sorry for coming by without notice.
It's okay.
So did you need something?
Yeah.
SIGH
Prince... ♡
I should've worn cuter pajamas!
PANIC!
And my hair is a mess!

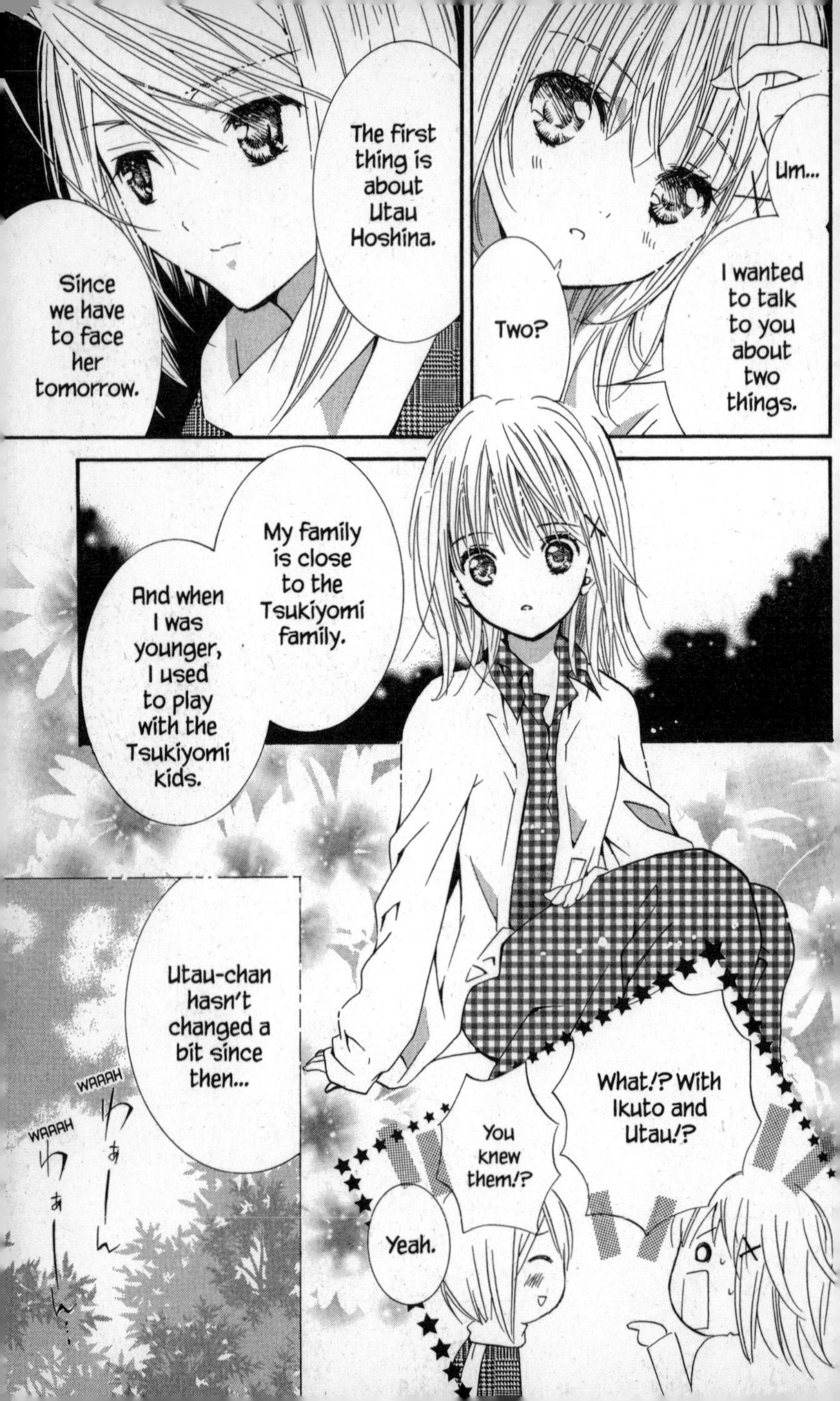
Um...
I wanted to talk to you about two things.
Two?
The first thing is about Utau Hoshina.
Since we have to face her tomorrow.
My family is close to the Tsukiyomi family.
And when I was younger, I used to play with the Tsukiyomi kids.
What!? With Ikuto and Utau!?
You knew them!?
Yeah.
Utau-chan hasn't changed a bit since then...
WAAAH
わぁーん
WAAAH
わぁーん…

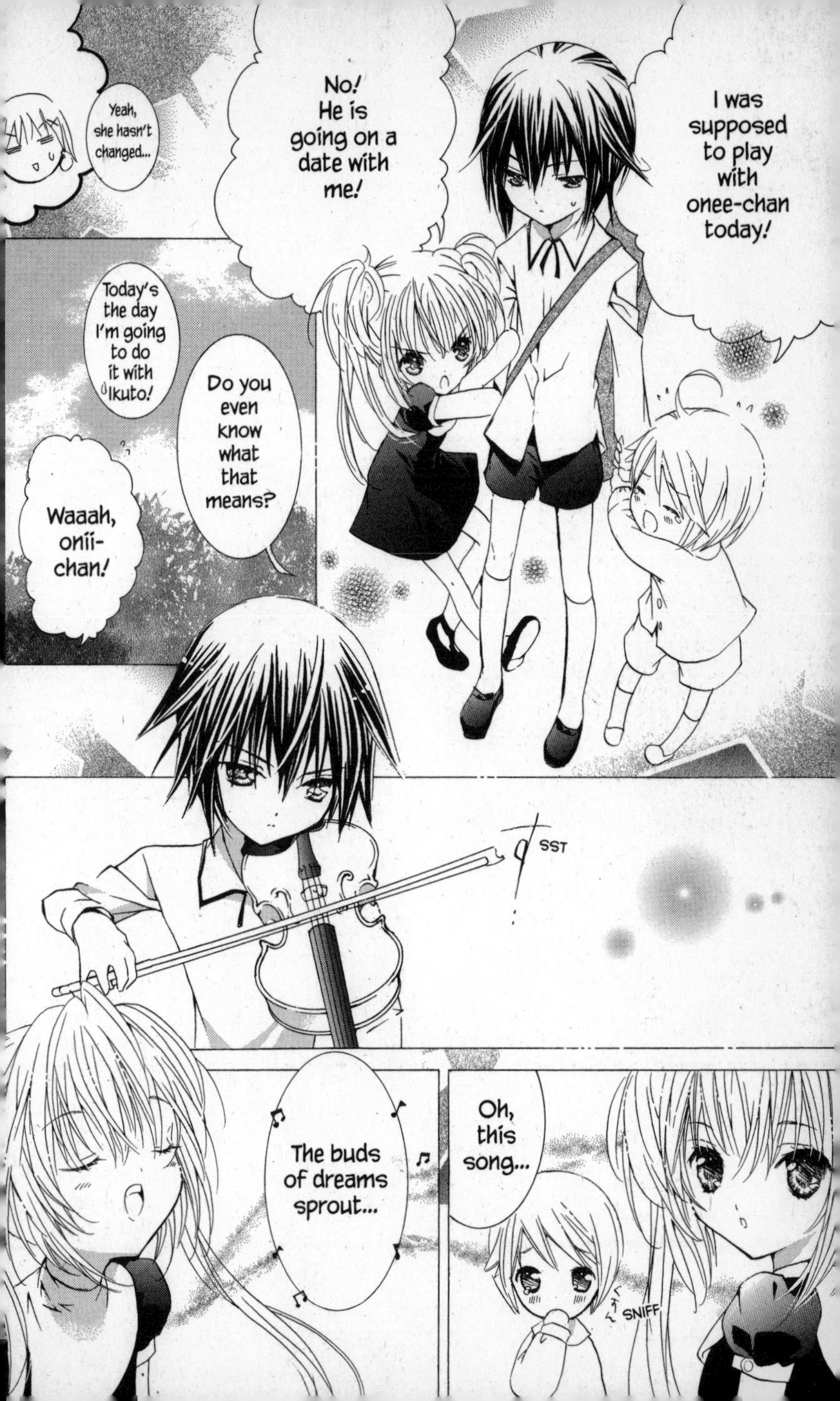

I was supposed to play with onee-chan today!
No! He is going on a date with me!
Yeah, she hasn't changed...
Today's the day I'm going to do it with Ikuto!
Do you even know what that means?
Waaah, onii-chan!
SST
Oh, this song...
SNIFF
The buds of dreams sprout...

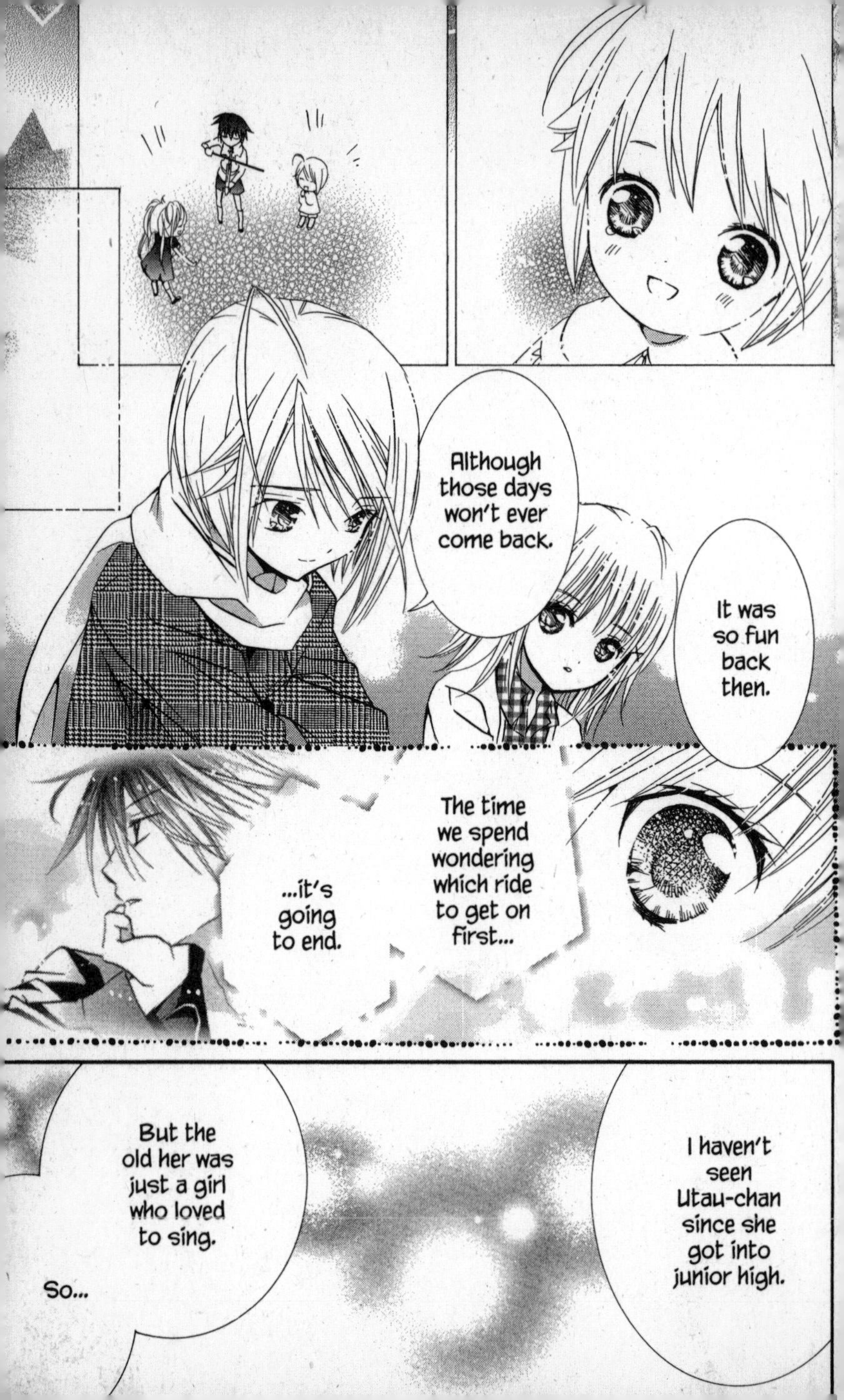
It was so fun back then.
Although those days won't ever come back.
The time we spend wondering which ride to get on first...
...it's going to end.
I haven't seen Utau-chan since she got into junior high.
But the old her was just a girl who loved to sing.
So...

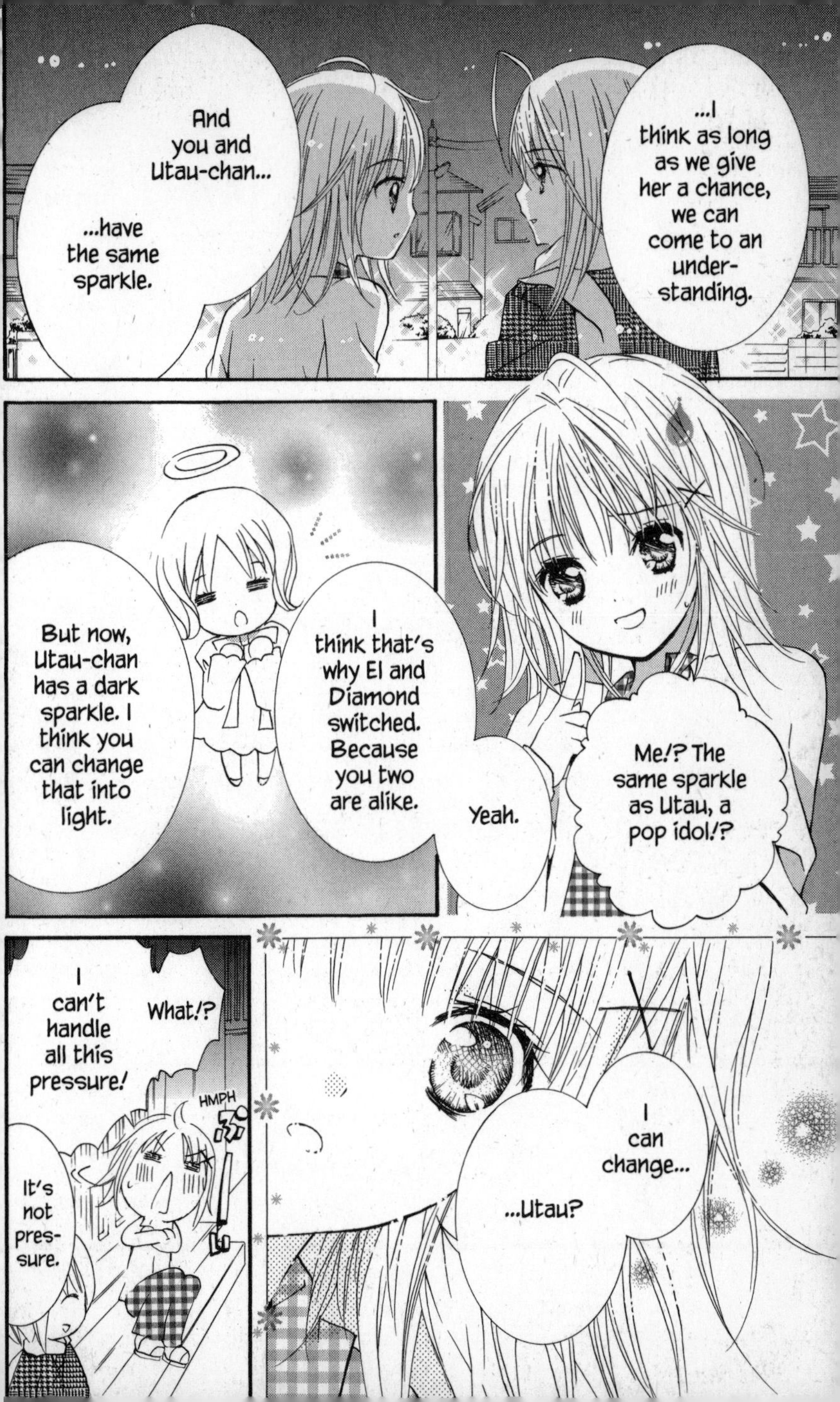
...I think as long as we give her a chance, we can come to an under-standing.
And you and Utau-chan...
...have the same sparkle.
Me!? The same sparkle as Utau, a pop idol!?
Yeah.
I think that's why El and Diamond switched. Because you two are alike.
But now, Utau-chan has a dark sparkle. I think you can change that into light.
I can change...
...Utau?
What!?
I can't handle all this pressure!
HMPH
It's not pres-sure.

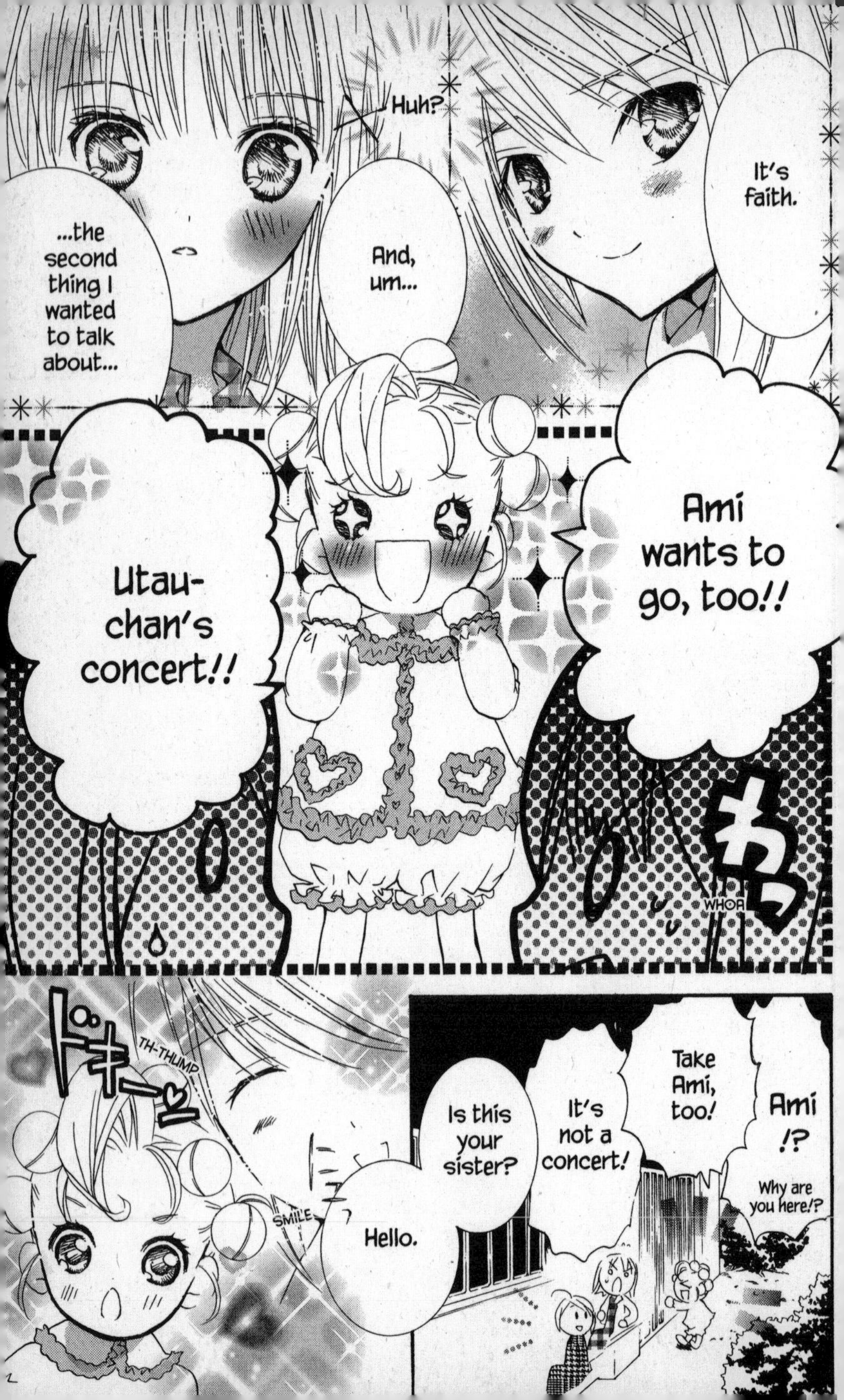
It's faith.
Huh?
And, um...
...the second thing I wanted to talk about...
Ami wants to go, too!!
WHOA
Utau-chan's concert!!
Ami !?
Why are you here!?
Take Ami, too!
It's not a concert!
Is this your sister?
Hello.
SMILE
TH-THUMP

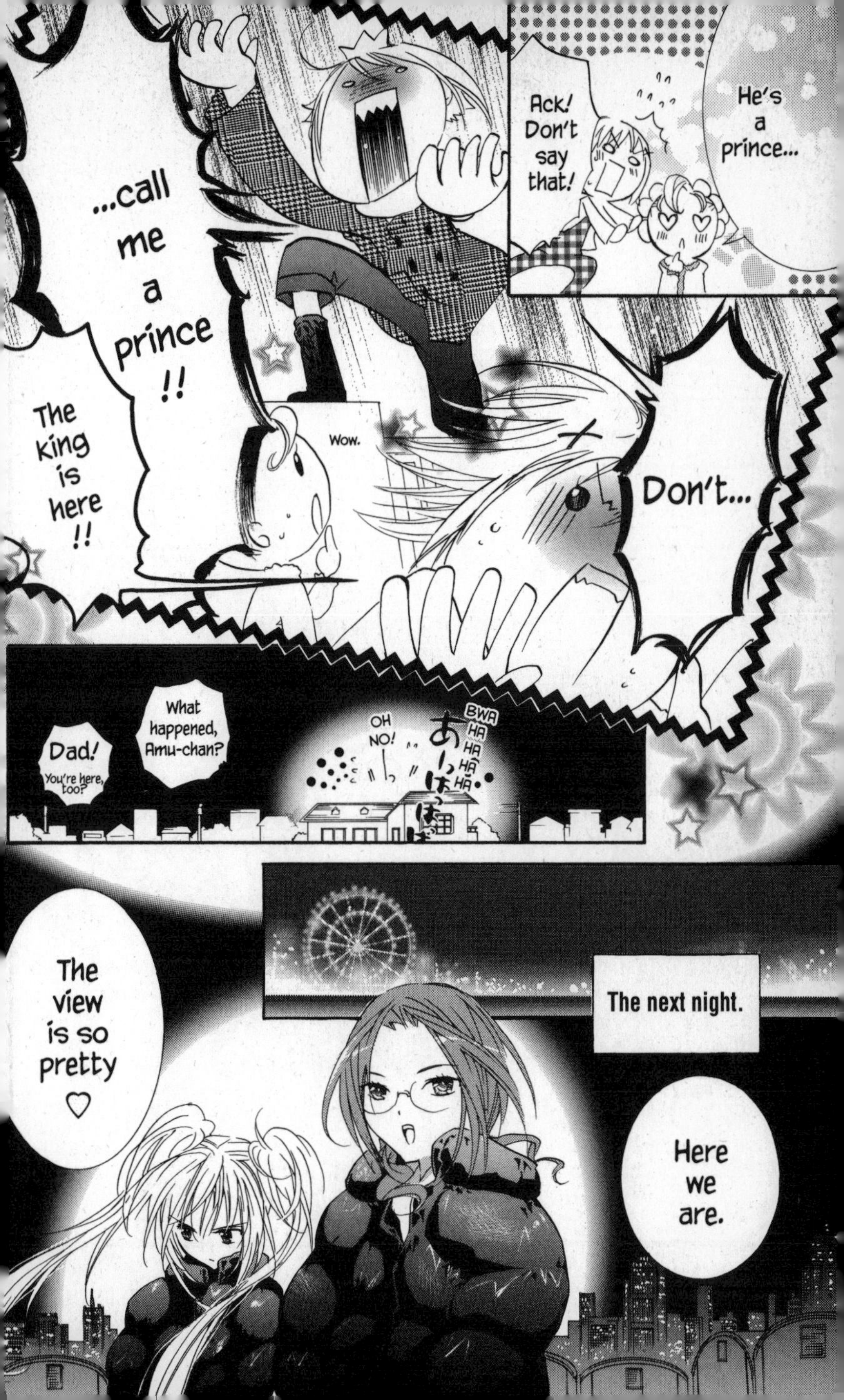

He's a prince...
Ack! Don't say that!
Don't...
...call me a prince!!
Wow.
The king is here!!
BWA HA HA HA HA
OH NO!
What happened, Amu-chan?
Dad! You're here, too?
The next night.
Here we are.
The view is so pretty ♡

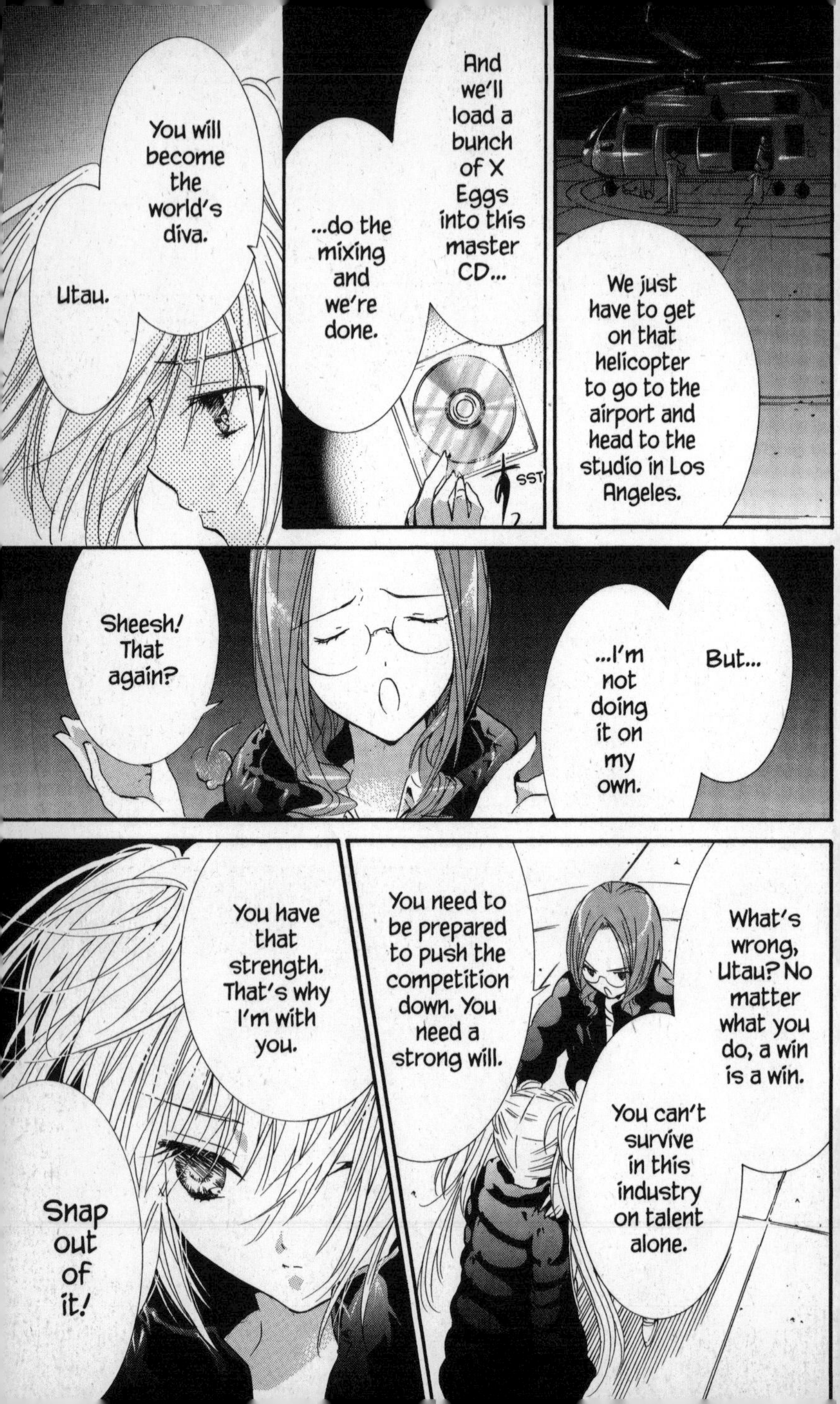
We just have to get on that helicopter to go to the airport and head to the studio in Los Angeles.
And we'll load a bunch of X Eggs into this master CD...
...do the mixing and we're done.
SST
You will become the world's diva.
Utau.
But...
...I'm not doing it on my own.
Sheesh! That again?
What's wrong, Utau? No matter what you do, a win is a win.
You can't survive in this industry on talent alone.
You need to be prepared to push the competition down. You need a strong will.
You have that strength. That's why I'm with you.
Snap out of it!

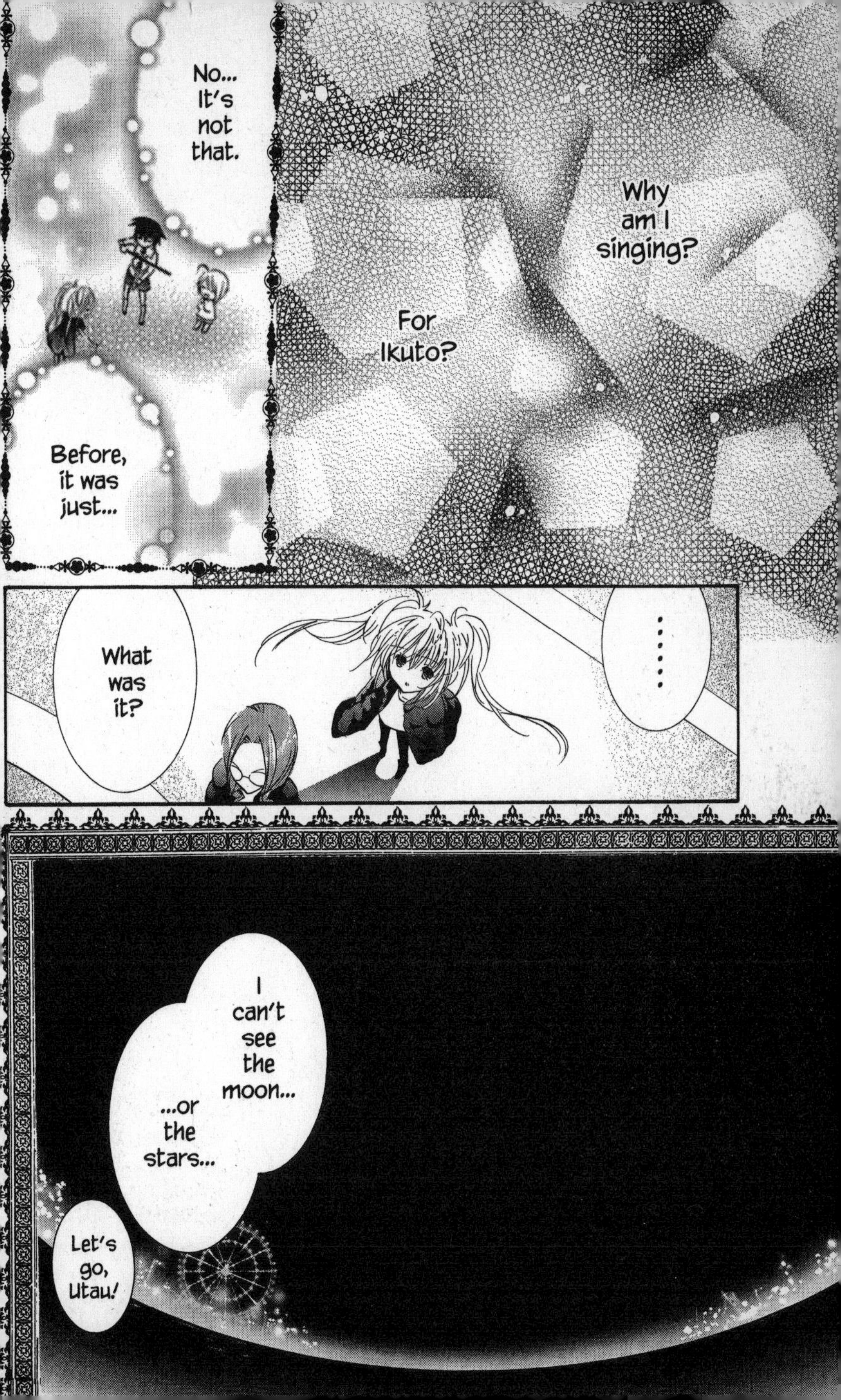
Why am I singing?
For Ikuto?
No... It's not that.
Before, it was just...
......
What was it?
I can't see the moon...
...or the stars...
Let's go, Utau!

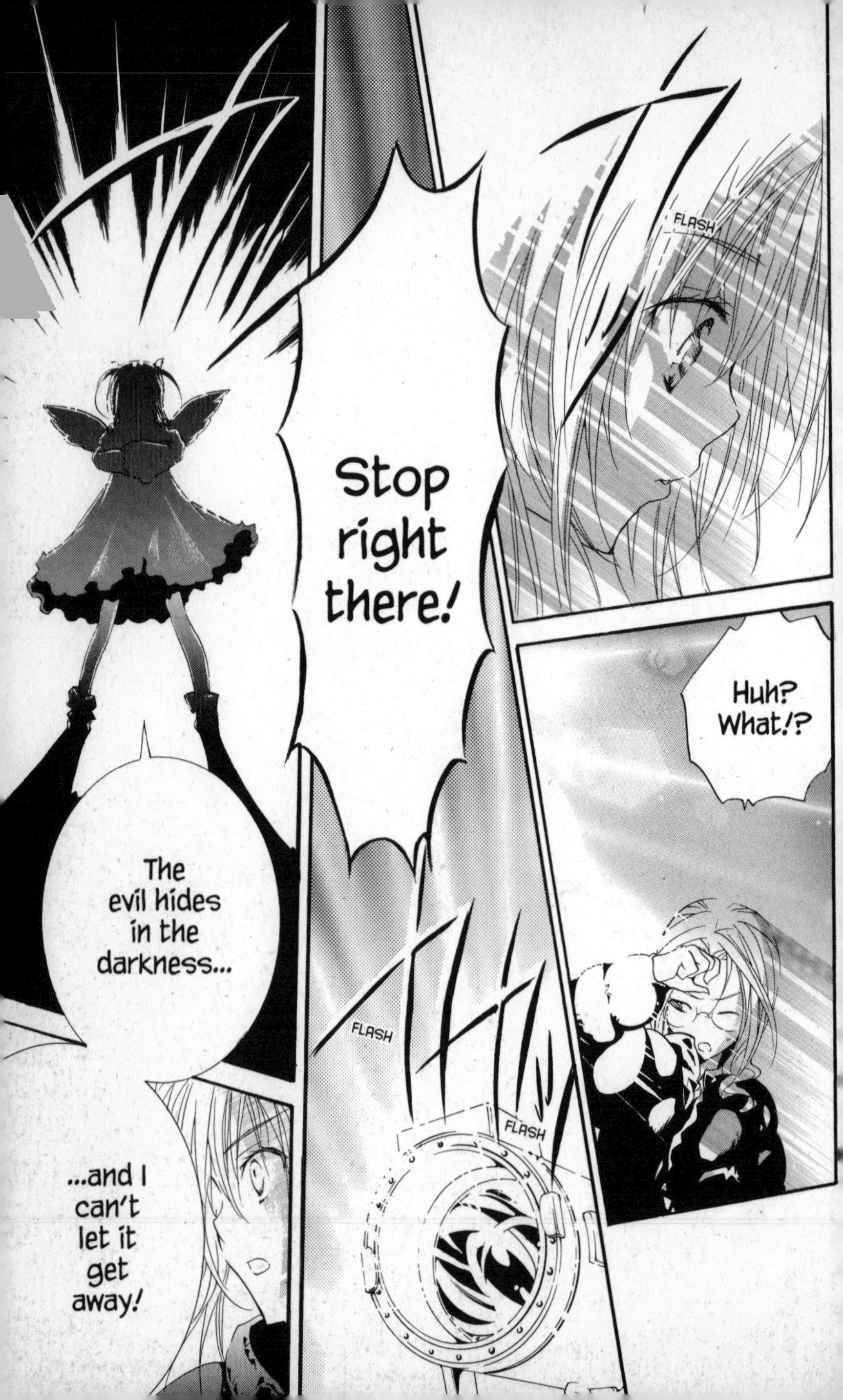
FLASH
Huh? What!?
Stop right there!
FLASH
FLASH
The evil hides in the darkness...
...and I can't let it get away!

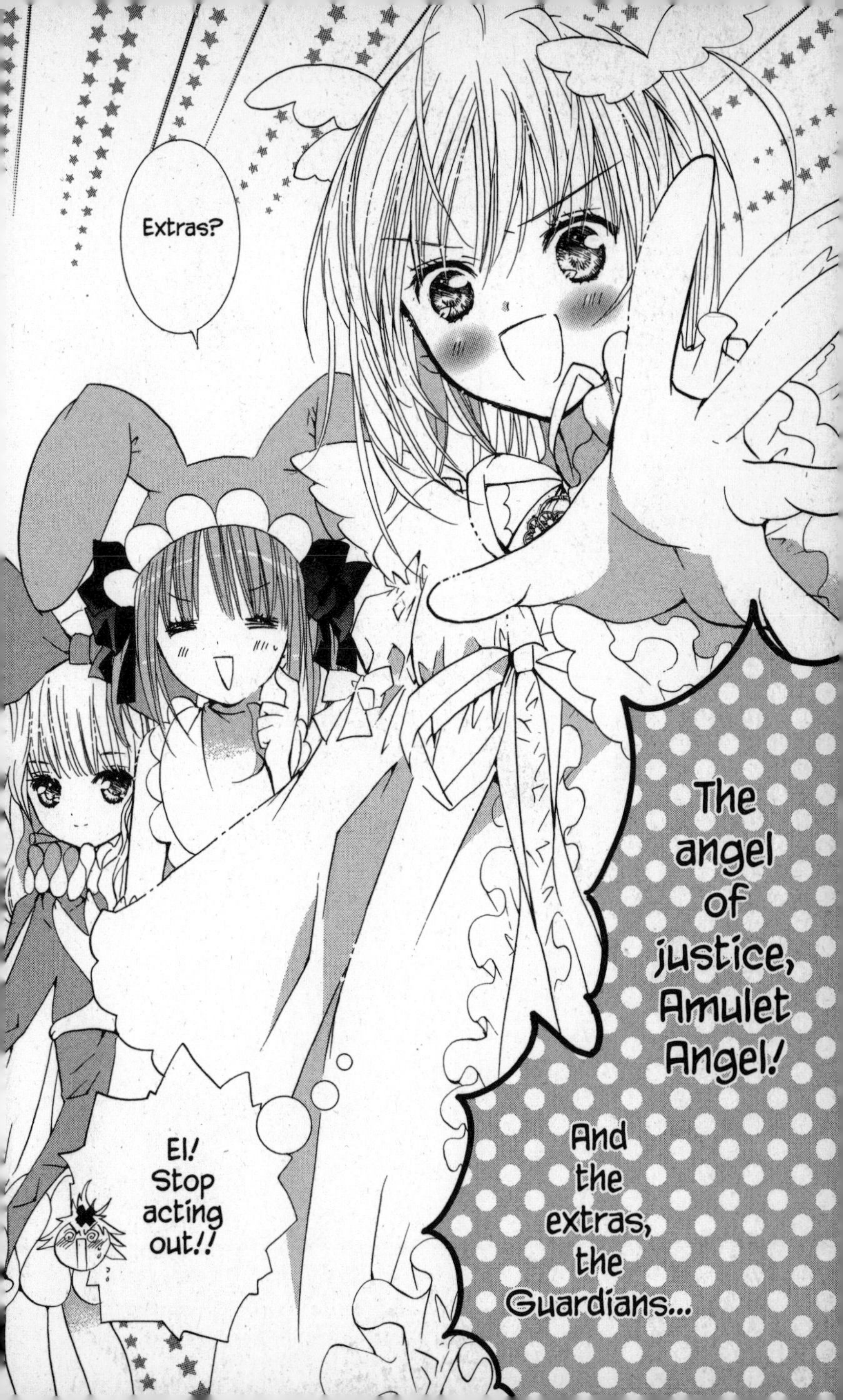
Extras?
The angel of justice, Amulet Angel!
And the extras, the Guardians...
El! Stop acting out!!

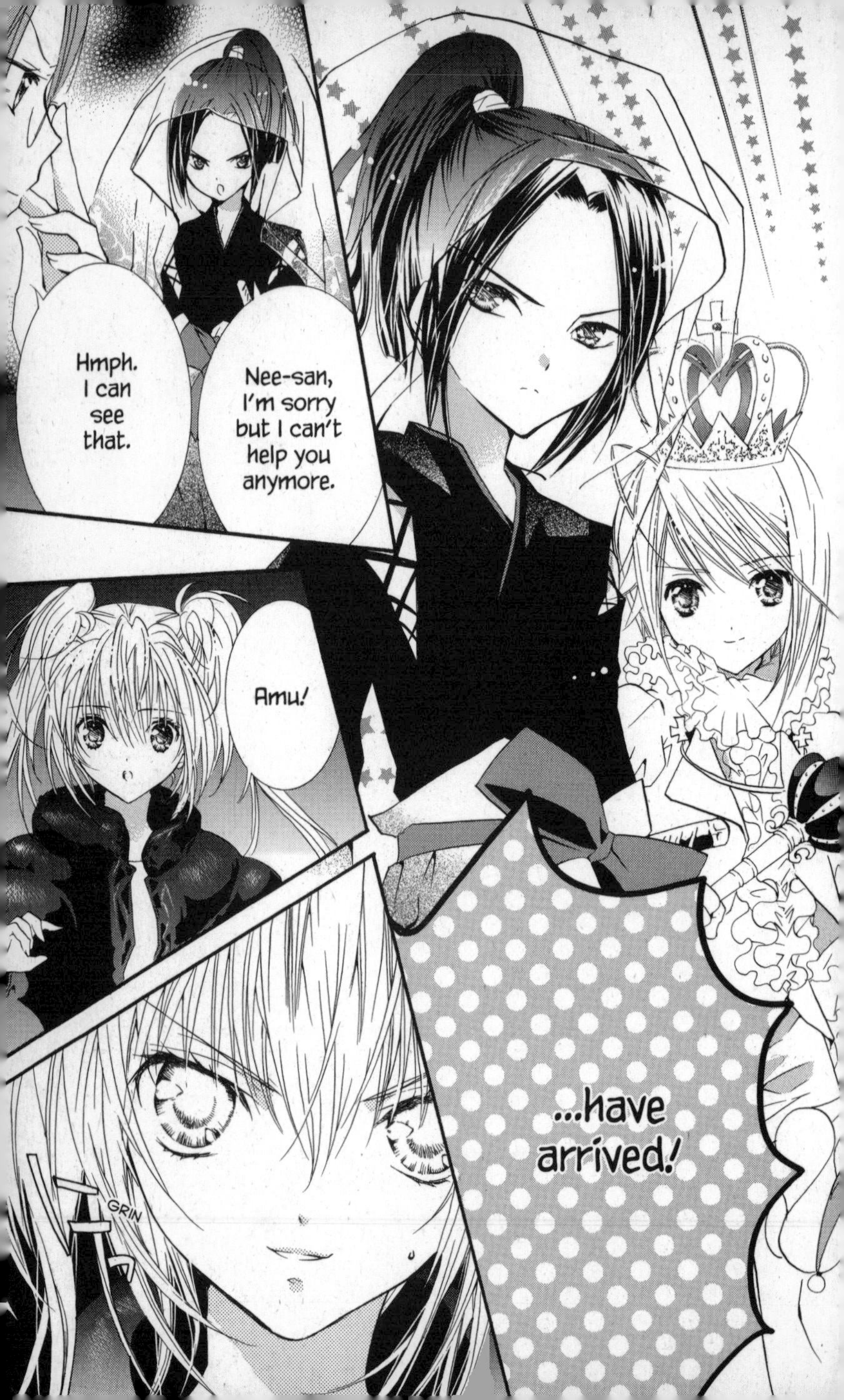
Nee-san, I'm sorry but I can't help you anymore.
Hmph. I can see that.
Amu!
GRIN
...have arrived!

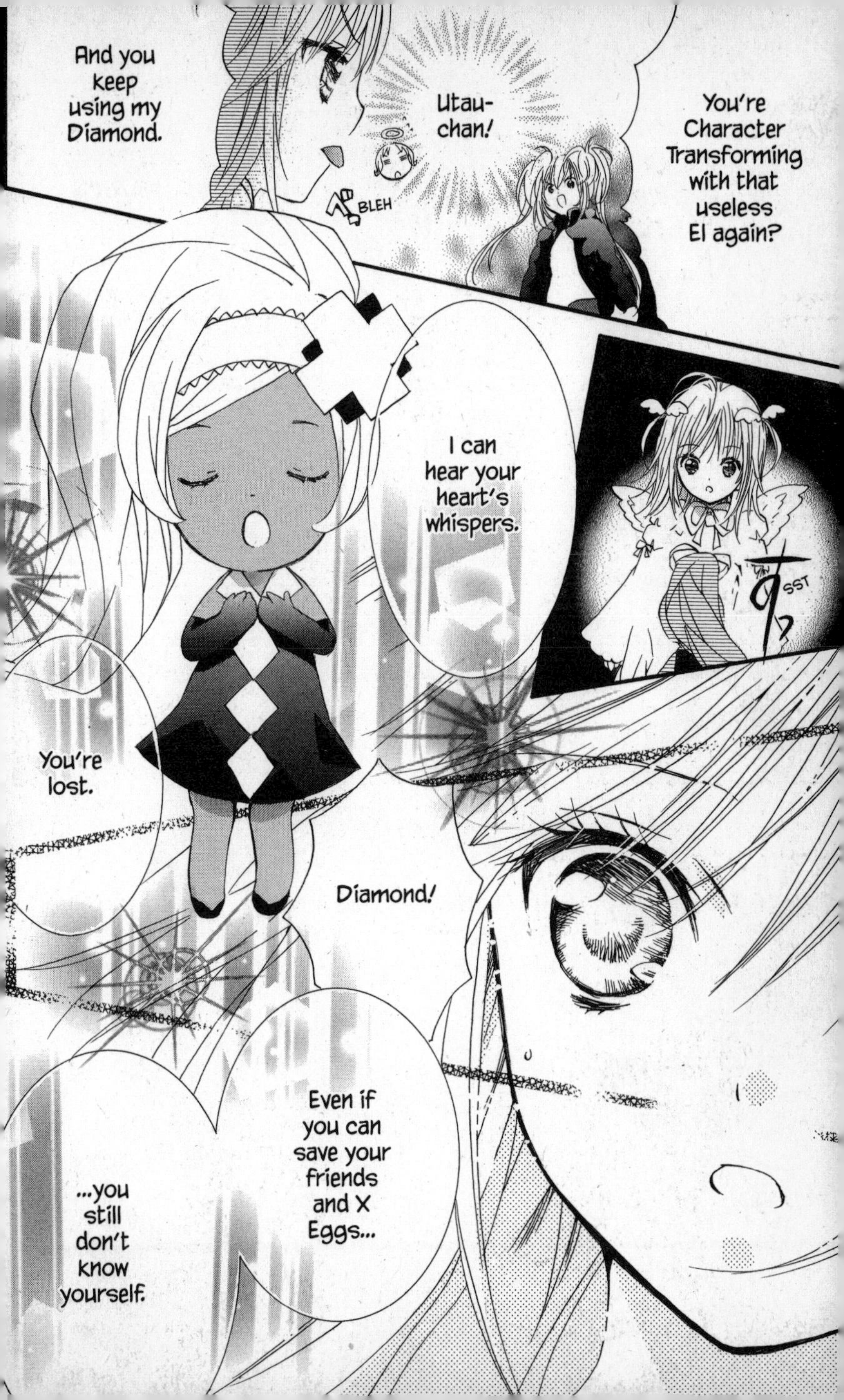
You're Character Transforming with that useless El again?
Utau-chan!
And you keep using my Diamond.
BLEH
SST
I can hear your heart's whispers.
You're lost.
Diamond!
Even if you can save your friends and X Eggs...
...you still don't know yourself.

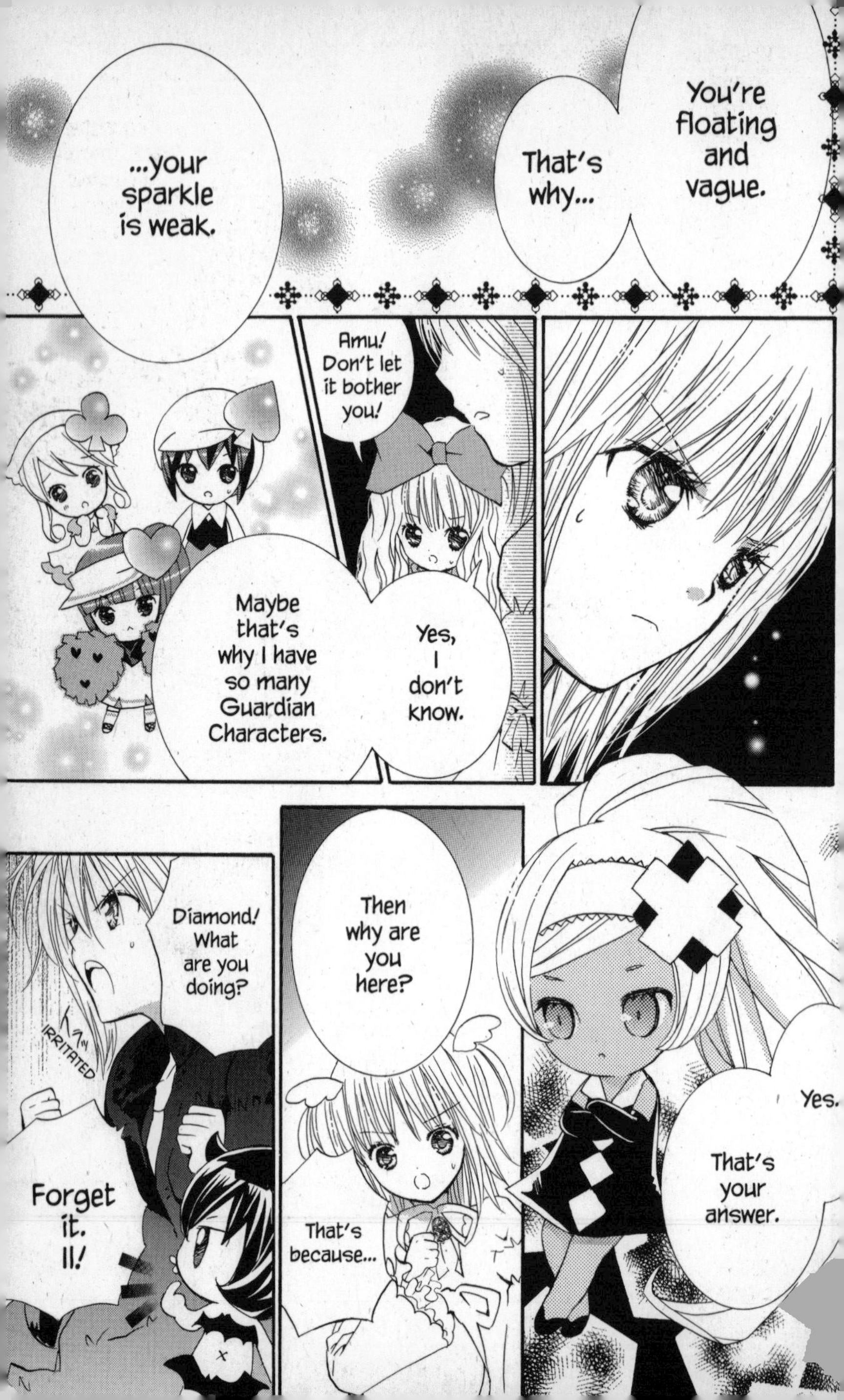

You're floating and vague.
That's why...
...your sparkle is weak.
Amu! Don't let it bother you!
Yes, I don't know.
Maybe that's why I have so many Guardian Characters.
Yes.
That's your answer.
Then why are you here?
That's because...
Diamond! What are you doing?
IRRITATED
Forget it. Il!

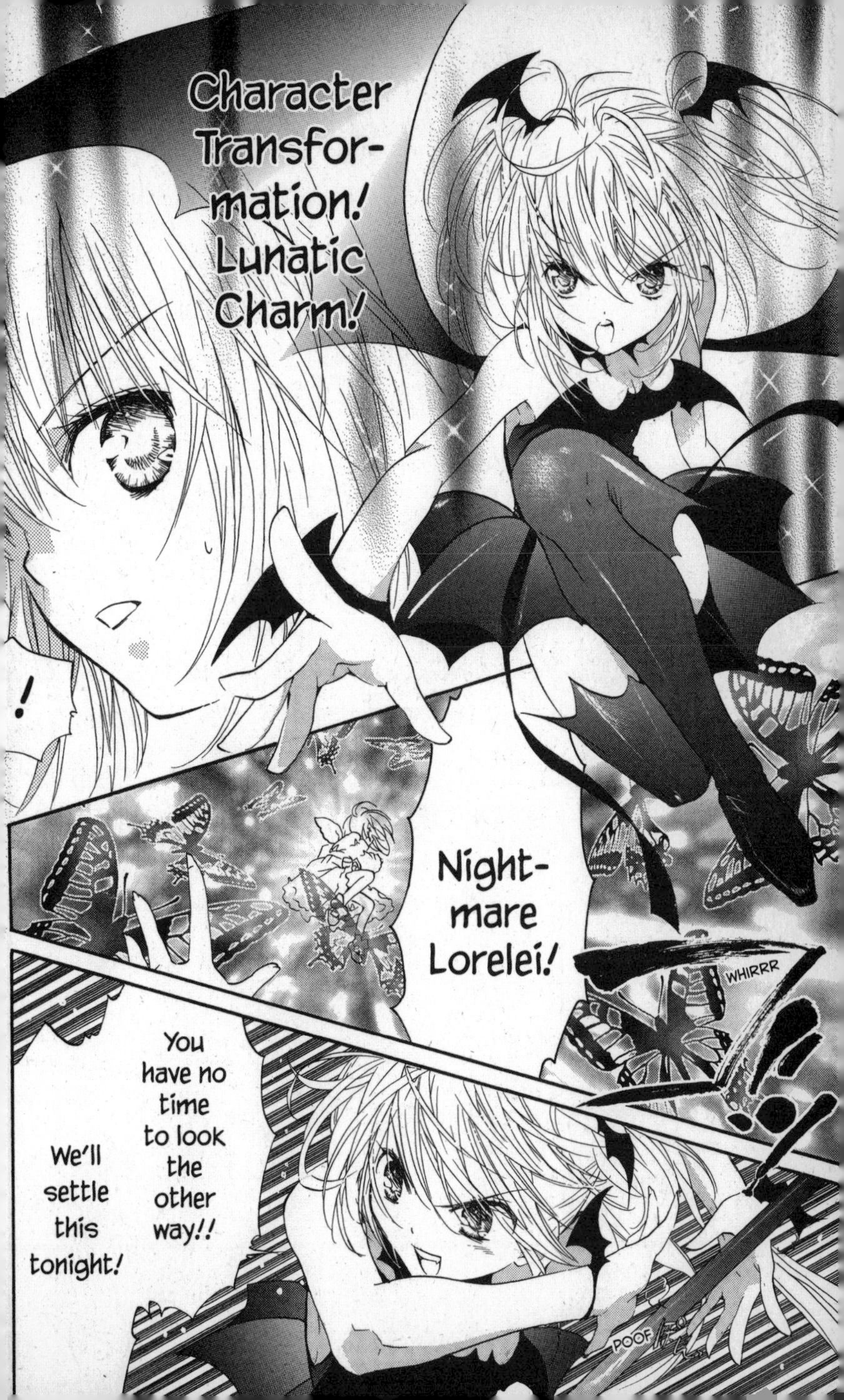
Character Transformation! Lunatic Charm!
!
Nightmare Lorelei!
WHIRRR
!
You have no time to look the other way!!
We'll settle this tonight!
POOF

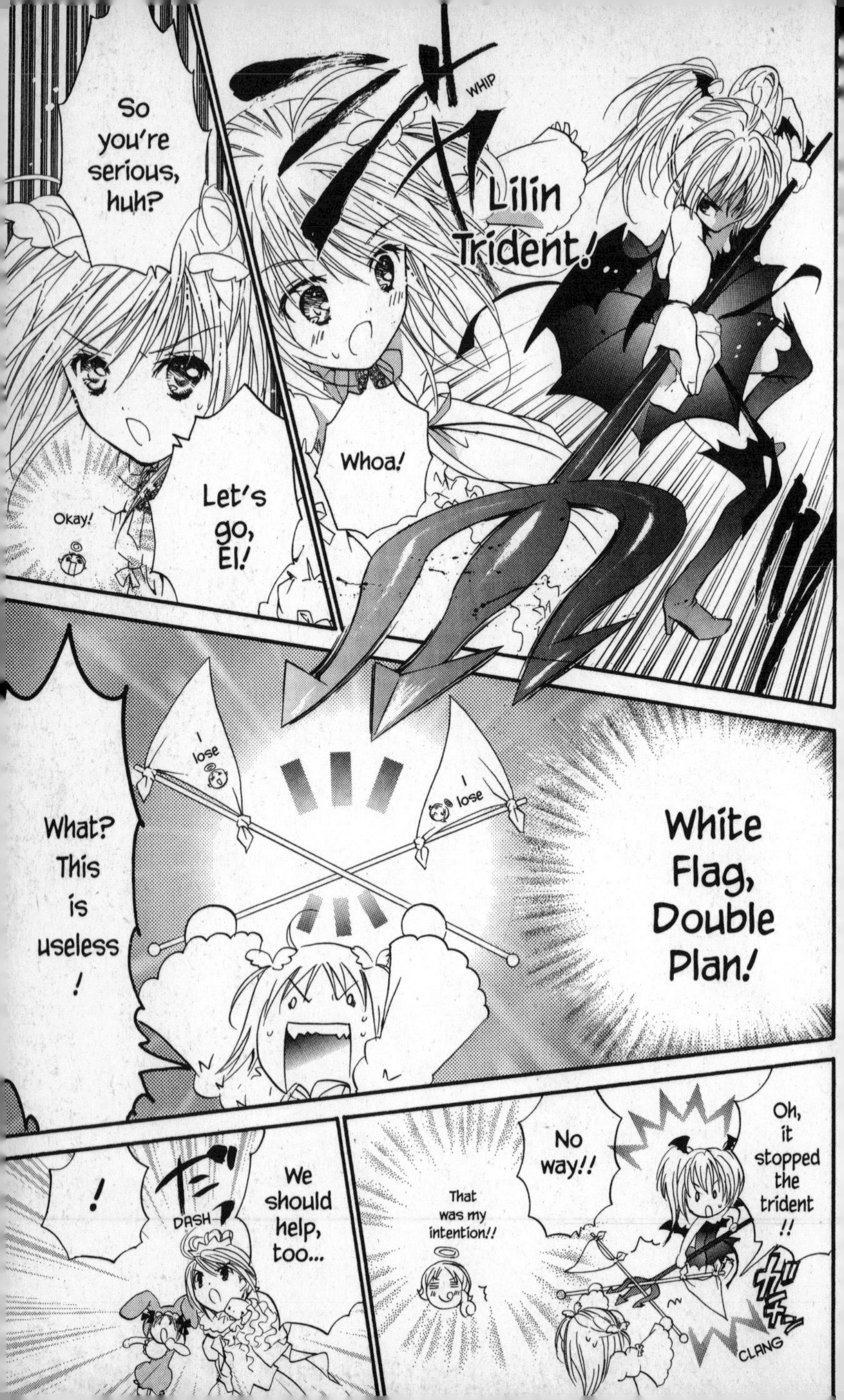
WHIP
Lilin Trident!
Whoa!
So you're serious, huh?
Let's go, El!
Okay!
White Flag, Double Plan!
I lose
I lose
What? This is useless!
Oh, it stopped the trident!!
CLANG
No way!!
That was my intention!!
We should help, too...
DASH
!

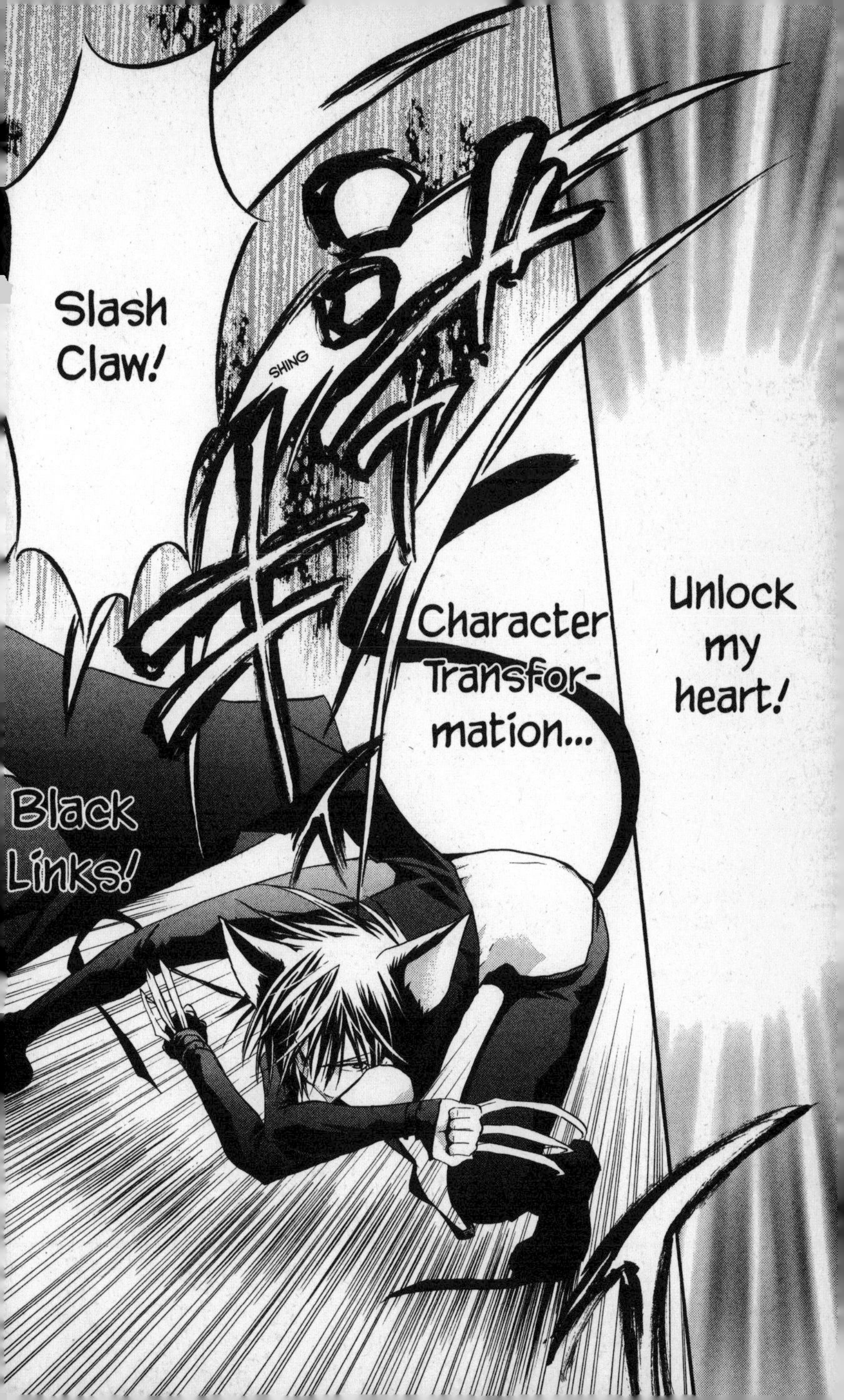

Unlock my heart!
Character Transformation...
Black Links!
Slash Claw!
SHING

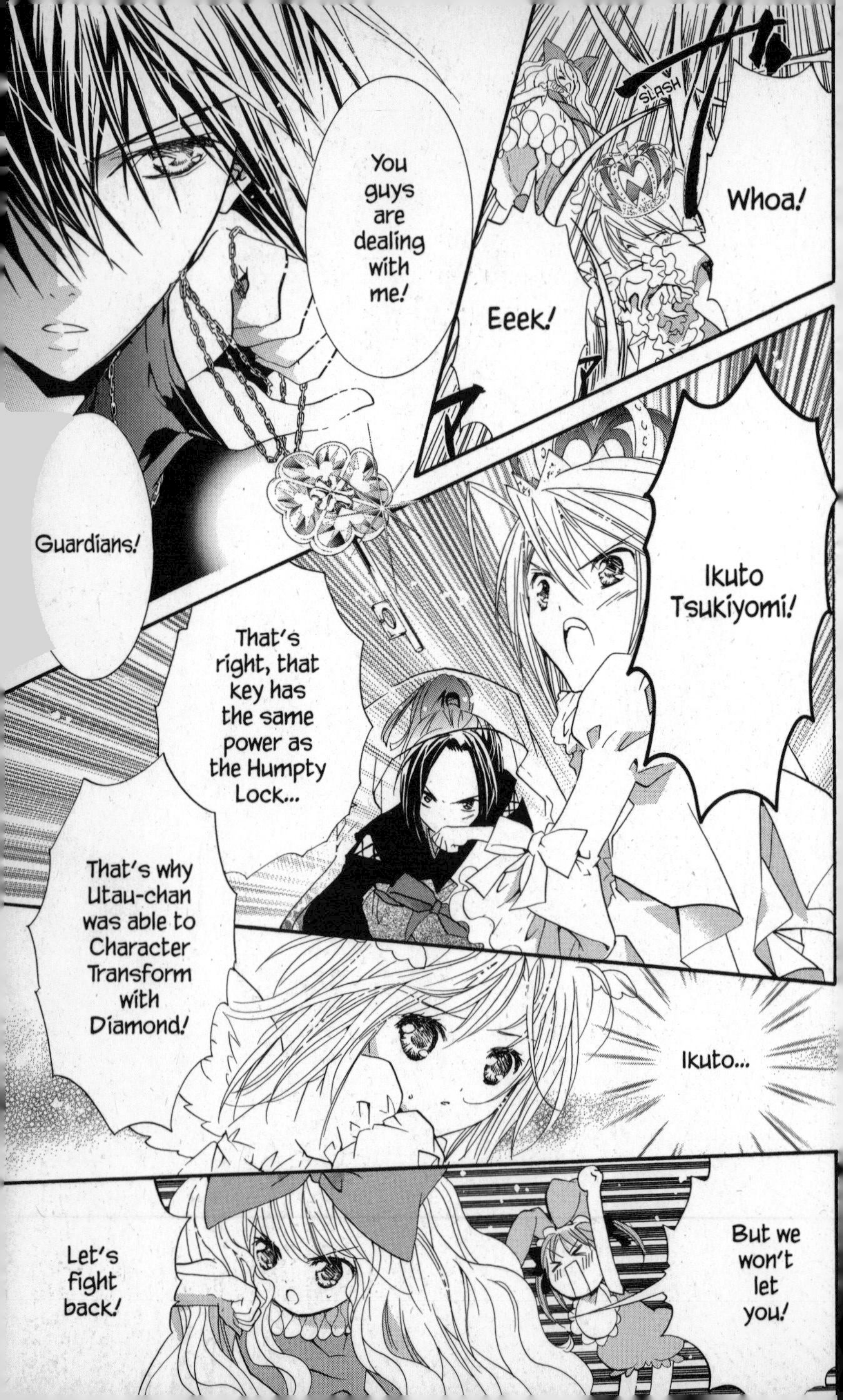
SLASH
Whoa!
Eeek!
You guys are dealing with me!
Guardians!
Ikuto Tsukiyomi!
That's right, that key has the same power as the Humpty Lock...
That's why Utau-chan was able to Character Transform with Diamond!
Ikuto...
But we won't let you!
Let's fight back!

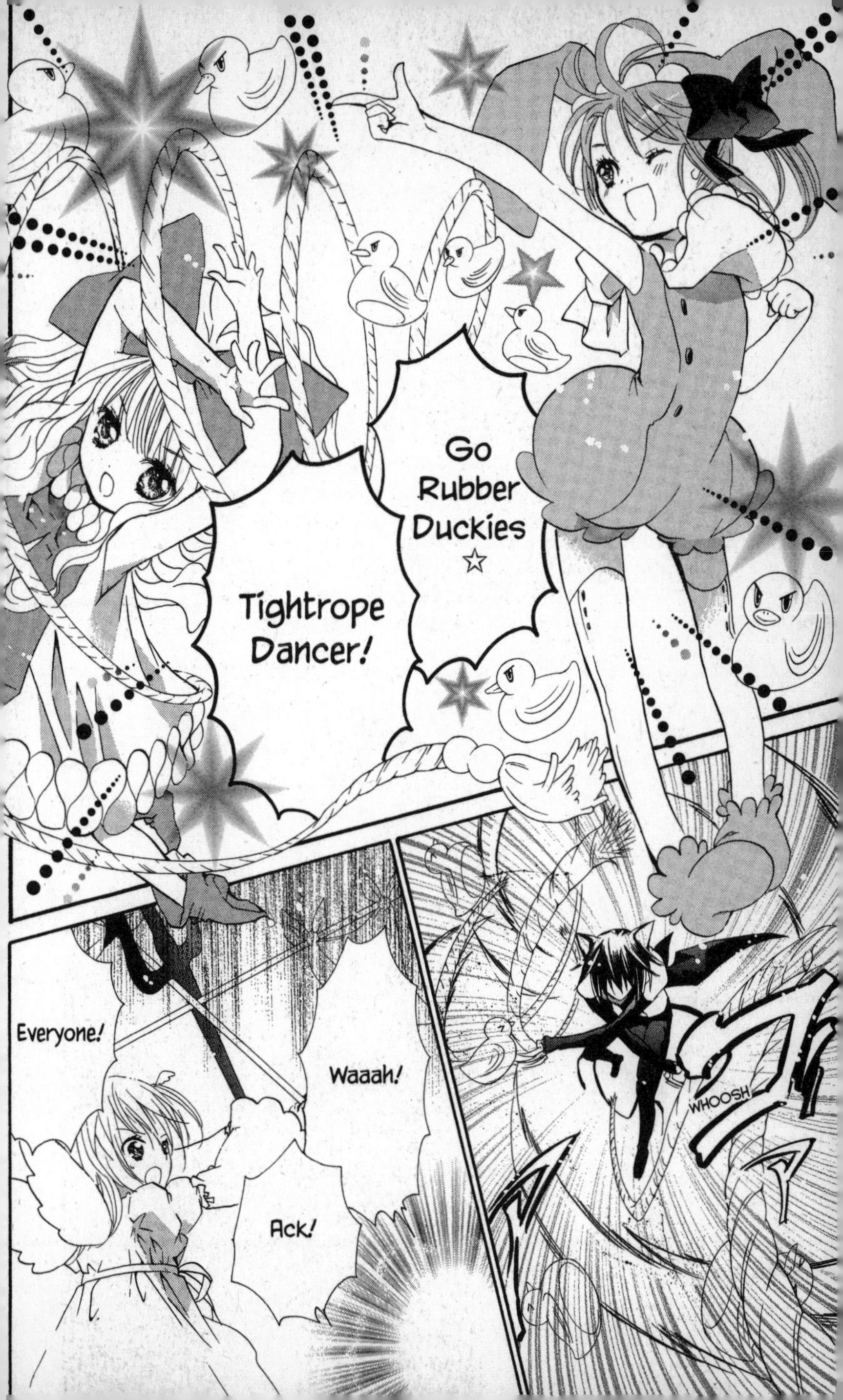
Go Rubber Duckies ☆
Tightrope Dancer!
WHOOSH
Waaah!
Everyone!
Ack!

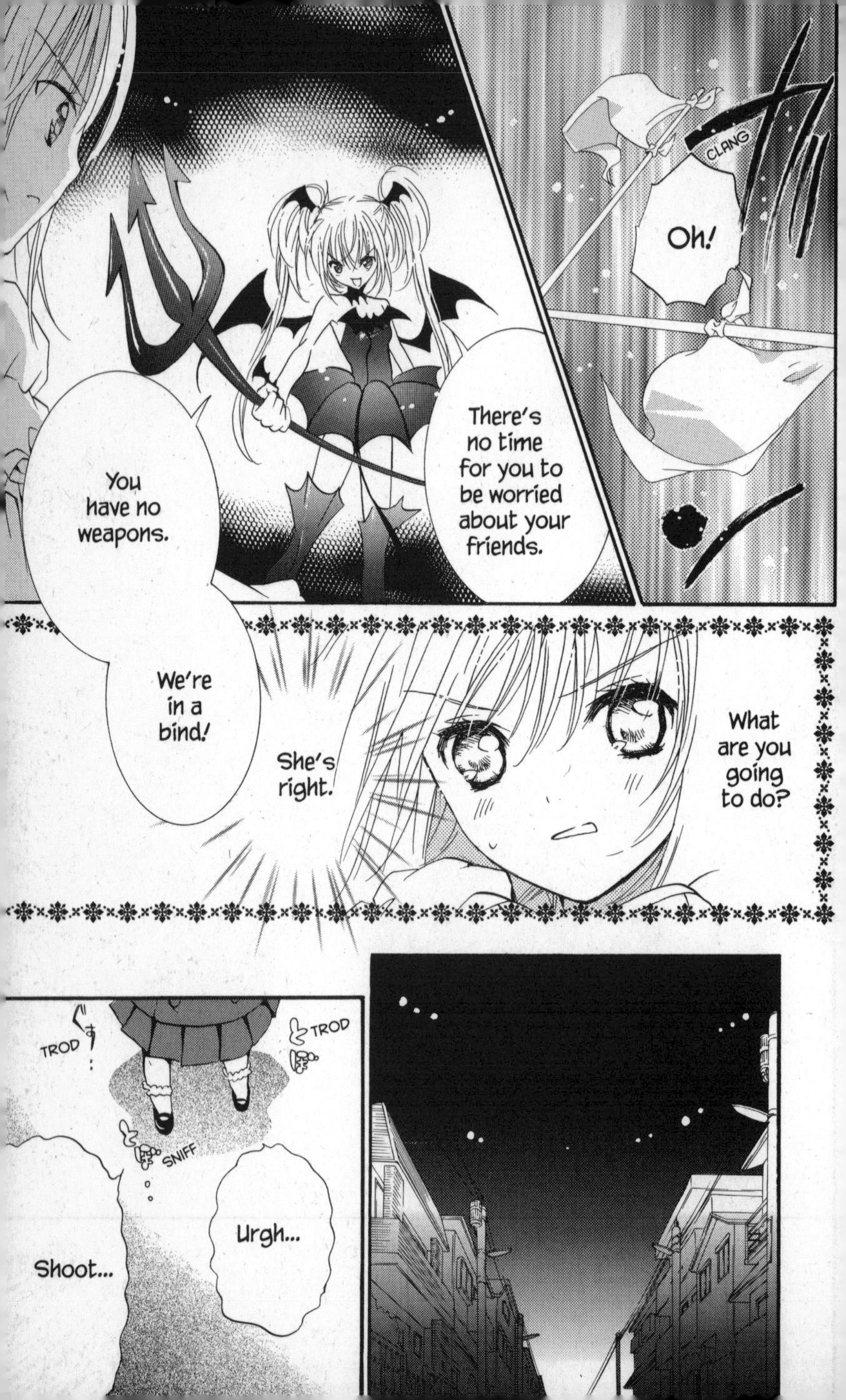
CLANG
Oh!
There's no time for you to be worried about your friends.
You have no weapons.
We're in a bind!
What are you going to do?
She's right.
TROD
TROD
SNIFF
Urgh...
Shoot...

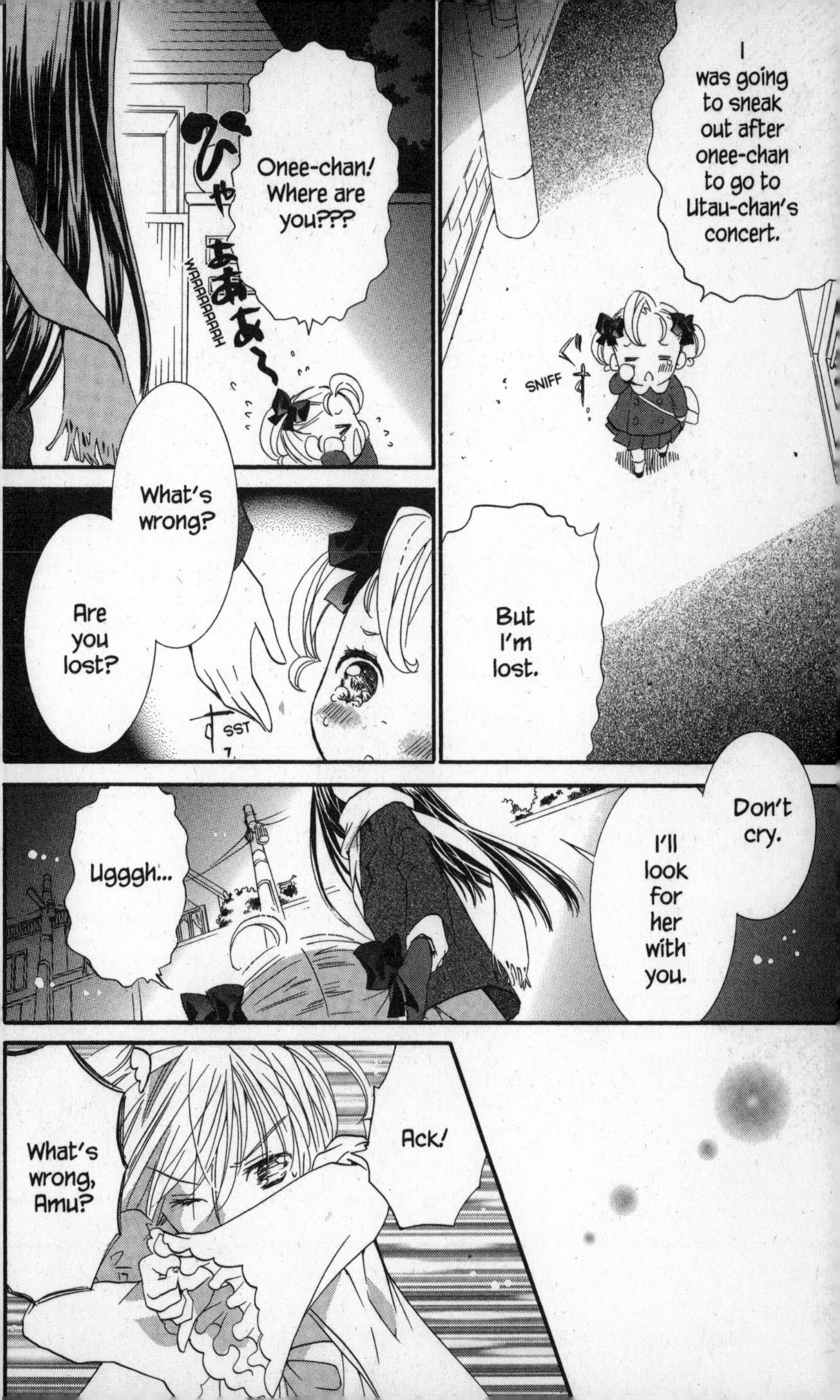
I was going to sneak out after onee-chan to go to Utau-chan's concert.
ぐすっ
SNIFF
Onee-chan! Where are you???
ぴゃああ~
WAAAAAAAAH
But I'm lost.
What's wrong?
Are you lost?
すっ
SST
Don't cry.
I'll look for her with you.
Ugggh...
Ack!
What's wrong, Amu?

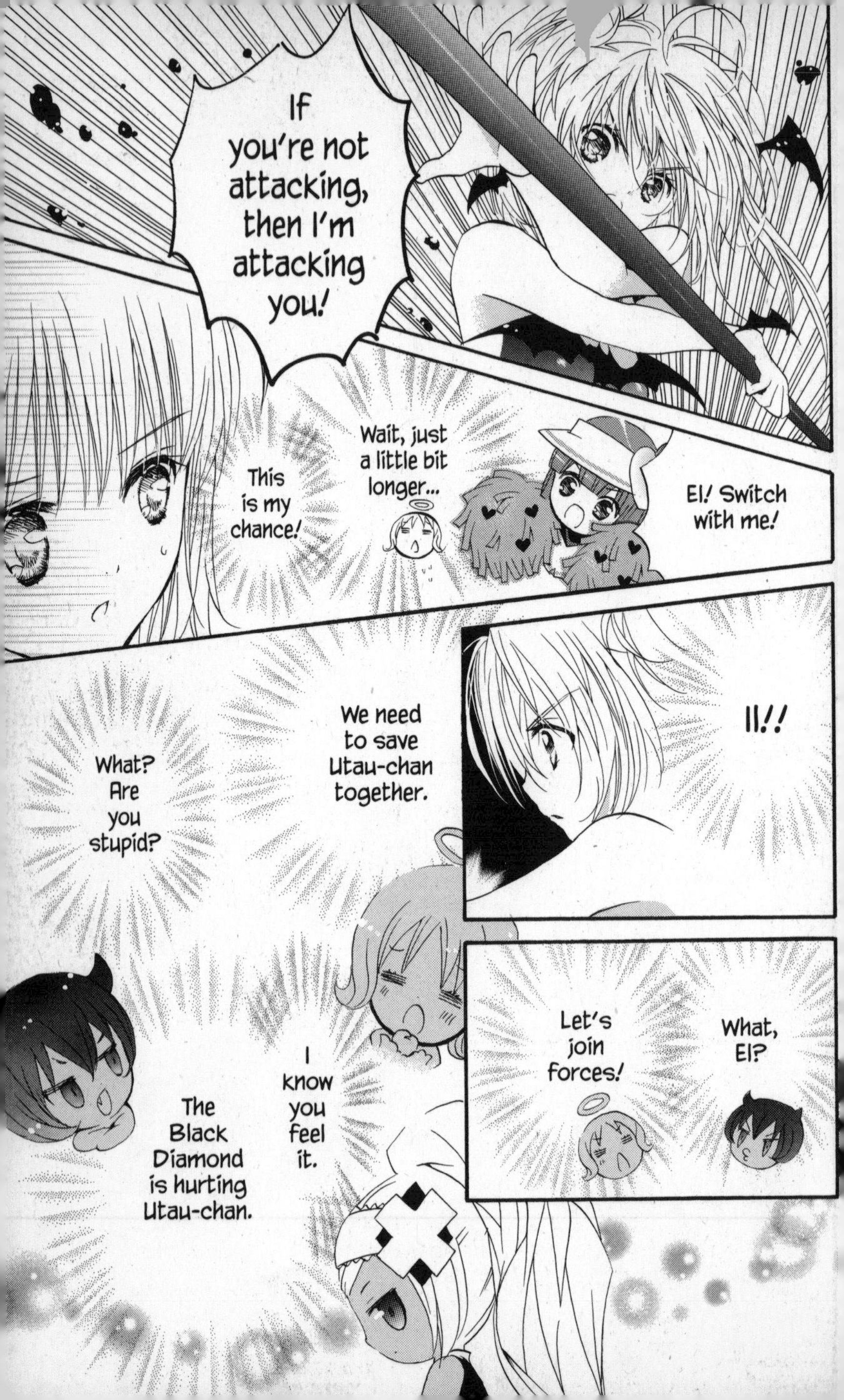
If you're not attacking, then I'm attacking you!
El! Switch with me!
Wait, just a little bit longer...
This is my chance!
!!!
What, El?
Let's join forces!
We need to save Utau-chan together.
What? Are you stupid?
I know you feel it.
The Black Diamond is hurting Utau-chan.

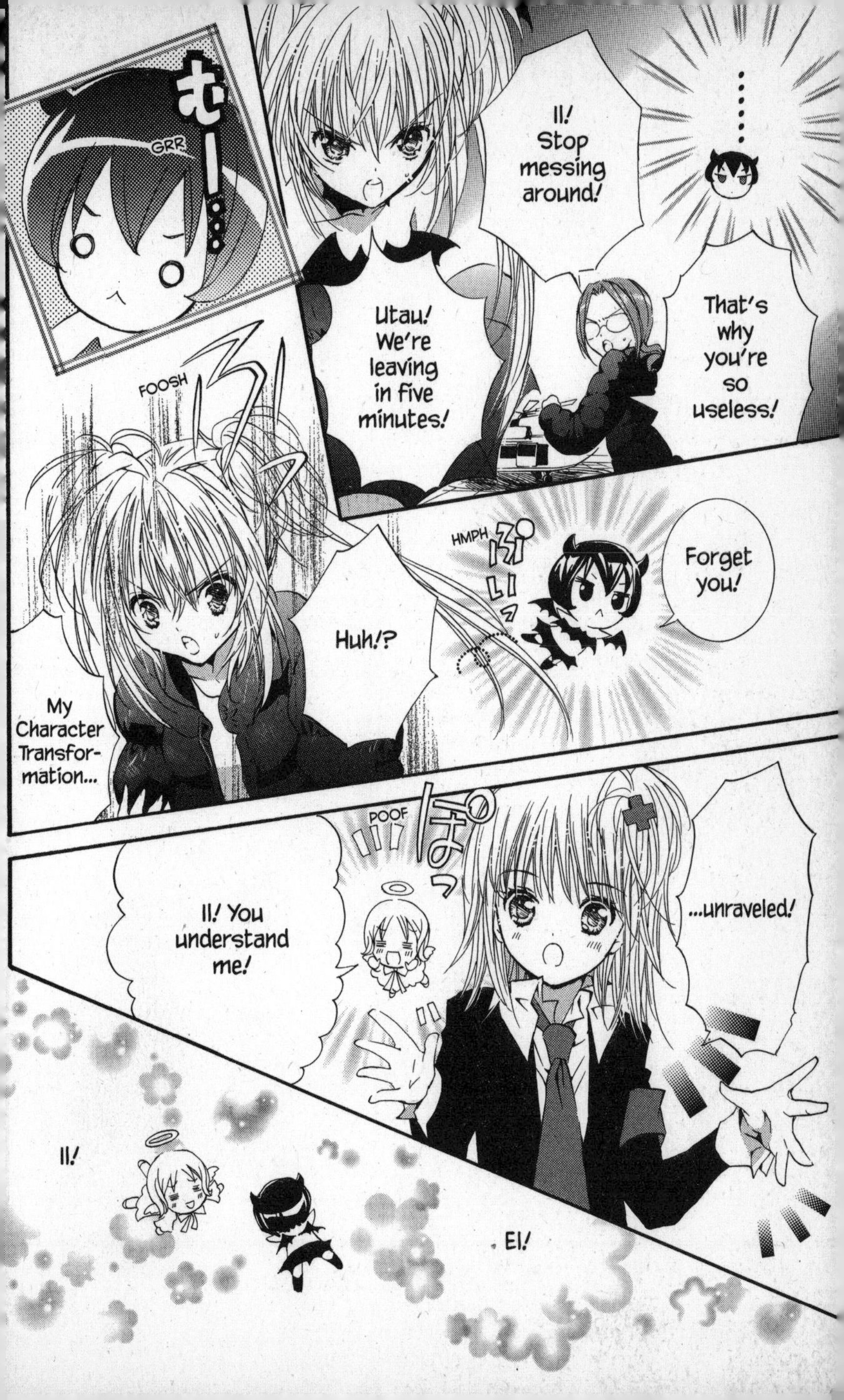
...
Il! Stop messing around!
That's why you're so useless!
Utau! We're leaving in five minutes!
GRR
HMPH
Forget you!
Huh!?
FOOSH
My Character Transformation...
POOF
...unraveled!
Il! You understand me!
Il!
El!

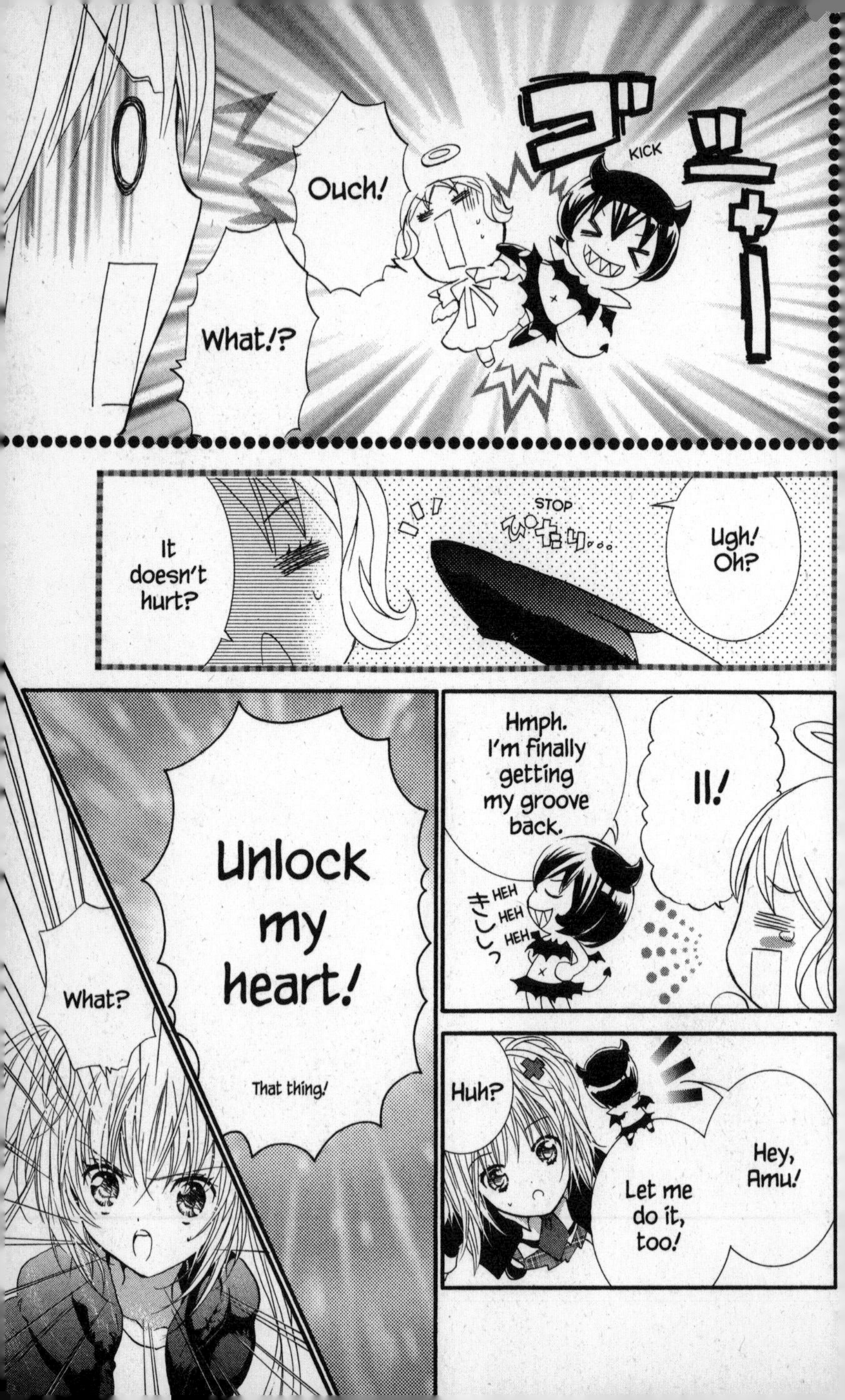
KICK
Ouch!
What!?
Ugh! Oh?
STOP
It doesn't hurt?
!!
Hmph. I'm finally getting my groove back.
HEH HEH HEH
Hey, Amu!
Let me do it, too!
Huh?
Unlock my heart!
That thing!
What?

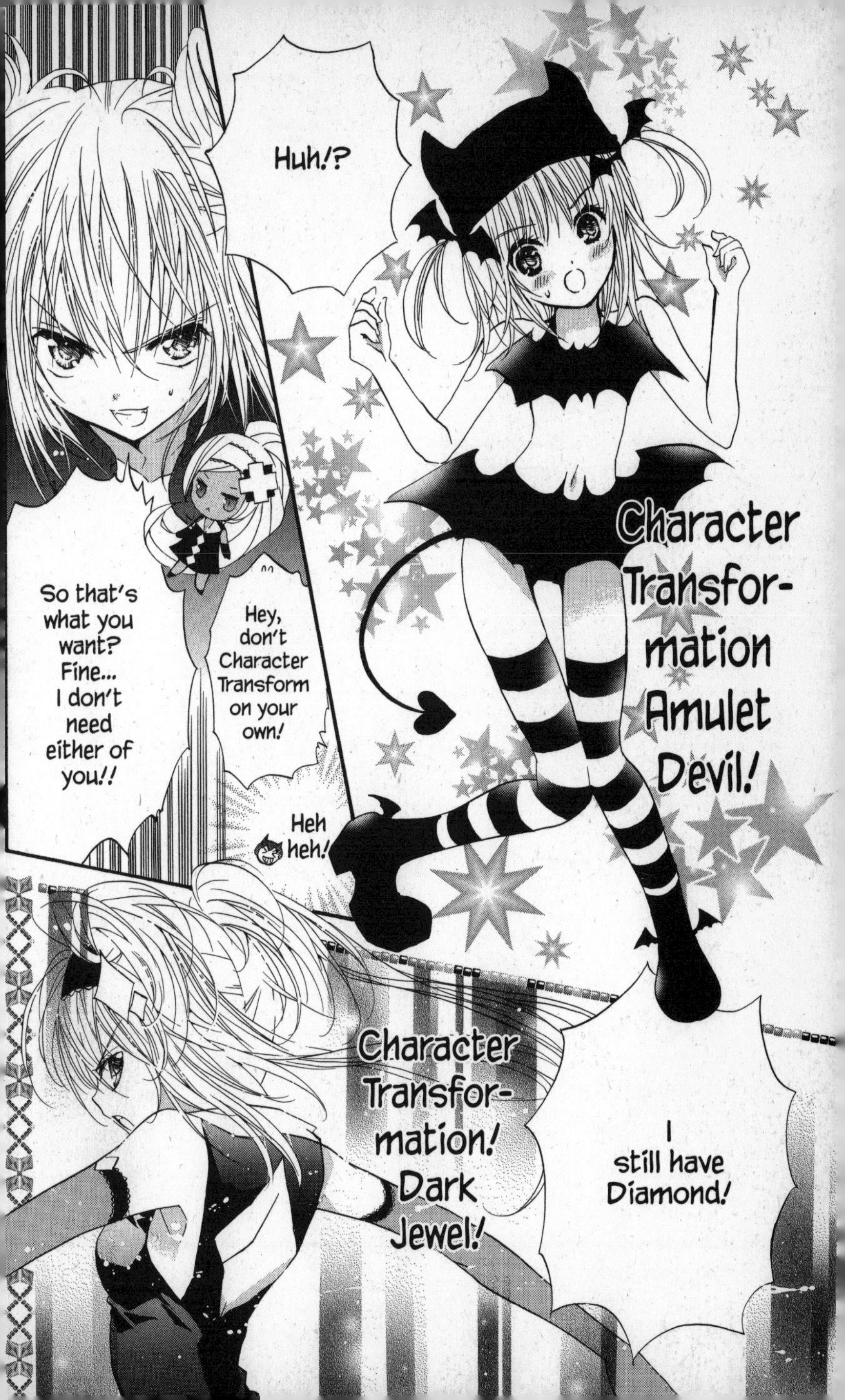
Huh!?
Character Transformation Amulet Devil!
Hey, don't Character Transform on your own!
Heh heh!
So that's what you want? Fine... I don't need either of you!!
I still have Diamond!
Character Transformation! Dark Jewel!

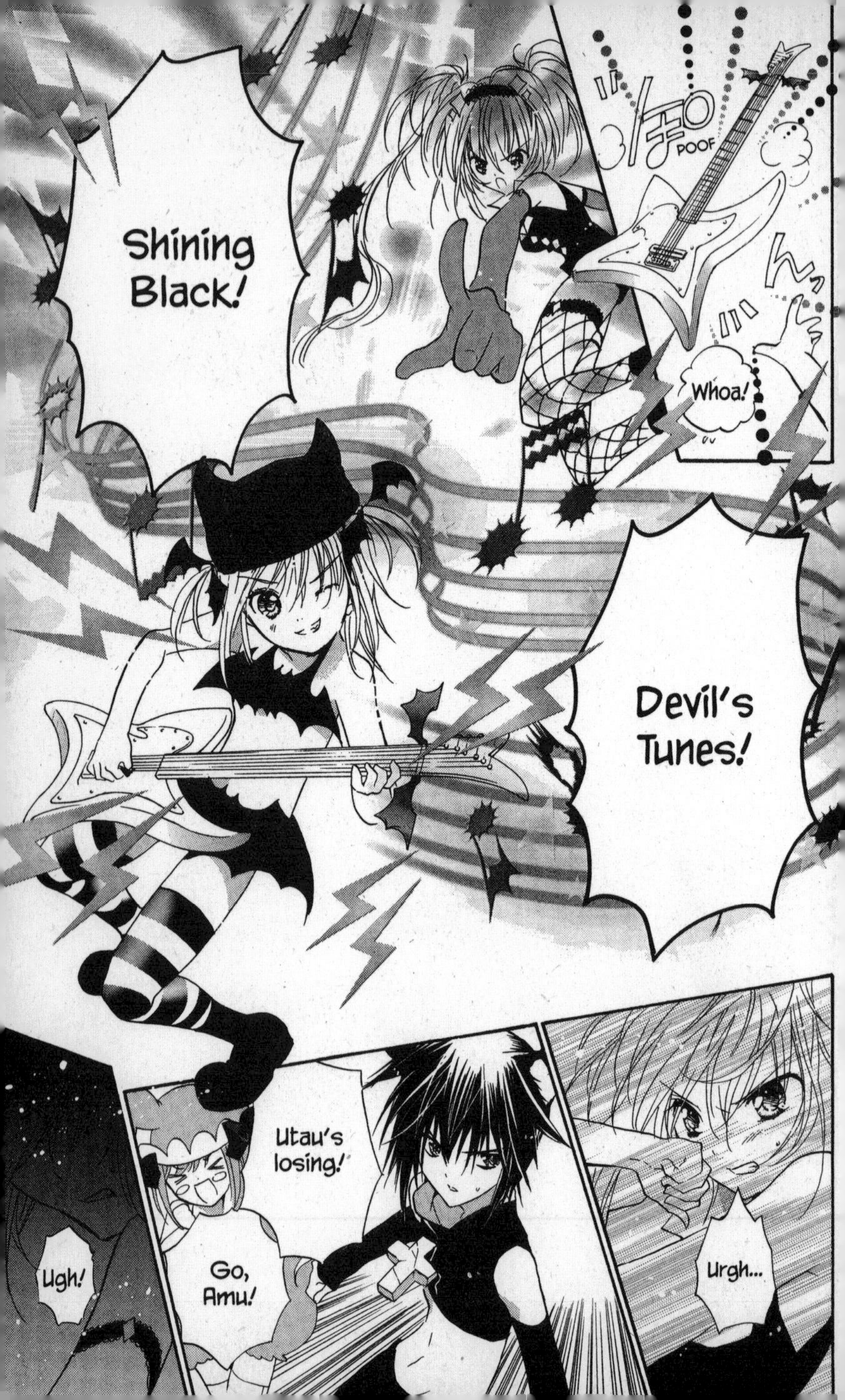
POOF
Whoa!
Shining Black!
Devil's Tunes!
Urgh...
Utau's losing!
Go, Amu!
Ugh!

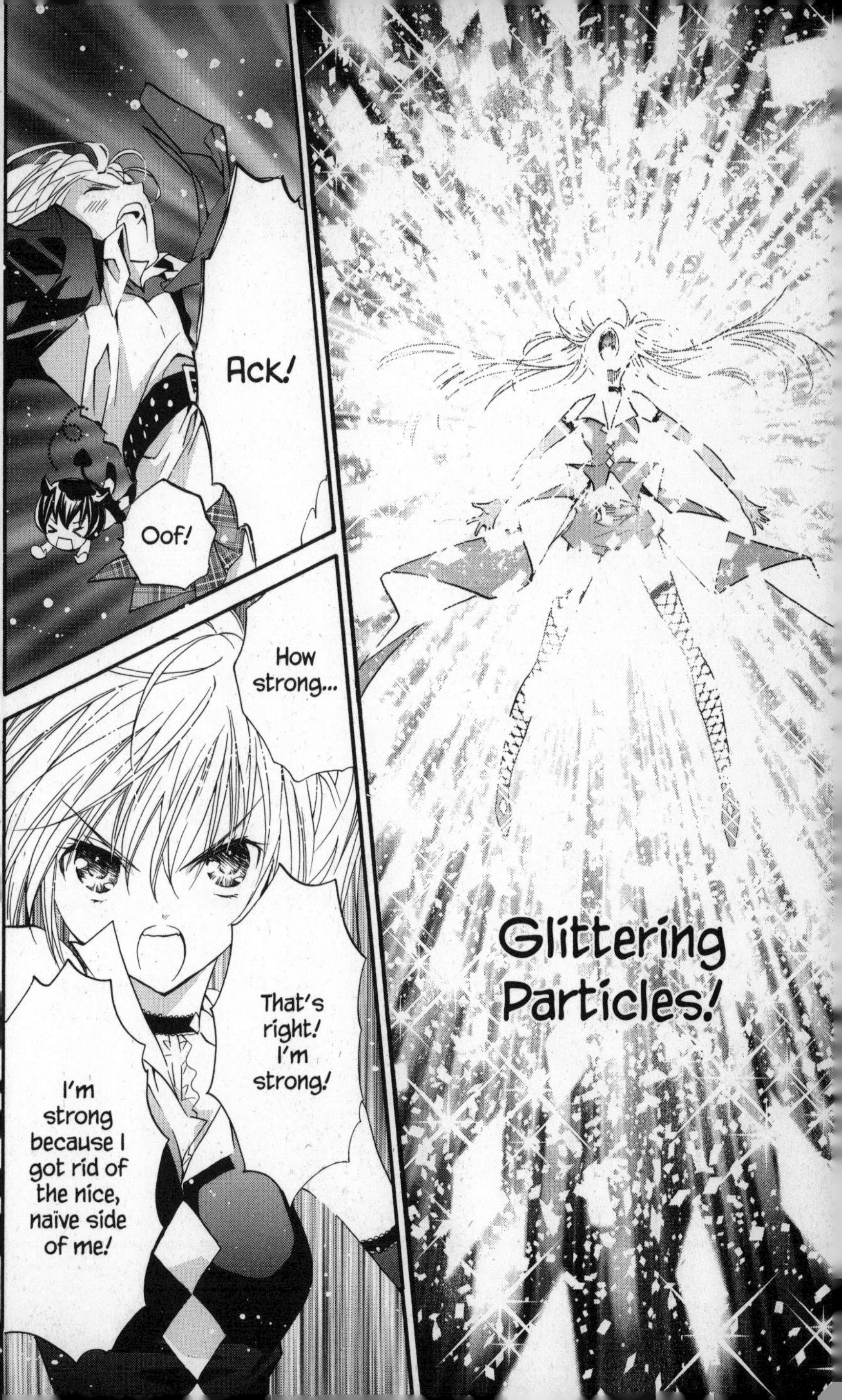
Glittering Particles!
Ack!
Oof!
How strong...
That's right! I'm strong!
I'm strong because I got rid of the nice, naïve side of me!

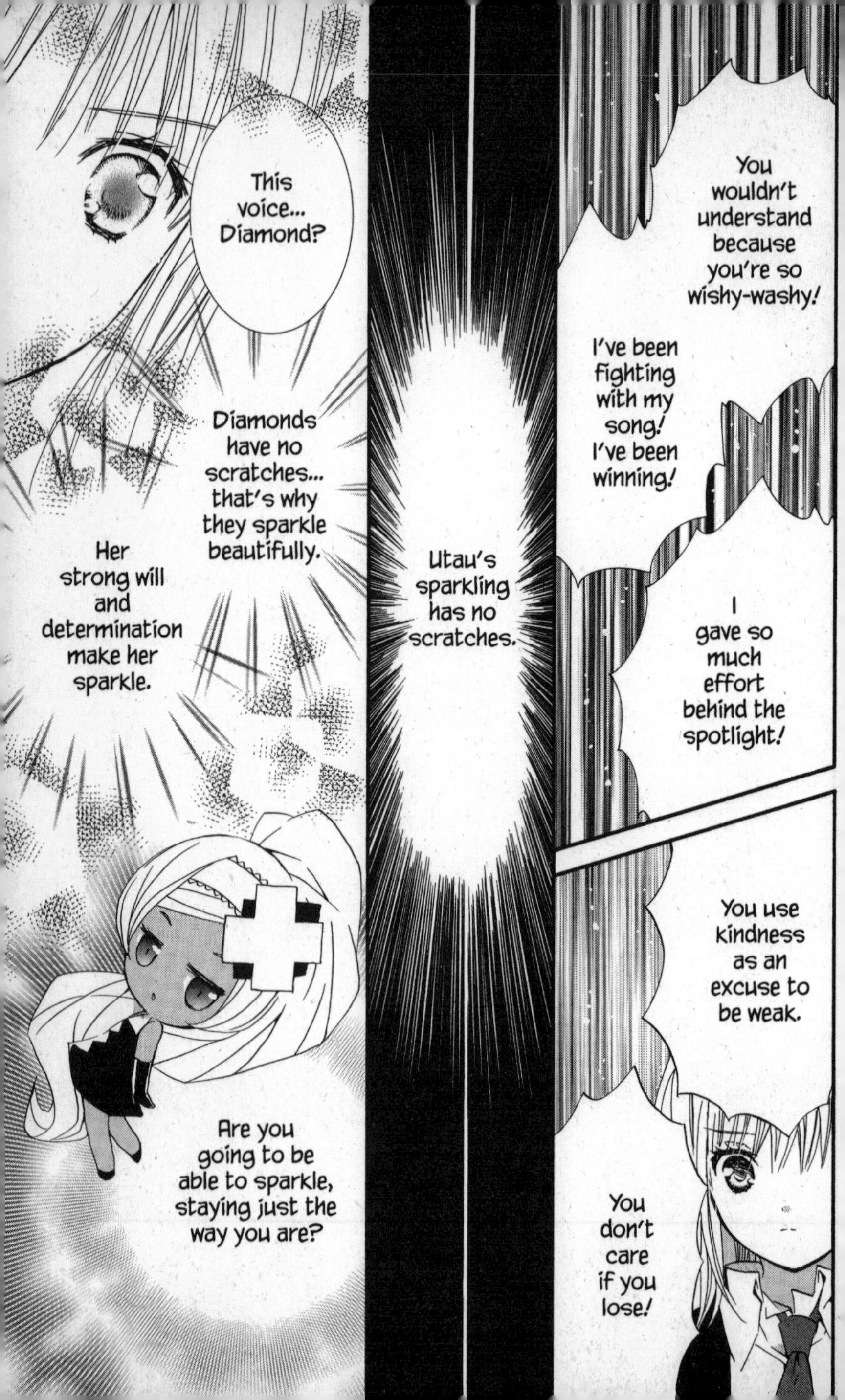

You wouldn't understand because you're so wishy-washy!
I've been fighting with my song! I've been winning!
I gave so much effort behind the spotlight!
You use kindness as an excuse to be weak.
You don't care if you lose!
Utau's sparkling has no scratches.
This voice... Diamond?
Diamonds have no scratches... that's why they sparkle beautifully.
Her strong will and determination make her sparkle.
Are you going to be able to sparkle, staying just the way you are?

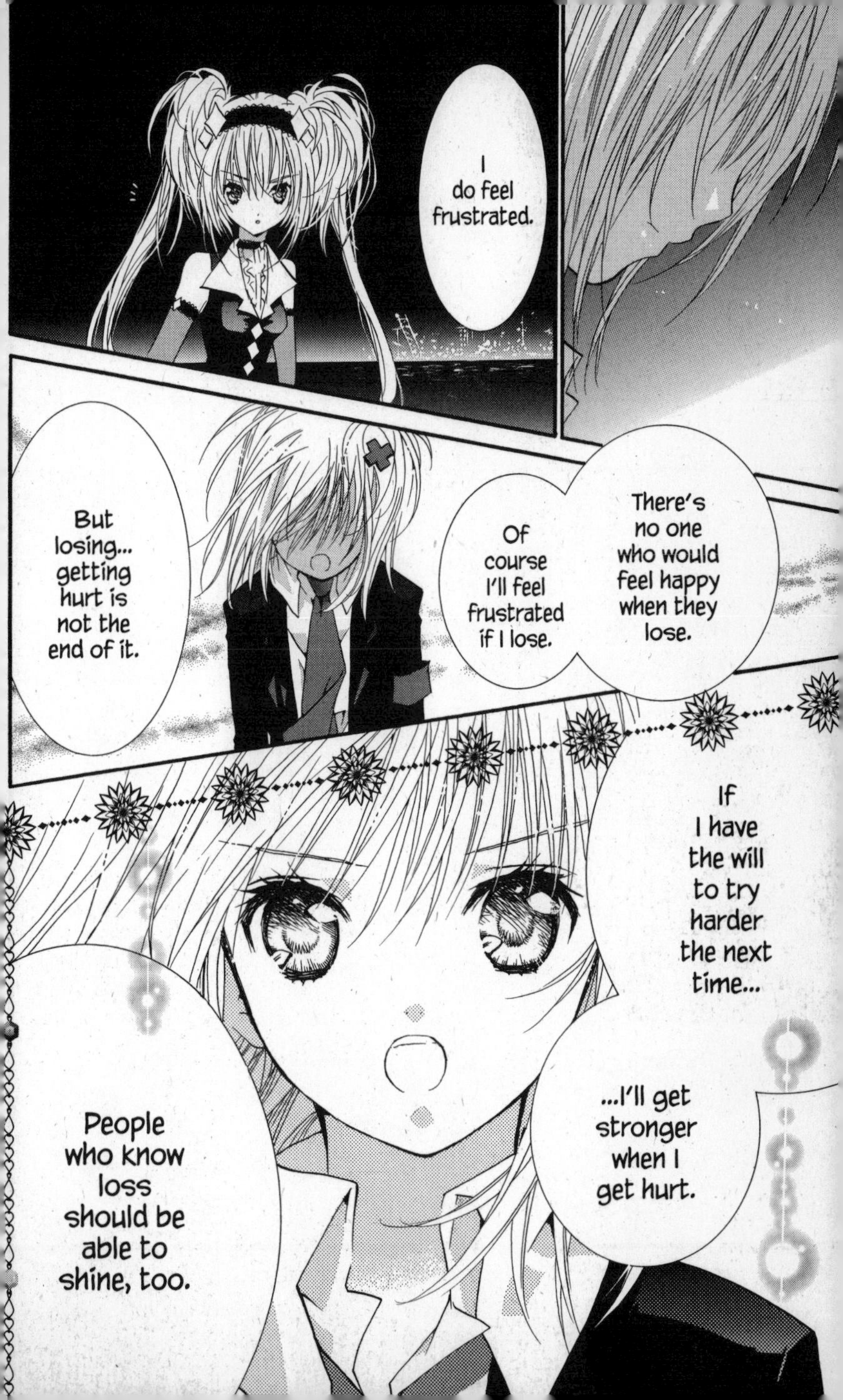
I do feel frustrated.
There's no one who would feel happy when they lose.
Of course I'll feel frustrated if I lose.
But losing... getting hurt is not the end of it.
If I have the will to try harder the next time...
...I'll get stronger when I get hurt.
People who know loss should be able to shine, too.

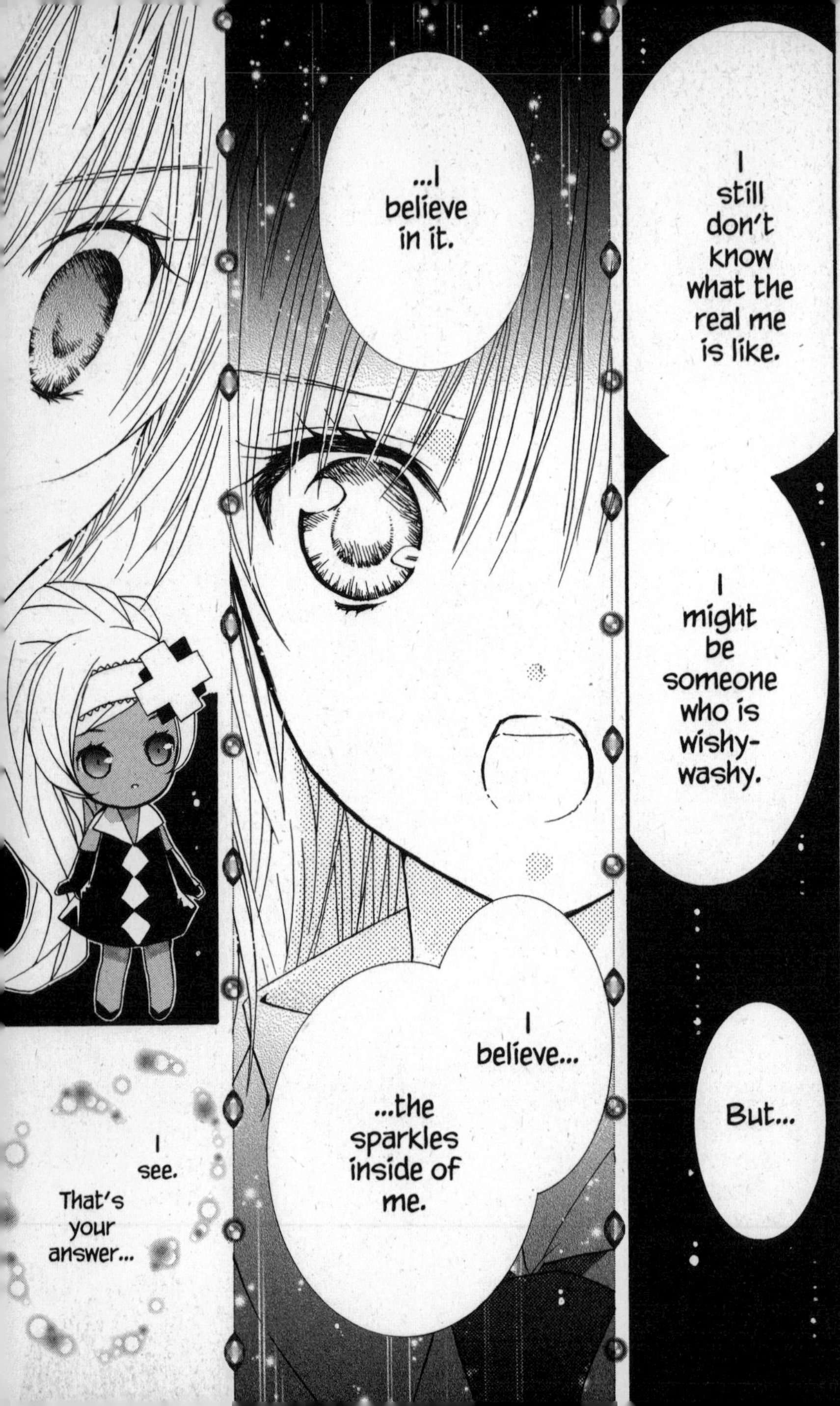
I still don't know what the real me is like.
I might be someone who is wishy-washy.
But...
...I believe in it.
I believe...
...the sparkles inside of me.
I see. That's your answer...

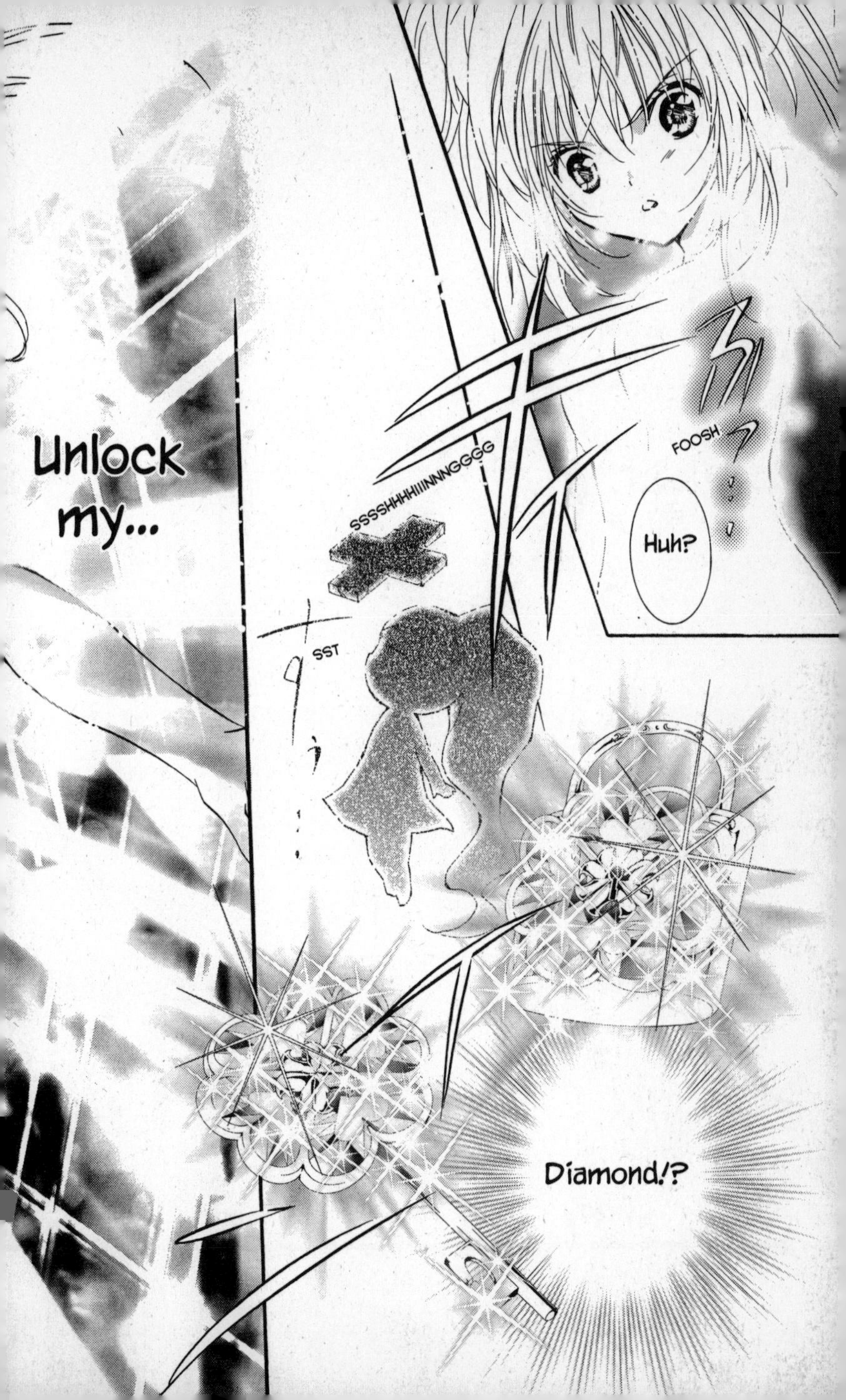
FOOSH
Huh?
SSSSHHHHIIIINNNGGGG
SST
Diamond!?
Unlock my...

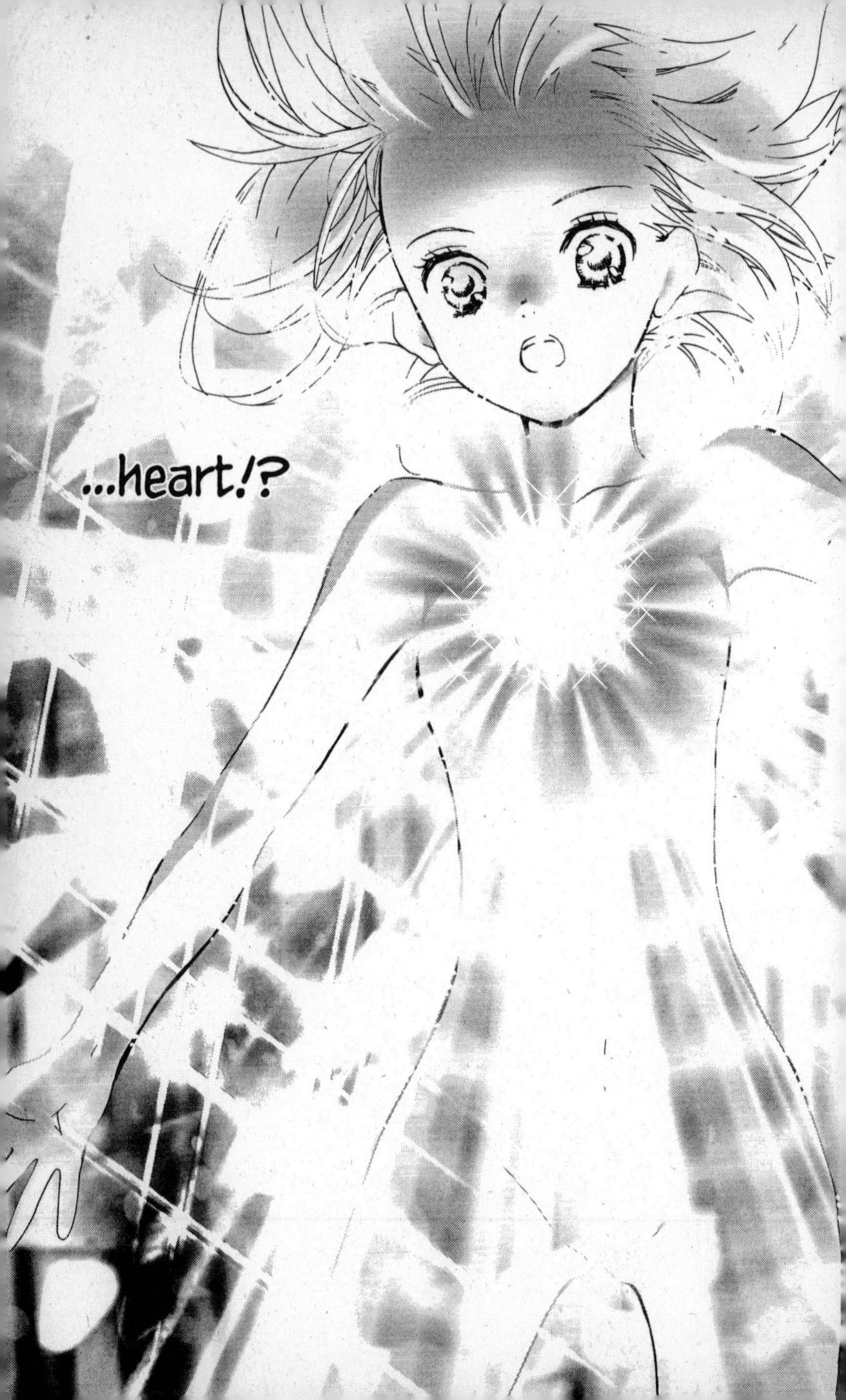
...heart!?

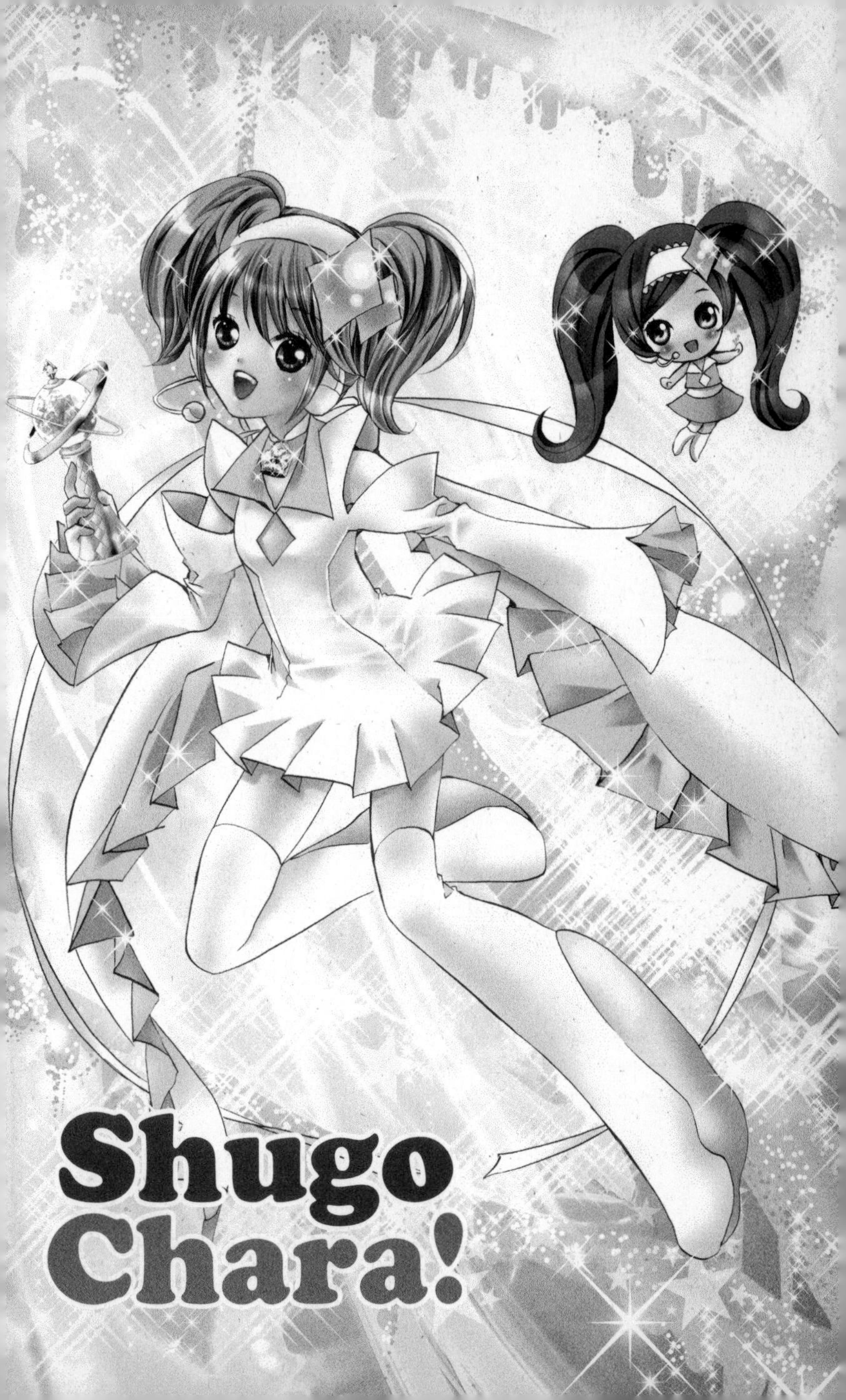
Shugo
Chara!

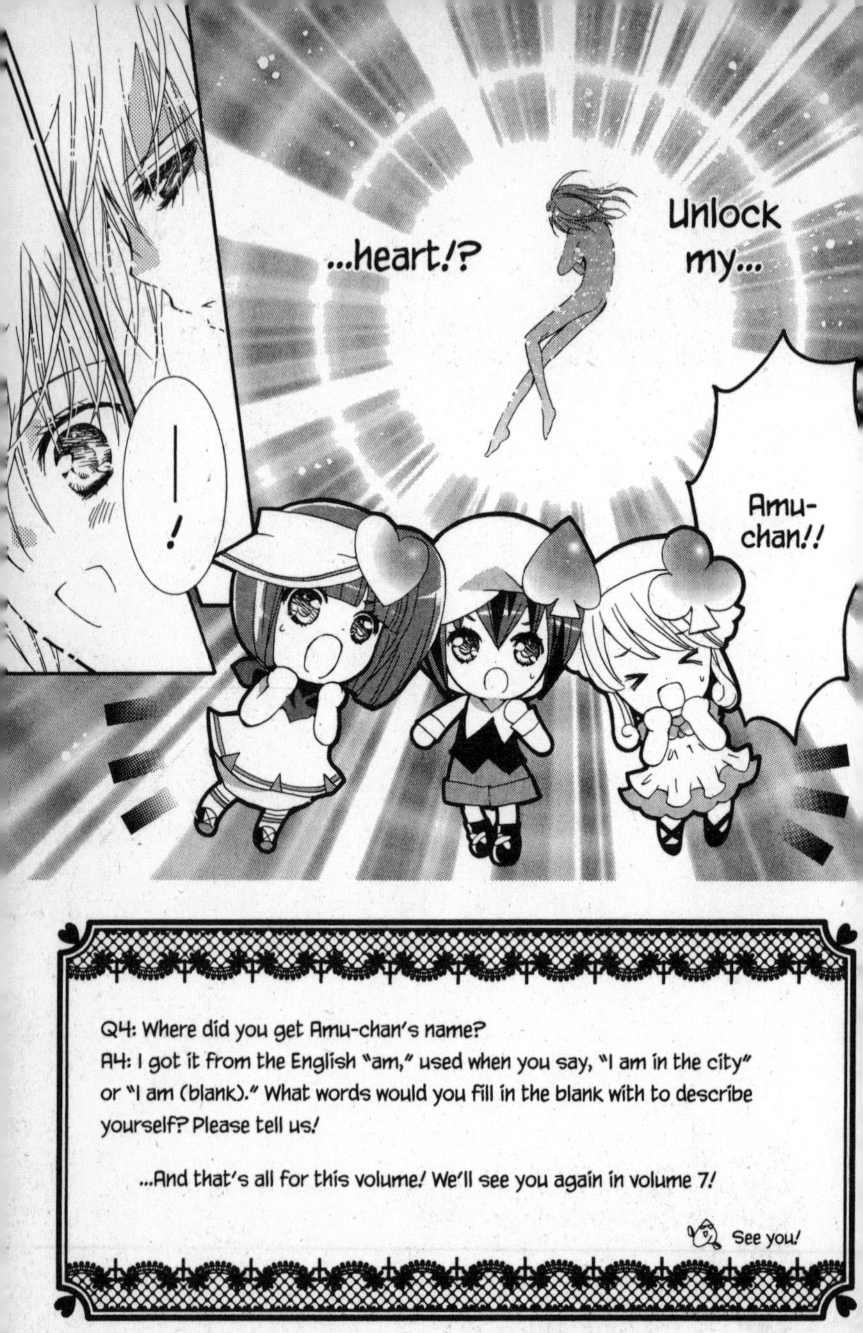
Unlock my...
...heart!?
Amu-chan!!
!

Q4: Where did you get Amu-chan's name?
A4: I got it from the English "am," used when you say, "I am in the city" or "I am (blank)." What words would you fill in the blank with to describe yourself? Please tell us!

...And that's all for this volume! We'll see you again in volume 7!

See you!

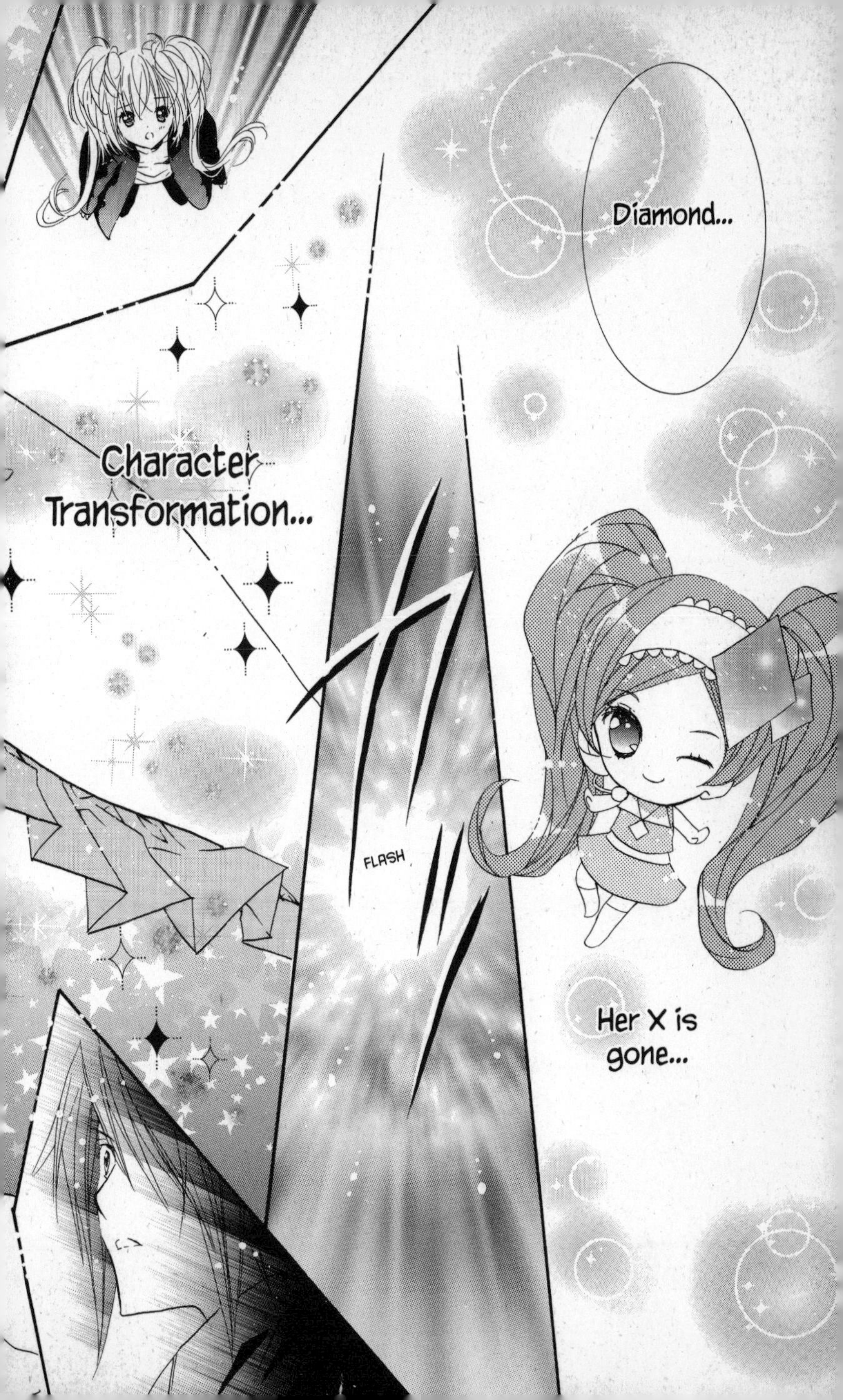
Diamond...
Her X is gone...
Character Transformation...
FLASH

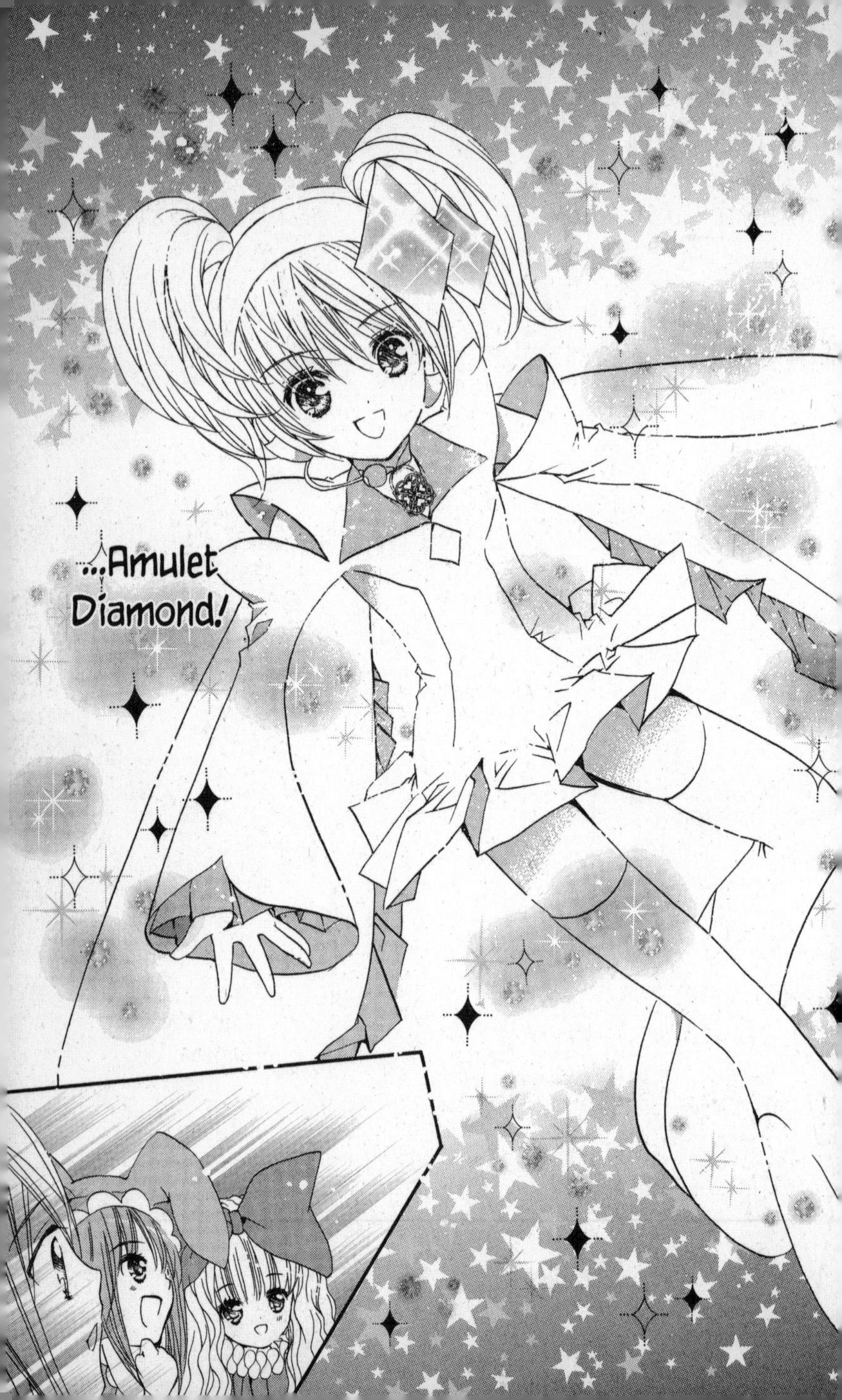
...Amulet Diamond!

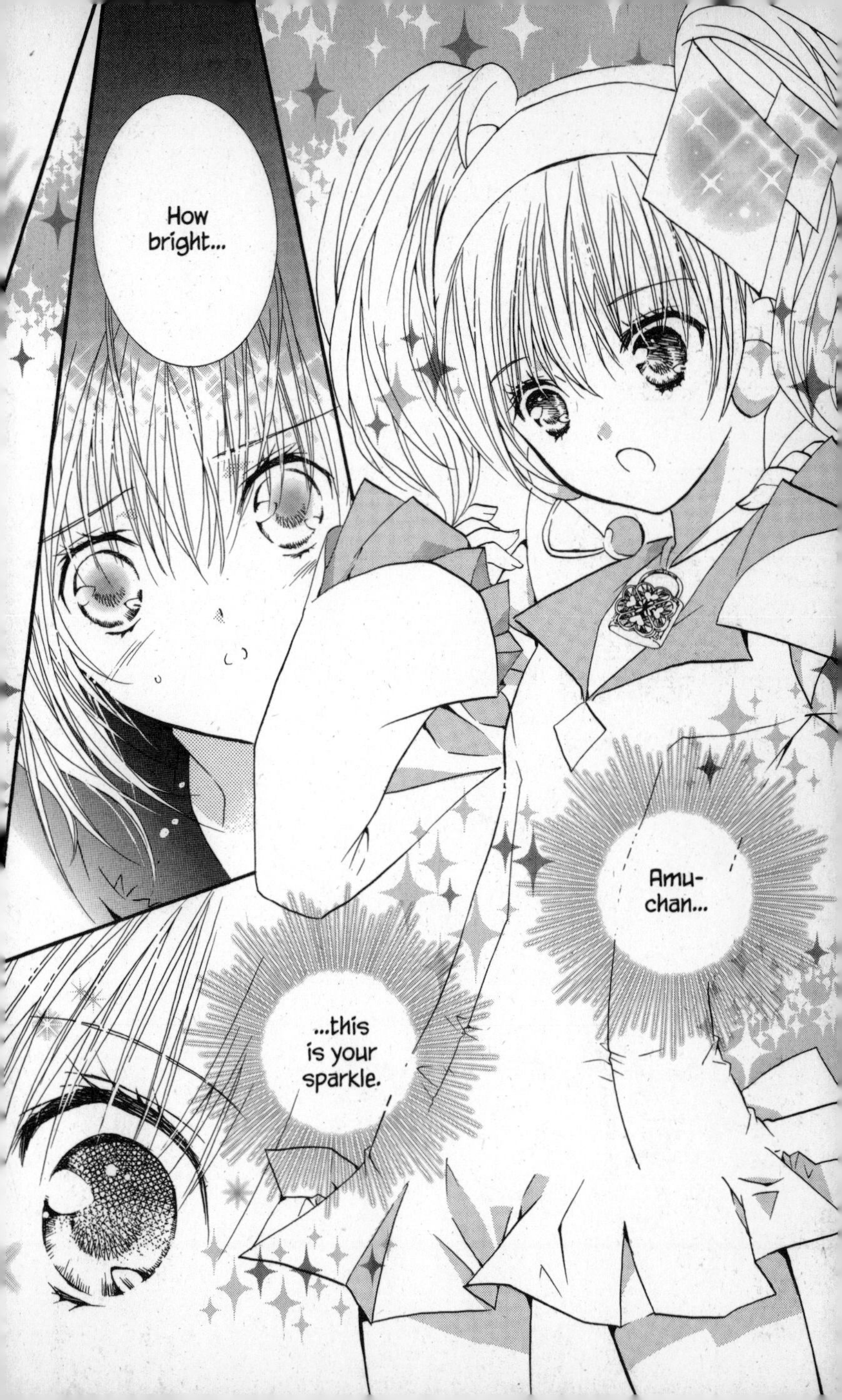
How bright...
Amu-chan...
...this is your sparkle.

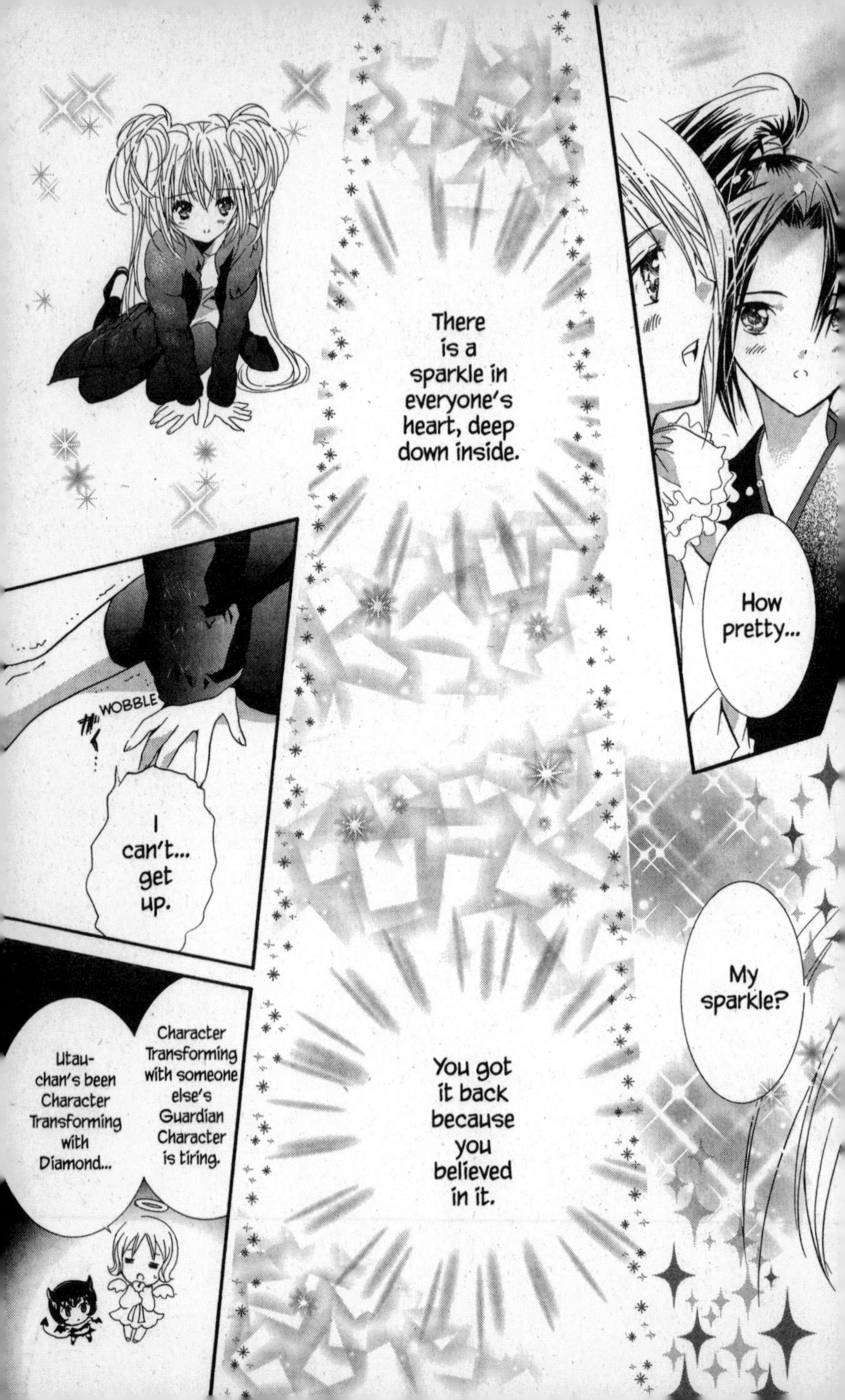
How pretty...
My sparkle?
There is a sparkle in everyone's heart, deep down inside.
You got it back because you believed in it.
WOBBLE
I can't... get up.
Character Transforming with someone else's Guardian Character is tiring.
Utau-chan's been Character Transforming with Diamond...

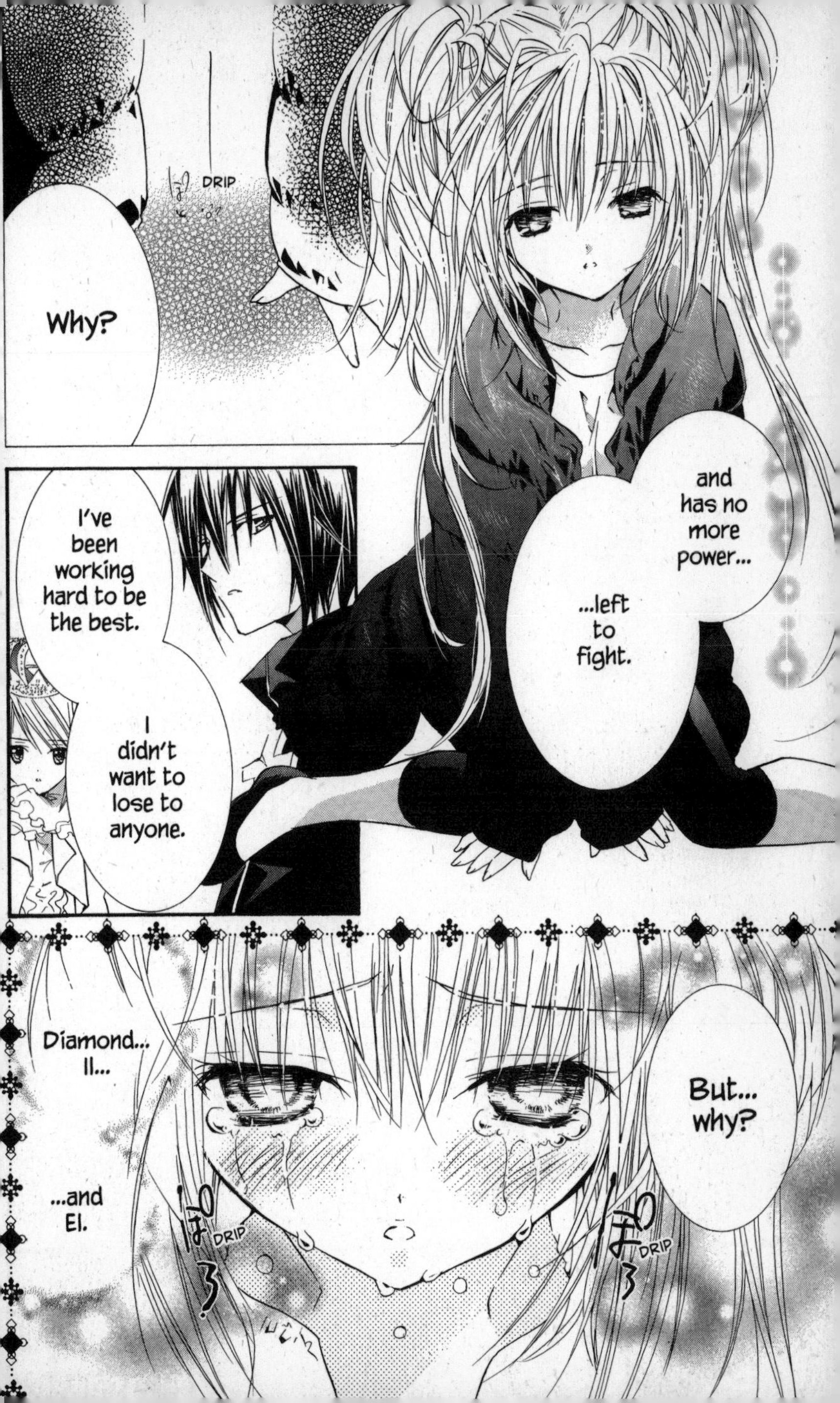

and has no more power...
...left to fight.
DRIP
Why?
I've been working hard to be the best.
I didn't want to lose to anyone.
But... why?
DRIP
DRIP
Diamond... II...
...and El.

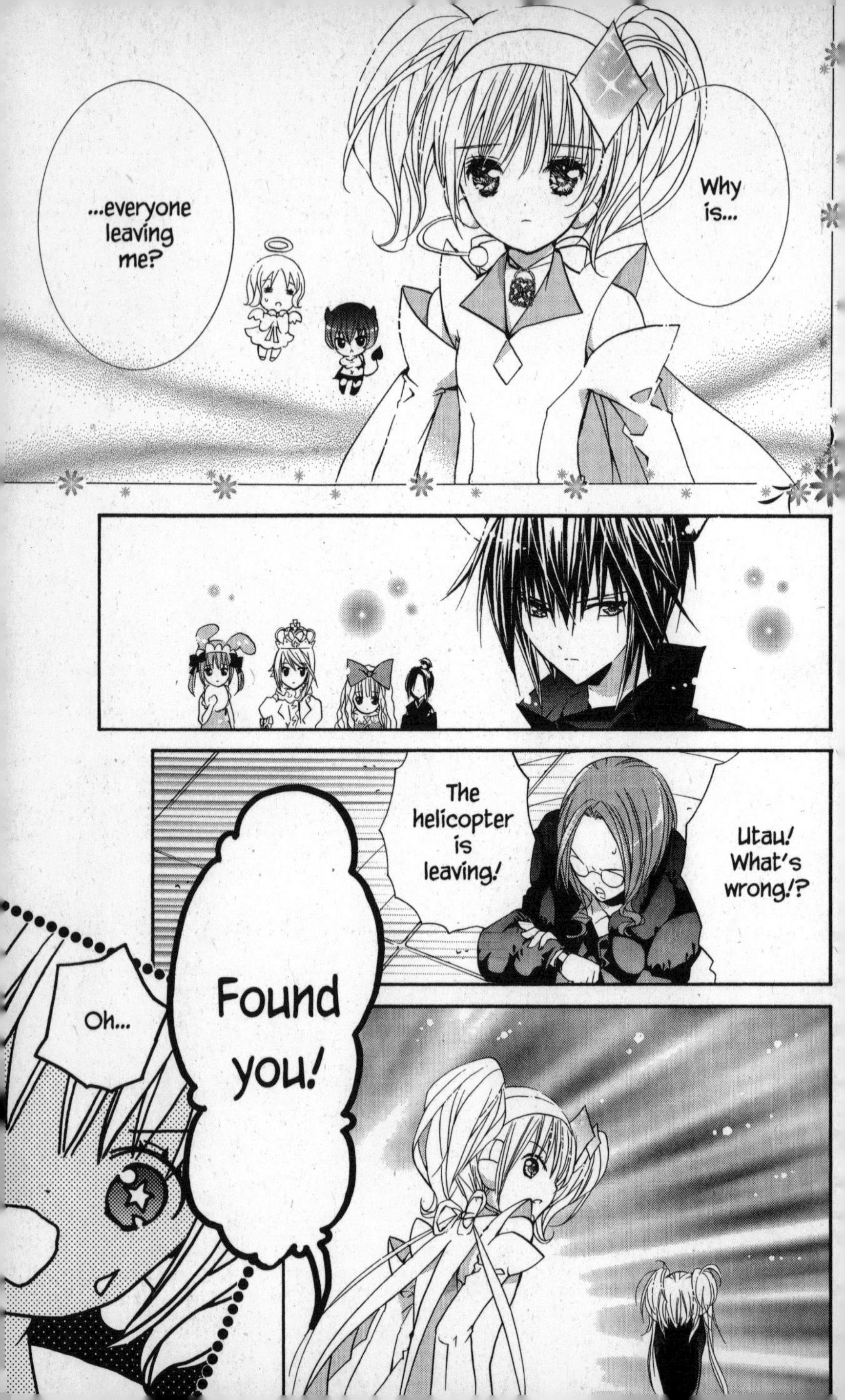

Why is...
...everyone leaving me?
Utau! What's wrong!?
The helicopter is leaving!
Found you!
Oh...

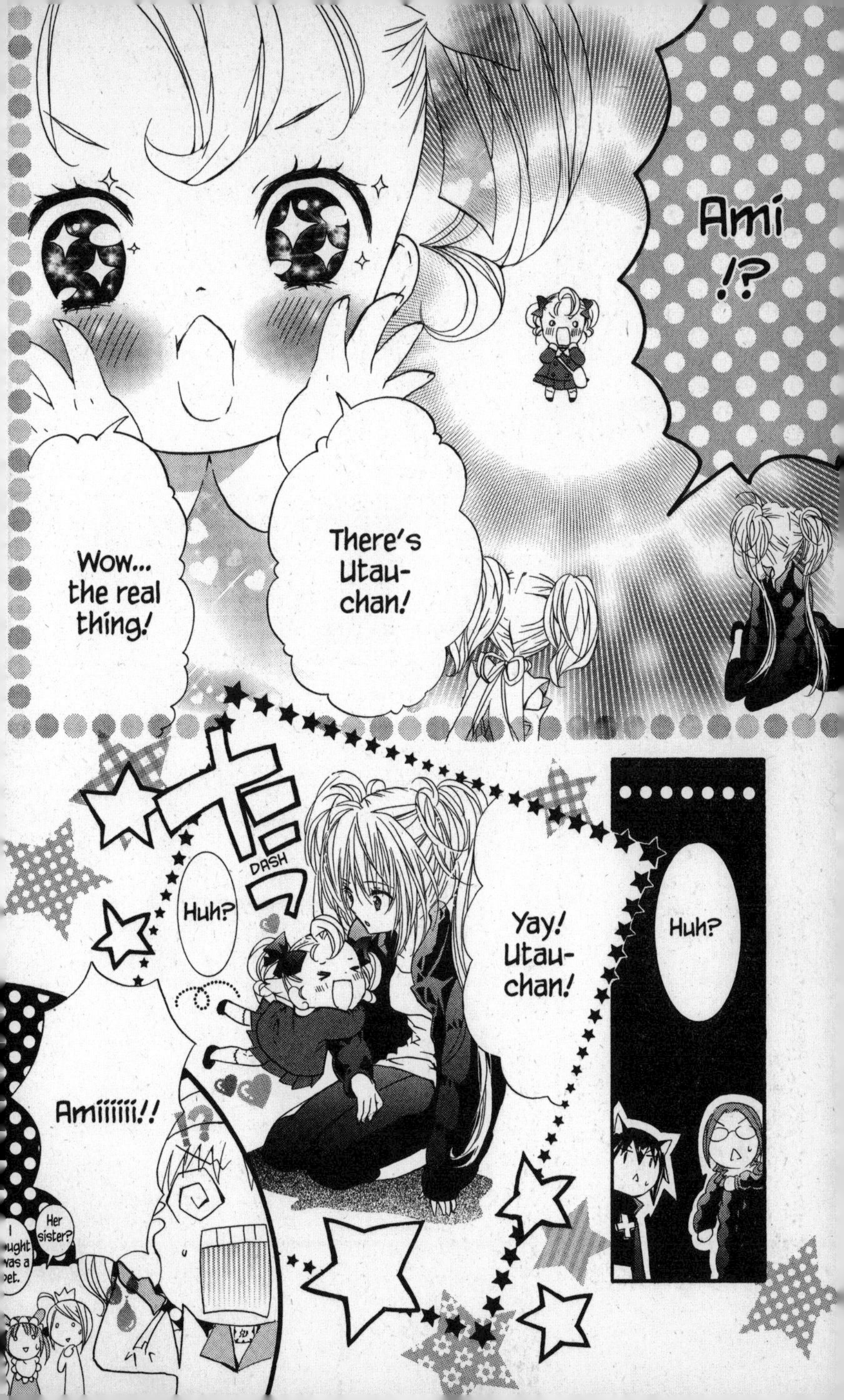

Ami !?
There's Utau-chan!
Wow... the real thing!
Huh?
Yay! Utau-chan!
DASH
Huh?
Amiiiiiii!!
Her sister?

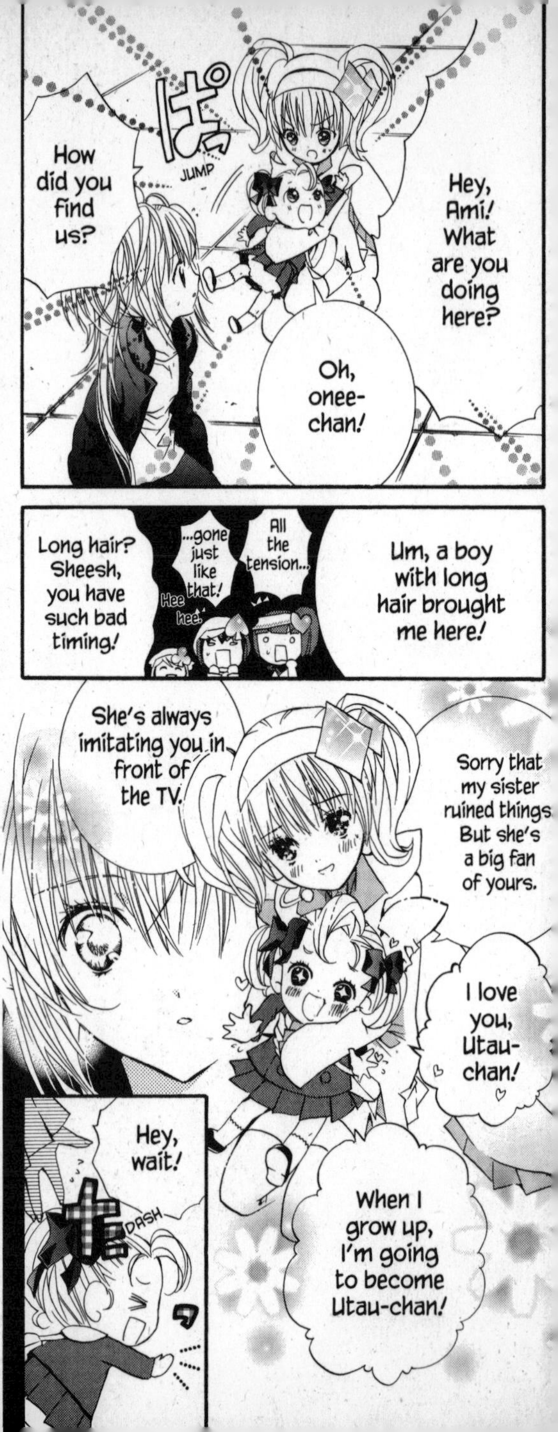
Hey, Ami! What are you doing here?
ぱっ
JUMP
Oh, onee-chan!
How did you find us?
Um, a boy with long hair brought me here!
All the tension...
...gone just like that!
Hee hee.
Long hair? Sheesh, you have such bad timing!
Sorry that my sister ruined things. But she's a big fan of yours.
She's always imitating you in front of the TV.
I love you, Utau-chan!
When I grow up, I'm going to become Utau-chan!
Hey, wait!
DASH

character profile

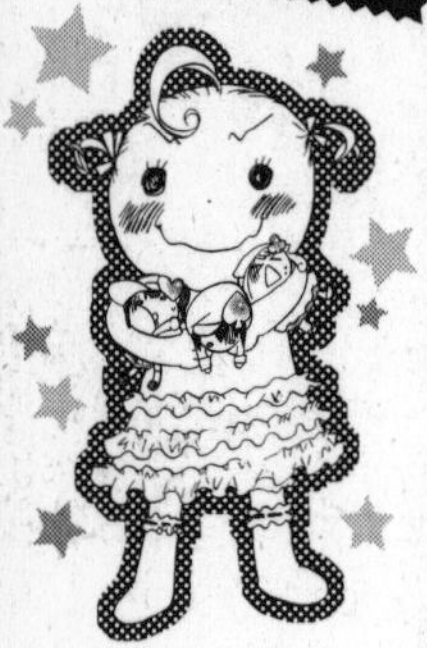

Ami Hinamori

Birthday: 3/21
Blood Type: O
Sign: Aries

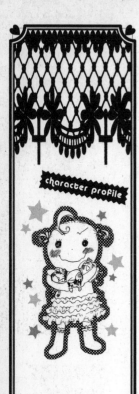

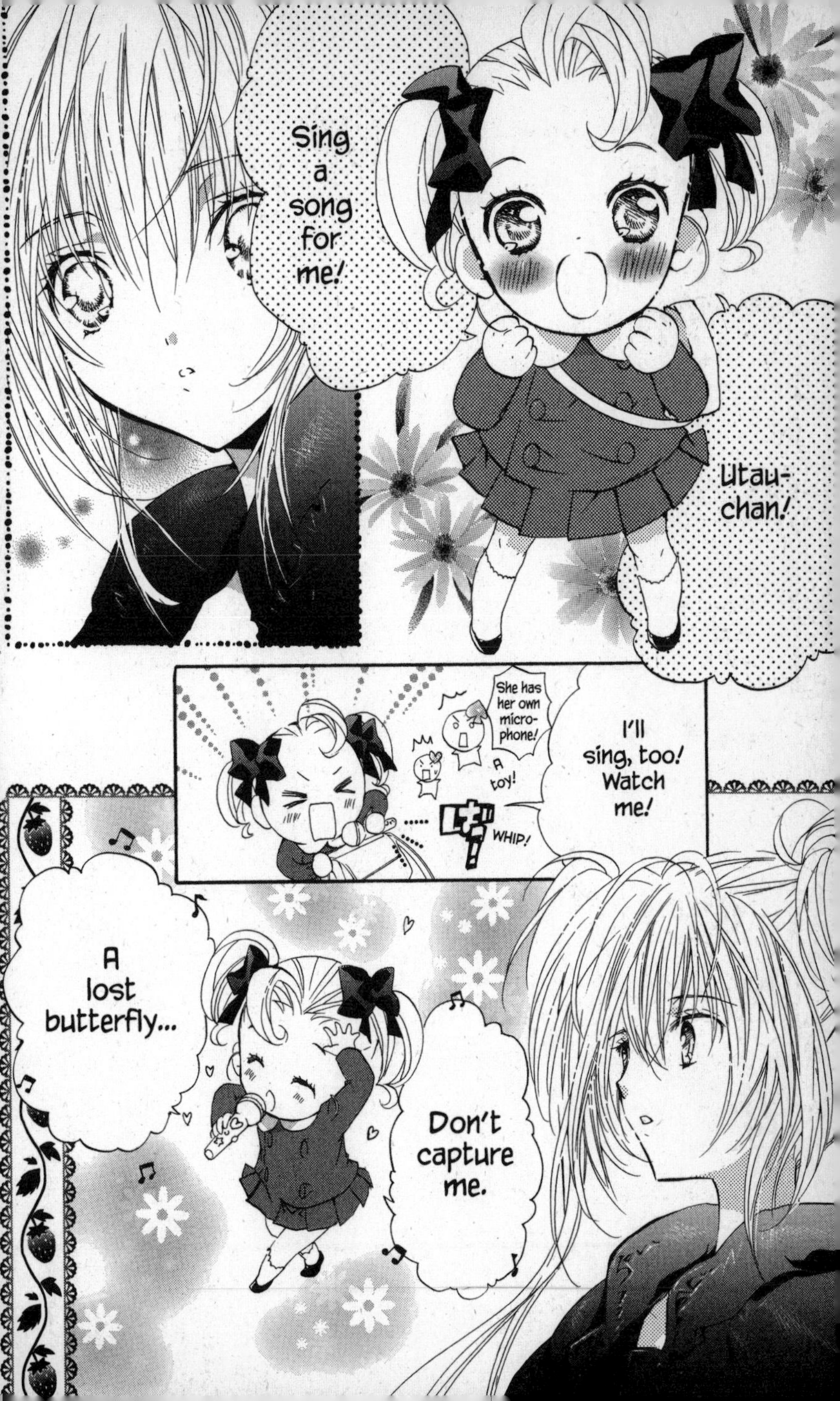
Utau-chan!
Sing a song for me!
I'll sing, too! Watch me!
She has her own microphone!
A toy!
WHIP!
A lost butterfly...
Don't capture me.

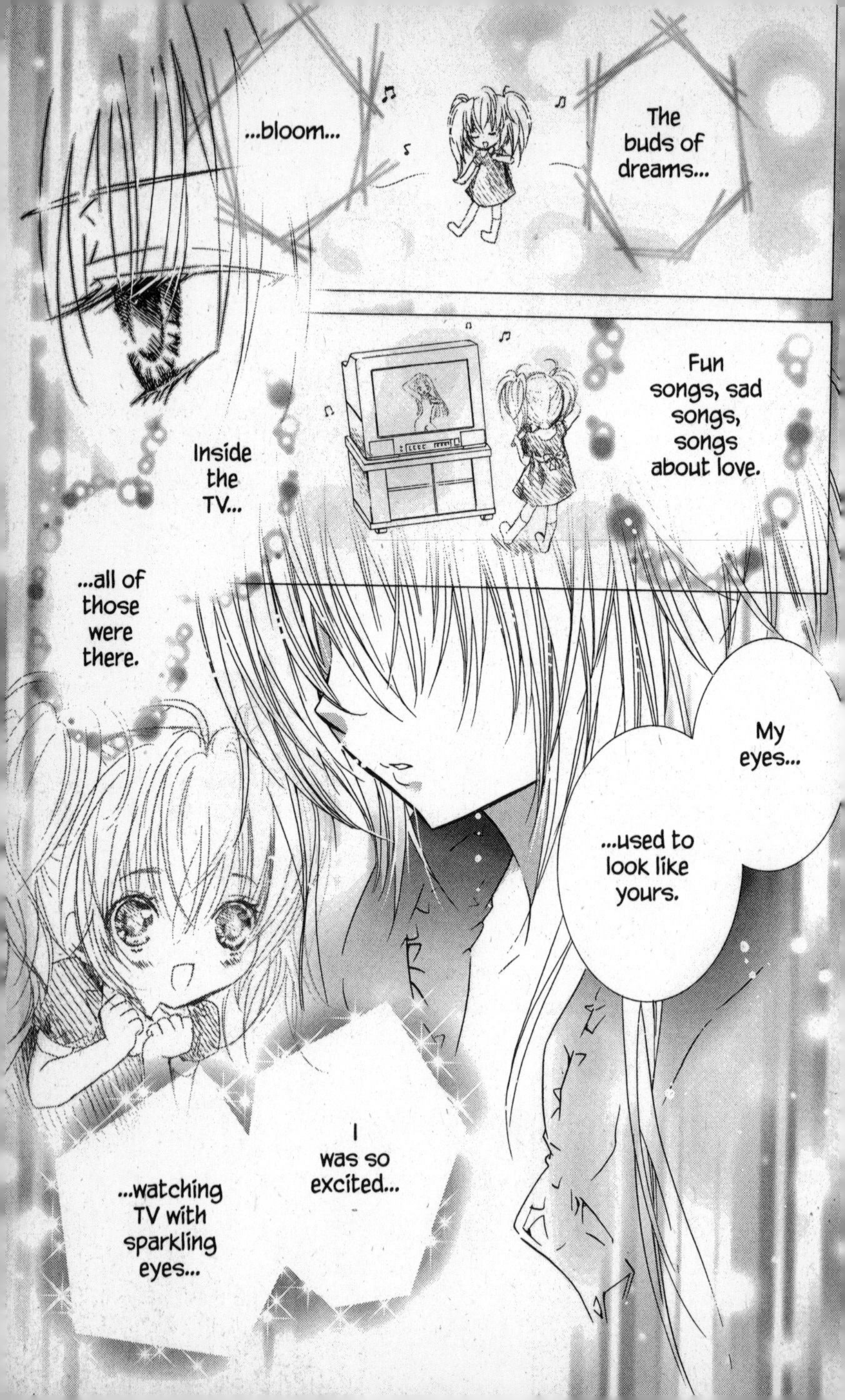
The buds of dreams...
...bloom...
Fun songs, sad songs, songs about love.
Inside the TV...
...all of those were there.
My eyes...
...used to look like yours.
I was so excited...
...watching TV with sparkling eyes...

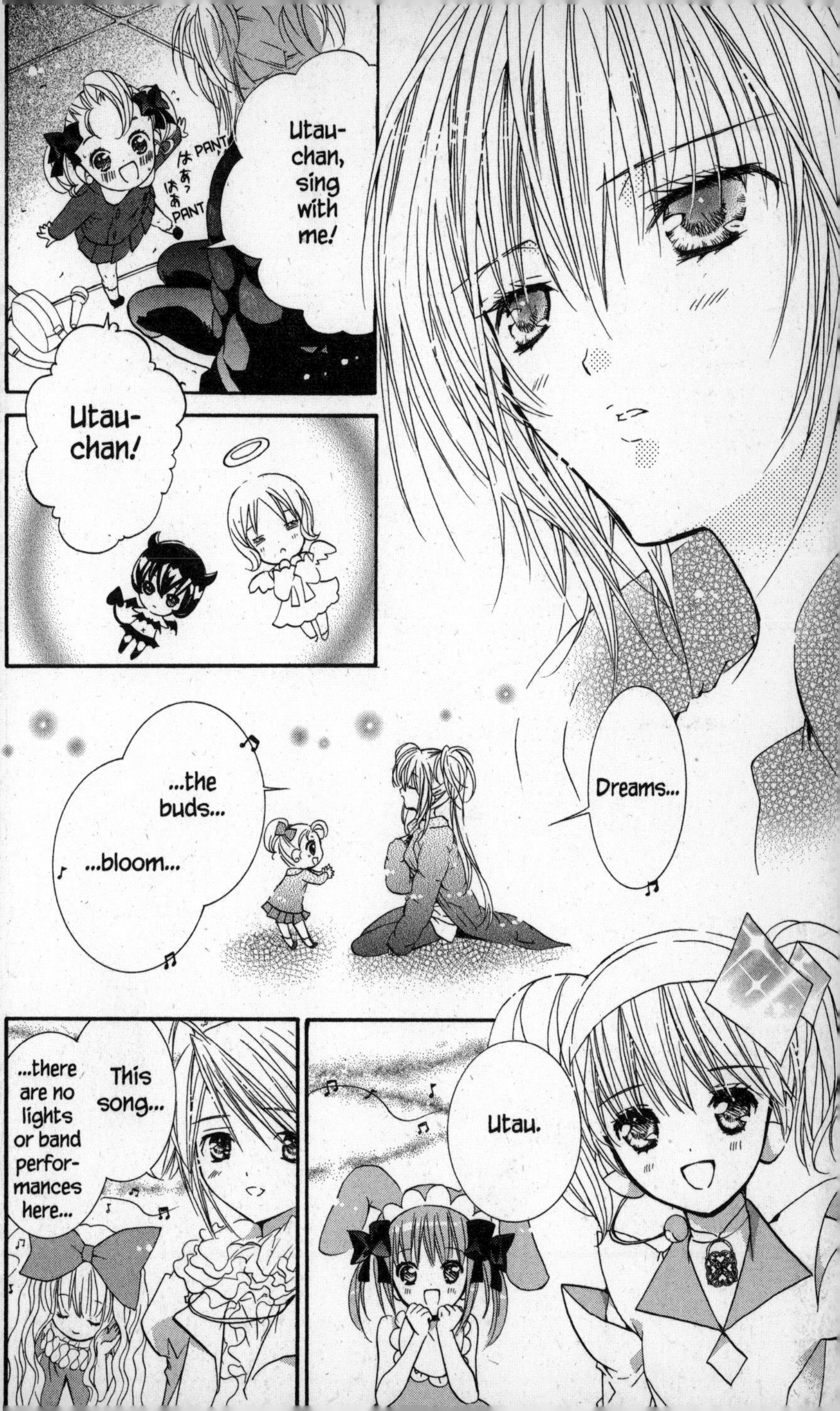

Utau-chan, sing with me!
はあっ PANT
はあ PANT
Utau-chan!
Dreams...
...the buds...
...bloom...
Utau.
This song...
...there are no lights or band performances here...

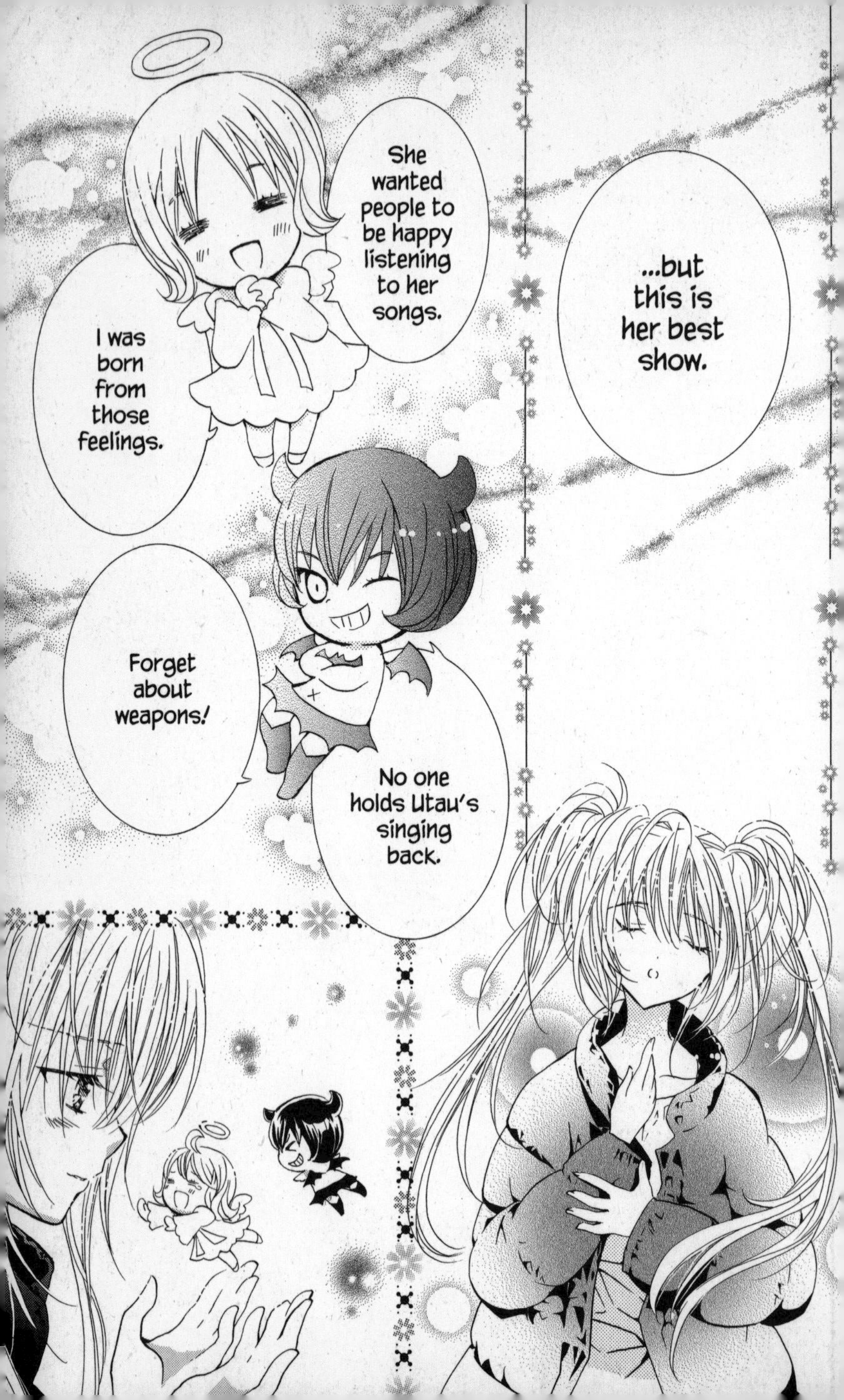
...but this is her best show.
She wanted people to be happy listening to her songs.
I was born from those feelings.
Forget about weapons!
No one holds Utau's singing back.

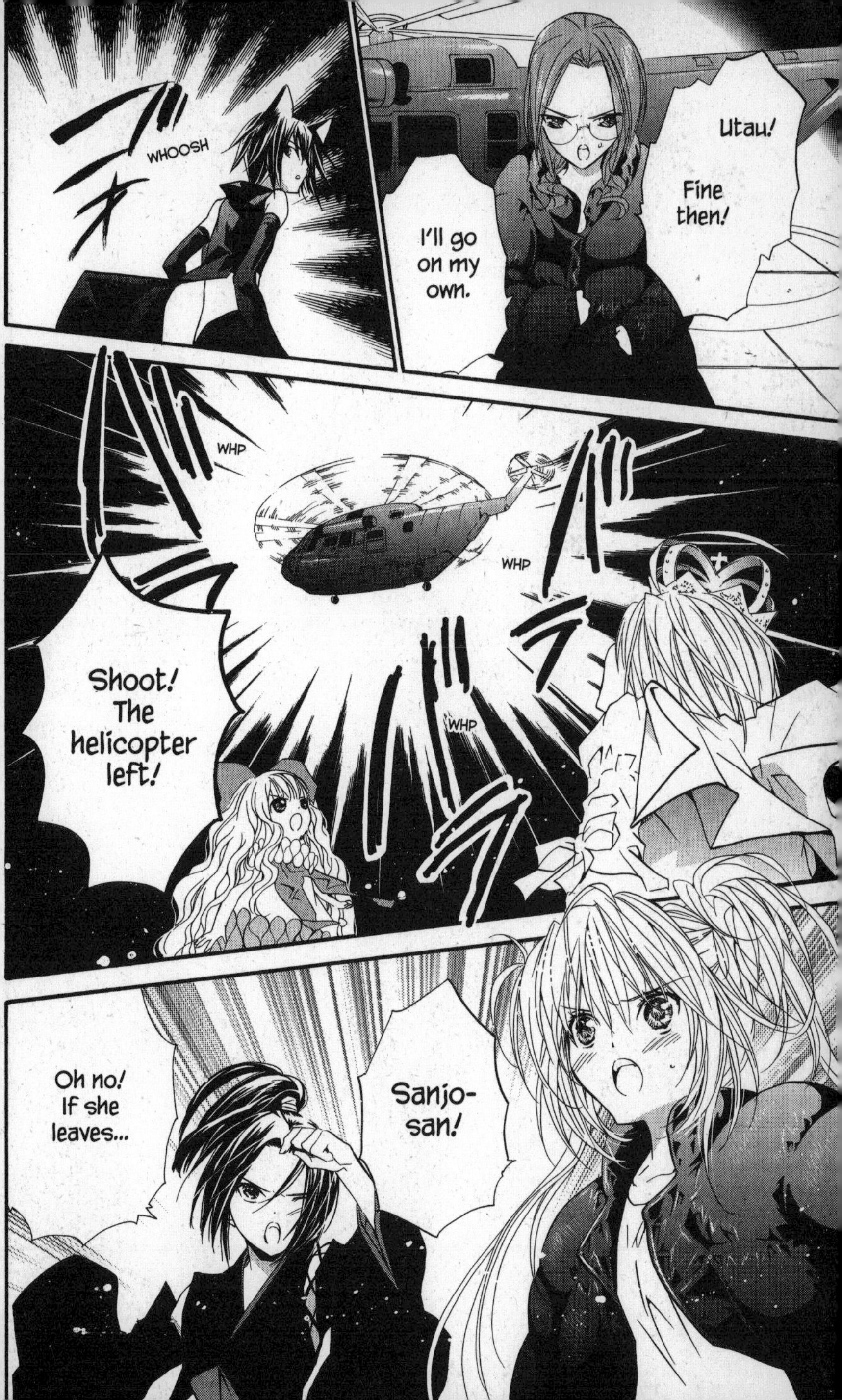
Utau!
Fine then!
I'll go on my own.
WHOOSH
WHP
WHP
WHP
Shoot! The helicopter left!
Sanjo-san!
Oh no! If she leaves...

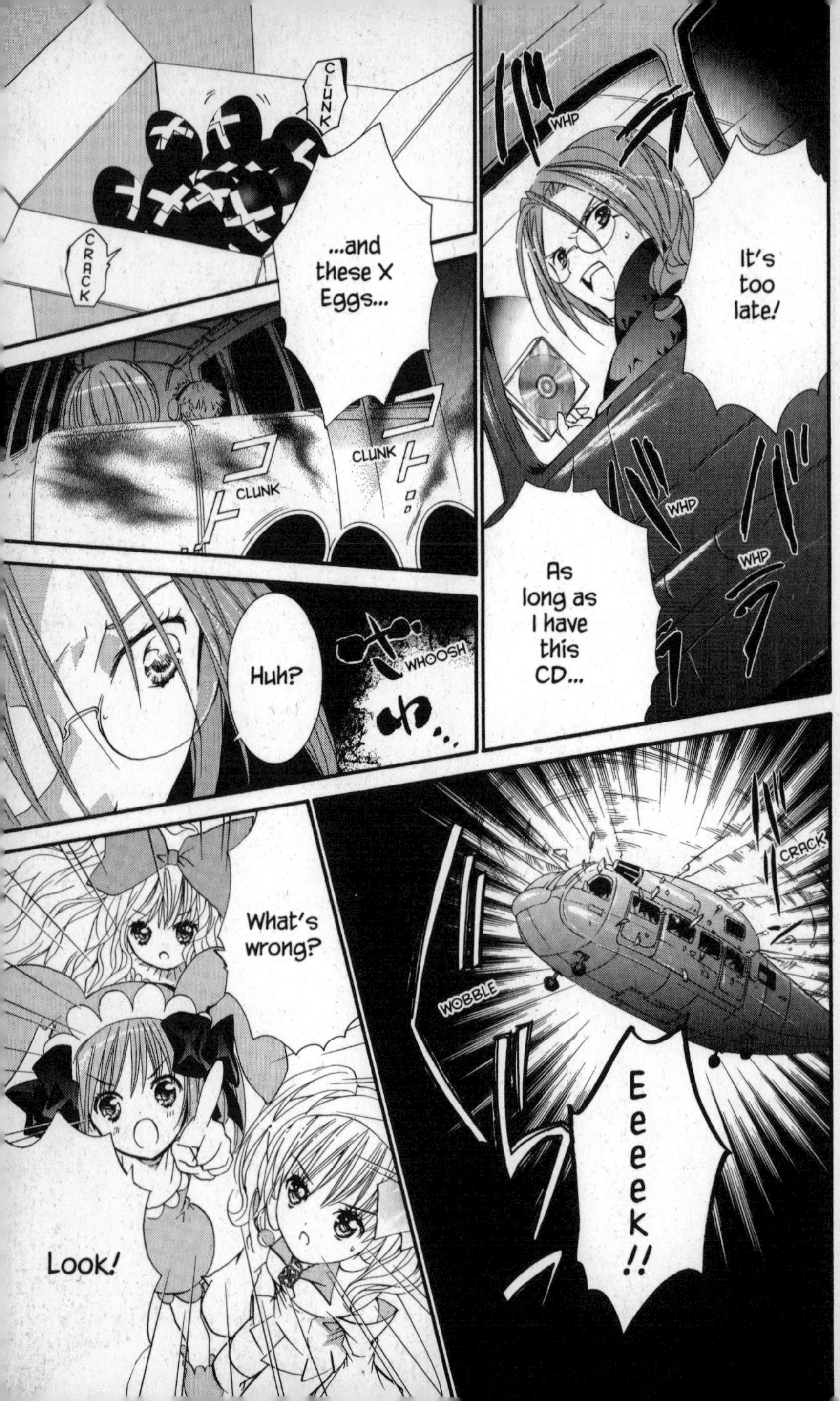
WHP
It's too late!
WHP
WHP
As long as I have this CD...
CLUNK
...and these X Eggs...
CRACK
CLUNK
CLUNK
WHOOSH
Huh?
CRACK
WOBBLE
Eeeek!!
What's wrong?
Look!

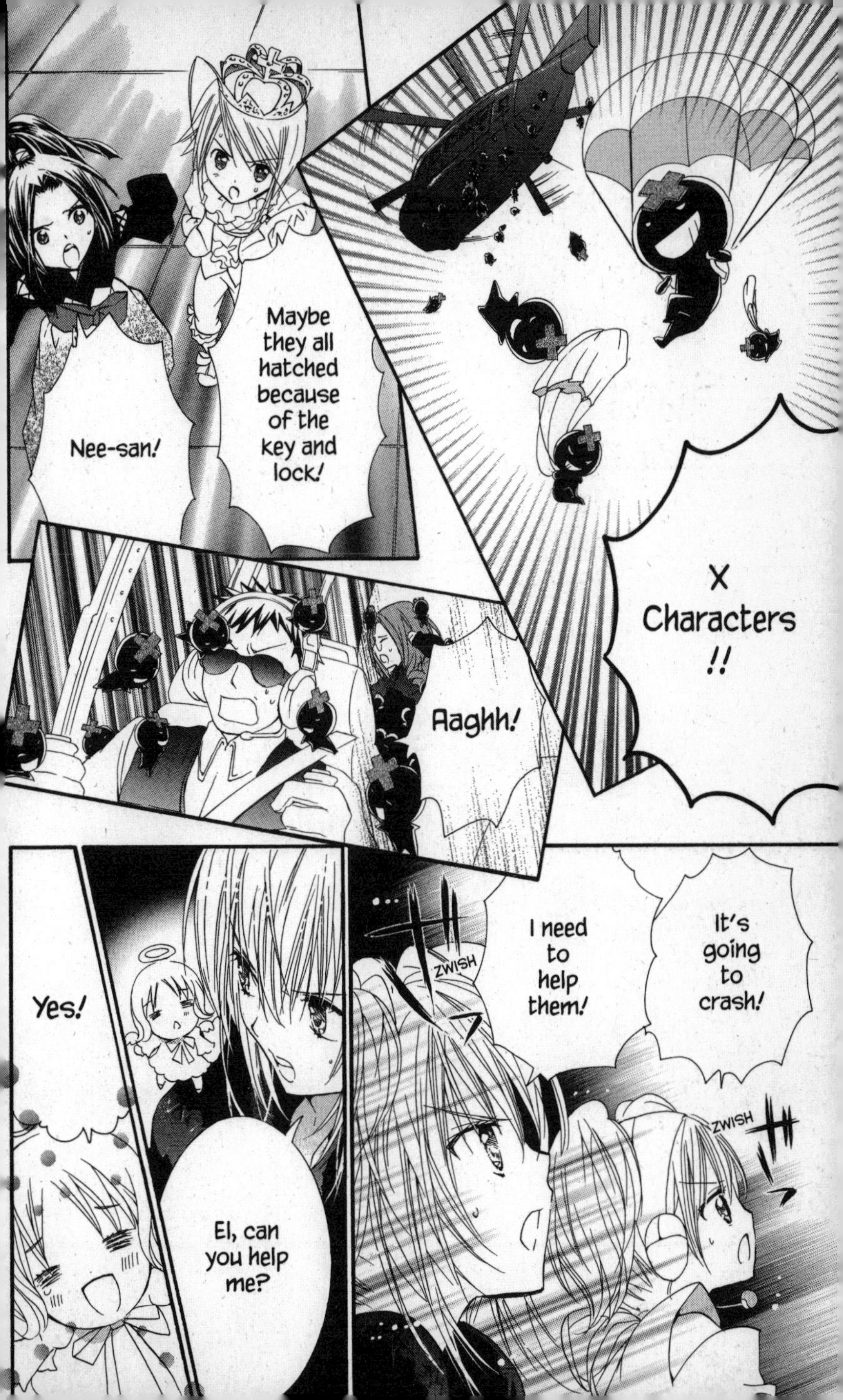

X Characters!!
Maybe they all hatched because of the key and lock!
Nee-san!
Aaghh!
It's going to crash!
I need to help them!
ZWISH
ZWISH
El, can you help me?
Yes!

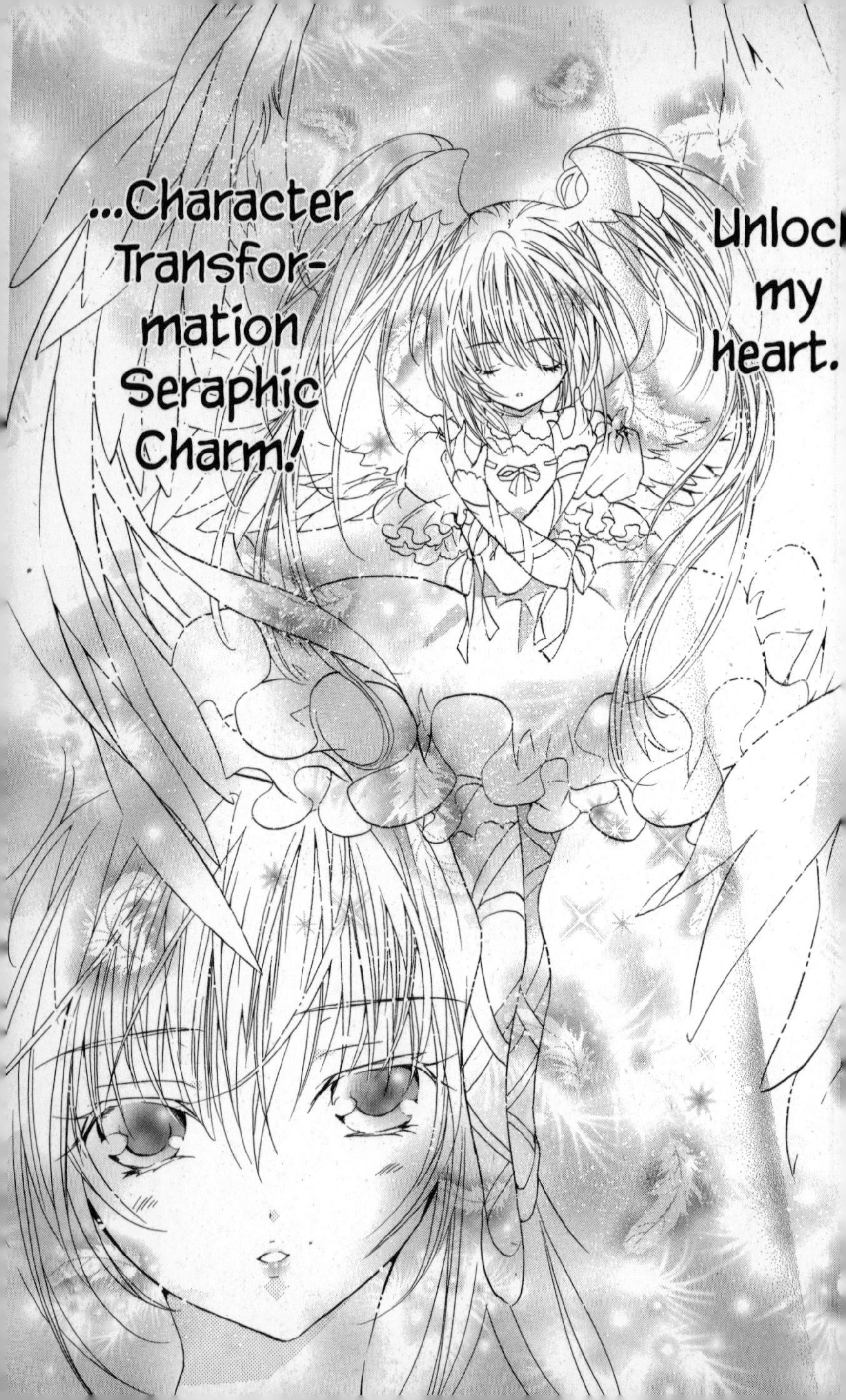
Unlock my heart.
...Character Transformation Seraphic Charm!

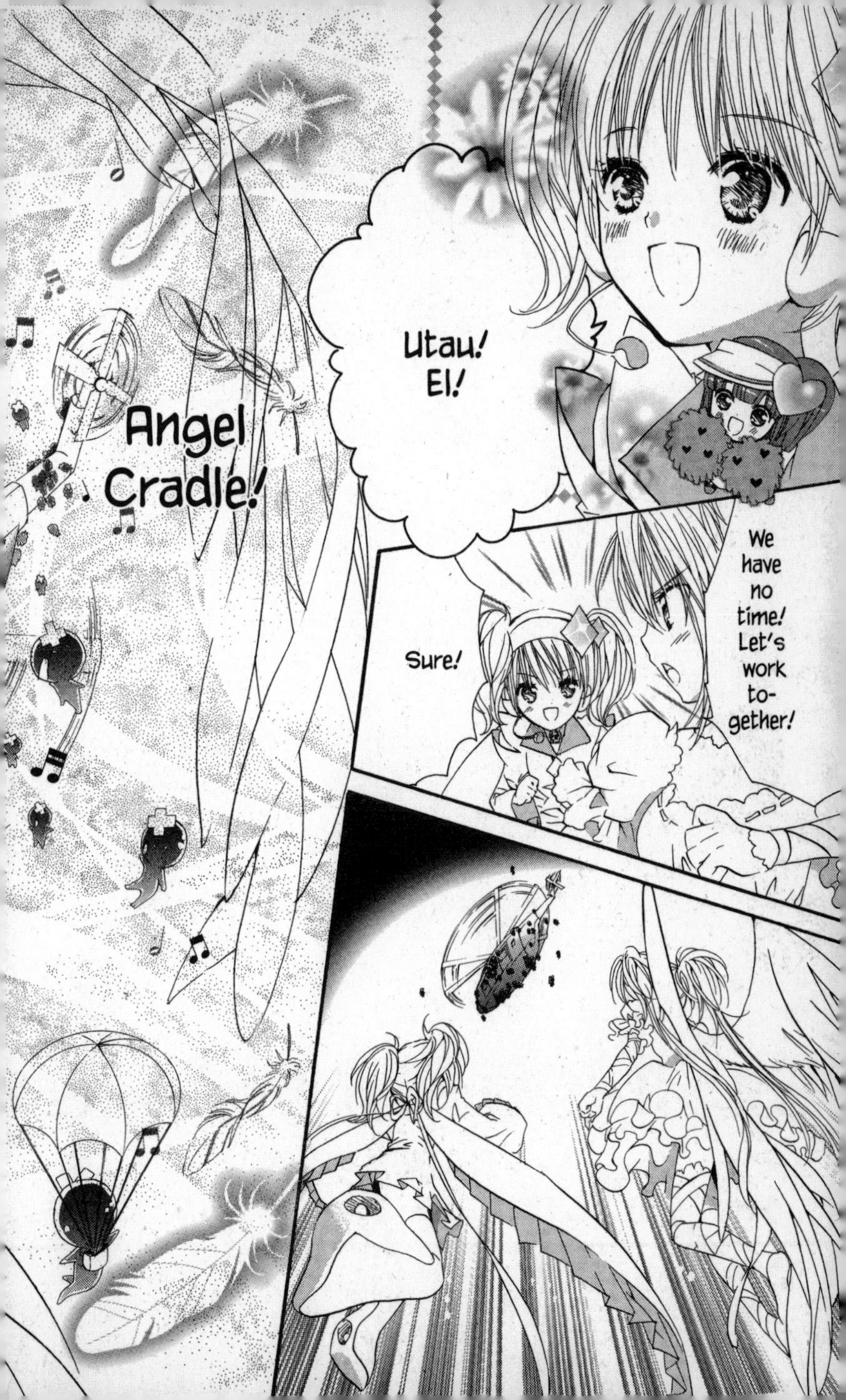
Utau! El!
We have no time! Let's work together!
Sure!
Angel Cradle!

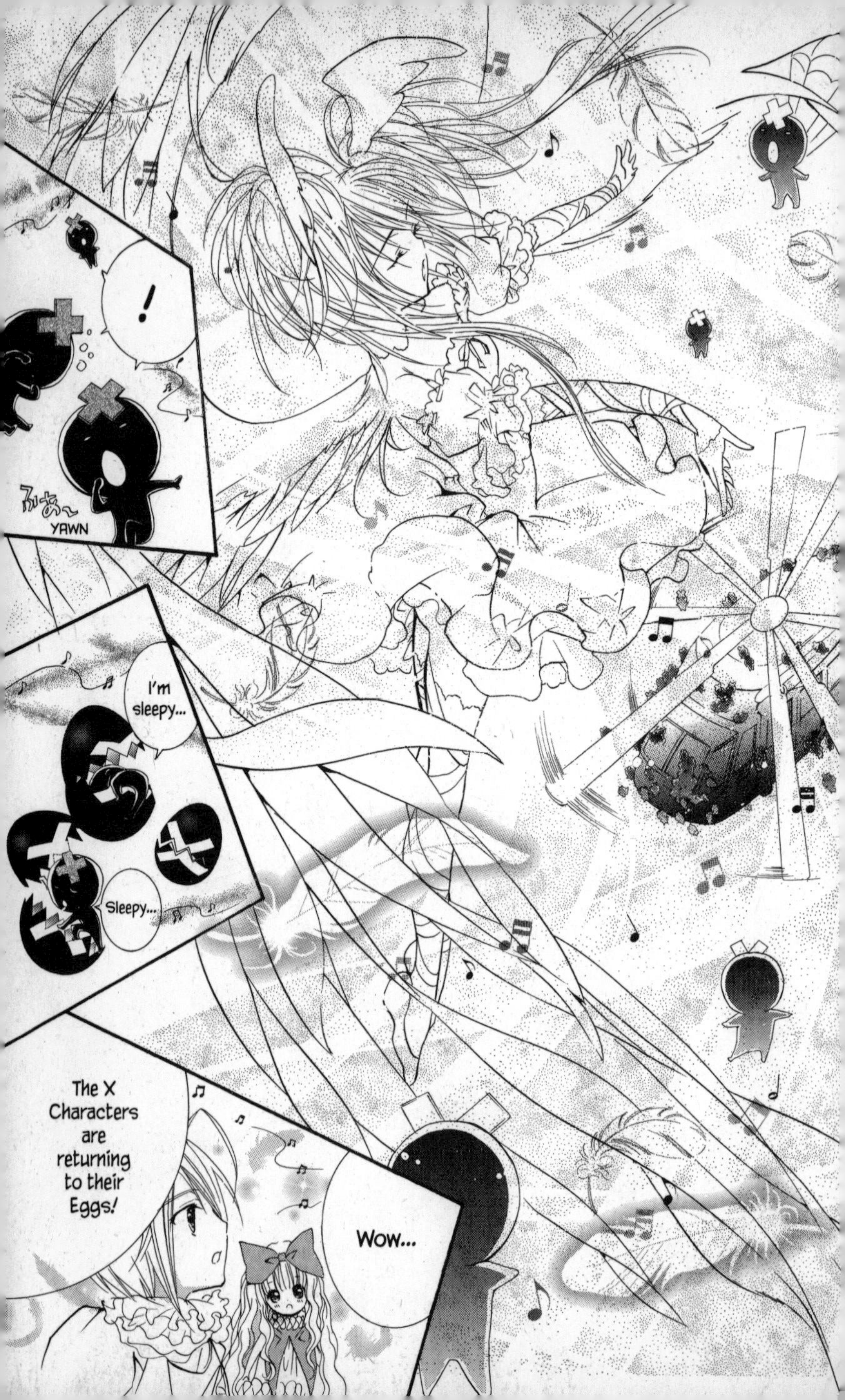
!
ふあ～
YAWN
I'm sleepy...
Sleepy...
Wow...
The X Characters are returning to their Eggs!

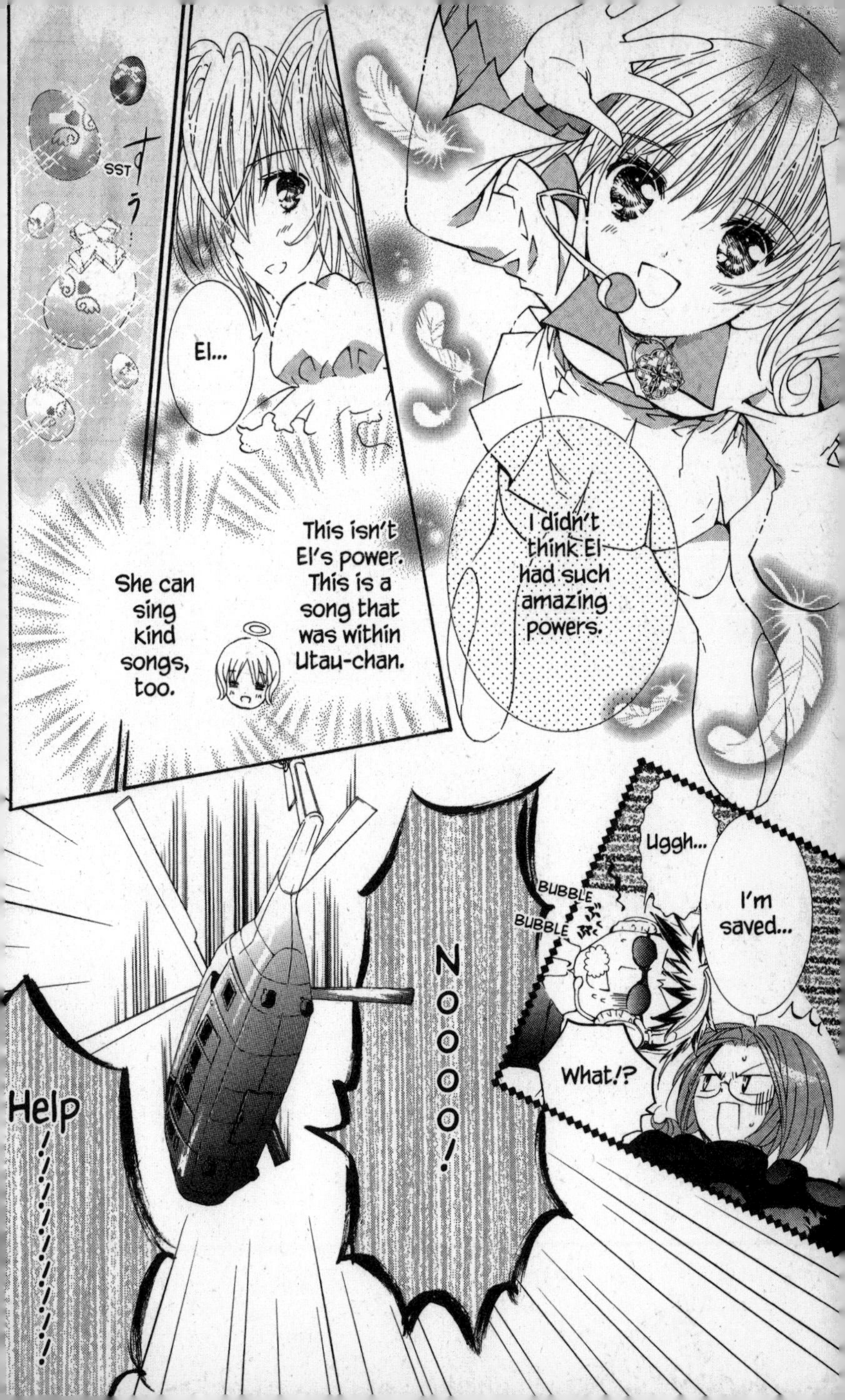
I didn't think El had such amazing powers.
El...
SST
This isn't El's power. This is a song that was within Utau-chan.
She can sing kind songs, too.
I'm saved...
Uggh...
BUBBLE
BUBBLE
What!?
NOOOOO!
Help!!!!!!!!!!!

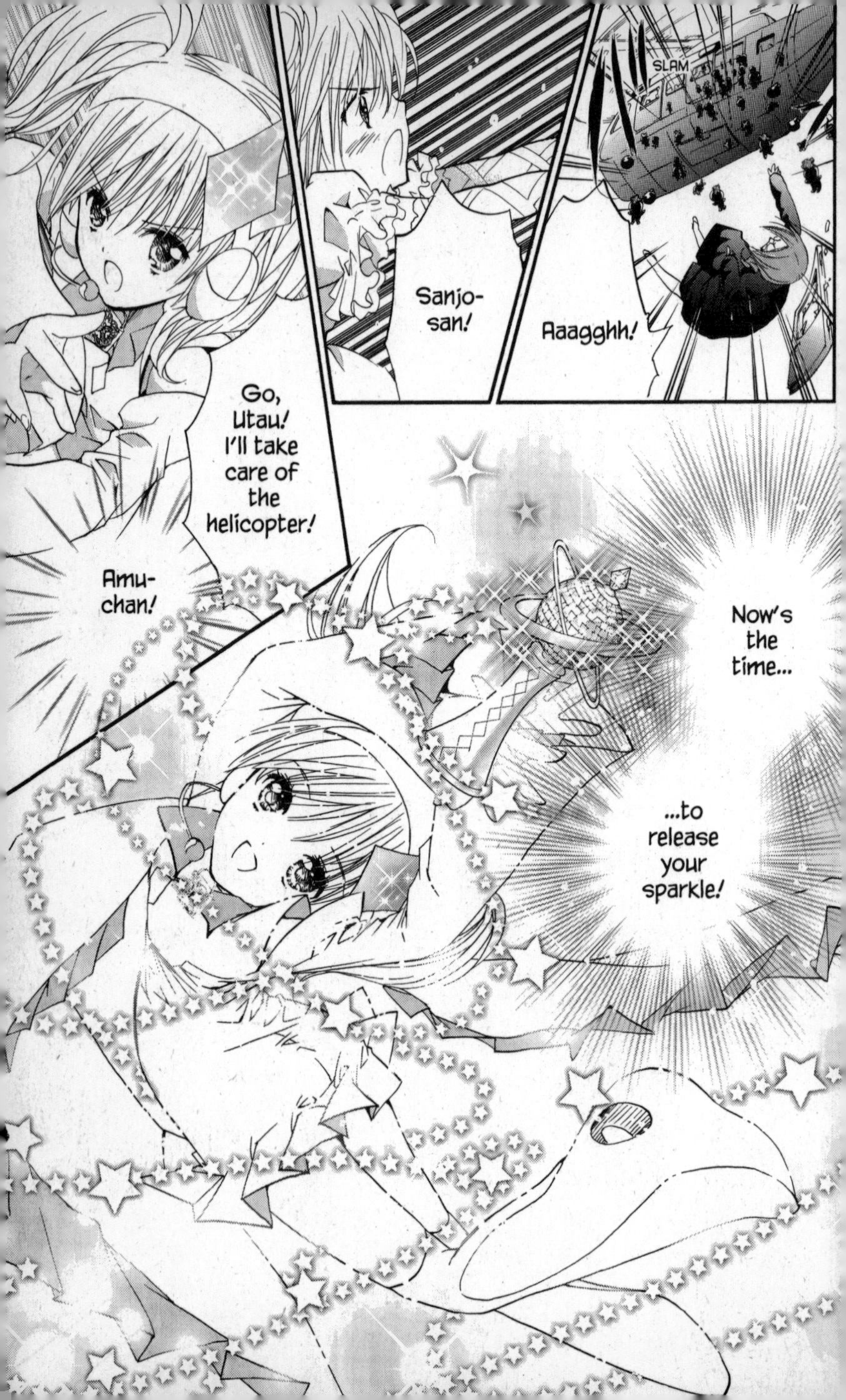
SLAM
Aaagghh!
Sanjo-san!
Go, Utau! I'll take care of the helicopter!
Amu-chan!
Now's the time...
...to release your sparkle!

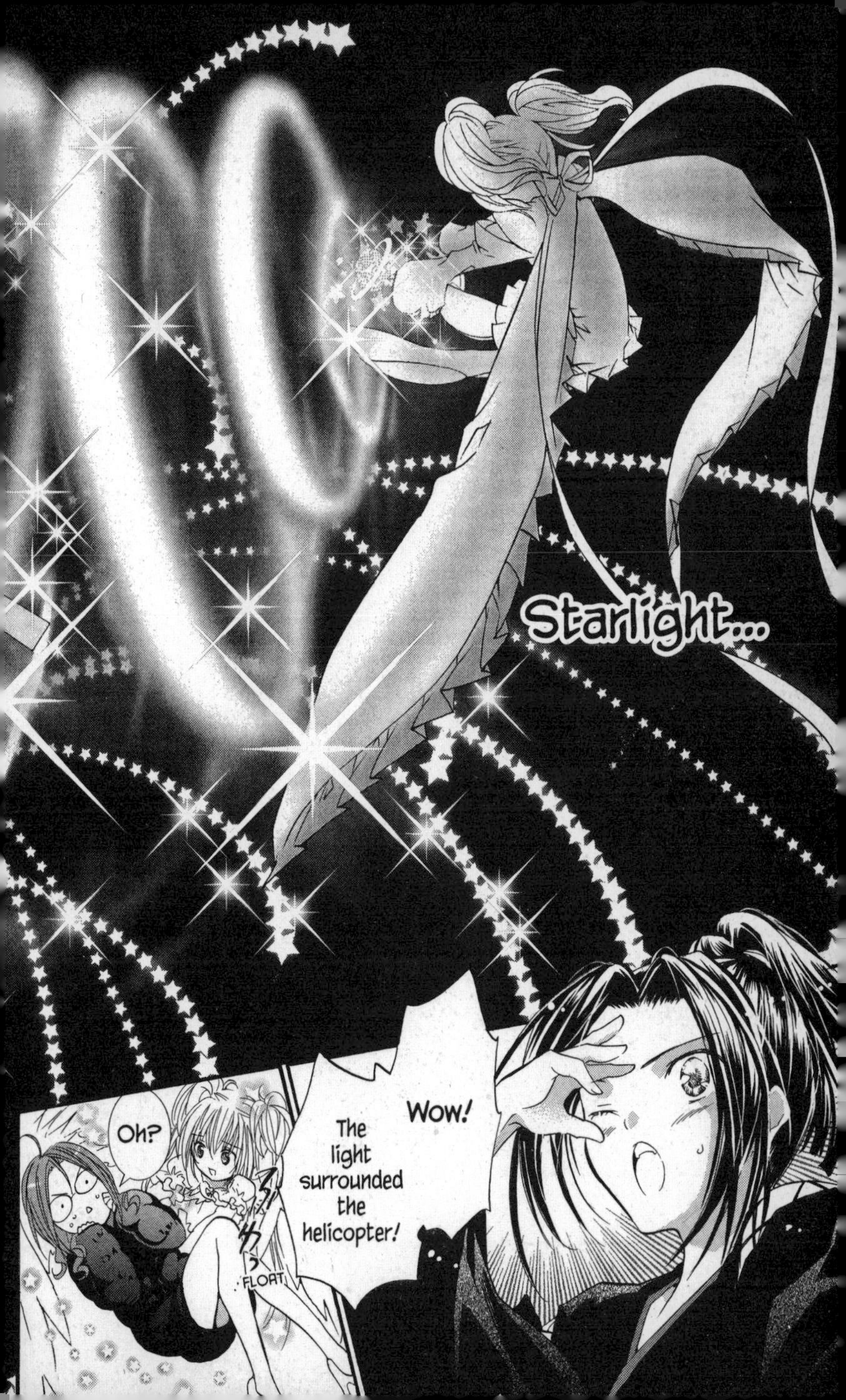
Starlight...
Wow!
The light surrounded the helicopter!
Oh?
FLOAT

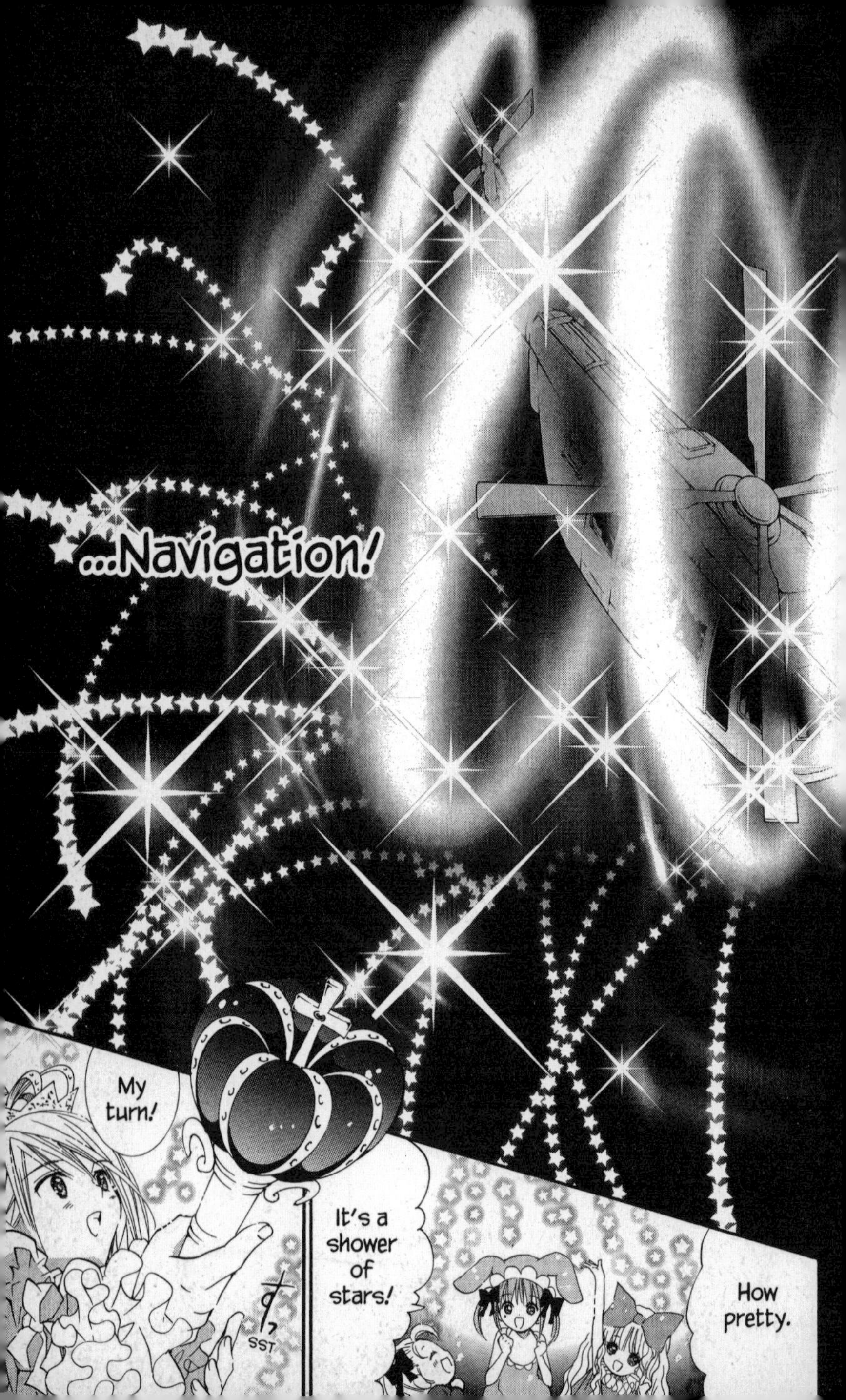

...Navigation!
How pretty.
It's a shower of stars!
My turn!
SST

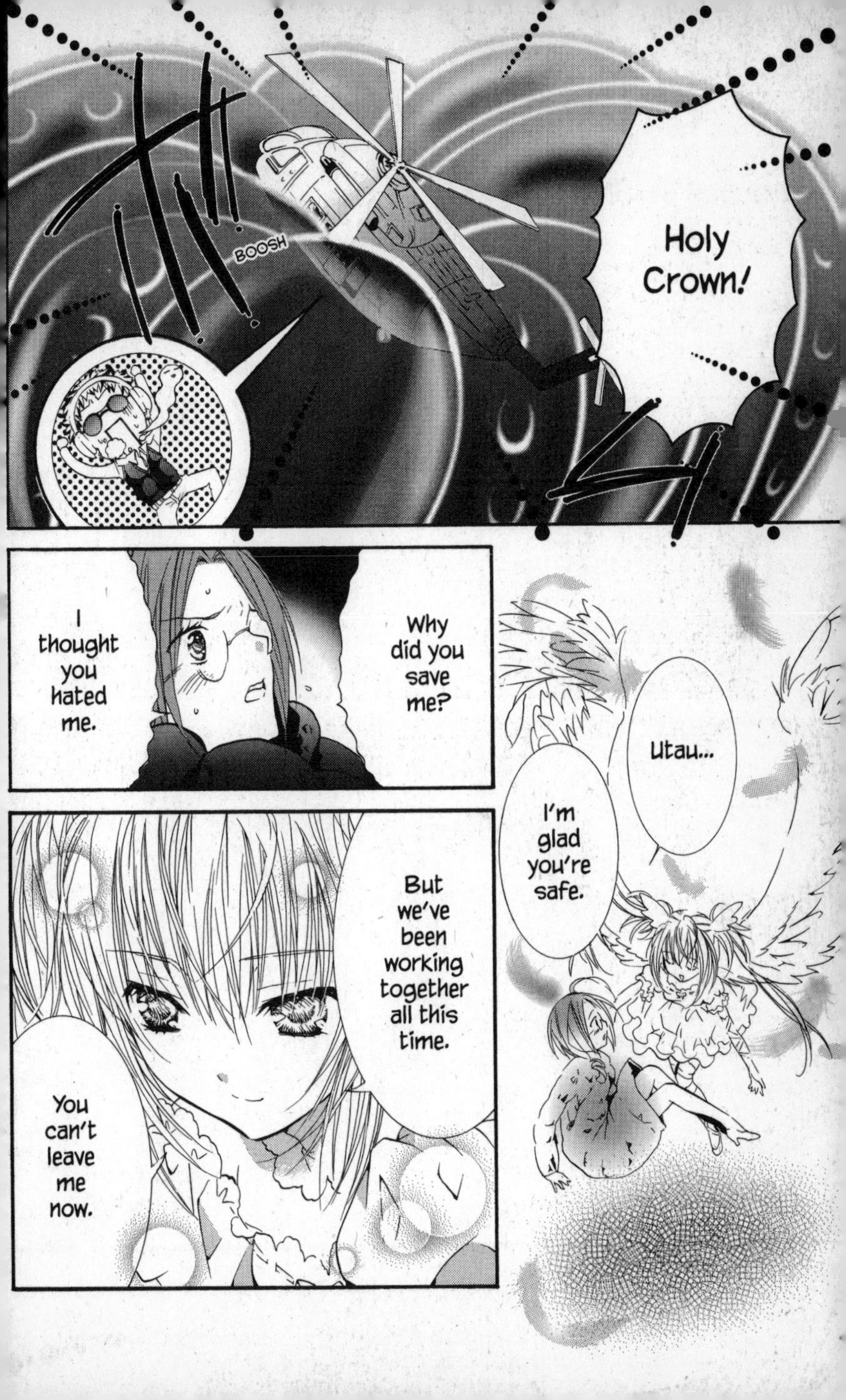
Holy Crown!
BOOSH
Utau...
I'm glad you're safe.
Why did you save me?
I thought you hated me.
But we've been working together all this time.
You can't leave me now.

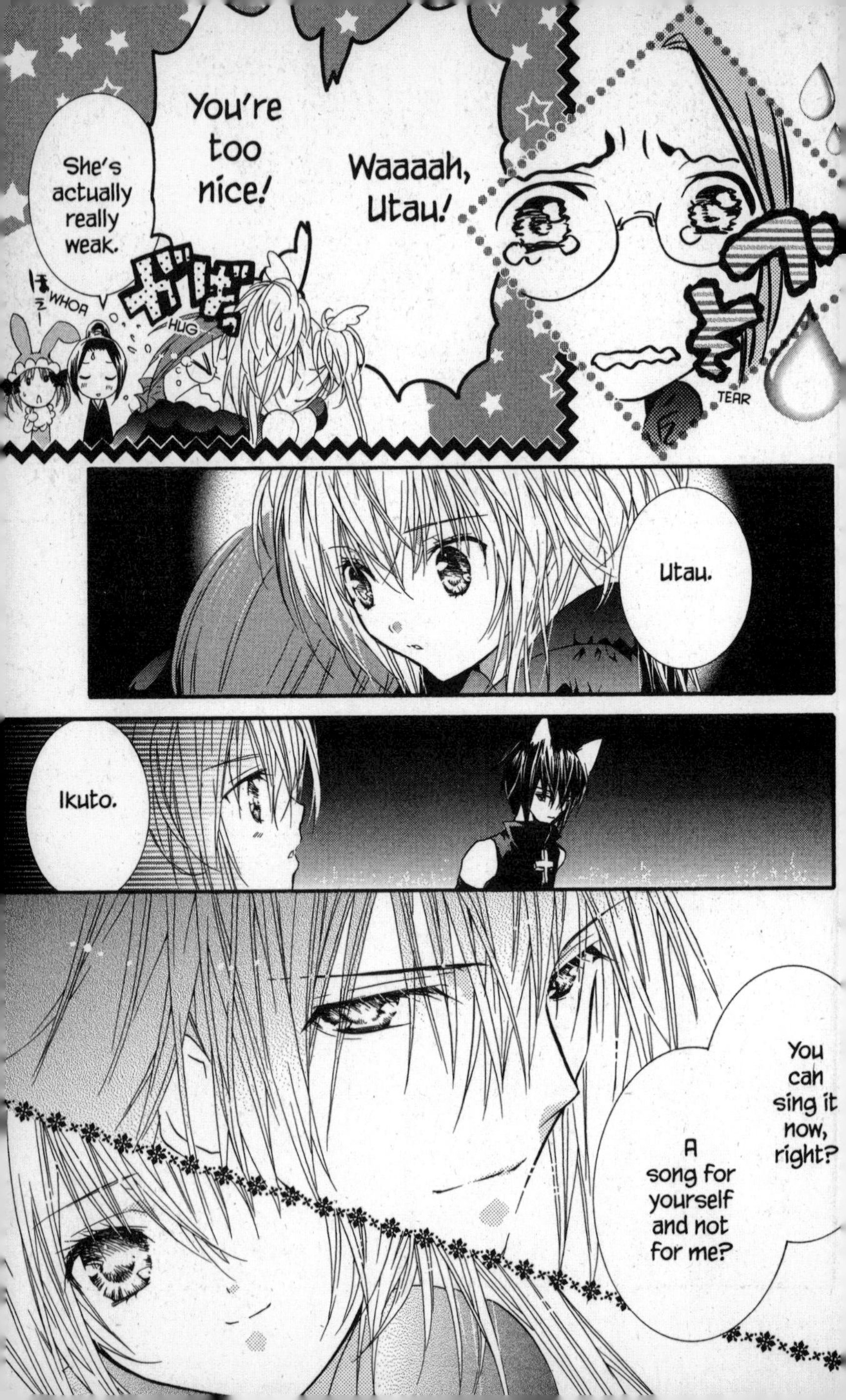
TEAR
Waaaah, Utau!
You're too nice!
She's actually really weak.
HUG
WHOA
Utau.
Ikuto.
You can sing it now, right?
A song for yourself and not for me?

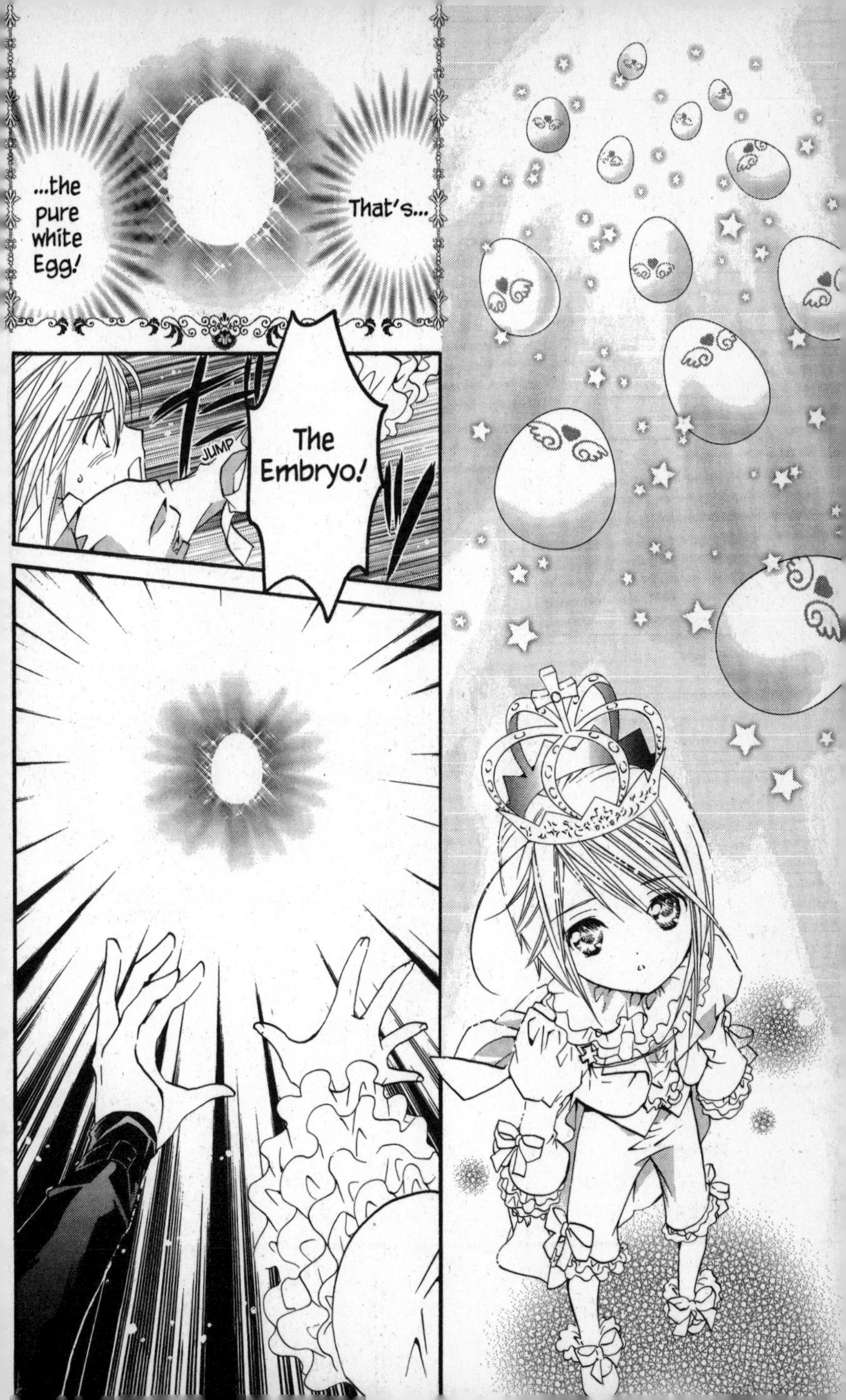
That's...
...the pure white Egg!
The Embryo!
JUMP

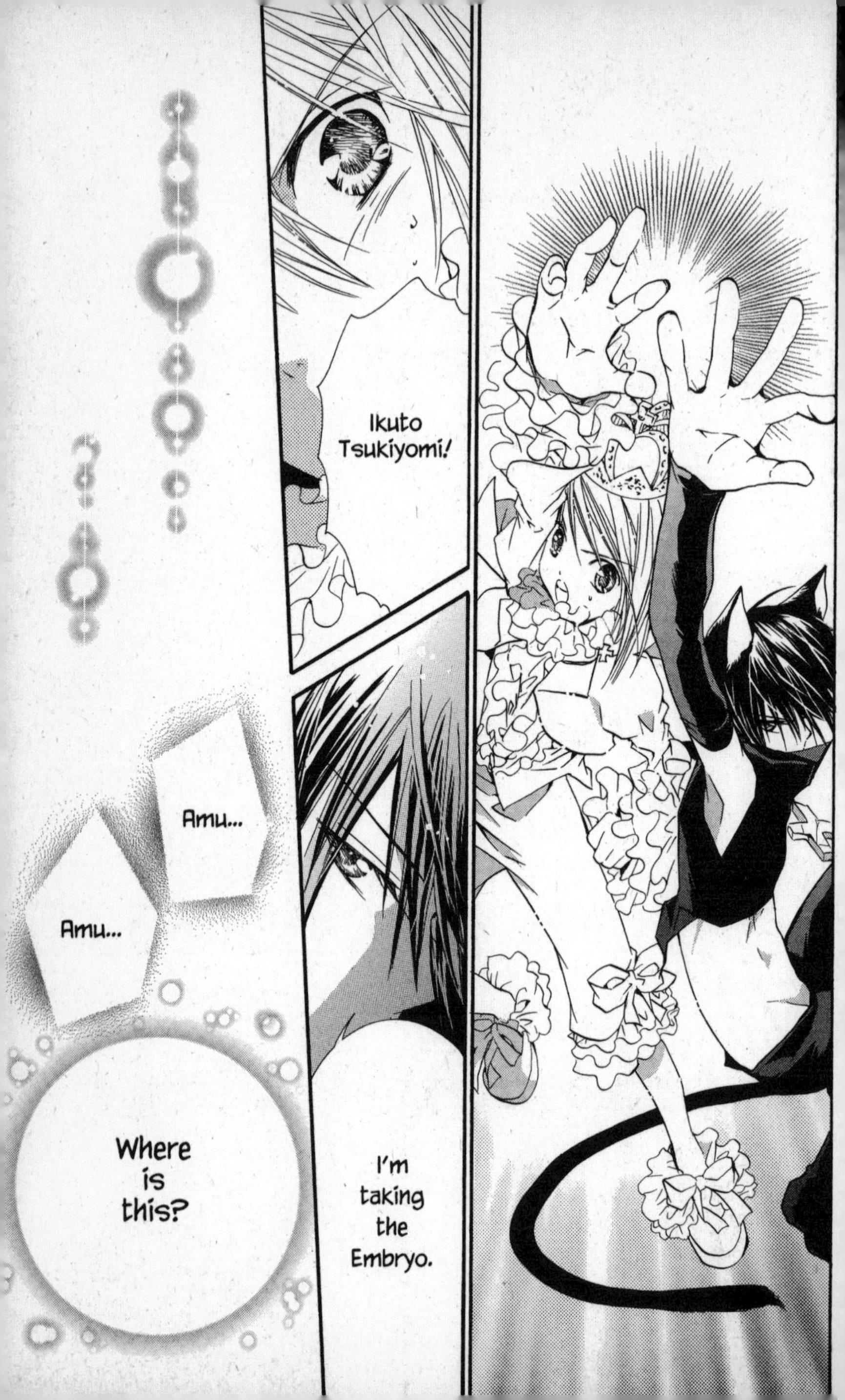
Ikuto Tsukiyomi!
I'm taking the Embryo.
Amu...
Amu...
Where is this?

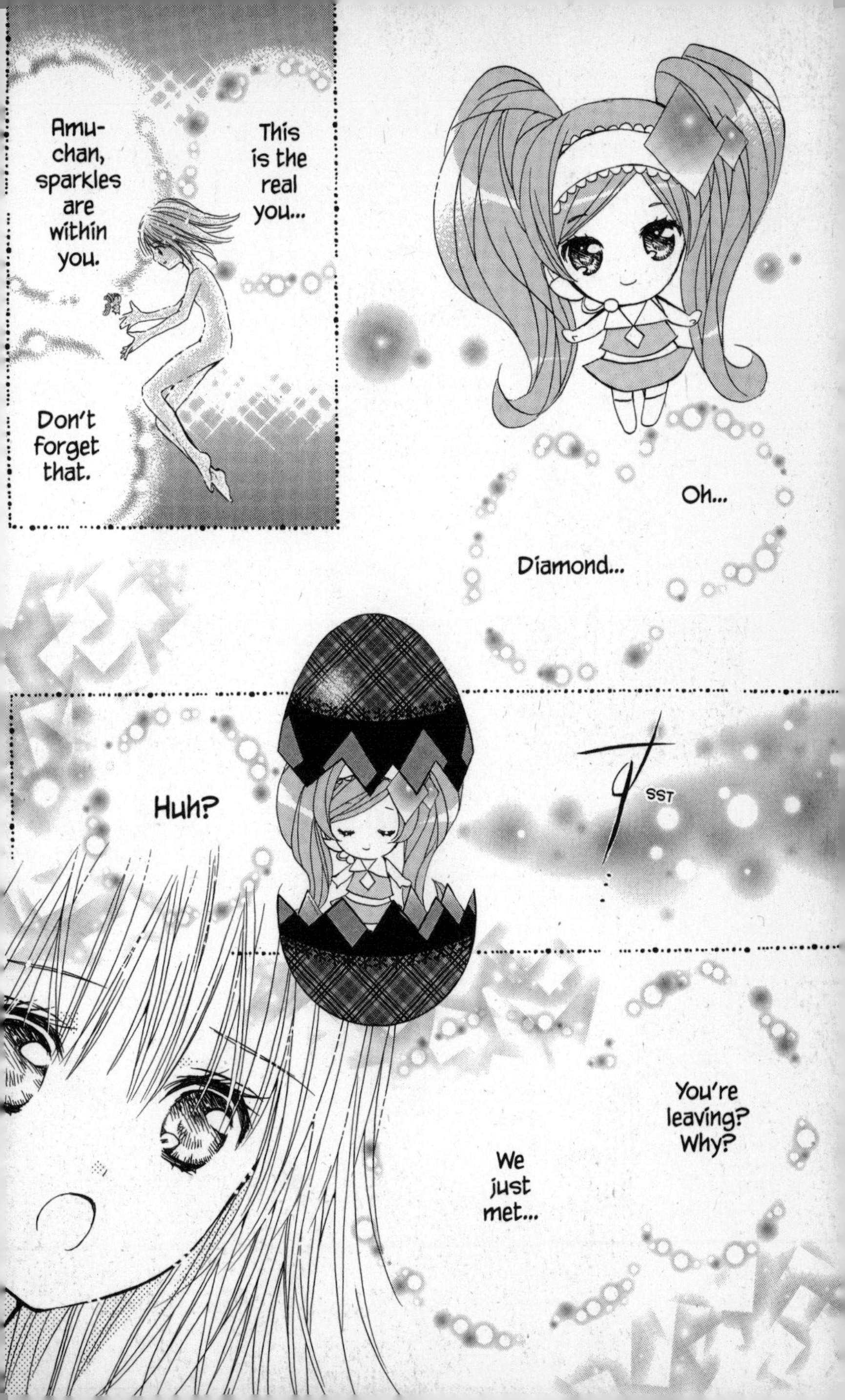

Oh...
Diamond...
This is the real you...
Amu-chan, sparkles are within you.
Don't forget that.
SST
Huh?
You're leaving? Why?
We just met...

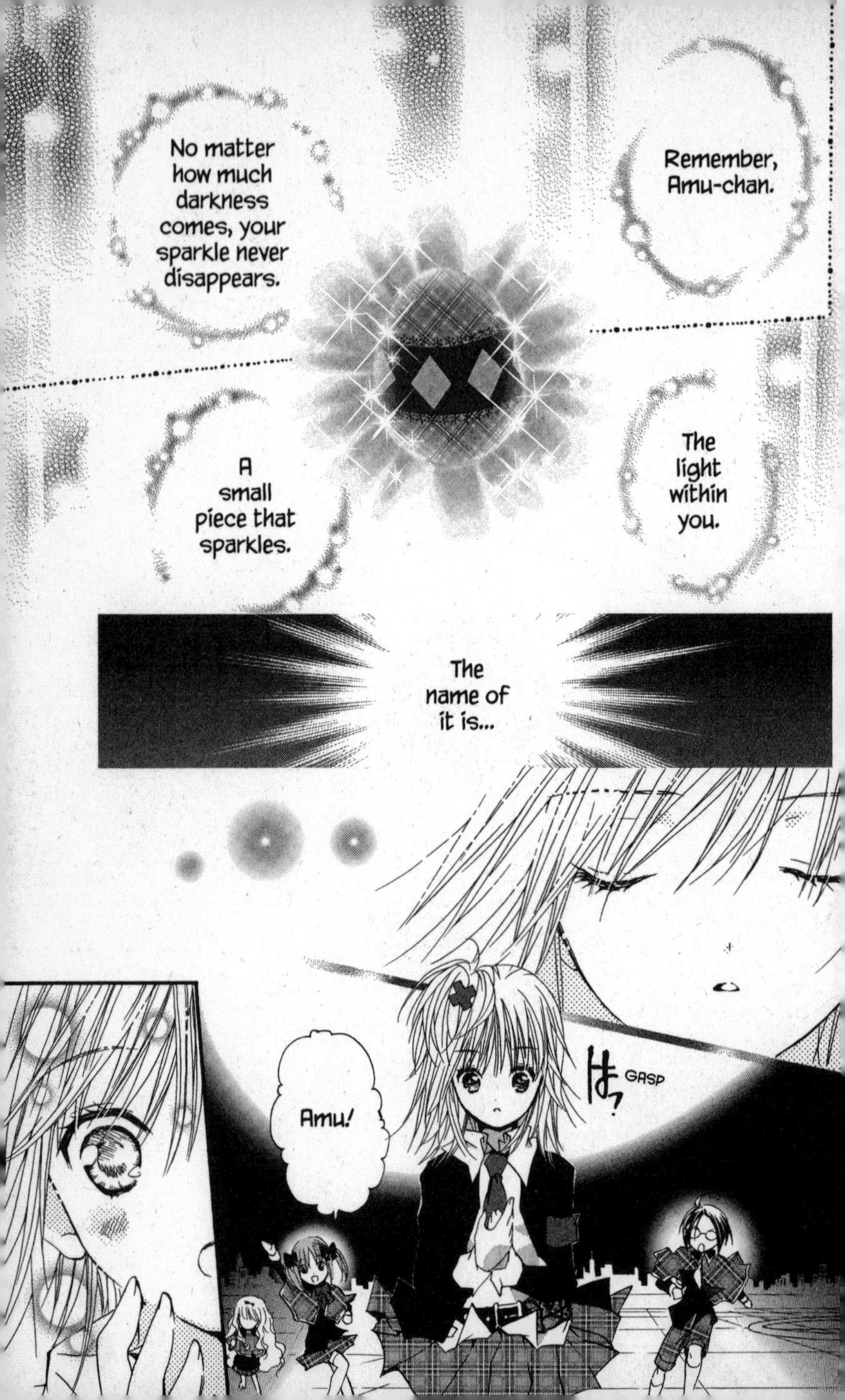
Remember, Amu-chan.
No matter how much darkness comes, your sparkle never disappears.
The light within you.
A small piece that sparkles.
The name of it is...
は GASP
Amu!

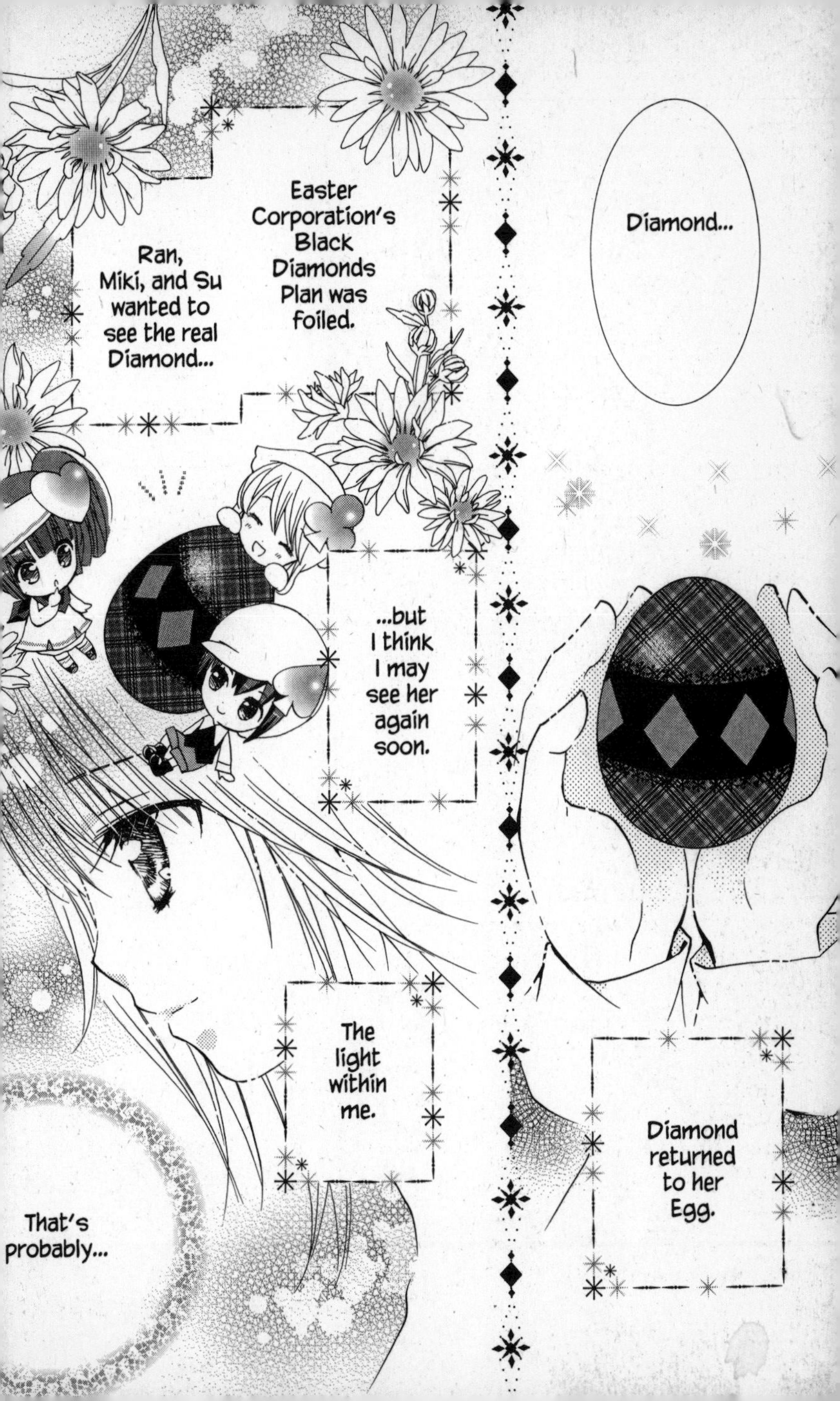
Diamond...
Diamond returned to her Egg.
Easter Corporation's Black Diamonds Plan was foiled.
Ran, Miki, and Su wanted to see the real Diamond...
...but I think I may see her again soon.
The light within me.
That's probably...

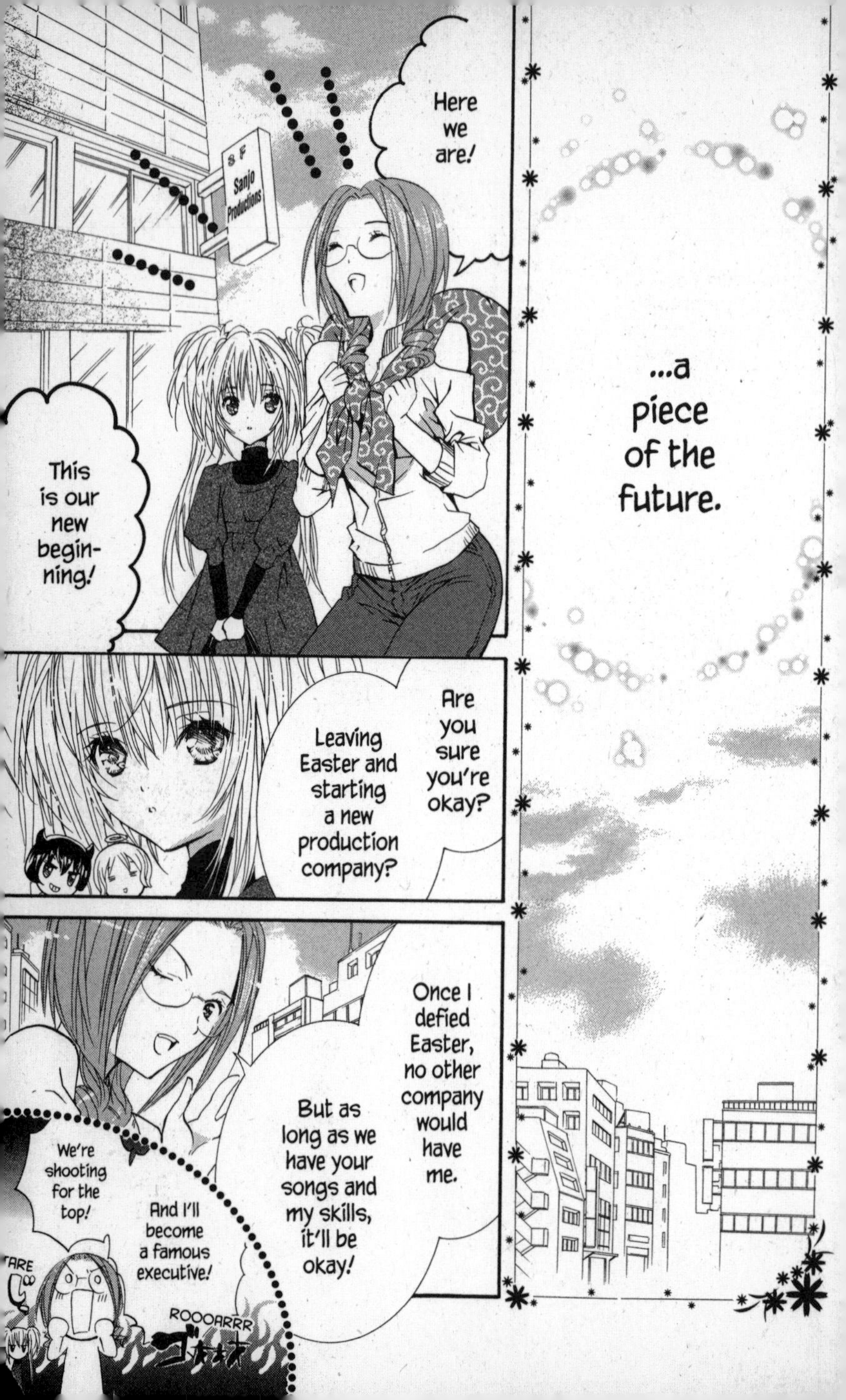
...a piece of the future.
Here we are!
3 F Sanjo Productions
This is our new beginning!
Are you sure you're okay?
Leaving Easter and starting a new production company?
Once I defied Easter, no other company would have me.
But as long as we have your songs and my skills, it'll be okay!
We're shooting for the top!
And I'll become a famous executive!
TARE
ROOOARRR

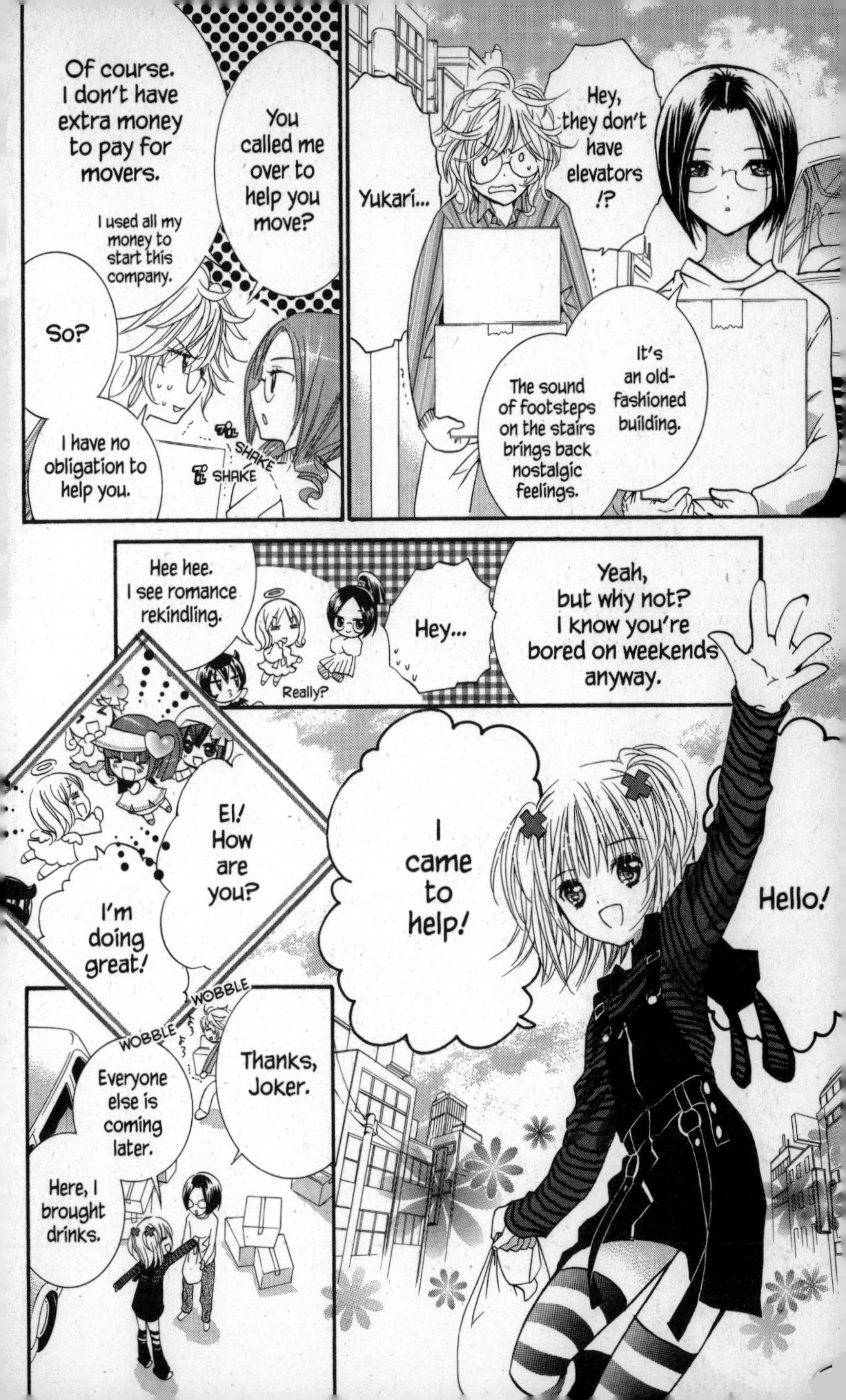
Hey, they don't have elevators !?
Yukari...
It's an old-fashioned building.
The sound of footsteps on the stairs brings back nostalgic feelings.
You called me over to help you move?
Of course. I don't have extra money to pay for movers.
I used all my money to start this company.
So?
SHAKE
SHAKE
I have no obligation to help you.
Yeah, but why not? I know you're bored on weekends anyway.
Hey...
Hee hee. I see romance rekindling.
Really?
Hello!
I came to help!
Ei! How are you?
I'm doing great!
Thanks, Joker.
WOBBLE
WOBBLE
Everyone else is coming later.
Here, I brought drinks.

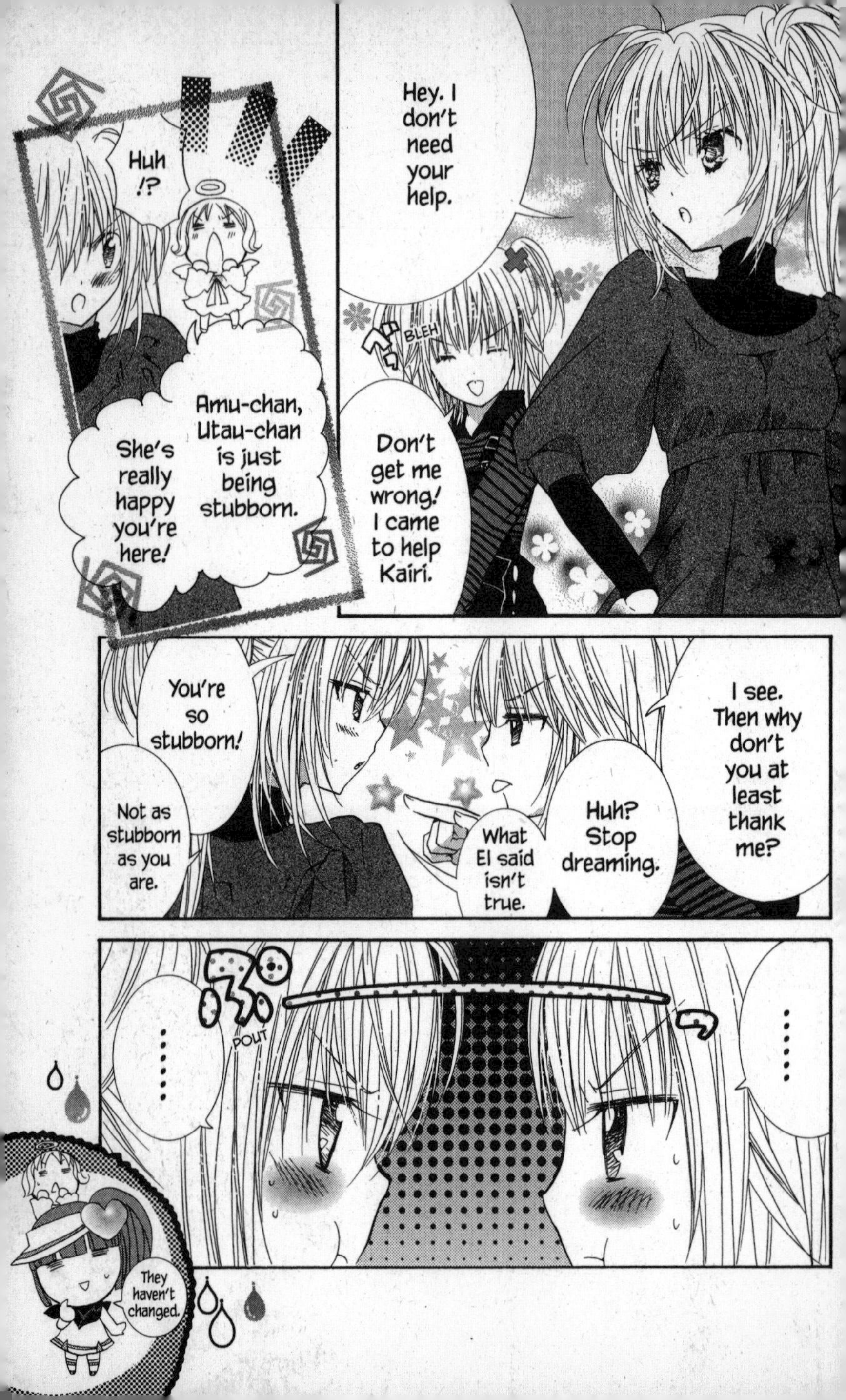
Hey. I don't need your help.
BLEH
Don't get me wrong! I came to help Kairi.
Huh!?
Amu-chan, Utau-chan is just being stubborn.
She's really happy you're here!
I see. Then why don't you at least thank me?
Huh? Stop dreaming.
What El said isn't true.
You're so stubborn!
Not as stubborn as you are.
......
POUT
......
They haven't changed.

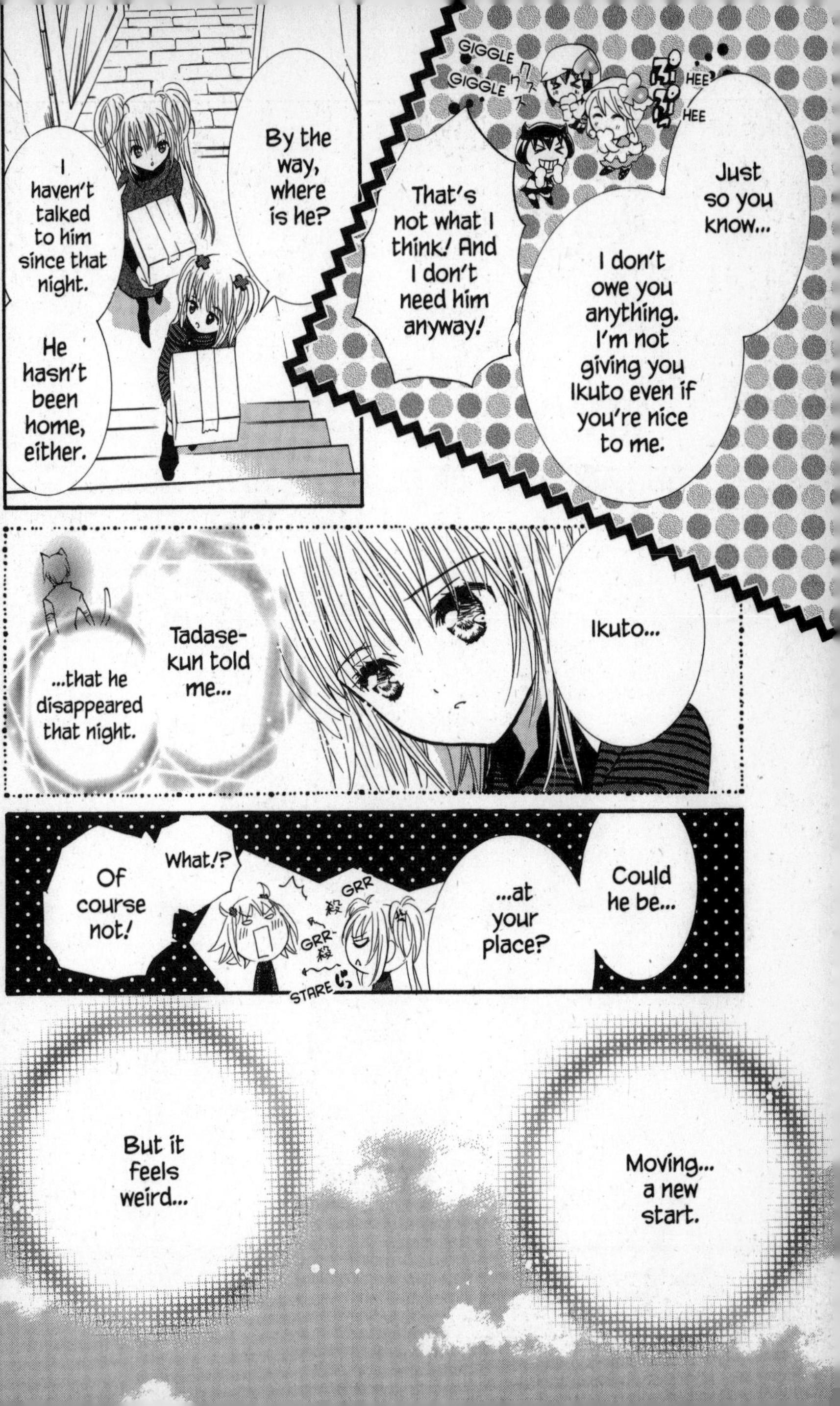
GIGGLE
GIGGLE
HEE
HEE
Just so you know...
I don't owe you anything. I'm not giving you Ikuto even if you're nice to me.
That's not what I think! And I don't need him anyway!
By the way, where is he?
I haven't talked to him since that night.
He hasn't been home, either.
Ikuto...
Tadase-kun told me...
...that he disappeared that night.
Could he be...
...at your place?
GRR
GRR-
STARE
What!?
Of course not!
Moving... a new start.
But it feels weird...

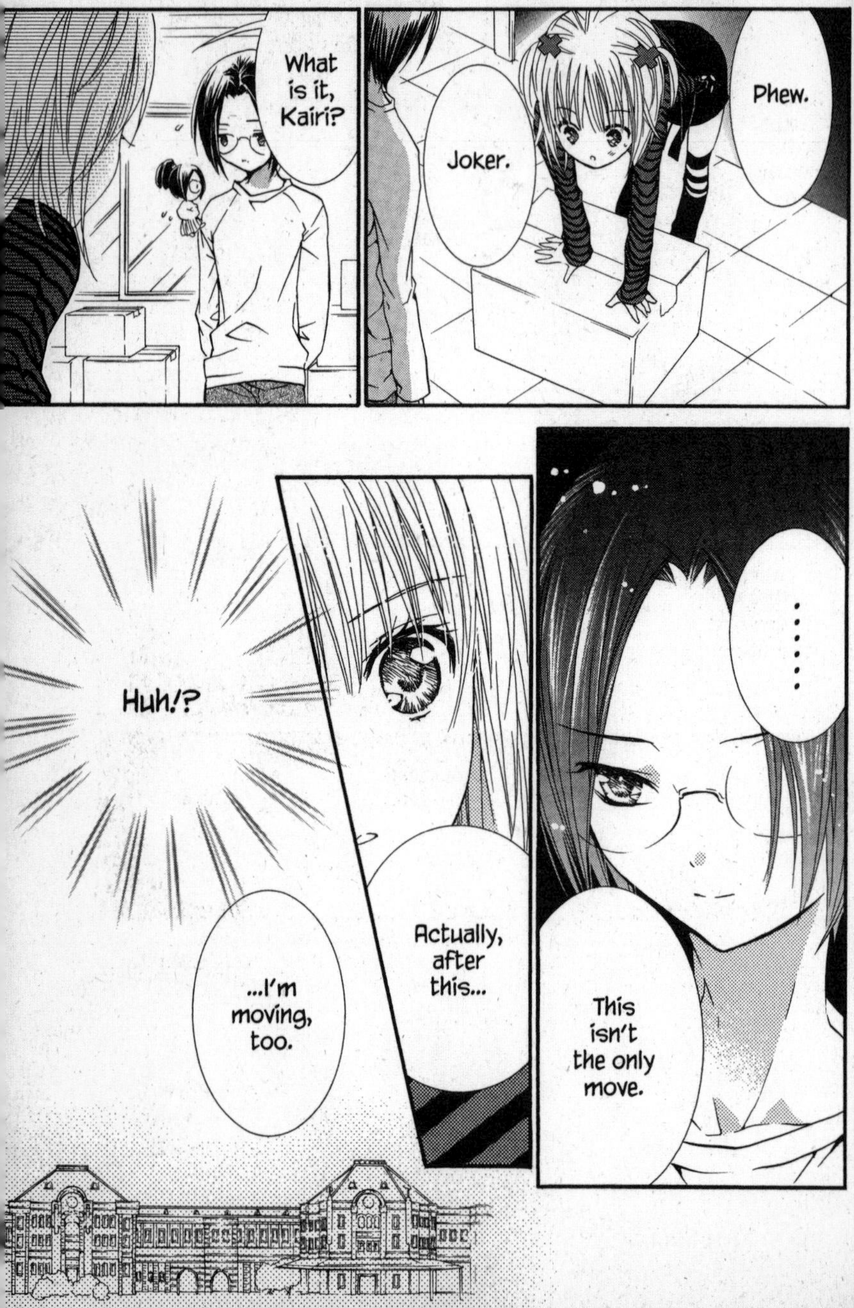
Phew.
Joker.
What is it, Kairi?
......
This isn't the only move.
Actually, after this...
...I'm moving, too.
Huh!?

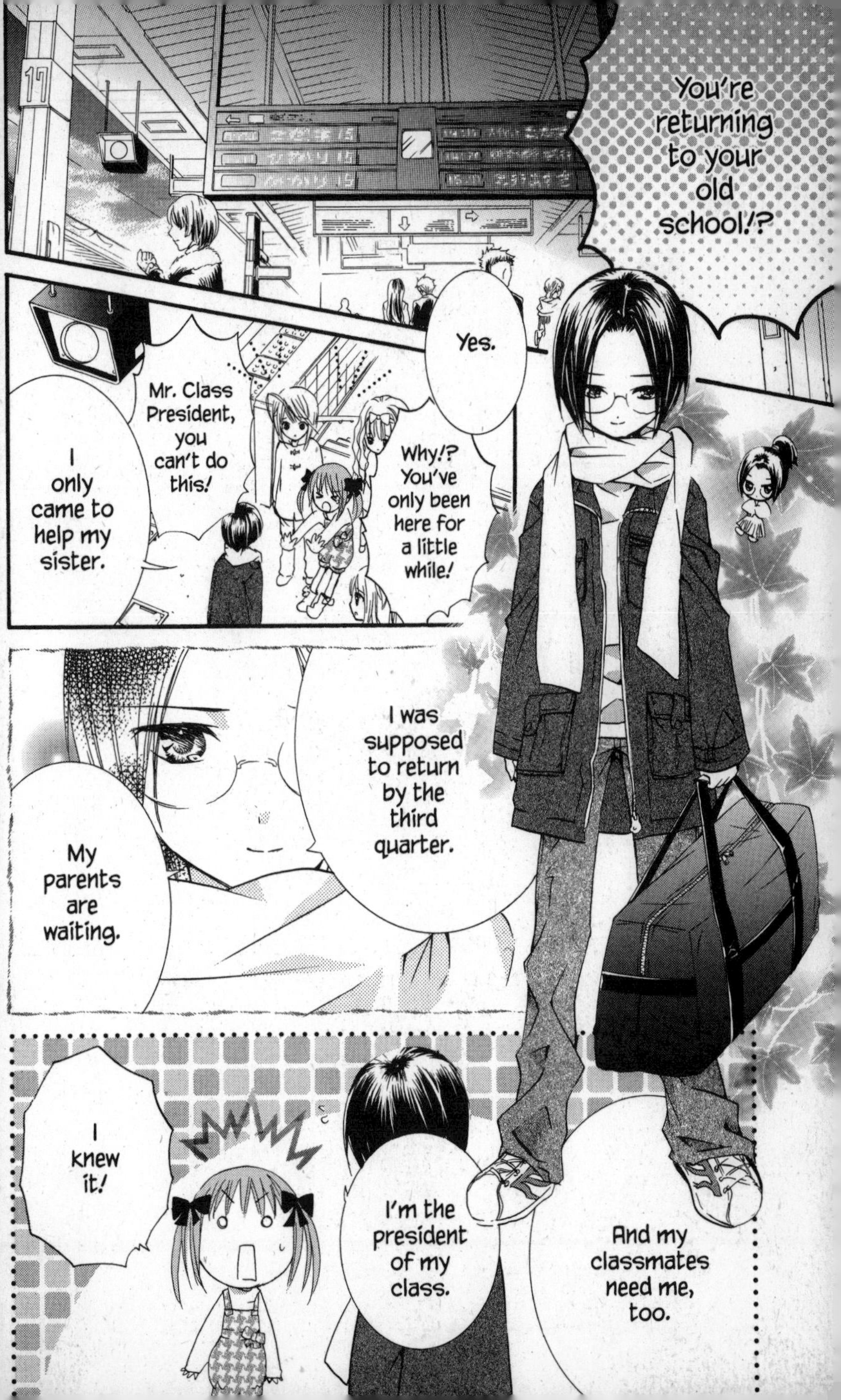
You're returning to your old school!?
Yes.
Why!? You've only been here for a little while!
Mr. Class President, you can't do this!
I only came to help my sister.
I was supposed to return by the third quarter.
My parents are waiting.
I'm the president of my class.
And my classmates need me, too.
I knew it!

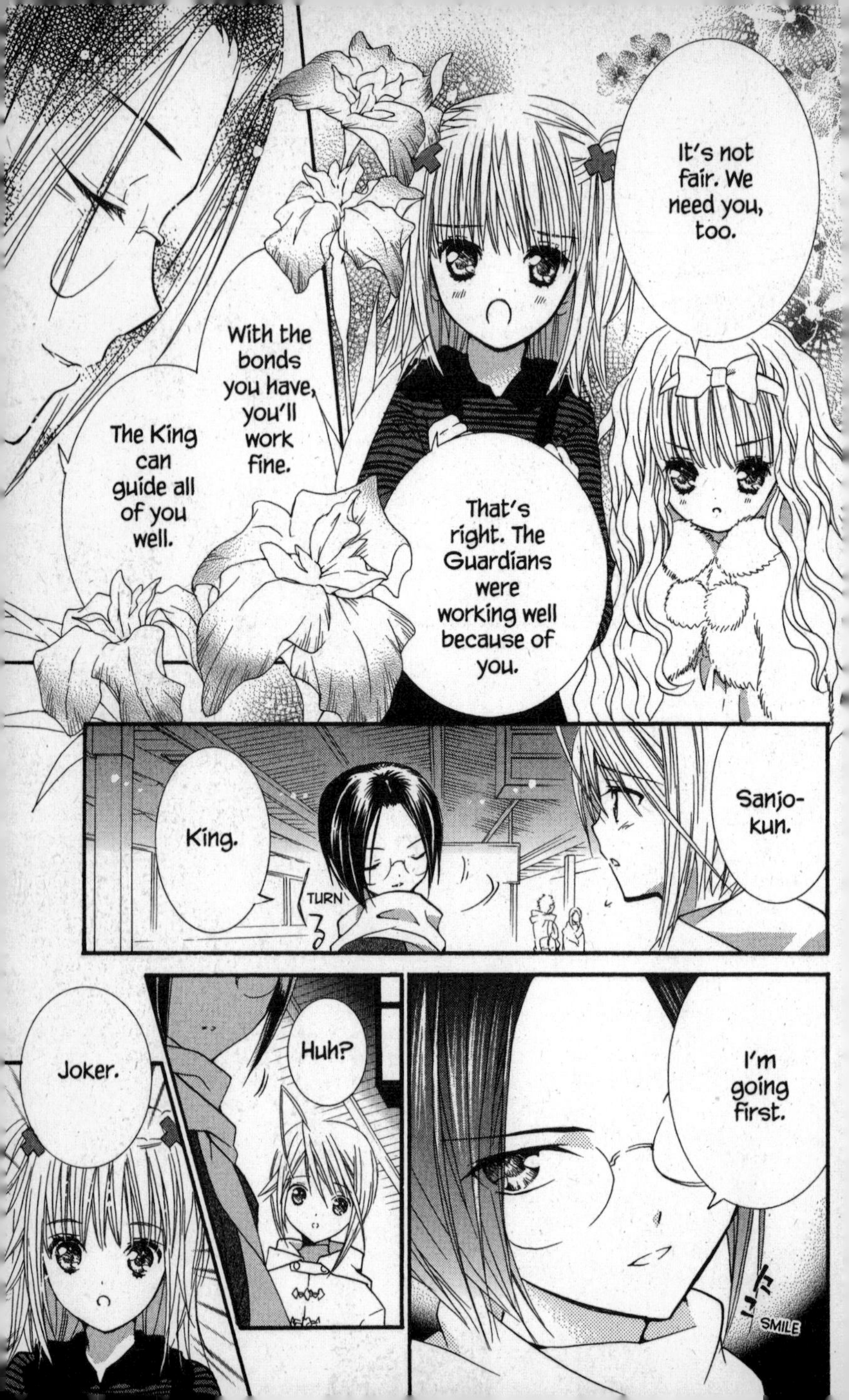
It's not fair. We need you, too.
That's right. The Guardians were working well because of you.
With the bonds you have, you'll work fine.
The King can guide all of you well.
Sanjo-kun.
King.
TURN
I'm going first.
SMILE
Huh?
Joker.

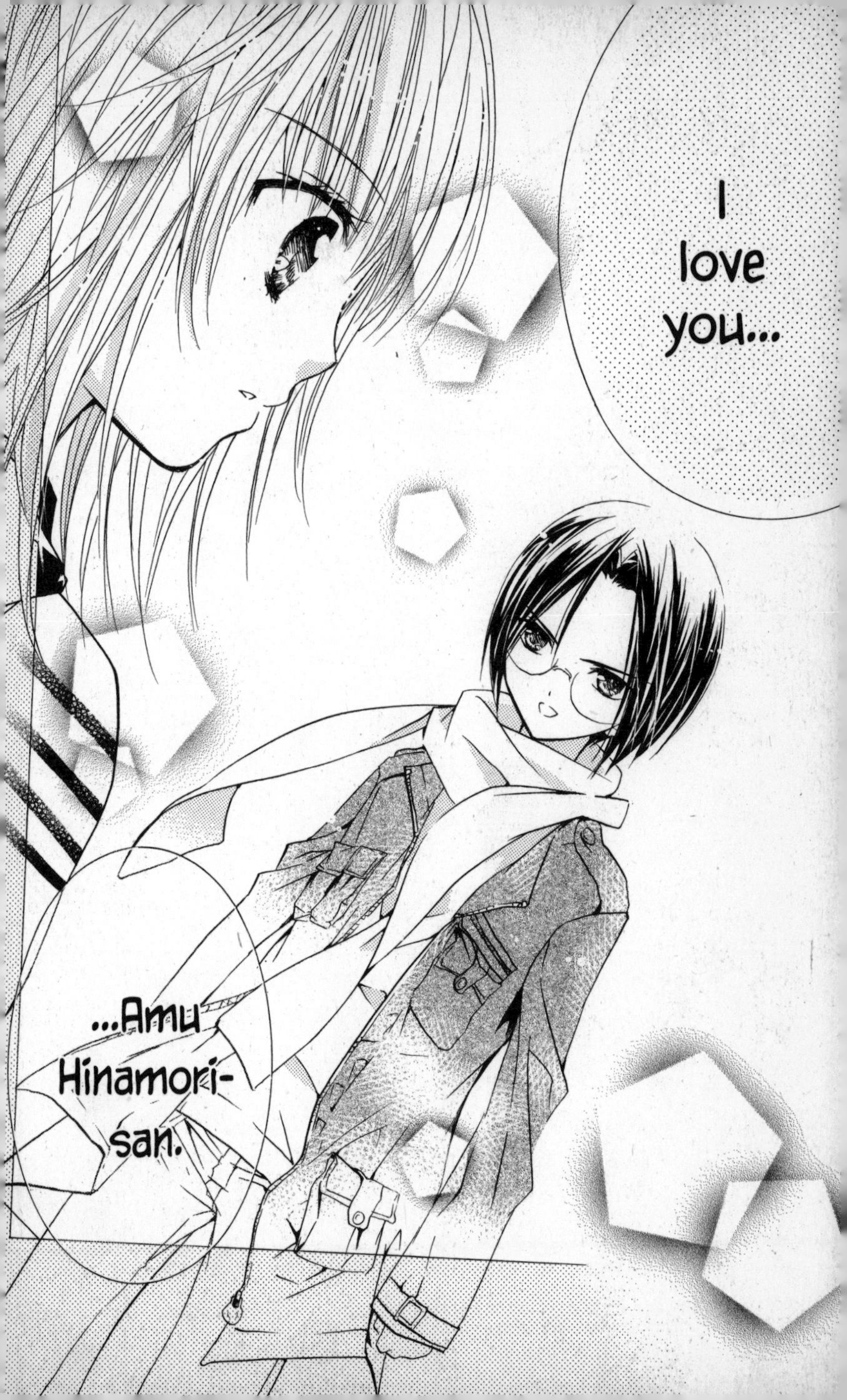
I love you...
...Amu Hinamori-san.

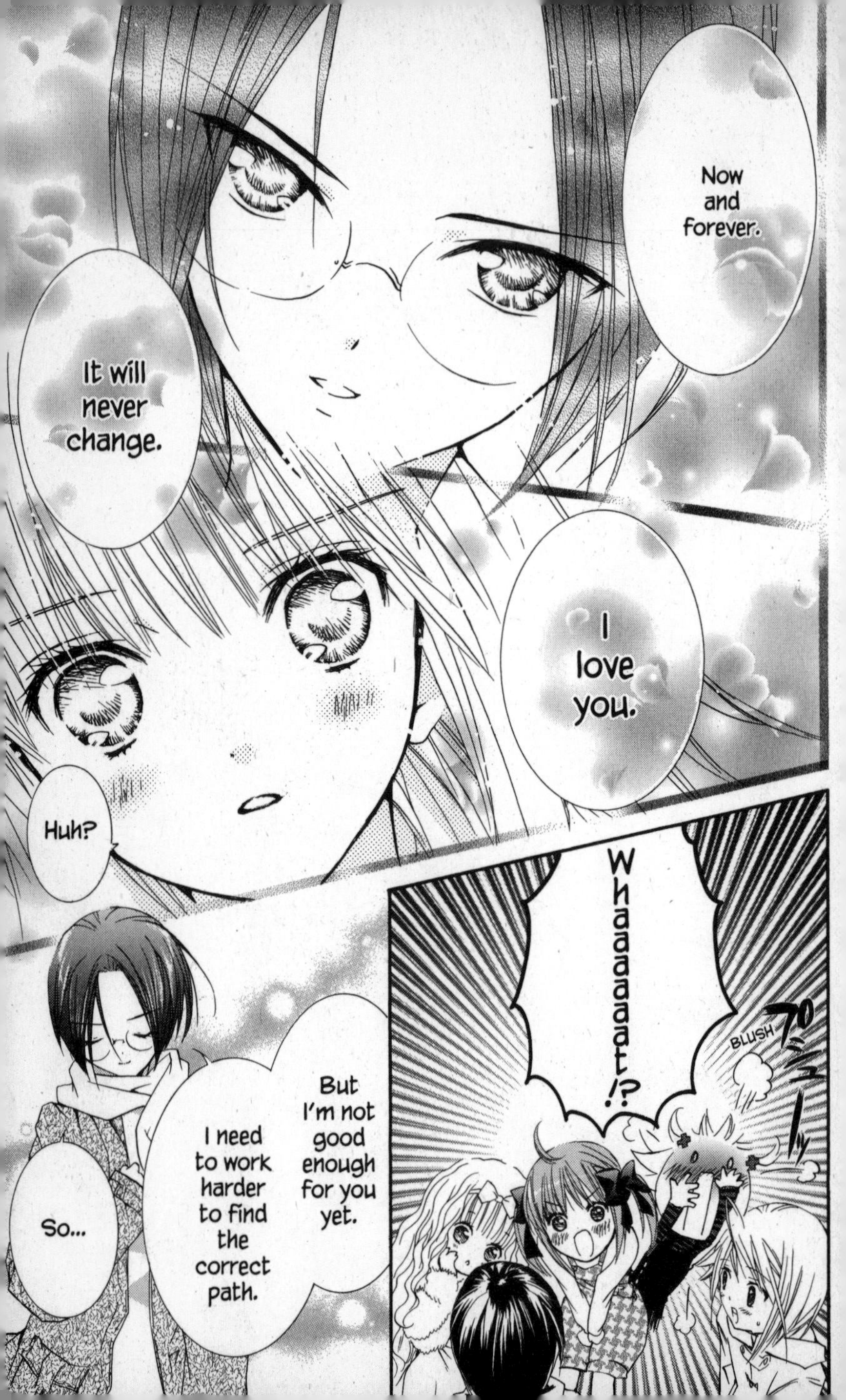
Now and forever.
It will never change.
I love you.
Huh?
Whaaaaaat!?
BLUSH
But I'm not good enough for you yet.
I need to work harder to find the correct path.
So...

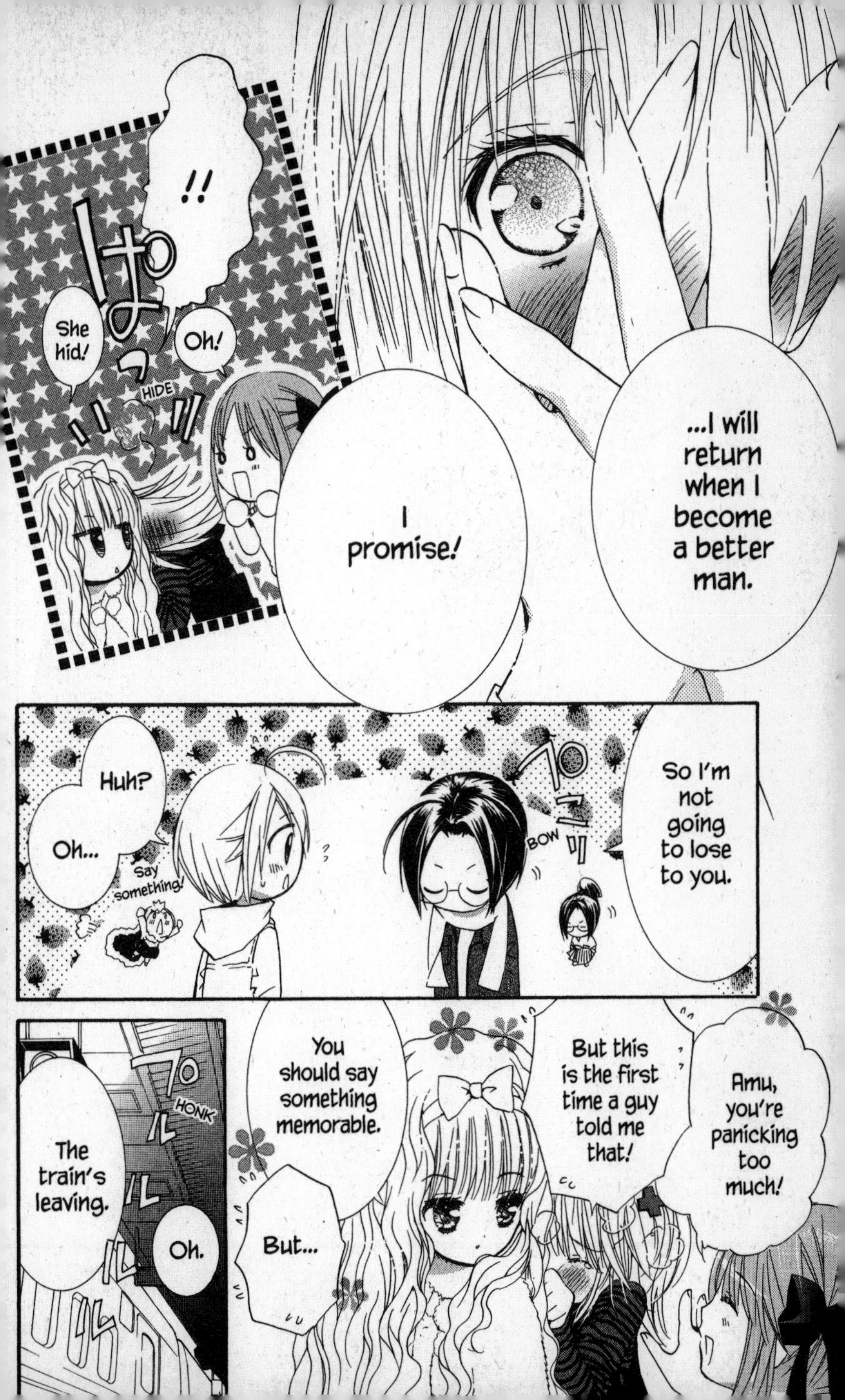

...I will return when I become a better man.
I promise!
!!
Oh!
She hid!
HIDE
So I'm not going to lose to you.
BOW
Huh?
Oh...
Say something!
Amu, you're panicking too much!
But this is the first time a guy told me that!
You should say something memorable.
But...
HONK
The train's leaving.
Oh.

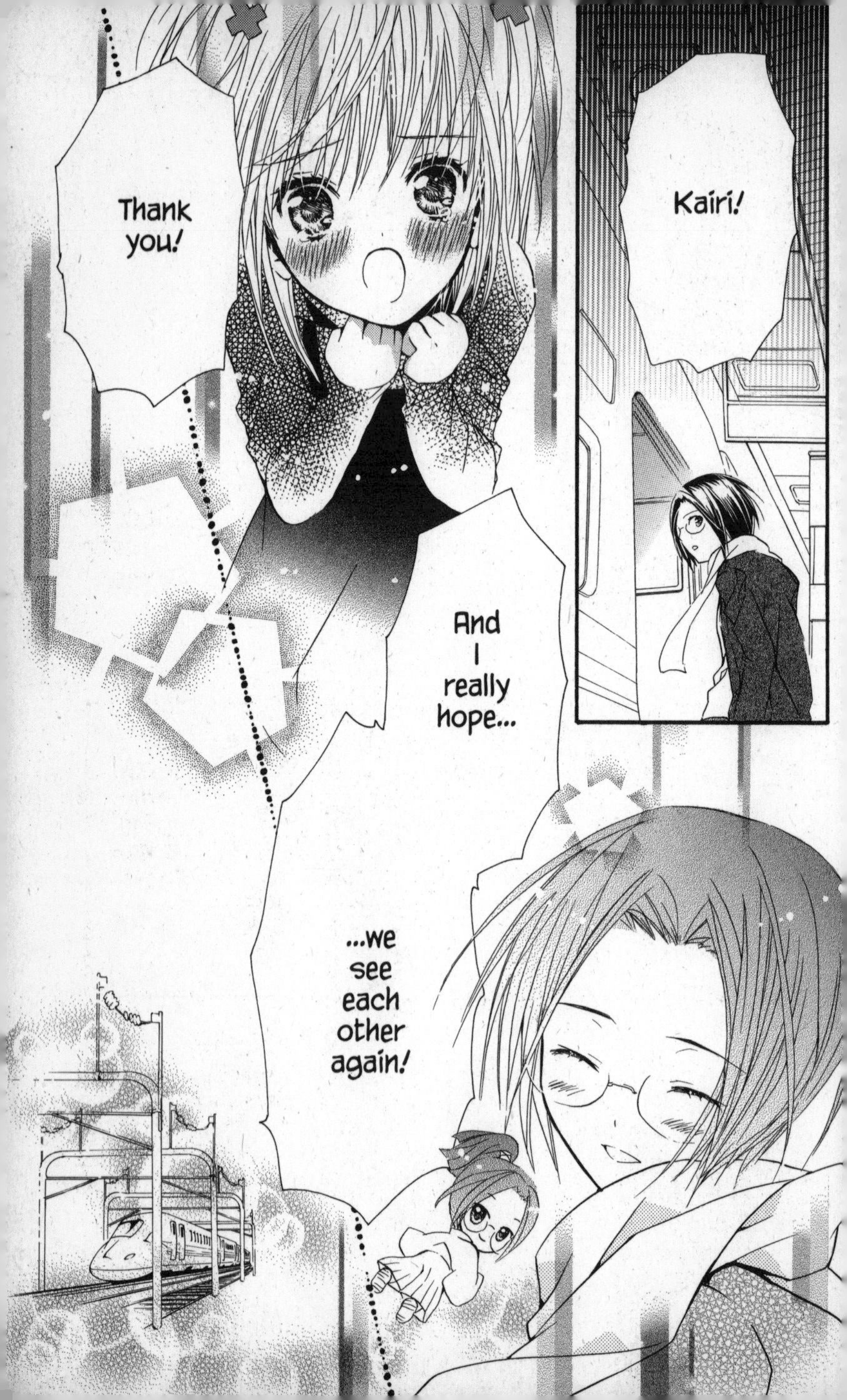
Kairi!
Thank you!
And I really hope...
...we see each other again!

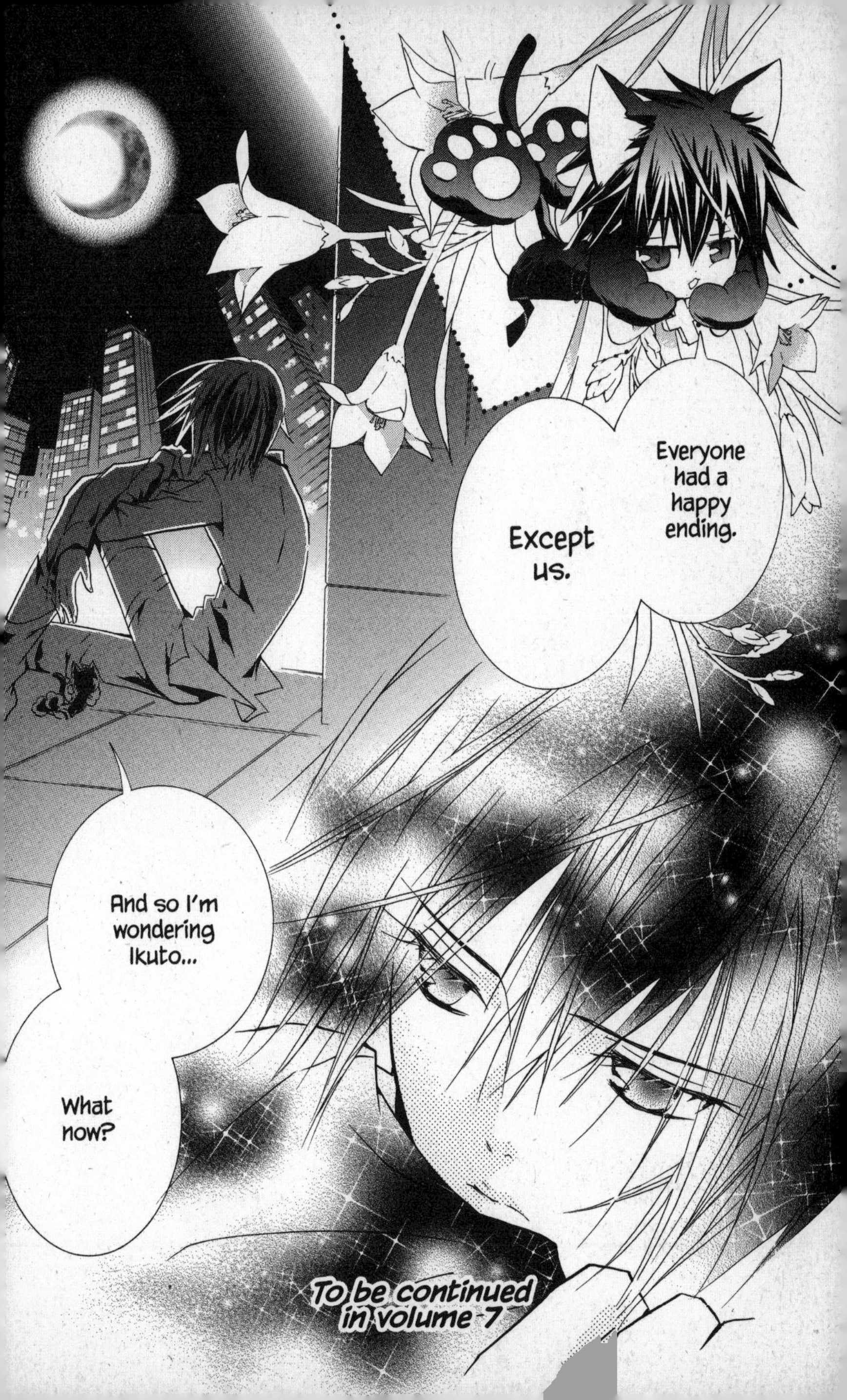
Everyone had a happy ending.
Except us.
And so I'm wondering Ikuto...
What now?
To be continued in volume 7

Shugo
Chara!

About the Creators

PEACH-PIT:
Banri Sendo was born on June 7.
Shibuko Ebara was born on June 21. They
are a pair of Gemini manga artists who
work together. Sendo likes to eat sweets,
and Ebara likes to eat spicy stuff.

"Whenever we draw manga, we try to decorate our
room with flowers. We hope that the soothing power
of the flower translates into the manga!"—PEACH-PIT

Translation Notes

Japanese is a tricky language for most Westerners, and translation is often more art than science. For your edification and reading pleasure, here are notes on some of the places where we could have gone in a different direction in our translation of the work, or where a Japanese cultural reference is used.

Nee-san, page 4

Nee-san is a Japanese honorific for big sister.

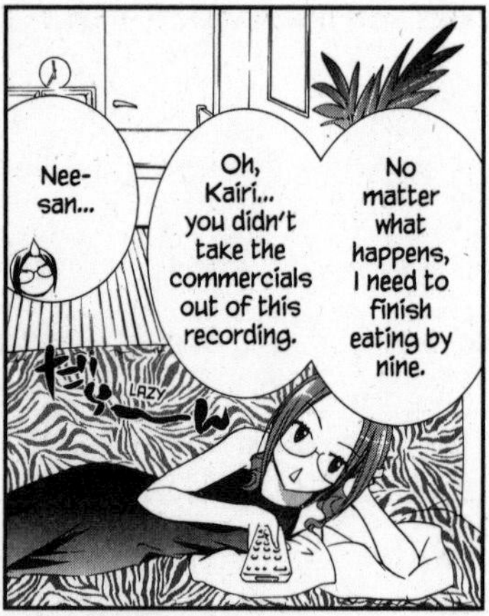
No matter what happens, I need to finish eating by nine.
Oh, Kairi... you didn't take the commercials out of this recording.
Nee-san...
LAZY

Musashi Miyamoto, page 78

Musashi Miyamoto is a famed swordsman from Japan. He is known for his many duels, his Niten-ryu style of swordsmanship, and his *Book of Five Rings*, which is a book on strategy, tactics, and philosophy.

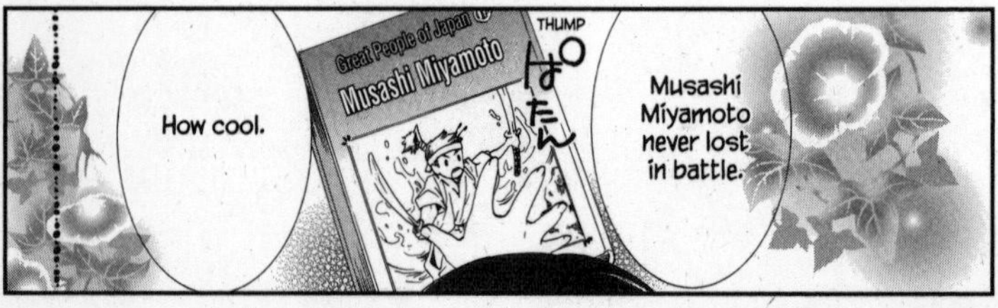
Musashi Miyamoto never lost in battle.
THUMP
Great People of Japan
Musashi Miyamoto
How cool.

Umeboshi, page 99

Umeboshi are pickled *ume* fruits. *Ume* are a type of fruit from the prunus family which are often called plums, but are actually closer to apricots. *Umeboshi* are quite common in Japan, and can often be found in boxed lunches, placed in the center of a bed of rice to make it look like the Japanese flag. *Umeboshi* are very salty and sour. They are made by putting ripe *ume* in a barrel with salt.

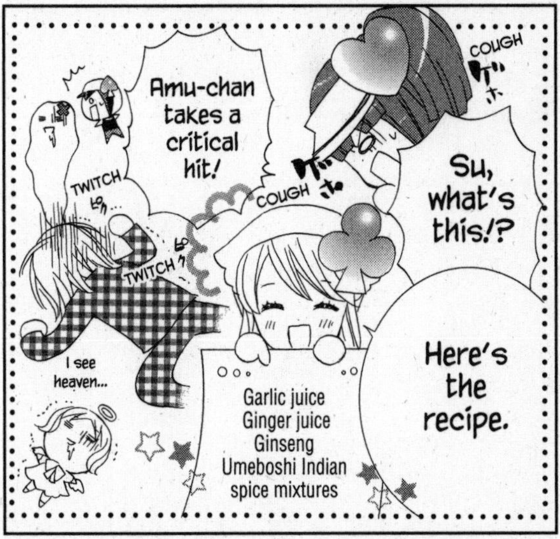
COUGH
Su, what's this!?
Amu-chan takes a critical hit!
COUGH
Here's the recipe.
Garlic juice
Ginger juice
Ginseng
Umeboshi Indian spice mixtures
TWITCH
TWITCH
I see heaven...

Onee-chan, page 102

Onee-chan is a Japanese honorific for "big brother."

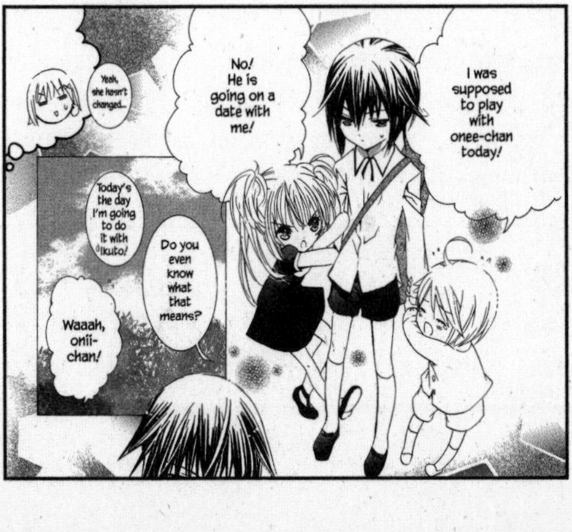
I was supposed to play with onee-chan today!
No! He is going on a date with me!
Yeah, she hasn't changed...
Today's the day I'm going to do it with Ikuto!
Do you even know what that means?
Waaah, onii-chan!

Preview of *Shugo Chara!*, volume 7

We are pleased to present you a preview from volume 7 of *Shugo Chara!* Please check our website (www.delreymanga.com) to see when this volume will be available in English. For now you'll have to make do with Japanese!

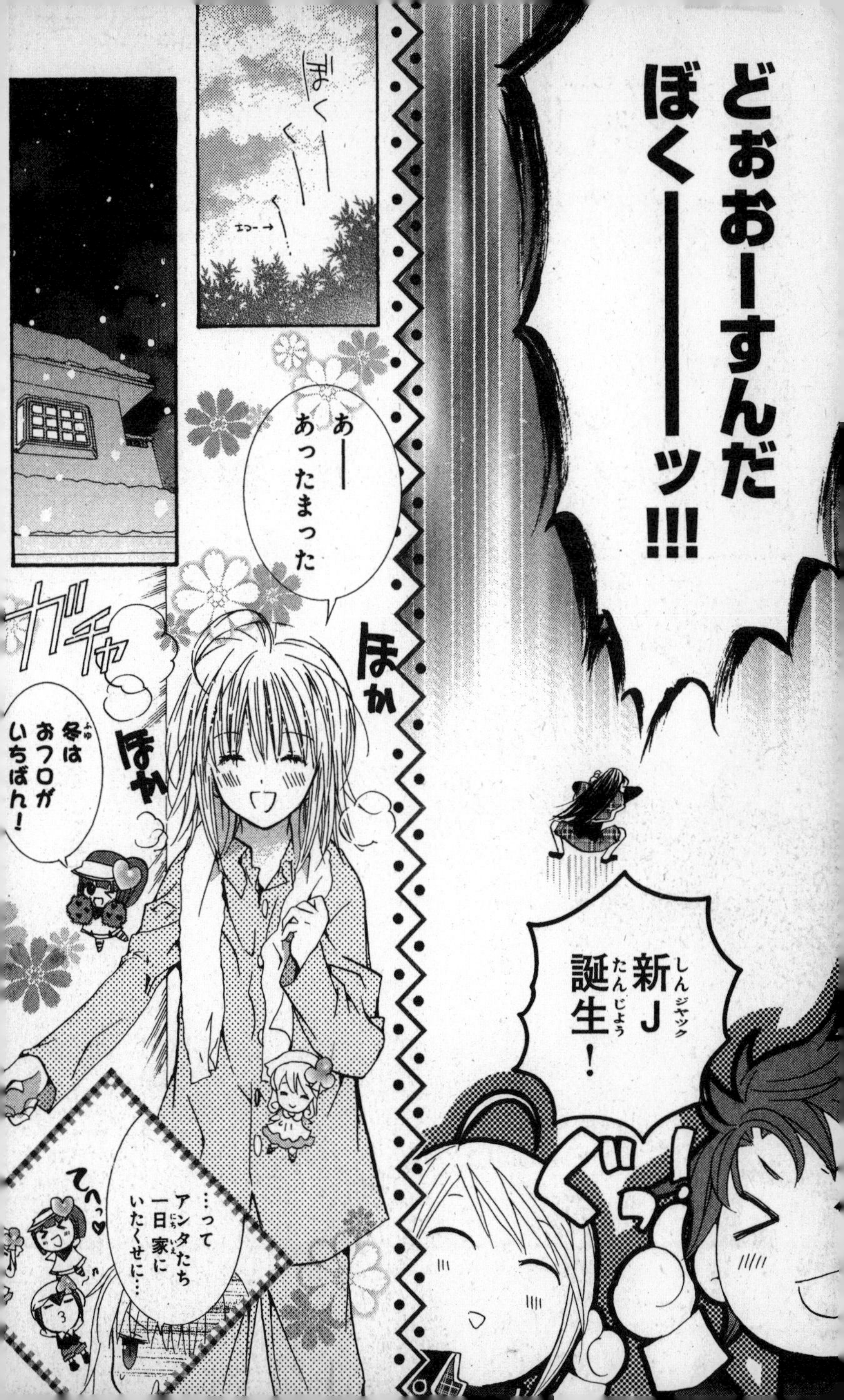

どぉおーすんだ
ぼくーーーッ!!!
新J誕生！
ぐっ
ぼくーー
くーー
くー…
エコー→
ガチャ
あーー
あったまった
ほか
ほか
冬はおフロがいちばん！
…ってアンタたち一日家にいたくせに…
てへっ♥

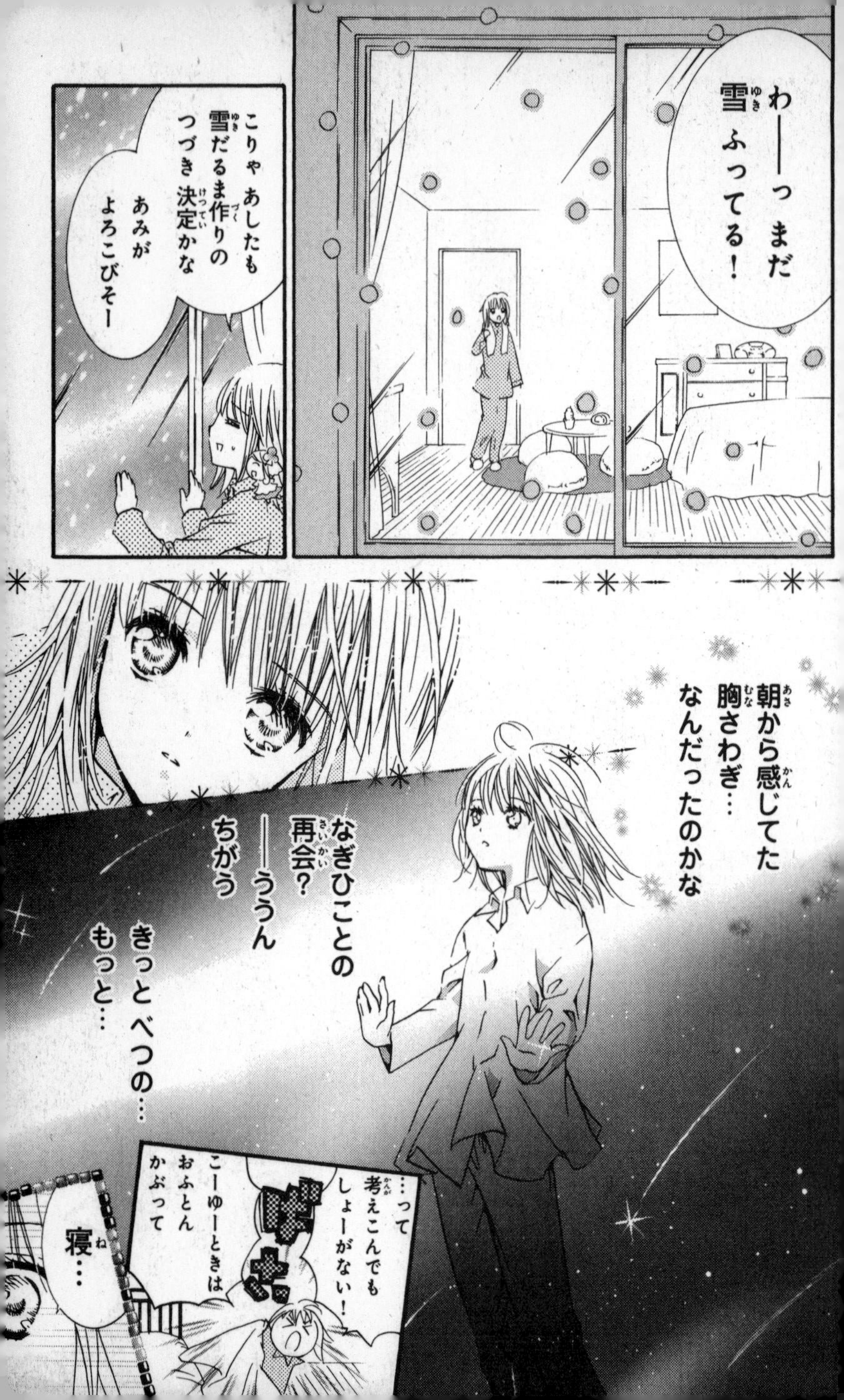
わーっまだ雪ふってる！
こりゃ あしたも雪だるま作りのつづき決定かな
あみがよろこびそー
朝から感じてた胸さわぎ…なんだったのかな
なぎひことの再会？
——ううん ちがう
きっとべつの… もっと…
…って考えこんでもしょーがない！
こーゆーときはおふとんかぶって
寝…

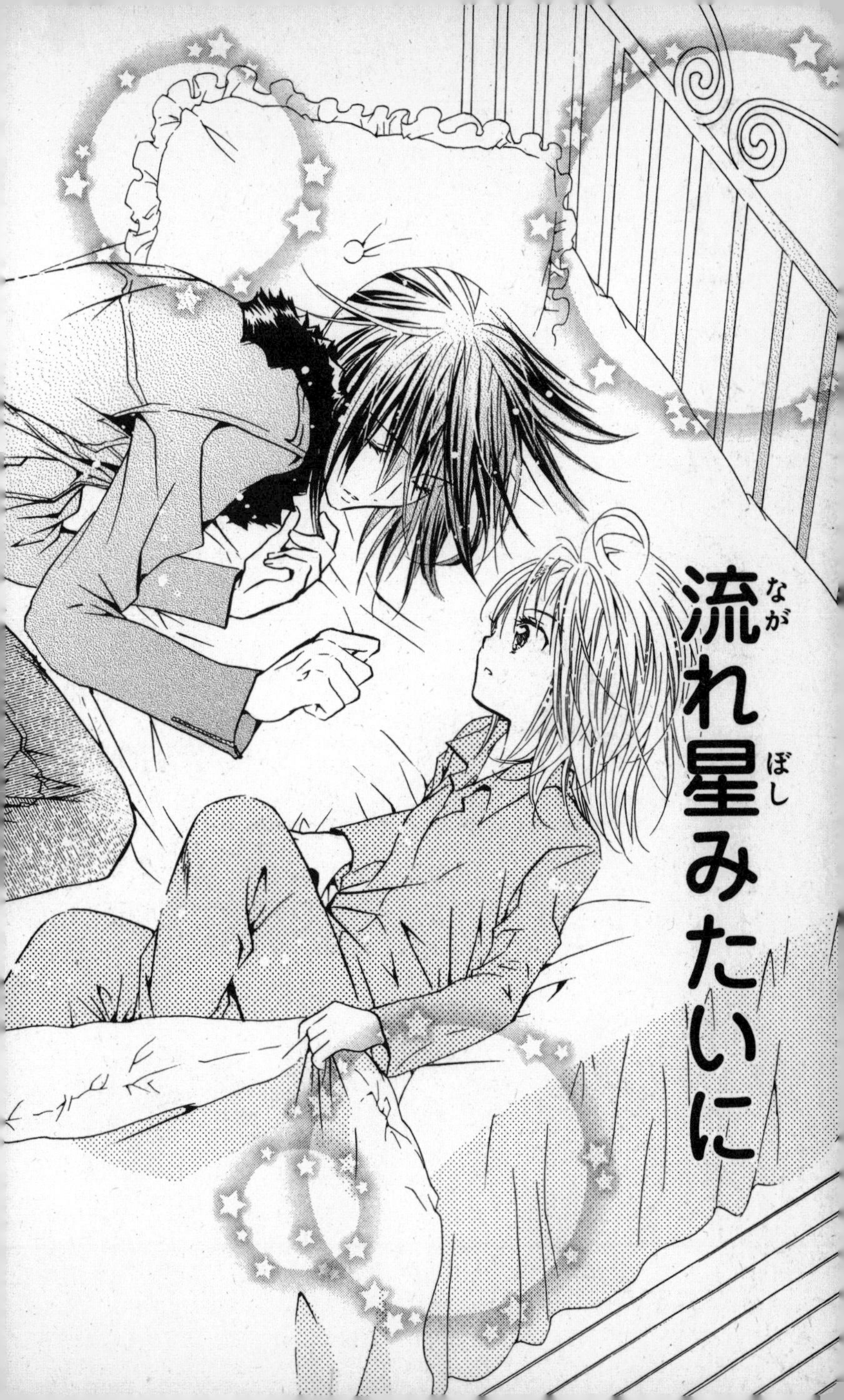
流れ星みたいに

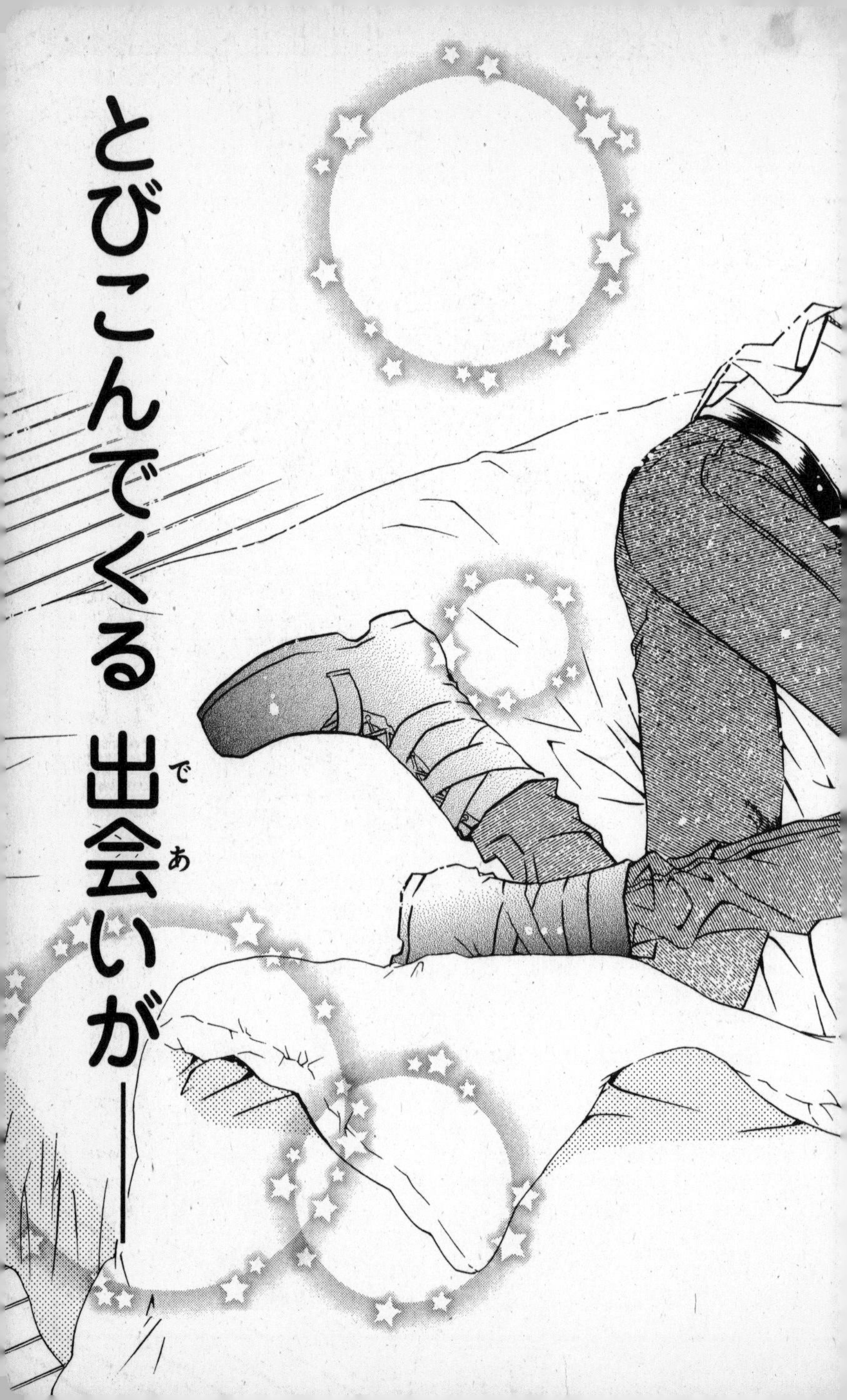
とびこんでくる出会いが——

FROM HIRO MASHIMA, CREATOR OF *RAVE MASTER*

FAIRY TAIL

FAIRY TAIL 1
Hiro Mashima Creator of Rave Master

FAIRY TAIL 2
Hiro Mashima Creator of Rave Master

Lucy has always dreamed of joining the Fairy Tail, a club for the most powerful sorcerers in the land. But once she becomes a member, the fun really starts!

Special extras in each volume! Read them all!

VISIT WWW.DELREYMANGA.COM TO:

- Read sample pages
- View release date calendars for upcoming volumes
- Sign up for Del Rey's free manga e-newsletter
- Find out the latest about new Del Rey Manga series

RATING T AGES 13+

DEL REY MANGA デルレイ

The Otaku's Choice™

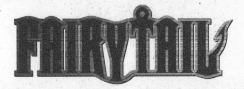

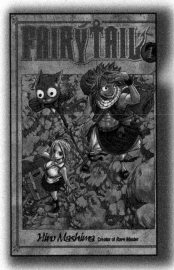

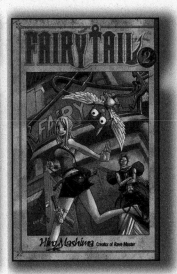

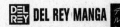

STORY BY SURT LIM
ART BY HIROFUMI SUGIMOTO

A DEL REY MANGA ORIGINAL

Exploring the woods, young Kasumi encounters an ancient tree god, who bestows upon her the power of invisibility. Together with classmates who have had similar experiences, Kasumi forms the Magic Play Club, dedicated to using their powers for good while avoiding sinister forces that would exploit them.

Special extras in each volume! Read them all!

VISIT WWW.DELREYMANGA.COM TO:
• Read sample pages
• View release date calendars for upcoming volumes
• Sign up for Del Rey's free manga e-newsletter
• Find out the latest about new Del Rey Manga series

RATING T AGES 13+

DEL REY MANGA
The Otaku's Choice™

TOMARE!

[STOP!]

You're going the wrong way!

Manga is a completely different type of reading experience.

To start at the *beginning*, go to the *end*!

That's right! Authentic manga is read the traditional Japanese way—from right to left, exactly the *opposite* of how American books are read. It's easy to follow: Just go to the other end of the book, and read each page—and each panel—from right side to left side, starting at the top right. Now you're experiencing manga as it was meant to be!